St Michael

THE GUINNESS BOOK OF EXTRAORDINARY RECORDS

Robin Cousins performs the rarely-seen back flip, reaching a height of 18 feet. ***(All-Sport)***

'The famous *Guinness Book of Records* is the fullest and most authoritative source of achievement in the world. Apart from covering every aspect of human endeavour – from the bizarre to the heroic – it also includes records from the natural world, science and technology. *The Guinness Book of Extraordinary Records* is the pick of these entries – most are extraordinary, some unbelievable, but all are true.'

STOP PRESS

Fastest trans-atlantic crossing **The 72 ft Virgin Atlantic II owned by Richard Branson and with a crew of 6 made the fastest West to East crossing for a monohull on 26–29 Jun 1986 in 3 days 8 hr 31 min. His Virgin Atlantic Challenger (I) on an earlier crossing covered 1786.71 km *963.87 nautical miles* in 24 hr.** **(See p.123)**

Largest cat **'Himmy' of Queensland, Australia, died on 12 Mar 1986, weight unchanged.**

Rarest birds **An Ivory-billed woodpecker (*Campephilus principalis bairdi*) was positively identified in the mountains of eastern Cuba in April 1986. It was last recorded in the island in 1972.**

Longest frog jump **'Rosie the Ribeter' owned and trained by Lee Giudici of Santa Clara, California, USA, leapt 6,55 m *21 ft 5¾ in* on 18 May 1986 at the annual Calaveras Jumping Jubilee at Angels Camp.**

Largest cucumber **Mrs Eileen Chappel of Bowen Hills, Queensland, Australia, grew a cucumber reported on 13 May 1986 to weigh 22 kg *48.5 lb*.**

Heaviest hailstones **Stones up to 1,02 kg *2¼ lb* are reported to have killed 92 in the Gopalganj district of Bangladesh on 14 Apr 1986.**

Most expensive British manuscript **John Paul Getty II acquired four manuscript leaves from the only known illustrated life of Thomas à Becket for £1,375,000 at Sotheby's, London on 24 Jun 1986.**

Fastest bagpipe playing **Sgt Mick Maitland, Pipe Major of No 111 RAF Fighter Squadron played 'Scotland The Brave' on his pipes at a speed of Mach 2.0 and a height of 12,190 m *40,000 ft*. He was flown in Phantom XV 574 by Wing Commander Phil W Roser, the Squadron Commander. This supersonic performance was given 64.3 km *40 miles* south of RAF Akrotiri, Cyprus on 3 June 1986.**

Highest paid TV performer **It was reported in July 1986 that Bill Cosby earned £6.5 million in 12 months on US TV shows and concerts and from advertisements and albums.**

Most expensive used car **A 1931 Bugatti Royale from the collection of the late William F Harrah made $6.5 million *£4.3 million* in auction at Reno, Nevada, USA on 27 June 1986.**

This edition published exclusively for Marks and Spencer p.l.c. by Guinness Superlatives Ltd, 33 London Road, Enfield, Middlesex, Great Britain

Designed and printed by Jarrold & Sons Ltd, Norwich, Norfolk

ISBN 0–85112–801–7

Contents

CHAPTER 1

HUMAN WONDERS

CHAPTER 2

WELLIE-WANGING AND OTHER WONDERS

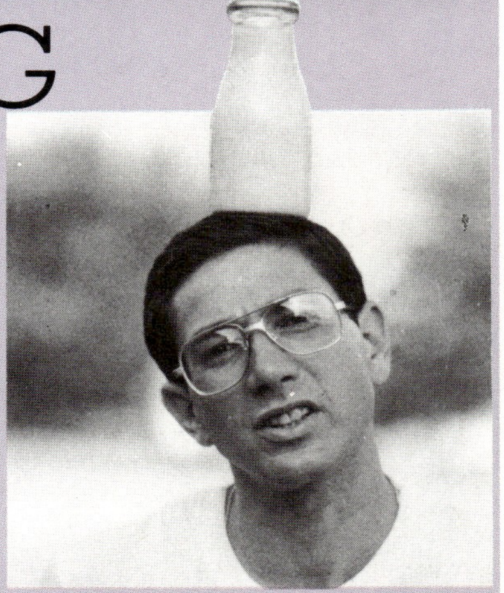

CHAPTER 3

ANIMAL SUPERLATIVES

CHAPTER 4

THE NATURAL WORLD

CHAPTER 5

BUILDING BIG

CHAPTER 6

THAT'S ENTERTAINMENT

CHAPTER 7

TRANSPORT RECORDS

CHAPTER 8

SPORTING RECORDS

Marks and Spencer is in
The Guinness Book of Records!

'*Highest sales per unit area.* The department store with the fastest-moving stock in the world is the Marks & Spencer premier branch, known as 'Marble Arch' at 458 Oxford Street, City of Westminster, Greater London. The figure of £1566 worth of goods per square foot of selling space per year is believed to be an understatement. The selling area is 8584 m^2 *92,400* ft^2. The company has 269 branches in the UK and operates on over 603 850 m^2 *6.5 million* ft^2 of selling space and now has stores on the Continent and Canada.'

CHAPTER 1

HUMAN WONDERS

The all-time tallest and shortest: Robert Wadlow (USA), 8 ft 11 in *b.* 1918 *d.* 1940. Pauline Musters (Holland) 24 in, *b.* 1876 *d.* 1895.

LITTLE & LARGE

'England's heaviest ever man Daniel Lambert (1770–1809) of Leicester who weighed 355 kg *52 stone 11 lb.* *(Leicestershire Museums & Art Galleries)*'

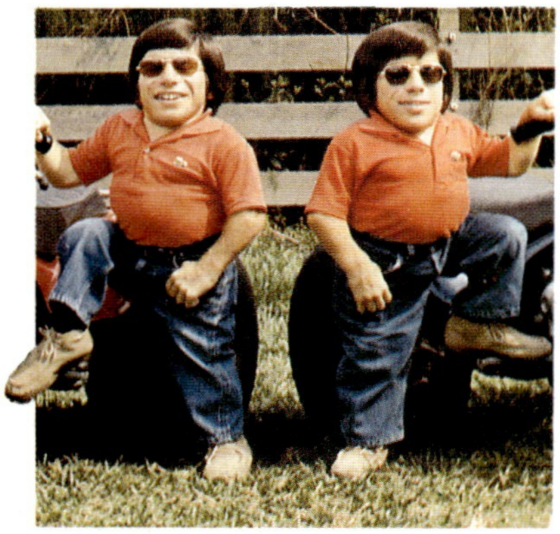

John and Greg Rice, the world's shortest twins. Together, their heights add up to 173 cm *68 in*.

Alton, Illinois's tallest police officer Raymond Galloway (188 cm *6 ft 2 in*) being dwarfed by the Mayor's son Robert Wadlow – the tallest human of all time at 2,72 m *8 ft 11.1 in*. (*Alton Telegraph*).

GIANT LEAGUE TABLE

1. Robert Pershing Wadlow (1918–40) of Alton, Illinois, USA 272 cm *8 ft 11 in.*
2. John F. Carroll (1932–69) of Buffalo, New York State, USA 263,5 cm *8 ft $7\frac{3}{4}$ in.*
3. John William Rogan (1871–1905), a Negro of Gallatin, Tennessee, USA 259,1 cm *8 ft 6 in.*
4. Väinö Myllyrinne (1909–63) of Helsinki, Finland 251,4 cm *8 ft 3 in.*
5. Bernard Coyne (1897–1921) of Anthon, Iowa, USA 248,9 cm *8 ft 2 in.*
6. Don Koehler (1925–81) of Denton, Montana, USA 248,9 cm *8 ft 2 in*, latterly lived in Chicago.
7. Patrick Cotter O'Brien (1760–1806) of Kinsale, County Cork, Ireland 246 cm *8 ft 1 in.*
8. 'Constantine' (1872–1902) of Reutlingen, West Germany 245,8 cm *8 ft 0.8 in.*
9. Gabriel Estevao Monjane (b. 1944–*fl.* 1984) of Monjacaze, Mozambique *c* 245,7 cm *8 ft $0\frac{3}{4}$ in.*
10. Sulaimān 'Ali Nashnush (b. 1943–*fl.* 1984) of Tripoli, Libya 245 cm *8 ft 0.4 in.*

TALLEST GIANTESS

Giantesses are rarer than giants but their heights are still spectacular. The tallest woman in history was Zeng Jinlian (pronounced San Chung Lin) (b. 26 June 1964) of Yujiang village in the Bright Moon Commune, Hunan Province, central China, who was 247 cm *8 ft 1 in* when she died on 13 Feb 1982. She began to grow abnormally from the age of 4 months and stood 156 cm *5 ft 1½ in* before her 4th birthday and 217 cm *7 ft 1½ in* when she was 13. Her hands measured 25,5 cm *10 in* and her feet 35,5 cm *14 in* in length. Her parents are 163 cm *5 ft 4 in* and 156 cm *5 ft 1½ in* while her brother was 158 cm *5 ft 2¼ in* aged 18.

SHORTEST DWARF

The shortest mature human of whom there is independent evidence was Pauline Musters ('Princess Pauline'), a Dutch midget. She was born at Ossendrecht, on 26 Feb 1876 and measured 30 cm *11.8 in* at birth. At the age of 9 she was 55 cm *21.65 in* tall and weighed only 1,5 kg *3 lb 5 oz.* She died, at the age of 19, of pneumonia, with meningitis, her heart weakened from alcoholic excesses, on 1 Mar 1895 in New York City, NY, USA. Although she was billed at 48 cm *19 in*, she had earlier been medically measured to be 59 cm *23.2 in* tall. A *post mortem* examination showed her to be exactly 61 cm *24 in*.

The 1400 lb CHAMPION FATTY

The heaviest human in recorded medical history was Jon Brower Minnoch (b. 29 Sept 1941) of Bainbridge Island, Washington, USA, who was carried on planking by a rescue team into the University Hospital, Seattle in March 1978. Dr Robert Schwartz estimated that he was 'probably more' than 635 kg *1400 lb (100 st)*. His highest actually recorded bodyweight was 442 kg *975 lb* in September 1976. To roll him over in his hospital bed it took 13 attendants. After nearly 2 years on a 1200 calorie per day diet he was discharged at 216 kg *476 lb (34 st)*. He had to be readmitted in October 1981 having reportedly gained 91 kg *200 lb (over 14 st)* in 7 days. He died on 10 Sept 1983. This former taxi-cab driver stood 1,85 m *6 ft 1 in* tall. He was 181 kg *400 lb* in 1963, and 317 kg *700 lb* in 1966.

HAPPY HUMPHREY – THE CHAMPION SLIMMER

The greatest recorded slimming feat was that of William J. Cobb (b. 1926), *alias* 'Happy Humphrey', a professional wrestler of Augusta, Georgia, USA. It was reported in July 1965 that he had reduced from 364 kg *57 st 4 lb* to 105 kg *16 st 8 lb*, a loss of 259 kg *40 st 11 lb* in 32 months. His waist measurement declined from 256 to 112 cm *101 to 44 in*. In October 1973 it was reported that 'Happy' was back to his normal weight of 295 kg *46½ st* or *651 lb*.

TALLEST LIVING WOMAN

The tallest living woman is Sandy Allen (b. 18 June 1955, Chicago) of Niagara Falls, Ontario, Canada. On 14 July 1977 she underwent a pituitary gland operation, which inhibited further growth at 231,7 cm *7 ft 7¼ in*. A 2,95 kg *6½ lb* baby, her acromegalic growth began soon after birth. She now weighs 209,5 kg *33 st* and takes a size 16EEE American shoe (=14½ UK or 50PP Continental).

TALLEST COUPLE

Anna Hanen Swan (1846–88) of Nova Scotia, Canada, was billed at 246 cm *8 ft 1 in* but actually measured 227 cm *7 ft 5½ in*. In London on 17 June 1871 she married Martin van Buren Bates (1845–1919) of Whitesburg, Letcher County, Kentucky, USA, who stood 219 cm *7 ft 2½ in* making them the tallest married couple on record.

Britain's tallest man – Chris Greener 229 cm *7 ft 6¼ in* – with past champion moustache of Britain – that of John Roy at 189 cm *74½ in*. The moustache record is now held by Mike Solomons at 83 cm *33 in*.

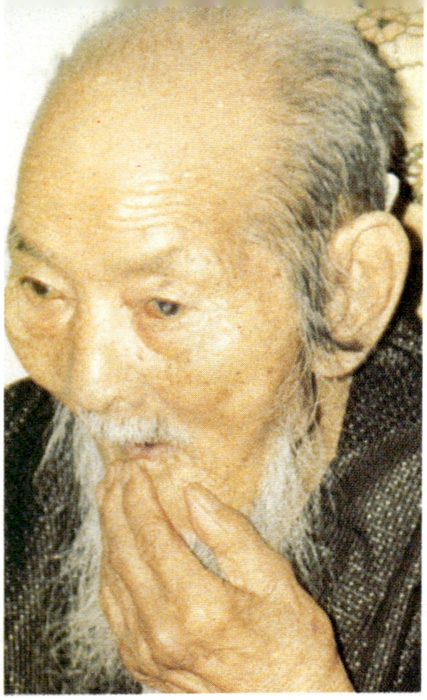

OLDEST HUMAN

OLDEST AUTHENTIC CENTENARIAN *WORLD*

The greatest *authenticated* age to which any human has ever lived is a unique 120 years 237 days in the case of Shigechiyo Izumi of Asan on Tokunoshima an island 1320 km *820 miles* SW of Tokyo, Japan. He was born at Asan on 29 June 1865 and recorded as a 6-year-old in Japan's first census on 1871. He died at his home at 12.15 GMT on 21 Feb 1986 after developing pneumonia.

Shigechiyo Izumi of Japan, aged 120 at his death in 1986.

AUTHENTIC NATIONAL LONGEVITY RECORDS

	Years	Days		Born		Died	
Japan	120	237	Shigechiyo Izumi	29 June	1865	21 Feb	1986
United States[1]	113	273	Fannie Thomas	24 Apr	1867	22 Jan	1981
Canada[2]	113	124	Pierre Joubert	15 July	1701	16 Nov	1814
United Kingdom[3]	113	+	Anna Eliza Williams (Mrs) (née Davies)	2 June	1873	*fl.* 2 June	1986
Spain[4]	112	228	Josefa Salas Mateo	14 July	1860	27 Feb	1973
France	112	66	Augustine Teissier (Sister Julia)	2 Jan	1869	9 Mar	1981
Morocco	> 112		El Hadj Mohammed el Mokri (Grand Vizier)		1844	16 Sept	1957
Poland	112	+	Roswlia Mielczarak (Mrs)		1868	7 Jan	1981
Ireland	111	327	The Hon. Katherine Plunket	22 Nov	1820	14 Oct	1932
Australia	111	235	Jane Piercy (Mrs)	2 Sept	1869	3 May	1981
South Africa[5]	111	151	Johanna Booyson	17 Jan	1857	16 June	1968
Czechoslovakia	111	+	Marie Bernatkova	22 Oct	1857	*fl.* Oct	1968
Channel Islands (Guernsey)	110	321	Margaret Ann Neve (*née* Harvey)	18 May	1792	4 Apr	1903
Northern Ireland	110	234	Elizabeth Watkins (Mrs)	10 Mar	1863	31 Oct	1973
Sweden	110	200+	Wilhelmine Sande (Mrs)	24 Oct	1874	*fl.* 12 May	1985
Yugoslavia	110	150+	Demitrius Philipovitch	9 Mar	1818	*fl.* Aug	1928
Netherlands[6]	110	141	Gerada Hurenkamp-Bosgoed	5 Jan	1870	25 May	1980
Greece[7]	110	+	Lambrini Tsiatoura (Mrs)		1870	19 Feb	1981
USSR[8]	110	+	Khasako Dzugayev	7 Aug	1860	*fl.* Aug	1970
Italy	110	+	Dimiana Sette (Sig)		1884	25 Feb	1985
Norway[9]	109	208	Marie Olsen (Mrs)	1 May	1850	24 Nov	1959
Tasmania (State of)	109	179	Mary Ann Crow (Mrs)	2 Feb	1836	31 July	1945
Scotland[10]	109	14	Rachel MacArthur (Mrs)	26 Nov	1827	10 Dec	1936
Belgium	108	327	Mathilda Vertommen-Hellemans	12 Aug	1868	4 July	1977
Germany[11]	108	128	Luise Schwarz	27 Sept	1849	2 Feb	1958
Iceland	108	45	Halldóra Bjarndóttir	14 Oct	1873	28 Nov	1981
Portugal[12]	108	+	Maria Luisa Jorge	7 June	1859	*fl.* July	1967
Finland	109	182	Andrei Akaki Kuznetsoff	17 Oct	1873	*fl.* 17 Apr	1983
Malaysia	106	+	Hassan Bin Yusoff	14 Aug	1865	*fl.* Jan	1972
Luxembourg	105	228	Nicolas Wiscourt	31 Dec	1872	17 Aug	1978

[1] *Ex-slave Mrs Martha Graham died at Fayetteville, North Carolina on 25 June 1959 reputedly aged 117 or 118. Census researches by Eckler show that she was seemingly born in Dec 1844 and hence aged 114 years 6 months. Mrs Rena Glover Brailsford died in Summerton, South Carolina, USA on 6 Dec 1977 reputedly aged 118 years. Mrs Rosario Reina Vasquez who died in California on 2 Sept 1980 was reputedly born in Sonora, Mexico on 3 June 1866, which would make her 114 years 93 days. The 1900 US Federal Census for Crawfish Springs Militia District of Walker County, Georgia, records an age of 77 for a Mark Thrash. If the Mark Thrash (reputedly born in Georgia in December 1822) who died near Chattanooga, Tennessee on 17 Dec 1943 was he, and the age attributed was accurate, then he would have survived for 121 years.*

[2] *Mrs Ellen Carroll died in North River, Newfoundland, Canada on 8 Dec 1943, reputedly aged 115 years 49 days. Research is underway on the Ontario 1881 Census records on the claim of David Trumble to have been born 15 Dec 1867.*

[3] *London-born Miss Isabella Shepheard was allegedly 115 years old when she died at St Asaph, Clwyd, North Wales, on 20 Nov 1948, but her actual age was believed to have been 109 years 90 days. Charles Alfred Nunez Arnold died in Liverpool on 15 Nov 1941 reputedly aged 112 years 66 days based on a baptismal claim (London, 10 Sept 1829). Mrs Elizabeth Cornish (née Veale) who was buried at Stratton, Cornwall on 10 Mar 1691/2 was reputedly baptized on 16 Oct 1578, 113 years 4 months earlier.*

[4] *Snr Benita Medrana of Avila died on 28 Jan 1979 allegedly aged 114 years 335 days.*

[5] *Mrs Susan Johanna Deporter of Port Elizabeth, South Africa, was reputedly 114 years old when she died on 4 Aug 1954. Mrs Sarah Lawrence, Cape Town, South Africa was reputedly 112 on 3 June 1968.*

[6] *Thomas Peters was recorded to have been born on 6 Apr 1745 in Leeuwarden and died aged 111 years 354 days on 26 Mar 1857 in Arnhem.*

[7] *The claim that Liakon Efdokia died 17 Jan 1982 aged 118 years 13 days is not substantiated by the censuses of 1971 or 1981. Birth registration before 1920 was fragmentary.*

[8] *There are allegedly 21,700 centenarians in USSR (cf. 7000 in USA). Of these 21,000 are ascribed to the Georgian SSR,* i.e. *one in every 232. In July 1962 it was reported that 128, mostly male, were in the one village of Medini.*

[9] *Mrs W. Sande was born in present-day Norway.*

[10] *Lachlen McDonald died 7 June 1858 in Harris, Outer Hebrides, was recorded as being '110 years' on his death certificate.*

[11] *West Germany: An unnamed female died in 1979 aged 112 years and an unnamed male died, aged also 112 years in 1969. The Austrian record is 108 years (female d. 1975) and the Swiss record is also 108 years (female d. 1967).*

[12] *Senhora Jesuina da Conceicao of Lisbon was reputedly 113 years old when she died on 10 June 1965.*

Note: *fl* is the abbreviation for *floruit*, Latin for he (or she) was living at the relevant date.

RECORD MUMS

RECORD MUMS

The greatest officially recorded number of children produced by a mother is 69 by the first of the two wives of Feodor Vassilyev (b. 1707), a peasant from Shuya, 241 km *150 miles* east of Moscow. In 27 confinements she gave birth to 16 pairs of twins, 7 sets of triplets and 4 sets of quadruplets. The case was reported by the Monastery of Nikolskiy on 27 Feb 1782 to Moscow. At least 67 survived infancy. Currently the world's most prolific mother is reported to be Leontina Albina (b. 1925) of San Antonio, Chile, who was reported pregnant in November 1980 having already produced 54 children. Her husband Gerardo Secunda Albina (b. 1921) states that he was married in Argentina in 1943 and they had 5 sets of triplets (all boys) before coming to Chile. 'Only' 40 (24 boys and 16 girls) survive. Eleven were lost in an earthquake.

MOST TWINS *GEOGRAPHICALLY*

In Chungchon, South Korea it was reported in September 1981 that there was unaccountably 38 pairs in only 275 families – the highest ever recorded ratio.

FASTEST TRIPLET BIRTH

The fastest recorded natural birth of triplets has been 2 minutes in the case of Mrs James E. Duck of Memphis, Tennessee (Bradley, Christopher and Carmon) on 21 Mar 1977.

QUINDECAPLETS

It was announced by Dr Gennaro Montanino of Rome that he had removed the foetuses of 10 girls and 5 boys from the womb of a 35-year-old housewife on 22 July 1971. A fertility drug was responsible for this unique and unsurpassed instance of quindecaplets.

LONGEST AND SHORTEST PREGNANCY

Claims up to 413 days have been widely reported but accurate data are bedevilled by the increasing use of oral contraceptive pills which is a cause of amenorrhoea. *The US Medical Investigator* of 27 Dec 1884 reported a case of 15 months 20 days and the *Histoire de l'Academie* of 1751 the most extreme case of 36 months. In the pre-pill era English law has accepted pregnancies with extremes of 174 days (*Clark* v. *Clark*, 1939) and 349 days (*Hadlum* v. *Hadlum*, 1949). Ernestine Hudgins was born weighing 482 g *17 oz* 18 weeks premature in San Diego, California, USA on 8 Feb 1983.

OLDEST MOTHER *WORLD*

Medical literature contains extreme but unauthenticated cases of septuagenarian mothers, such as Mrs Ellen Ellis, aged 72, of Four Crosses, Clwyd, who allegedly produced a still-born 13th child on 15 May 1776 in her 46th year of marriage. Many very late maternities will be cover-ups for illegitimate grandchildren. The oldest recorded mother for whom the evidence satisfied medical verification was Mrs Ruth Alice Kistler (*née* Taylor), formerly Mrs Shepard (1899–1982), of Portland, Oregon, USA. A birth certificate indicates that she gave birth to a daughter, Suzan, at Glendale, near Los Angeles, California, on 18 Oct 1956, when her age was 57 years 129 days. After her death a person purporting to be a relative alleged for an unknown motive that Mrs Kistler had 'changed the birth date'.

Leontina Albina of San Antonio, Chile; who built her unrivalled family of 54 children with 5 sets of triplets before she was 22.

BODY MEASUREMENTS

West Germany's Georgia Sebrantke: contender for today's title for having the world's longest tresses at 296 cm *9 ft 8½ in.*

LONGEST AND SHORTEST BONES

There are 206 bones in the human body, of which the *femur* is the longest. It constitutes usually 27½% of a person's stature, and may be expected to be 50 cm *19¾ in* long in a 183 cm *6 ft*-tall man. The longest recorded bone was the femur of the German giant Constantine, who died in Mons, Belgium, on 30 Mar 1902, aged 30. It measured 76 cm *29.9 in*. The femur of Robert Wadlow, the tallest man ever recorded, measured an estimated 75 cm *29½ in*.

The *stapes* or stirrup bone, one of the three in the middle ear, is the smallest human bone, measuring from 2,6 to 3,4 mm *0.10 to 0.17 in* in length and weighing from 2,0 to 4,3 mg *0.03 to 0.065 g*.

SMALLEST WAISTS

Queen Catherine de Medici (1519–89) decreed a waist measurement of 33 cm *13 in* for ladies of the French Court. This was at a time when females were more diminutive. The smallest recorded waist among women of normal stature in the 20th century is a reputed 33 cm *13 in* in the case of the French actress Mlle Polaire (1881–1939) and Mrs Ethel Granger (1905–82) of Peterborough who reduced from a natural 56 cm *22 in* over the period 1929–39.

CHAMPION BLOOD DONOR

Since 1966 Allen Doster, a self-employed beautician, has (to 1 Jan 1983) donated 1508 US pints at Roswell Park Memorial Institute, New York, USA as a plasmapheresis donor. The present-day normal limit on donations is 5 pints per annum. A 50-year-old haemophiliac Warren C. Jyrich required 2400 donor units *1080 l* of blood when undergoing open heart surgery at the Michael Reese Hospital, Chicago, USA in December 1970.

LONGEST NECKS

The maximum measured extension of the neck by the successive fitting of copper coils, as practised by the Padaung or Kareni people of Burma, is 40 cm *15¾ in*.

LONGEST HAIR

Swami Pandarasannadhi, the head of the Tirudadutural monastery, Tanjore district, Madras, India was reported in 1949 to have hair 7,92 m *26 ft* in length. The length of hair of Miss Skuldfrid Sjorgren (b. Stockholm) was reported from Toronto, Canada in 1927 to have reached twice her height at 3,20 m *10 ft 6 in*.

FASTEST TALKER

Few people are able to speak *articulately* at a sustained speed above 300 words per min. The fastest broadcaster has been regarded as Gerry Wilmot (b. Victoria, BC, Canada, 6 Oct 1914) the ice hockey commentator in the post-World War II period. Raymond Glendenning (1907–74), the BBC horseracing commentator, once spoke 176 words in 30 sec while commentating on a greyhound race. In public life the highest speed recorded is a 327 words per min burst in a speech made in December 1961 by John Fitzgerald Kennedy (1917–63), then President of the United States. Tapes of attempts to recite Hamlet's 262-word Soliloquy in under 24 sec (655 w.p.m.) have proved unintelligible.

The world's longest necks are among the Padaung or Kareni people of Burma. The record is 40 cm *15¾ in*.

LONGEST BEARD

The longest beard preserved was that of Hans N. Langseth (b. 1846 near Eidsroll, Norway) which measured 5,33 m *17½ ft* at the time of his burial at Kensett, Iowa in 1927 after 15 years residence in the United States. The beard was presented to the Smithsonian Institution, Washington, DC in 1967. The beard of the bearded lady Janice Deveree (b. Bracken Co., Kentucky, USA, 1842) was measured at 36 cm *14 in* in 1884. The beard of Mlle Helene Antonia of Liège, Belgium, a 17th century exhibitionist was said to have reached her hips.

LONGEST MOUSTACHE

The longest moustache on record was that of Masuriya Din (b. 1908), a Brahmin of Uttar Pradesh, India. It grew to an extended span of 2,59 m *8 ft 6 in* between 1949 and 1962. Karna Ram Bheel (b. 1928) was granted permission by a New Delhi prison governor in February 1979 to keep his 238 cm *7 ft 10 in* moustache grown since 1949 during his life sentence. Birger Pellas (b. 21 Sept 1934) of Malmö, Sweden has a 2,64 m *8 ft 8 in* moustache grown since 1973. The longest moustache in Great Britain is that of Mr Mike Solomons of Long Dilton, Surrey. It measured 83,8 cm *33 in* as at 24 Mar 1986.

LARGEST CHEST MEASUREMENTS

George Macaree (formerly Britain's heaviest man) has a chest measurement of 190,5 cm *75 in* (waist 177,8 cm *70 in*), at a bodyweight of 196,8 kg *31 st* (height 177,8 cm *5 ft 10 in*) and Martin Ruane has a chest measurement of 185,4 cm *73 in* (waist 172,7 cm *68 in*).

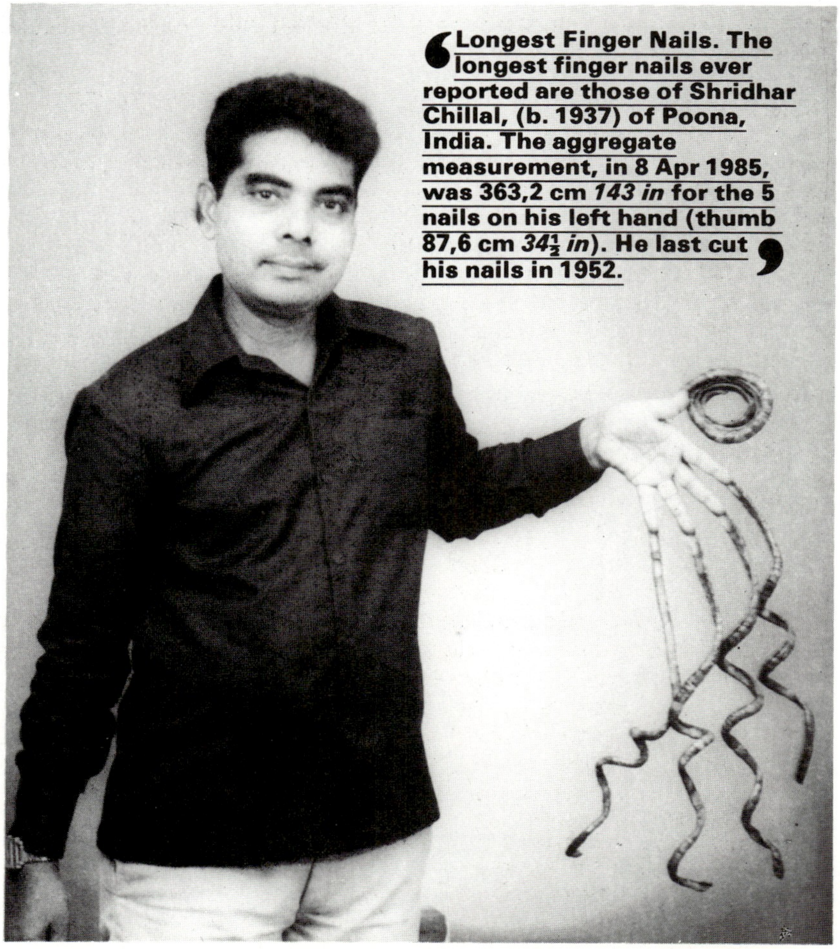

'Longest Finger Nails. The longest finger nails ever reported are those of Shridhar Chillal, (b. 1937) of Poona, India. The aggregate measurement, in 8 Apr 1985, was 363,2 cm *143 in* for the 5 nails on his left hand (thumb 87,6 cm *34½ in*). He last cut his nails in 1952.'

'Sergei Vassilevitch Rachmaninov (1873–1943) had a span of 12 white notes and could play a left hand chord of C, Eb, G, C, G.'

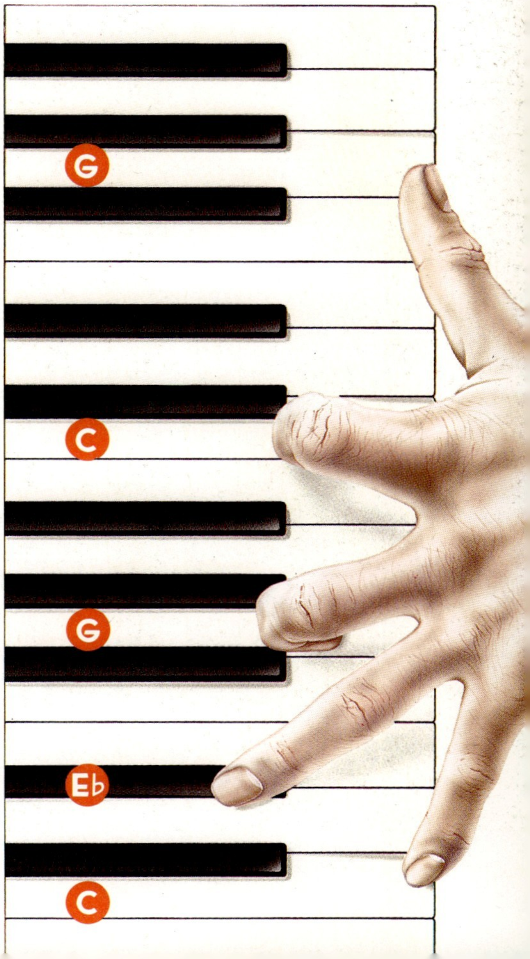

BODY MEASUREMENTS

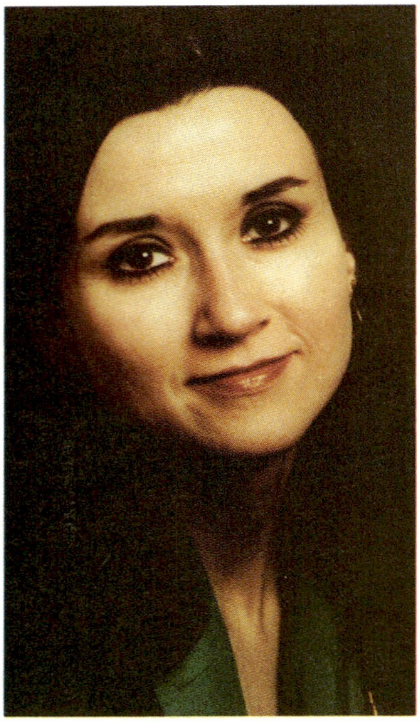

❛*Highest IQ.* The highest childhood score has been achieved by Marilyn Mach vos Savant of St Louis, Missouri, USA who as a 10 year old achieved a ceiling score for 23 year olds thus giving her an IQ of 230.❜

IVAN THE SUPER-BRAIN

The brain of an average adult male (*i.e.* 20–55 years) weighs 1424 g *3 lb 2.2 oz*, decreasing gradually to 1395 g *3 lb 1.1 oz* with advancing age. The heaviest non-diseased brain on record was that of Ivan Sergeyvich Turgenev (1818–83), the Russian author. His brain weighed 2012 g *4 lb 6.9 oz*.

THE FASTEST BRAIN IN THE EAST

Mrs Shakuntala Devi of India demonstrated the multiplication of 7,686,369,774,870 × 2,465,099,745,779 at the Computer Department of Imperial College, London on 18 June 1980, in 28 sec. Her correct answer was 18,947,668,177,995,426,462,773,730.

THE LONGEST MEMORY

Bhandanta Vicitsara recited 16,000 pages of Bhuddist canonical texts in Rangoon, Burma in May 1974. Rare instances of eidetic memory – the ability to re-project and hence 'visually' recall material – are known to science.

SUPER TOTS

HEAVIEST BABY

The heaviest babies on record, of normal parentage, were boys of 10,2 kg *22 lb 8 oz* born to Sig Carmelina Fedele of Aversa, Italy in September 1955 and by caesarian section to Mrs Christian Samane at Sipetu Hospital, Transkei, South Africa on 24 May 1982. The latter boy weighed 34,9 kg *77 lb* at 16 months.

LIGHTEST BABY

The lowest birth weight recorded for a surviving infant, of which there is definite evidence, is 283 g *10 oz* in the case of Mrs Marian Taggart *née* Chapman (b. 5 June 1938, d. 31 May 1983) who was born six weeks premature in South Shields, Tyne and Wear. She was born unattended (length 31 cm $12\frac{1}{4}$ *in*) and was nursed by Dr D. A. Shearer, who fed her hourly for the first 30 hours with brandy, glucose and water through a fountain-pen filler. At three weeks she weighed 821 g *1 lb 13 oz* and by her first birthday 6,29 kg *13 lb 14 oz*. Her weight on her 21st birthday was 48,08 kg *7 st 8 lb*. The smallest viable baby reported from the United States has been Jacqueline Benson born at Palatine, Illinois, on 20 Feb 1936, weighing 340 g *12 oz*.

1181 sets of twins gathered at Twinsberg, Ohio, USA 3–4 August 1985. This photograph shows about a quarter of the total.

SUPER TOTS

MOST BOUNCING BABY

The most bouncing baby on record was probably James Weir (1819–1821) who, according to his headstone in Cambushnethan, Old Parish Cemetery, Wishaw, Strathclyde, Scotland was 50,8 kg *8 st or 112 lb* at 13 months, 1,01 m *3 ft 4 in* in height and 99 cm *39 in* in girth.

FIRST TEST-TUBE TOT

Louise Brown (2,6 kg *5 lb 12 oz*) was delivered by Caesarian section from Lesley Brown, 31, in Oldham General Hospital, Lancashire, at 11.47 p.m. on 25 July 1978. She was externally conceived on 10 Nov 1977.

MOST SOUTHERLY BIRTH

Emilio Marcos Palma (Argentina) born 7 Jan 1978 at the Sargento Cabral Base, Antarctica is the only infant who can claim to be first born on any continent.

MEDICAL RECORDS

HIGHEST BODY TEMPERATURE

Willie Jones, 52 year old, was admitted to Grady Memorial Hospital, Atlanta, Georgia on 10 July 1980 with heat stroke on a day when the temperature reached 32,2 °C *90 °F* with 44% humidity. His temperature was found to be 46,5 °C *115.7 °F*. After 24 days he was discharged.

FASTEST AND SLOWEST PULSE RATES

A normal adult pulse rate is 70–72 beats per min at rest for males and 78–82 for females. Rates increase to 200 or more during violent exercise and drop to as low as 12 in the extreme cases of Dorothy Mae Stevens and Jean Hilliard (b. 1962) of Fosston, Minnesota, USA on 20 Dec 1980.

LONGEST COMA

It was reported in January 1985 that Alice Collins (b. 1891) of Columbia, South Carolina, USA, had regained consciousness after lapsing into a coma 75 years 2 months earlier. She had fallen down two flights of stairs in October 1909.

LONGEST DREAM

Dreaming sleep is characterized by rapid eye movements known as REM discovered in 1953 by William Dement of the University of Chicago. The longest recorded period of REM is one of 2 hr 23 min on 15 Feb 1967 at the department of Psychology, University of Illinois, Chicago on Bill Carskadon, who had had his previous sleep interrupted. In July 1984 The Sleep Research Centre, Halifa, Israel recorded nil REM in a 33-year-old male who had a shrapnel brain injury.

RAREST DISEASE

Medical literature periodically records hitherto undescribed diseases. A disease as yet undescribed but predicted by a Norwegian doctor is podocytoma of the kidney – a tumour of the epithelial cells lining the glomerulus of the kidney.

The last case of endemic Smallpox was recorded in Ali Maow Maalin in Merka, Somalia on 26 Oct 1977. In Britain Paul Braddon of Rusper, West Sussex was reported on 2 Aug 1983 to be the first case to contract malaria for more than 35 years.

'The lightest surviving baby for which there is definite evidence is 283 g *10 oz* in the case of Mrs Marian Chapman née Taggart (1938–83) in South Shields, Tyne and Wear, UK.'

Paul Braddon of Rusper, West Sussex who on 2 Aug 1983 was reported to be the first case of malaria contracted for more than 35 years.

MEDICAL RECORDS

The loudest snore recorded was 87.5 decibels in the early hours of 28 June 1984 by Melvyn Switzer who was 1 ft from the meter. His wife is deaf in one ear.

MOST INFECTIOUS DISEASE

The most infectious of all diseases is the pneumonic form of plague, which has a mortality rate of about 99.99%. This is matched by rabies and AIDS (Acquired immune deficiency syndrome). Leprosy, transmissible by coughing, sneezing or spitting, is the most bacilliferous of communicable diseases. The bacillus is *Mycobacterium leprae* discovered by G. H. A. Hansen (Norway) (1841–1912) in 1871.

THE MOST INFECTIOUS PERSON

The most publicized of all typhoid carriers has been Mary Mallon, known as Thyphoid Mary, of New York City, NY, USA. She was the source of nine outbreaks, notably that of 1903. She was placed under permanent detention from 1915 until her death in 1938. A still anonymous dairy farmer from Camden, NY was the source of 409 cases (40 fatal) in August 1909.

THE BIGGEST YAWN

In Lee's case, reported in 1888, a 15-year-old female patient yawned continuously for a period of 5 weeks.

Fifty-one year old Joseph Ascough who can still smile after averaging over six operations a year since he was born.

THE LOUDEST SNORE

The highest measured sound level recorded by any chronic snorer is 87.5 decibels at Hever Castle, Kent in the early hours of 28 June 1984. Melvyn Switzer of Hampshire was 30 cm *1 ft* from the meter. His wife Julie is deaf in one ear.

LONGEST HEART STOPPAGE

The longest recorded heart stoppage is a minimum of 3 hr 40 min in the case of Miss Jean Jawbone, 20, was revived by a team of 26, using peritoneal dialysis, in Health Sciences Centre, Winnipeg, Manitoba, Canada on 8 Jan 1977. A 'Mammalian diving reflex' can be triggered in humans falling into water cooler than 21 °C *70 °F*. In February 1974 Vegard Slettmoen, 5, fell through the ice on the river Nitselv, Norway. He was found 40 min later 2,5 m *8 ft* down but was revived in Akershus Central Hospital without brain-damage.

LONGEST IN IRON LUNG

The longest recorded period in an 'iron lung' is 37 years 58 days by Mrs Laurel Nisbet (b. 17 Nov 1912) of La Crescenta, California, USA, who died on 22 Aug 1985. She had been in an 'iron lung' continuously since 25 June 1948. The longest survival in an 'iron lung' in Britain has been 30 years by Denis Atkin in Lodge Moor Hospital, Sheffield, South Yorkshire. Mr John Prestwich (b. 24 Nov 1938) of Kings Langley, Hertfordshire has been dependent on a negative pressure respirator since 24 Nov 1955.

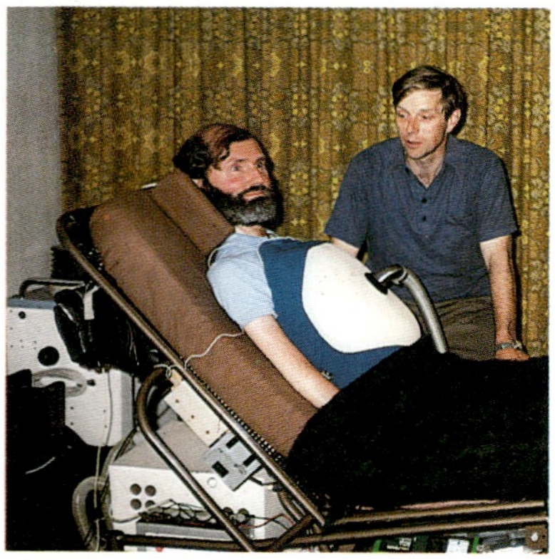

Longest in an Iron Lung. John Prestwich's life has been prolonged by 30 years by dint of a negative pressure respirator.

THE GREAT HICCOUGH

The longest recorded attack of hiccoughs or singultus is that afflicting Charles Osborne (b. 1894) of Anthon, Iowa, USA, for 60 years from 1922. He contracted it when slaughtering a hog and has hiccoughed about 430 million times in the interim period. He was unable to find a cure, but has led a reasonably normal life in which he had two wives and fathered eight children. He did admit, however, that he could not keep in his false teeth.

SUPER SNEEZING

The most chronic sneezing fit ever recorded is that of Donna Griffiths (b. 1969) of Pershore, Hereford & Worcester. She started sneezing on 13 Jan 1981 and surpassed the previous duration record of 194 days on 27 July 1981. She sneezed an estimated million times in the first 365 days. She achieved her first sneeze-free day on 16 Sept 1983 – the 978th day. The highest speed at which expelled particles have ever been measured to travel is 167 km/h *103.6 mph*.

MOST MOTIONLESS
The longest that anyone has continuously remained motionless is 13 hr by Willie Nugent, 38, Northern Ireland on 24 June 1985. The longest recorded case of involuntarily being made to stand to attention was when Staff Sgt Samuel B. Moody USAF, was so punished in Narumi prison camp, Nagoya, Japan for 53 hr in the spring of 1945. He survived to write *Reprieve from Hell.*

SUPER SWALLOWING
The worst reported case of compulsive swallowing was an insane female Mrs H. aged 42, who complained of a 'slight abdominal pain'. She proved to have 2533 objects, including 947 bent pins, in her stomach. These were removed by Drs Chalk and Foucar in June 1927 at the Ontario Hospital, Canada. The heaviest object extracted from a human stomach has been a 2,53 kg *5 lb 3 oz* ball of hair in Swain's case from a 20-year-old female compulsive swallower in the South Devon and East Cornwall Hospital, England on 30 Mar 1895.

RECORD NUMBER OF DOCTORS
The country with the most physicians is the USSR, with 831,300, or one to every 307 persons. China had an estimated 1.4 million para-medical personnel known as 'bare foot doctors' by 1981. In the United Kingdom there were 154,318 doctors qualified to work as specialists, in general practice or in industry as at 1 Jan 1984.

The country with the lowest recorded proportion is Upper Volta, with 58 physicians (one for every 92,759 people) in 1970.

THE LIGHTEST SLEEPER
The longest recorded period for which a person has voluntarily gone without sleep is 449 hr (18 days 17 hr) by Mrs Maureen Weston of Peterborough, Cambridgeshire in a rocking chair marathon on 14 Apr–2 May 1977. Though she tended to hallucinate toward the end of this surely ill-advised test, she surprisingly suffered no lasting ill-effects. Victims of the very rare condition chronic colestites (total insomnia) have been known to go without definable sleep for many years. An example has been Jesus de Frutos (b. 1925) of Segovia, Spain who claims only to have dozed since 1954.

RECORD NUMBER OF DENTISTS
The country with the most dentists is the United States, where 145,000 were registered members of the American Dental Association in 1983.

RECORD NUMBER OF PSYCHIATRISTS
The country with the most psychiatrists is the United States. The registered membership of the American Psychiatric Association (inst. 1894) was 27,000 in 1983. The membership of the American Psychological Association (inst. 1892) was 65,000 in 1983.

WORLD'S LARGEST HOSPITAL
The largest mental hospital in the world is the Pilgrim State Hospital, West Brentwood, Long Island, NY, USA, with 3618 beds. It formerly contained 14,200 beds.

WORLD'S BUSIEST MATERNITY HOSPITAL
The busiest maternity hospital in the world is the Mama Yemo Hospital, Kinshasa, Zaïre with 41,930 deliveries in 1976. The record 'birthquake' occurred on a day in May 1976 with 175 babies born. It has 599 beds.

'Donna Griffiths (b. 1969) of Pershore, Hereford and Worcester, started sneezing on 13 Jan 1981 and surpassed the previous record of 194 days. She sneezed an estimated million times in the first year and achieved her first sneeze-free day on 16 Sept 1983 – the 978th day.'

'The largest general hospital in Great Britain – St James's University Hospital (which is also a teaching hospital), Leeds, West Yorkshire, with 1470 staffed beds.'

'Charles Osborne has hiccoughed 430 million times since slaughtering a hog in 1922. He has none the less married twice and fathered eight children.'

WHAT'S IN A NAME?

The most common name in the world is the Chinese family name Chang. At the last count there were well over 104 million.

The longest place-name in the United Kingdom is a Welsh station named for commercial rather than toponymic reasons by the proprietors of the Fairbourne Steam Railway, near Barmouth, North Wales who posted the 67 letter name on a station board 19,5 m *64 ft* long.

LONGEST CHRISTIAN NAME

The longest Christian or given name on record is one of 622 letters given by Mr Scott Roaul Sör-Lökken of Missoula, Montana, USA to his daughter Miss S. Ellen Georgianna Sör Lökken (b. 1979). The 'S' stands for a 598 letter name designed to throw a monkey wrench into the computers of federal bureaucracy. She is known as 'Snow Owl' for short or 'Oli' for shorter.

THE MOST POPULAR ENGLISH SURNAME

The commonest surname in the English-speaking world is Smith. The most recent published count showed 659,050 nationally insured Smiths in Great Britain, of whom 10,102 were plain John Smith and another 19,502 were John (plus one or more given names) Smith. Including uninsured persons there were over 800,000 Smiths in England and Wales alone, of whom 81,493 were called A. Smith. There were an estimated 2,382,509 Smiths in the USA in 1973. It is no secret that by 1984 there were some 90,000 Singhs in Britain – the name means 'in secret'.

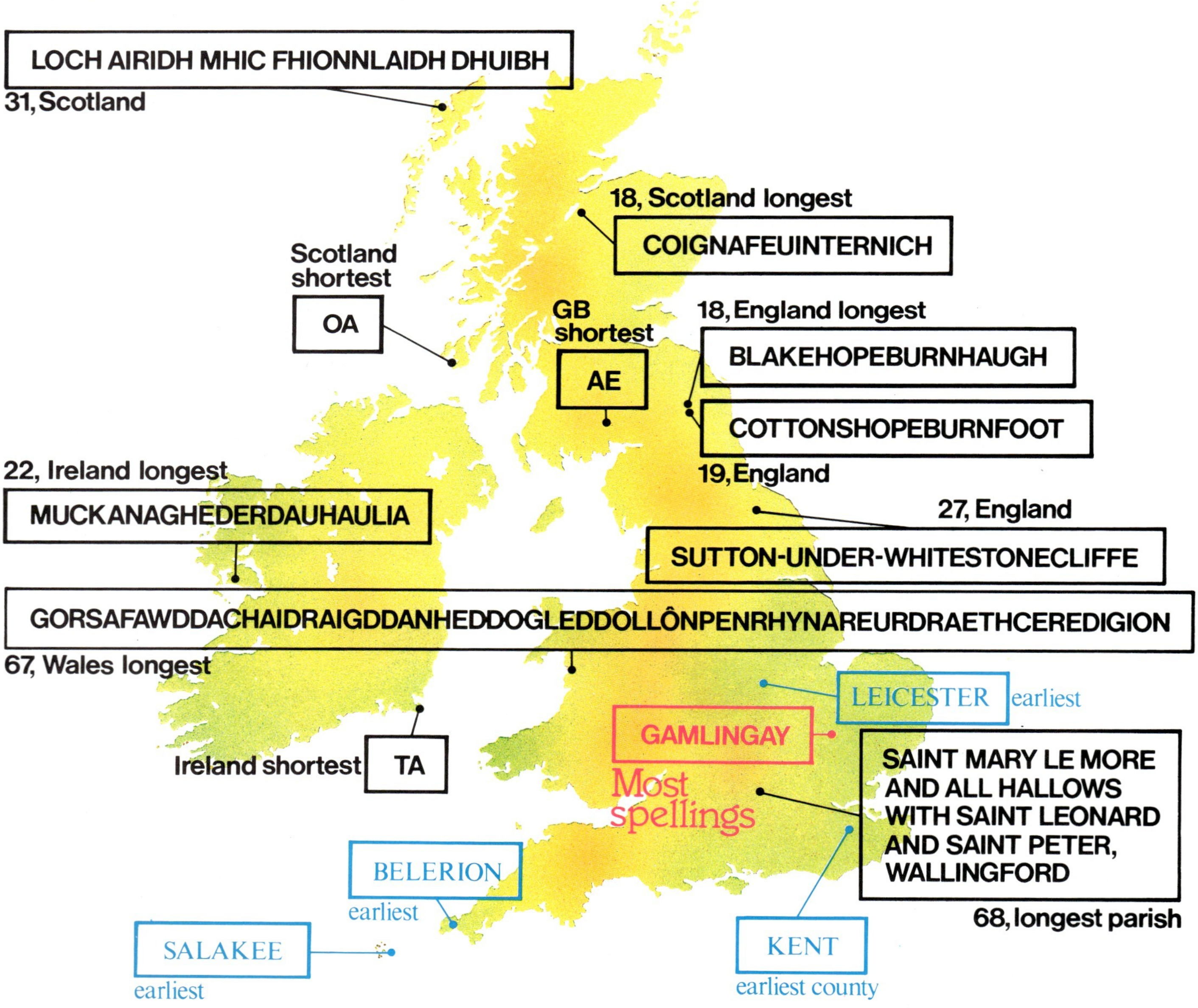

THE LONGEST SURNAME IN THE UNITED KINGDOM

The longest surname in the United Kingdom was the six-barrelled one borne by the late Major L.S.D.O.F. (Leone Sextus Denys Oswolf Fraudatifilius) Tollemache-Tollemache-de Orellana-Plantagenet-Tollemache-Tollemache, who was born on 12 June 1884 and died of pneumonia in France on 20 Feb 1917. Of non-repetitious surnames, the last example of a five-barrelled one was that of the Lady Caroline Jemima Temple-Nugent-Chandos-Brydges-Grenville (1858–1946). The longest single English surname is Featherstonehaugh (17 letters), correctly pronounced on occasions (but improbably on the correct occasion) Featherstonehaw or Festonhaw or Fessonhay or Freestonhugh or Feerstonhaw or Fanshaw.

LONGEST NAME IN THE WORLD

The longest name appearing on a birth certificate is that of Rhoshandiatellyneshiaunneveshenk Koyaanfsquatsiuty Williams born to Mr and Mrs James L. Williams in Beaumont, Texas, USA on 12 Sept 1984. On 5 Oct 1984 the father filed an amendment which expanded his daughter's first name to 1,019 letters and the middle name to 36 letters.

THE WORLD'S COMMONEST FAMILY NAME

The commonest family name in the world is the Chinese name Chang which is borne, according to estimates, by between 9.7 and 12.1% of the Chinese population, so indicating even on the lower estimate that there are at least some 104 million Changs – more than the entire population of all but 7 of the 170 other sovereign countries of the world.

THE WORLD'S LONGEST PLACE NAME

The official name for Bangkok, the capital city of Thailand, is Krungtep Mahanakhon. The full name is however: Krungthep Mahanakhon Bovorn Ratanakosin Mahintharayutthaya Mahadilokpop Noparatratchathani Burirom Udomratchanivetmahasathan Amorpiman Avatarnsathit Sakkathattiyavisnukarmprasit (167 letters) which in its most scholarly transliteration emerges with 175 letters. The longest place name now in use in the world is Taumatawhakatangihangakoauauotamatea(turipukakapikimaungahoronuku)pokaiwhenuakitanatahu, the unofficial 85-letter version of the name of a hill (305 m *1002 ft* above sea-level) in the Southern Hawke's Bay district of North Island, New Zealand. This Maori name means 'the hill whereon was played the flute of Tamatea, circumnavigator of lands, for his lady love'. The official version has 57 letters (1 to 36 and 65 to 85). Ijouaououene, a mountain in Morocco, has 8 consecutive vowel letters as rendered by the French.

THE WORLD'S SHORTEST PLACE NAMES

The shortest place names in the world are the French village of Y (population 143), so named since 1241, the Danish village Å on the island Fyn, the Norwegian village of Å (pronounced 'Aw'), the Swedish place Å in Vikholandet, U in the Caroline Islands, Pacific Ocean; and the Japanese town of Sosei which is alternatively called Aioi or O. There was once a '6' in West Virginia, USA. The shortest place names in Great Britain are the two-lettered places of Ae (population 199 in 1961) Dumfries and Galloway; Oa on the island of Islay, Strathclyde and Bu on Wyre, Orkney Islands. In the Shetland Islands there are skerries called Ve and two stacks called Aa. The island of Iona was originally I. The River E flows into the southern end of Loch Mhór, Invernessshire, and O Brook flows on Dartmoor, Devon. The shortest place name in Ireland is Ta (or Lady's Island) Lough, a sea-inlet on the coast of County Wexford.

'The world's longest place name is TAUMATAWHAKATANGI-HANGAKOAUAUOTAMA-TEAPOKAIWHENUAKA-TANATAHU a hill in New Zealand.'

A plasmid of bacterial DNA whose systematic name contains over 200,000 letters – the world's longest scientific name. (Science Photo Library).

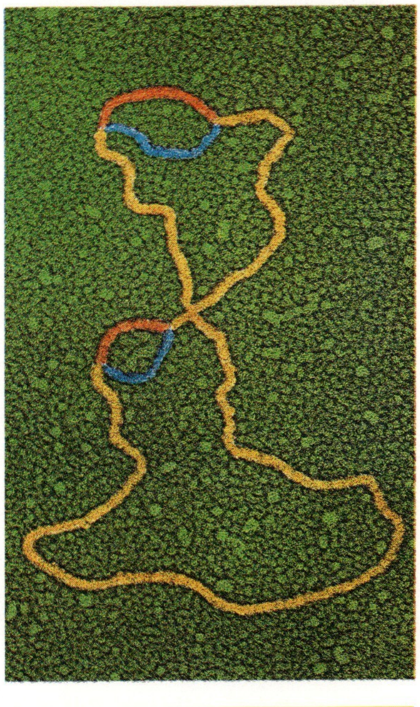

BIRTHS, DEATHS & MARRIAGES

'The tallest married couple. Canadian Anna Hanen Swan who married Martin van Buren Bates in London in 1871 (not shown here). Anna measured 227 cm *7 ft 5½ in* and Martin stood 220 cm *7 ft 2½ in.* *(Gary Doidge)*'

MAN OR WOMAN?

There were estimated to be 1003.5 men in the world for every 1000 women (1975). The country with the largest recorded shortage of males is the USSR, with 1145.9 females to every 1000 males (1981 census). The country with the largest recorded woman shortage is Pakistan, with 885 to every 1000 males in 1972. The figures are, however, probably under-enumerated due to *purdah*. The ratio in the United Kingdom was 1056 females to every 1000 males at mid-1982, and is expected to be 1014.2/1000 by AD 2000.

LIFE EXPECTATION

World expectation of life is rising from 47.4 years (1950–55) towards 64.5 years (1995–2000). There is evidence that life expectation in Britain in the 5th century AD was 33 years for males and 27 years for females. In the decade 1890–1900 the expectation of life among the population of India was 23.7 years.

Based on the latest available data, the highest recorded expectation of life at age 12 months is 73.7 years for males and 79.7 for females in Iceland (1979–80).

The lowest recorded expectation of life at birth is 27 years for both sexes in the Vallée du Niger area of Mali in 1957 (sample survey, 1957–8). The figure for males in Gabon was 25 years in 1960–1 but 45 for females.

The latest available figures for England and Wales (1978–80) are 70.2 years for males and 76.2 years for females. Scotland and Northern Ireland are both 68.4 years for males and 74.6 years for females, and for the Republic of Ireland (1980) 70.0 years for males and 75.0 for females. The British figure for 1901–10 was 48.53 years for males and 52.83 years for females.

HIGHEST AND LOWEST BIRTH RATES

The rate for the whole world was 27.5 per 1000 in 1982. The highest estimated by the UN is 54.6 per 1000 for Kenya in 1980. A world wide survey published in 1981 showed only Nepal (48.9) with a still rising birth rate.

Excluding Vatican City, where the rate is negligible, the lowest recorded rate is 10.1 for the Federal Republic of Germany and San Marino (1982). The fastest falling is in Thailand where the 3.3 average number of children per family has fallen to 1.8 in 10 years.

HIGHEST AND LOWEST DEATH RATES

The death rate for the whole world was 10.7 per 1000 in 1982. The highest of the latest available estimated death rates is 29.4 deaths per 1000 of the population in Kampuchea in 1975–80.

The lowest of the latest available recorded rates is 3.1 deaths/1000 in Samoa in 1980.

MARRIAGE

The country with the lowest average ages for marriage is India, with 20.0 years for males and 14.5 years for females. At the other extreme is Ireland, with 31.4 for males and 26.5 for females. In the People's Republic of China the *recommended* age for marriage for men has been 28 and for women 25. In England and Wales the peak ages for marriage are 22.8 years (male) and 19.6 years (female).

'The oldest couple to marry were Dyura Avramovich, 101 yr, and Yula Zhivich, 95 yr.'

DIVORCE

The country with most divorces is the United States with a total of 1,180,000 in 1982 – a rate of 47.29% on the then current annual total of marriages (*cf* 50.65% in 1979).

WORLD'S MOST MARRIED PEOPLE

The greatest number of marriages accumulated in the monogamous world is 26 by the former Baptist minister Glynn 'Scotty' Wolfe (b. 25 July 1908) of Blythe, California, who first married in 1927. His latest wife was the tattooed Cristine Sue Camacho, 38, married on 28 Jan 1984 but who left in May. His previous oldest wife was 22. His total number of children is, he says, 41. He has additionally suffered 24 mothers-in-law.

Mrs Beverly Nina Avery, then aged 48, a bar-maid from Los Angeles, California, USA, set a monogamous world record in October 1957 by obtaining her sixteenth divorce from her fourteenth husband, Gabriel Avery. She alleged outside the court that five of the 14 had broken her nose.

The record for bigamous marriages is 104 by Giovanni Vigliotto, one of some 50 aliases used by either Fred Jipp (b. New York City, 3 Apr 1936) or Nikolai Peruskov (b. Siracusa, Sicily, 3 Apr 1929) over the span 1949–1981 in 27 US States and 14 other countries. Four victims were aboard one ship in 1968 and two in London. On 28 Mar 1983 in Phoenix, Arizona he was sentenced to 28 years for fraud, 6 years for bigamy and fined $336,000.

Glynn 'Scotty' Wolfe of California who has accumulated the greatest number of marriages, 26 to date, his experience of mothers-in-law is unrivalled.

OLDEST BRIDE AND BRIDEGROOM

The oldest recorded bridegroom has been Harry Stevens, 103, married Thelma Lucas, 84, at the Caravilla Retirement Home, Wisconsin on 3 Dec 1984.

'The average age at which girls marry in India is 14½ yr.'

LONGEST ENGAGEMENTS

The longest engagement on record was between Octavio Guillen, and Adriana Martinez. They finally took the plunge after 67 years in June 1969 in Mexico City, Mexico. Both were then 82.

WORLD'S LONGEST MARRIAGE

The longest recorded marriages are of 86 years between Sir Temulji Bhicaji Nariman and Lady Nariman from 1853 to 1940 resulting from a cousin marriage when both were five. Sir Temulji (b. 3 Sept 1848) died, aged 91 years 11 months, in August 1940 at Bombay. Lazurus Rowe (b. Greenland, New Hampshire, 1725) and Molly Webber were recorded as marrying in 1743. He died first in 1829 after 86 years of marriage.

MOST MARRIED

Jack V. and Edna Moran of Seattle, Washington, USA have married each other 40 times since the original and only really necessary occasion on 27 July 1937 in Seaside, Oregon. Subsequent ceremonies have included those at Banff, Canada (1952), Cairo, Egypt (1966) and Westminster Abbey, London (1975).

'The controversial Rev. Moon officiated over a mass wedding ceremony involving 5837 couples from 83 different countries at the Holy Spirit Association for the Unification of World Christianity, Seoul, S. Korea on 14 Oct 1982.'

BIRTHS, DEATHS & MARRIAGES

'The highest alimony ever awarded was $2,261,000 (then £983,000) against broadcasting executive George Storer Snr, aged 74 on 29 October 1974 in Miami, Florida. He also had to pay his wife's legal costs of $200,000 (then £86,950).'

GOLDEN WEDDINGS
Despite the advent of the computer, records on golden (or 50 years long) weddings remain still largely uncollated. Unusual cases reported include that of Mrs Agnes Mary Amy Mynott (b. 25 May 1887) who attended the golden wedding of her daughter Mrs Violet Bangs of St Albans on 20 Dec 1980, 23 years after her own. The 3 sons and 4 daughters of Mr and Mrs J. Stredwick of East Sussex *all* celebrated golden weddings between May 1971 and April 1981. Triplets Lucille (Mrs Vogel), Marie (Mrs McNamara) and Alma (Mrs Prom) Pufpaff all celebrated their golden weddings on 12 Apr 1982 having all married in Cleveland, Minnesota in 1932.

MASS CEREMONY
The largest mass wedding ceremony was one of 5837 couples from 83 countries officiated over by Sun Myung Moon (b. 1920) of the Holy Spirit Association for the Unification of World Christianity in the Chamsil Gymnasium, Seoul, South Korea on 14 Oct 1982. The response to the question 'Will you swear to love your spouse for ever?' is 'Ye'.

MOST EXPENSIVE WEDDING
The wedding of Mohammed, son of Shaik Zayid ibn Sa'id al-Makhtum, to Princess Salama in Abu Dhabi in May 1981 lasted 7 days and cost an estimated £22 million in a purpose built stadium for 20,000.

LATEST DIVORCE
In March 1980 a divorce was reported in the Los Angeles Superior Court, California between Bernardine and Leopold Delpes in which both parties were aged 88. The British record age is 101 years by Harry Bidwell at Brighton, Sussex on 21 Nov 1980.

ROYAL RECORDS

OLDEST RULING HOUSE AND LONGEST REIGN
The Emperor of Japan, Hirohito (born 29 Apr 1901), is the 124th in line from the first Emperor, Jimmu Tenno or Zinmu, whose reign was traditionally from 660 to 581 BC, but more probably from *c* 40 BC to *c* 10 BC. The present Emperor, who succeeded on 25 Dec 1926 is currently the world's longest reigning monarch.

Her Majesty Queen Elizabeth II (b. 21 Apr 1926) represents dynasties historically traceable at least back until the 4th century AD; in the case of Tegid, great grandfather of Cunedda, founder of the House of Gwynedd in Wales; she is 54th in line. If the historicity of some early Scoto-Irish and Pictish kings were acceptable, the lineage could be extended to about 70 generations.

Emperor Hirohito, the world's longest reigning monarch and 124th in line from Japan's first Emperor whose reign was before Christ.

LONGEST REIGN OF ALL TIME
The longest recorded reign of any monarch is that of Phiops II or Neferkare, a Sixth Dynasty Pharaoh of ancient Egypt. His reign began in *c* 2281 BC, when he was aged 6, and is believed to have lasted *c* 94 years. Musoma Kanijo, chief of the Nzega district of western Tanganyika (now part of Tanzania), reputedly reigned for more than 98 years from 1864, when aged 8, until his death on 2 Feb 1963. The longest reign of any major European monarch was that of King Louis XIV of France, who ascended the throne on 14 May 1643, aged 4 years 231 days, and reigned for 72 years 110 days until his death on 1 Sept 1715, four days before his 77th birthday. Alfonso I Henrigues of Portugal reigned first as a Count and then as the first King for 73 years 220 days from 30 Apr 1112 to 6 Dec 1185.

ROYAL RECORDS

ROMAN OCCUPATION
During the 369 year long Roman occupation of England, Wales and parts of southern Scotland there were 40 sole and 27 co-Emperors of Rome. Of these the longest reigning was Constantinus I (The Great) from 31 Mar 307 to 22 May 337.

HIGHEST NUMBERED ROYAL
The highest post-nominal number ever used to designate a member of a Royal House was 75 briefly enjoyed by Count Heinrich LXXV Reuss (1800–1). All male members of this branch of this German family are called Heinrich and are successively numbered from I upwards *each* century.

British regnal numbers date from the Norman conquest. The highest is 8, used by Henry VIII (1509–47) and by Edward VIII (1936) who died as HRH the Duke of Windsor, on 28 May 1972. Jacobites liked to style Henry Benedict, Cardinal York (b. 1725), the grandson of James II, as Henry IX in respect of his 'reign' from 1788 to 1807 when he died as last survivor in the male line of the House of Stuart.

LONGEST LIVED 'ROYALS'
The longest life among the Blood Royal of Europe has been that of the late HSH Princess Elizabeth Maria Auguste of Ysenburg and Büdingen, West Germany. She was born on 12 Nov 1883 and died, as Duchess of Vandières, on 10 Oct 1982 aged 98 years 332 days. The greatest age among European Royal Consorts is the 101 years 268 days of HSH Princess Leonilla Bariatinsky (b. Moscow, 9 July 1816), who married HSH Prince Louis of Sayn-Wittgenstein-Sayn and died in Ouchy, Switzerland on 1 Feb 1918. The longest-lived Queen on record has been the Queen Grandmother of Siam, Queen Sawang (b. 10 Sept 1862), 27th daughter of King Mongkut (Rama IV); she died on 17 Dec 1955 aged 93 years 3 months.

HRH Princess Alice Mary, VA, GCVO, GBE, Countess of Athlone (b. 25 Feb 1883) became the longest ever lived British 'royal' on 15 July 1977 and died aged 97 years 313 days on 3 Jan 1981. She fulfilled 20,000 engagements, including the funerals of five British monarchs.

YOUNGEST KING AND QUEEN
Forty-six of the world's 169 sovereign states are not republics. They are lead by 1 Emperor, 14 Kings, 3 Queens, 4 princely rulers, 1 Sultan, 3 Amirs, the Pope, a Shaik, a Ruler and one elected monarch. Queen Elizabeth II is Head of State of 16 other Commonwealth countries. That with the youngest King is Swaziland where King Mswati III was crowned on 25 Apr 1986 aged 18. He was born Makhosetive, the 67th son of King Subhusa II. That with the youngest Queen is Denmark with Queen Margrethe II (b. 16 Apr 1940).

HEAVIEST MONARCH
The world's heaviest monarch is the 1,90 m *6 ft 3 in* tall King Taufa'ahau of Tonga who in Sept 1976 was weighed on the only adequate scales in the country at the airport recording 209,5 kg *33 st (462 lb)*. By 1985 he was reported to have slimmed to 139,7 kg *308 lb*.

MOST PROLIFIC
The most prolific monogamous 'royals' have been Prince Hartmann of Liechtenstein (1613–86) who had 24 children, of whom 21 were live born, by Countess Elisabeth zu Salm-Reifferscheidt (1623–88). HRH Duke Roberto I of Parma (1848–1907) also had 24 children but by two wives. One of his daughters HIM Empress Zita of Austria (b. 9 May 1892) was exiled on 23 Mar 1919 but visited Vienna, her titles intact on 17 Nov 1982 reminding republicans that her father succeeded to the throne of Parma in 1854.

'The shortest reign of all time was King Virabahu of the Kalinga Kshatriya dynasty of Ceylon (Sri Lanka) who was assassinated a few hours after he was crowned at Polonnaruwa in 1196.'

King Taufa'ahau of Tonga, heaviest of the world's fourteen kings. He is the son of the former Queen Salote.

The 93-year-old HIM Empress Zita of Austria one of HRH Duke Roberto I of Parma's 24 children.

RITZY RECORDS

'The most expensive musical box is this 1901 cylinder musical box which set an auction record of £19,000 in 1985. It was made for the special envoy to the Shah of Persia. *(Sotheby's, London)*'

ART NOUVEAU
The highest auction price for any piece of art nouveau is $360,000 (*then £163,600*) for a spider-web leaded glass mosaic and bronze table lamp by L. C. Tiffany at Christie's, New York on 8 Apr 1980.

The *c* 245-year-old porcelain thimble which fetched a record price of £8000 in December 1979.

BED
A 1930 black lacquer kingsize bed made by Jean Durand was auctioned at Christie's, New York City on 2 Oct 1983 for £49,668.

BLANKET
The most expensive blanket was a Navajo Churro handspun serape of *c* 1852 sold for $115,500 (*then £79,000*) at Sotheby's, New York City on 22 Oct 1983.

CARPET
In 1946 the Metropolitan Museum, New York, privately paid $1 million (*then £248,138*) for the 807×414 cm *26.5×13.6 ft* Anhalt Medallion carpet made in Tabriz or Kashan, Persia *c* 1590. The highest price ever paid at auction for a carpet is £231,000 for a 17th century 'Polonaise' silk and metal thread carpet at Sotheby's, London on 13 Oct 1982.

CERAMICS
The Greek urn painted by Euphronios and thrown by Euxitheos in *c* 530 was bought by private treaty by the Metropolitan Museum of Art, New York, for $1.3 million (*then £541,666*) in August 1972.

A carpet upon which even angels might fear to tread – the 17th-century 'Polonaise' silk and metal thread carpet auctioned at Sotheby's for a world record £231,000 on 13 Oct 1982.

CHAIR
The highest price ever paid for a single chair is $275,000 (*then £177,500*) on 23 Oct 1982 at Sotheby's in Manhattan, for the Chippendale side chair attributed to Thomas Affleck of Philadelphia, USA and made in *c* 1770.

CIGARETTE CARD
The most valuable card is one of the 6 known baseball series cards of Honus Wagner, who was a non-smoker, which was sold in New York in December 1981 for $25,000 (*then £13,900*).

DOLL
The highest price paid at auction for a doll is £16,000 for a William and Mary English wooden doll *c* 1690 at Sotheby's, London on 29 May 1984.

FURNITURE
The highest price ever paid for a single piece of furniture is £1,300,000 (*FF 15 million*) at Ader Picard Tajan, Monaco on 11 Nov 1984 for a mahogany and ebony collector's chest of drawers thought to have been made for Queen Marie-Antoinette (1755–1793) by G. Benneman.

The English furniture record was set by a black-japanned bureau-bookcase of *c* 1705. Formerly owned by Queen Mary, it made $860,000 (*then £463,366*) at Christie's, New York on 18 Oct 1981.

GLASS
The auction record is £520,000 for a Roman glass cage-cup of *c* AD 300 measuring 17,78 cm *7 in* in diameter and 10,16 cm *4 in* in height; sold at Sotheby's, London, on 4 June 1979 to Robin Symes.

GOLD PLATE
The auction record for any gold artefact is £950,400 for the 22 carat font made by the English silver- and goldsmith Paul Storr (1771–1844) to the design of Humphrey Repton in 1797. It was sold by Lady Anne Cavendish-Bentinck and bought by Armitage of London at Christie's on 11 July 1985.

GUN
The highest price ever paid for a single gun is £125,000 given by the London dealers F. Partridge for a French flintlock fowling piece made for Louis XIII, King of France in *c* 1615 and attributed to Pierre le Bourgeoys of Lisieux, France (d. 1627). This piece was included in the collection of the late William Goodwin Renwick of the United States sold by Sotheby's, London on 21 Nov 1972. It is now in the Metropolitan Museum, New York, USA.

HAT
The highest price ever paid for a hat is $66,000 (*then £34,750*) by the Alaska State Museum at a New York City auction in Nov 1981 for a Tlingit Kiksadi ceremonial frog helmet from *c* 1600.

ICON
The record auction price for an icon is $150,000 (*then £67,500*) paid at Christie's, New York on 17 Apr 1980 for the *Last Judgement* (from the George R. Hann collection, Pittsburgh, USA) made in Novgorod in the 16th century.

'The annual cost of keeping a pupil at the Le Rosey School, Gstaad, Switzerland in 1983/4 was reputed to be $20,000.'

The highest price ever paid for a single chair was £177,500 with a premium on 23 Oct 1982 at Sotheby's in Manhattan.

'The world's most expensive bottle of wine; a jeroboam (equivalent to six bottles of Bordeaux) of Mouton Rothschild, 1870, was bought for resale by Bill Burford of Dallas, Texas, from Whitwham Wines, Altrincham for £26,500 on 16 July 1984.'

RITZY RECORDS

Most Expensive Armour. The highest auction price paid for a suit of armour is £1,925,000 by B. H. Trupin (US) on 5 May 1983 at Sotheby's, London for the suit made in Milan by Giovanni Negroli in 1545 for Henri II, King of France from the Hever Castle Collection in Kent, England.

PAPERWEIGHT
The highest price ever paid for a glass paperweight is $143,000 (*£97,278*) at Sotheby's, New York City, USA on 2 Dec 1983 for a blue glass weight made at Pantin, Paris *post* 1850.

PISTOL
The highest price paid at auction for a pistol is £110,000 at Christie's London on 8 July 1980 for a Sadeler wheel-lock holster pistol from Munich dated *c* 1600.

PLAYING CARDS
The highest price paid for a deck of playing cards is $143,352 (*then £98,850*) by the New York Metropolitan Museum at Sotheby's, London on 6 Dec 1983.

PORCELAIN AND POTTERY
The highest auction price for any ceramic or any Chinese work of art is £792,000 for a blue and white Ming vase of 1426–35 bought by Hirano of Japan at Sotheby's, London on 15 Dec 1981.

POT LID
The highest price paid for a pot lid is £3300 for a seaweed patterned 'Spanish Lady' lid sold at Phillips, London on 19 May 1982.

SILVER
The highest price ever paid for silver is £612,500 for the pair of Duke of Kingston tureens made in 1735 by Meissonnier and sold by Christie's, Geneva on 8 Nov 1977. The English silver record is £484,000 at Sotheby's, London on 3 May 1984 for the Duke of Northumberland's Shield of Achilles, made in 1822 by Rundell, Bridge and Rundell.

SNUFF BOX
The highest price ever paid for a snuff box is Sw. Fr 1,540,000 (*then £435,028*) in a sale at Christie's, Geneva on 11 May 1982 for a gold snuff box dating from 1760–65 and once owned by Frederick the Great of Prussia. It was purchased by S. J. Phillips, the London dealers, for stock.

SPOONS
A Wiener werkstaffe spoon by Josef Hoffmann, Austria *c* 1905, was sold at Sotheby's, London for £17,600 on 28 Apr 1983. A set of 13 Henry VIII Apostle spoons owned by Lord Astor of Hever were sold for £120,000 on 24 June 1981 at Christie's, London.

SWORD
The highest price paid for a sword is the $145,000 (*then £85,800*) paid for the gold sword of honour, presented by the Continental Congress of 1779 to General Marie Jean Joseph Lafayette, at Sotheby Parke Bernet, New York City, USA on 20 Nov 1976.

TAPESTRY
The highest price for a tapestry is £550,000 for a Swiss medieval tapestry frieze in two parts dated 1468–1476 at Sotheby's, Geneva, on 10 Apr 1981 by the Basle Historische Museum.

THIMBLE
The record auction price for a thimble is £8000 paid by the London dealer Winifred Williams at Christie's, London on 3 Dec 1979 for a Meissen dentil-shaped porcelain piece of *c* 1740.

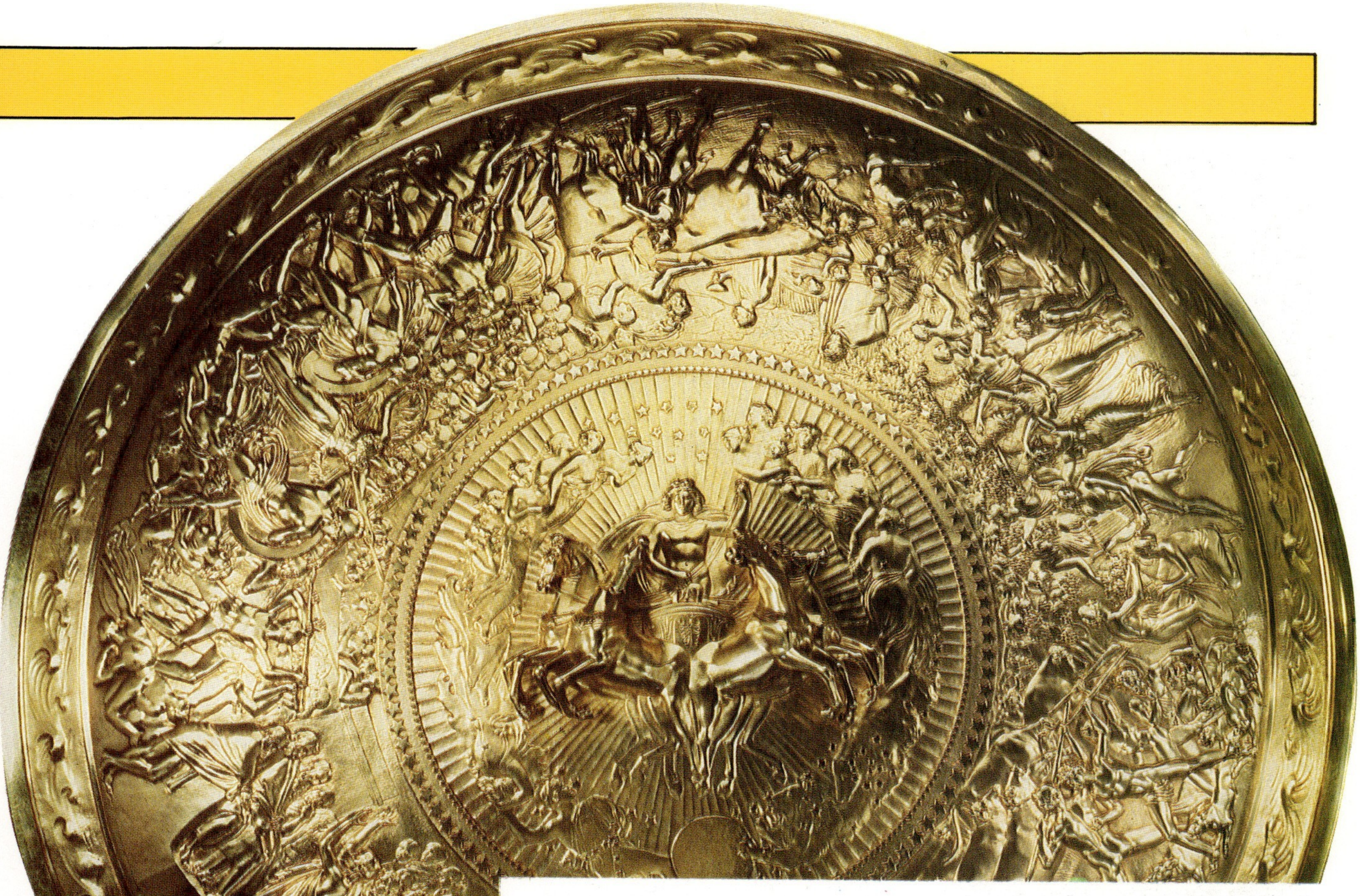

The Shield of Achilles which made a record price at auction for English silver.

Paul Storr's gold-plate font, made in 1797 and sold for a record £950,400 in 1985.

MOST EXPENSIVE WATCH

Excluding watches with jewelled cases, the most expensive standard men's pocket watch is the Swiss *Grande Complication* by Audemars-Piguet which retailed for £72,000 in January 1985. The *Kallista* watch with 130 carats of precious stones by Vacheron et Constantin of Geneva was valued in Apr 1981 at $5 million (*then £2,272,000*). The record price for an antique watch is $166,300 (*then £75,000*) paid to Capt. Peter Belin USN by L. C. Mannheimer of Zurich at Sotheby Parke Bernet, New York on 29 Nov 1979 for a gold studded case watch of *c.* 1810 by William Anthony of London.

RITZY RECORDS

The unique 1930 Silent Speed Six Bentley (*above*) which attracted a second hand car auction record of £270,600 at Sotheby's, London on 10 Dec 1984.

❛*Special.* The most expensive car to build has been the US Presidential 1969 Lincoln Continental Executive delivered to the US Secret Service on 14 Oct 1968. It has an overall length of 6,56 m *21 ft 6.3 in* with a 4,06 m *13 ft 4 in* wheel-base and with the addition of 2,03 tonnes *2 tons* of armour plate, weighs 5,43 tonnes *5.35 tons* (5443 kg *12,000 lb*). The estimated research, development and manufacture cost was $500,000 (*then £208,000*) but it is rented at $5000 (*now £2300*) per annum. Even if all four tyres were shot out it can travel at 80 km/h *50 mph* on inner rubber-edged steel discs. Carriage House Motor Cars Ltd of New York City in March 1978 completed 4 years' work on converting a 1973 Rolls Royce including lengthening it by 76,3 cm *30 in*. The price tag was $500,000 (*then £263,157*).❜

MOST EXPENSIVE LAND IN THE WORLD

The world's most expensive land is in central Hong Kong. In May 1982 freehold land for highrise building reportedly realized up to £11,000 per square foot. The freehold price for a grave site with excellent *Fung Shui* in Hong Kong may cost HK$200,000 for 1,21 × 3,04 m *4 ft × 10 ft* or £19,400 per ft^2. The real estate value per square metre of the two topmost French vineyards, Grande and Petite Cognac vineyards in Bordeaux, has not been recently estimated. The China Square Inch Land Ltd at a charity auction on 2 Dec 1977 sold 1 cm^2 *0.155 in^2* of land at Sha Tau Kok for HK$2000 (the equivalent of US$17,405,833,737 per acre). The purchasers were Stephen and Tony Nicholson. The most expensive land in Britain is that in the City of London. The freehold price on small prime sites reached £21,230/m^2 (*£1950/ft^2*) in mid 1973.

THE MOST EXPENSIVE SHARE

The highest denomination of any share quoted in the world is a single share in F. Hoffmann-La Roche of Basel worth Sw. Fr 101,000 (*£21,992*) on 23 Apr 1976.

THE MOST EXPENSIVE CIGAR

The most expensive standard cigar in the world is the 29,2 cm *11½ in* long Don Miguel 'Cervantes', which retails in Britain at £15.00.

❛The world's most expensive toy (right) – the £25,500 tin-plate model of Stephenson's *Rocket* made in Germany in 1909 *(Sotheby's, London)*.❜

1932 Bugatti. Sold for a record-breaking £440,000

CHOCOLATES
The most expensive chocolates are by Charbonel et Walker at $35 (*then £21.88*) per 453 g *1 lb* box.

CIGARETTE LIGHTER
The Dunhill Lighthouse Table Lighter is made in 18 ct gold – designed in the shape of a lighthouse set on an island base of amethyst which alone weighs 50 kg *1 cwt*. It weighs 1600 g *51.4 oz troy* and the windows on the lighthouse stem are amethyst. It was sold for £37,500 at Alfred Dunhill, St James's, London.

PRICIEST CLOTHES
The EVA suits for extra-vehicular activity worn by space shuttle crews from 1982 had a unit cost of $2.3 million (*then £1,437,000*). The dress with the highest price tag ever exhibited by a Paris fashion house was one in the Schiaparelli spring/summer collection on 23 Jan 1977. 'The Birth of Venus' designed by Serge Lepage with 512 diamonds was priced at Fr. 7,500,000 (*then £880,000*).

The coronation robe for Emperor Field-Marshal Jean-Bédel Bokassa with a 11,8 m *39 ft* long train was encrusted with 785,000 pearls and 1,220,000 crystal beads by Guiselin of Paris for £77,125. It was used at Bangui, Central African Empire (now Republic) on 4 Dec 1977.

MOST EXPENSIVE FABRIC
The most expensive fabric obtainable is Vicuña cloth manufactured by Fuji Keori Ltd of Osaka, Japan at $3235 (*£2087*) per metre in July 1983.

MOST EXPENSIVE SHOES
Emperor Bokassa of the Central African Republic commissioned pearl-studded shoes from the House of Berluti, Paris for his self-coronation in Dec 1977 at a cost of $85,000 (*then £38,800*).

The most expensive standard shoes obtainable are mink-lined golf shoes with 18 carat gold embellishments and ruby-tipped spikes made by Stylo Matchmakers International Ltd, of Northampton, England which retail for £7700, or $9625 per pair in the USA.

SNUFF
The most expensive snuff obtainable in Britain is 'Café Royale' sold by G. Smith and Sons (est. 1869) of 74 Charing Cross Road, City of Westminster, Greater London. It sells at £2.06 per oz as at 1 April 1986.

WREATH
The most expensive wreath on record was that presented to Sri Chinmoy in New York City, USA on 11 July 1983 by Ashrita Furman and Pahar Meltzer. It was handled by the Garland of Divinity's Love Florist, contained 10,000 flowers, and cost $3500 (*£2260*).

***Stuffed Bird.* The highest price ever paid for a stuffed bird is £9000. This was given on 4 Mar 1971 at Sotheby's, London, by the Iceland Natural History Museum for a specimen of the Great Auk (*Alca impennis*) in summer plumage, which was taken in Iceland *c* 1821; this particular specimen stood 57 cm *22½ in* high. The Great Auk was a flightless North Atlantic seabird, which was finally exterminated on Eldey, Iceland in 1844, becoming extinct through hunting. The last British sightings were at Co. Waterford in 1834 and St Kilda, Western Isles *c* 1840.**

RITZY RECORDS

Part of the unique block of 39 Norwegian 4 Skilling Blues, auctioned in London in 1981 for a record £105,000.

CHEESE

The world's most expensive cheese in its home market is Le Leruns made from ewes' milk at 90 francs per kilo (*now £3.40 per lb*). Cheese made to the Liederkranz formula in Van Wert, Ohio, USA retails at $2.25 per 4 oz; equivalent to $9.00 (*£6.40*) per lb. Britain's most costly traditional cheese is Blue Wensleydale which has no fixed price but is obtainable from some shops for between £2.50 and £3.00 per lb. The unlawfully made English Blue Vinney 'changes hands' for *c* £4.00 per lb.

WORLD'S MOST EXPENSIVE YACHT

King Khalid's Saudi Arabian 64,6 m *212 ft* Royal yacht was upstaged as the most expensive in 1979 by a five-deck 85,95 m *282 footer* built by the Benetti Shipyard, Viareggio, Italy for a reputed hull price of $24 million (*then £10.9 million*) to the order of Adnan Khashoggi. It has a helicopter and 5 speed boats.

STANDARD CAR

The most expensive British standard car is the Rolls-Royce 8 cylinder 6750 cc Camargue, quoted in May 1984 at £83,122 (incl. tax). More expensive are custom built models. Jack Barclay Ltd of Berkeley Square, London W1 quote £300,000 for an armour-plated Rolls-Royce Phantom VI (including tax).

The only owner of 25 new Rolls-Royces is believed to be Bhagwan Shri Rajneesh (b. 1931), the Indian mystic of Rajneeshpusam, Oregon, USA. His disciples have bestowed these upon him.

USED CAR

The greatest price paid for any used car is $2,229,000 (then £1,768,000) for John Lennon's 1965 Phantom V Rolls Royce at Sotheby's New York on 29 June 1985. In Great Britain £440,000 was paid in auction at Sotheby's for a Bugatti Type 55 roadster.

SPECIAL CAR

The most expensive special production was the US Presidential 1969 Lincoln Continental Executive. Its estimated cost was $500,000 (then £208,000).

Stamp Price Records

HIGHEST PRICE (TENDER) WORLD	**$1 million (*then £495,000*)**	**5 cent Blue Alexandria USA cover, Nov 25 1846 by George Normann *via* David Feldmans of Geneva on 9 May 1981.**
HIGHEST PRICE (AUCTION) (WORLD)	**£615,000**	**Baden 9 kr black on blue-green, colour error 1851 from the John R. Boker collection sold by Heinrich Köhler in Weisbaden, West Germany on 16 Mar 1985.**
HIGHEST PRICE (ERROR)	**$500,000 (*£227,500*)**	**US 1918 24 cent airmail invert of Jenny biplane 'Princeton' block of 4, by Myron Kaller syndicate on 19 July 1979. A single example reached $180,000 at auction in New York City in May 1982.**
HIGHEST PRICE (AUCTION) (UK)	**£105,000**	**Norwegian 4 Skilling Blue, 1855 block of 39 used – found in Trondheim railway station *c* 1923 by Phillips, New Bond Street, London on 5 Mar 1981.**
LARGEST PHILATELIC PURCHASE	**$11,000,000 (*then £4,945,000*)**	**Marc Haas collection of 3000 US postal and pre-postal covers to 1869 by Stanley Gibbons International Ltd of London in August 1979.**

MONEY

Britain's most expensive bid for a coin was £71,500 for a Henry III gold 20 pence (6 known) at Spink's, London on 13 June 1985.

EARLIEST PAPER MONEY

Paper money is an invention of the Chinese first tried in AD 910 and prevalent by AD 970. The world's earliest banknotes (*banco-sedler*) were issued in Stockholm, Sweden, in July 1661. The oldest surviving banknote is one of 5 dalers dated 6 Dec 1662. The oldest surviving printed Bank of England note is one for £555 to bearer, dated 19 Dec 1699 (11,4×19,6 cm *4½×7½ in*).

LARGEST AND SMALLEST PAPER MONEY

The largest paper money ever issued was the 1 kwan note of the Chinese Ming dynasty issue of 1368–99, which measured 22,8×33,0 cm *9×13 in.* In Oct 1983 one sold for £340. The smallest national note ever issued was the 10 bani note of the Ministry of Finance of Romania, in 1917. It measured (printed area) 27,5×38 mm *1.09×1.49 in.* Of German *notgeld* the smallest are the 1–3 pfg of Passau (1920–21) measuring 18×18,5 mm *0.70×0.72 in.*

WORLD'S MOST VALUABLE BANKNOTES

The highest denomination notes in circulation are US Federal Reserve Bank notes for $10,000 (*£5260*). They bear the head of Salmon Portland Chase (1808–73). None has been printed since July 1944 and the US Treasury announced in 1969 that no further notes higher than $100 would be issued. Only 350 $10,000 bills remain in circulation or unretired.

WORLD'S LEAST VALUABLE BANKNOTE

The lowest denomination legal tender banknote is the 1 sen (or 1/100th of a rupiah) Indonesian note. Its exchange value in mid 1984 was 140 to the new penny.

CHEQUE THE RECORD

The greatest amount paid by a single cheque in the history of banking has been one for Rs. 16,640,000,000 equivalent to £852,791,660 handed over by Hon. Daniel P. Moynihan, Ambassador of the USA to India in New Delhi on 18 Feb 1974. An internal US Treasury cheque for $4,176,969,623.57 was drawn on 30 June 1954.

GREATEST COIN COLLECTION

The highest price paid for a coin collection has been $7,300,000 (*then £3,550,000*) for a hoard of 407,000 US silver dollars from the La Vere Redfield estate in a courtroom auction in Reno, Nevada on 27 Jan 1976 by Steven C. Markoff of A-Mark Coin Co. Inc. of Beverley Hills, California.

The earliest example of a coin being dated. The year 494 BC on the Sicilian silver tetradrachm was designated as Year A.

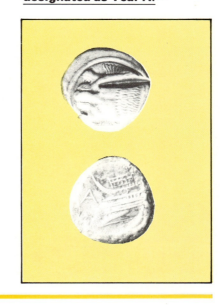

WORLD'S LARGEST HOARD OF MONEY

The largest hoard ever found was one of about 80,000 aurei in Brescello near Modena, Italy in 1814 believed to have been deposited *c* 37 BC. The numerically largest hoard ever found was the Brussels hoard of 1908 containing *c* 150,000 coins. A hoard of 56,000 Roman coins was found at Cunetio near Marlborough, Wiltshire on 15 Oct 1978.

The greatest discovery of treasure is the estimated $2000 million of gold coins and platinum ingots from the sunken Tsarist battleship *Admiral Nakhimov* 8524 tons 60 m *200 ft* down off the Japanese island of Tsushima. She sank on 27 May 1905.

COIN-COLUMN RECORD

The most valuable column of coins ever amassed for charity was a 15,6 km *9.69 miles* of pfennig pieces (worth DM 74,205.80) organized by soldiers of 21 Engineer Regiment stationed at Nienberg/Weser, West Germany on 23–24 Sep 1983.

RAGS AND RICHES

Paul McCartney MBE with his wife Linda. Paul is reputed to have earned the highest gross income in a year for a UK subject with a figure of £25 million.

'The record number of company directorships is 457 set in 1961 by Hugh T. Nicholson (1914–85).'

RICHEST FAMILIES

It has been tentatively estimated that the combined value of the assets nominally controlled by the du Pont family of some 1600 members may be of the order of $150,000 million. The family arrived in the USA from France on 1 Jan 1800. Capital from Pierre du Pont (1730–1817) enabled his son Eleuthère Irénée du Pont to start his explosives company in the United States. It was estimated in 1985 that both sons and both daughters of Haroldson Lafayette Hunt were billionaires.

LARGEST DOWRY

The largest recorded dowry was that of Elena Patiño, daughter of Don Simón Iturbo Patiño (1861–1947), the Bolivian tin millionaire, who in 1929 bestowed £8,000,000 from a fortune at one time estimated to be worth £125,000,000.

GREATER MISER

If meanness is measurable as a ratio between expendable assets and expenditure then Henrietta (Hetty) Howland Green (*née* Robinson) (1835–1916), who kept a balance of over $31,400,000 (*then £6.2 million*) in one bank alone, was the all-time world champion. Her son had to have a leg amputated because of her delays in finding a *free* medical clinic. She herself ate cold porridge because she was too thrifty to heat it. Her estate proved to be of $95 million (*then £19 million* [*and now worth £270 million*]).

RETURN OF CASH

The largest amount of *cash* ever found and returned to its owners was $500,000 (US) found by Lowell Elliott, 61 on his farm at Peru, Indiana, USA. It had been dropped in June 1972 by a parachuting hi-jacker.

Jim Priceman, 44, assistant cashier at Doft & Co. Inc. returned an envelope containing $37.1 million (*then £20.6 million*) in *negotiable* bearer certificates found outside 110 Wall Street to A. G. Becker Inc. of New York City on 6 April 1982. In announcing a reward of $250 (*then £140*) Beckers were acclaimed as 'being all heart'.

MILLIONAIRESSES

The world's wealthiest woman was probably Princess Wilhelmina Helena Pauline Maria of Orange-Nassau (1880–1962), formerly Queen of the Netherlands from 1890 to her abdication, 4 Sept 1948, with a fortune which was estimated at over £200 million. The largest amount proved in the will of a woman in the United Kingdom has been the £7,607,168 of the Rt Hon. Countess of Sefton in 1981. Mrs Anna Dodge (later Mrs Hugh Dillman) who was born in Dundee, Scotland, died on 3 June 1970 in the United States, aged 103, and left an estate of £40,000,000.

The cosmetician Madame Charles Joseph Walker, *née* Sarah Breedlove (b. Delta, Louisiana, USA 23 Dec 1867, d. 1919) is reputed to have become the first self-made millionairess. She was an uneducated Negro orphan scrub-woman whose fortune was founded on a hair straightener.

THE YOUNGEST MILLIONAIRE AND MILLIONAIRESS

The youngest person ever to accumulate a million dollars was the child film star Jackie Coogan (b. Los Angeles, 26 Oct 1914) co-star with Sir Charles Chaplin (1889–1977) in 'The Kid' made in 1920. Shirley Temple (b. Santa Monica, California 23 Apr 1928), formerly Mrs John Agar, Jr, now Mrs Charles Black, accumulated wealth exceeding $1,000,000 (*then £209,000*) before she was 10. Her child actress career spanned the years 1934–9.

GREATEST BEQUESTS

The greatest bequests in a lifetime of a millionaire were those of the late John Davison Rockefeller (1839–1937), who gave away sums totalling $750,000,000 (*now £350 million*). The greatest benefactions of a British millionaire were those of William Richard Morris, later the Viscount Nuffield, GBE, CH (1877–1963), which totalled more than £30,000,000 between 1926 and his death on 22 Aug 1963. The Scottish-born US citizen Andrew Carnegie (1835–1919) is estimated to have made benefactions totalling £70 million during the last 18 years of his life. These included 7689 church organs and 2811 libraries. He had started life in a bobbin factory at $1.20 per week.

The largest bequest made in the history of philanthropy was the $500,000,000 (*then £178,570,000*) gift, announced on 12 Dec 1955, to 4157 educational and other institutions by the Ford Foundation (established 1936) of New York City, NY, USA.

THE WORLD'S LARGEST LANDOWNER

The world's largest landowner is the United States Government, with a holding of 729,800,000 acres (2 953 000 km² *1,140,000 miles²*) which is more than the area of the world's 8th largest country Argentina and 12.8 times larger than the United Kingdom. The world's largest *private* landowner is reputed to be International Paper Co. with 3,64 million ha *9 million acres*. The United Kingdom's greatest ever private landowner was the 3rd Duke of Sutherland, George Granville Sutherland-Leveson-Gower, KG (1828–92), who owned 549 560 ha *1,358,000 acres* in 1883. Currently the largest landholder in Great Britain is the Forestry Commission (instituted 1919) with 1 209 000 ha *2,987,933 acres*. Currently the landowner with the largest known acreage is the 9th Duke of Buccleuch (b. 1923) with 136 035 ha *336,000 acres*. The longest tenure is that by St Paul's Cathedral of land at Tillingham, Essex, given by King Ethelbert before AD 616.

THE RICHEST MEN IN THE WORLD

Many of the riches of most of the world's 29 remaining monarchs are national rather than personal assets. The least fettered and most monarchical is H.M. Sir Muda Hassanal Bolkiah Mu'izzaddin Waddaulah Hon GCMG (b. 15 July 1946). He appointed himself Prime Minister, Finance and Home Affairs Minister on 1 Jan 1984. Brunei's annual oil revenue is £3000 million and its foreign reserves are £10,000 million all of which is effectually at his disposal.

The richest man in the United States has been Gordon Peter Getty (b. 1930), fourth son of Jean Paul Getty by his fourth wife Ann Rork, and sole trustee of the Sarah C. Getty Trust valued in Sept 1984 at $4100 million (*£3400 million*) but reduced by taxes and an estate split to under £1 billion by 1986.

The annual rankings in *Forbes Magazine* in 1985 list 13 billionaires headed by Sam Moore Walton, 67 of Wal-Mart Stores of Bentonville, Arkansas.

SALARY HIGHEST *WORLD*

The highest reported remuneration of any US businessman was $51,544,000 (*£33¾ million*) in salary, bonus and stock options received by Mr Frederick W. Smith, board chairman, of Federal Express in 1982. The highest amount in salary in 1985 was $12.7 million (*£8.8 million*) paid by DWE Corporation of Miami Beach, Florida to Victor Posner their Chairman of the Board.

'The comparison and estimations of extreme personal wealth are beset with difficulties. As Jean Paul Getty (1892–1976) once said 'if you can count your millions you are not a billionaire'. The term millionaire was invented *c* 1740 and billionaire (in the American sense of one thousand million) in 1861. The earliest dollar centi-millionaire was Cornelius Vanderbilt (1794–1877) who left $100 million in 1877. The earliest billionaires were John Davison Rockefeller (1839–1937); Henry Ford (1863–1947) and Andrew William Mellon (1855–1937). In 1937, the last year in which all 3 were alive, a billion US dollars were worth £205 million but that amount of sterling would today have a purchasing power exceeding £5000 million.'

RAGS AND RICHES

'The largest life policy ever written was one for $44 million (£24 million) in 1982.'

HIGHEST FEES

The highest paid investment consultant in the world is Dr Harry D. Schultz, who operates from Western Europe. His standard consultation fee for 60 minutes is $2000 on weekdays and $3000 at weekends. His quarterly retainer permitting companies to call on him on a daily basis is $28,125. He writes and edits an information packed International Newsletter instituted in 1964 now sold at $25 or £11 per copy.

GOLDEN HANDSHAKE

The highest carat handshake reported was one of 'nearly £700,000' attributed to Mr Bill Fieldhouse CBE (b. 1 Jan 1932) from Letraset of which he had been a director since 1969.

INSURANCE

It was estimated in 1978 that the total premiums paid in the United States first surpassed $100 billion (*then £52,600 million*) or $1400 *£736* per household. The company with the highest volume of insurance in force in the world is the Prudential Insurance Company of America of Newark, New Jersey, USA with $532,990 million at 31 Dec 1983, which is more than 2½ times the UK National Debt figure. The admitted assets are $78,924 million.

'The largest life assurance company in the United Kingdom is the Prudential Corporation plc. At 1 Jan 1984 the tangible assets were £16,713,800,000 and the total amount assured was £72,445,300,000.'

LIFE POLICIES LARGEST

The largest life assurance policy ever written was one for $44 million (*£24.4 million*) for a Calgary land developer Victor T. Uy in February 1982 by Transamerica Occidental Life Assurance Co. The salesman was local manager Lorenzo F. Reyes. The highest pay-out on a single life has been some $18 million (*then £7.5 million*) to Mrs Linda Mullendore, wife of an Oklahoma rancher, reported on 14 Nov 1970. Her murdered husband had paid $300,000 in premiums in 1969.

PROVED WILLS AND DEATH DUTIES

Sir John Reeves Ellerman, 2nd Bt (1909–73) left £53,238,370 on which all-time record death duties were payable. This is the largest will ever proved in the United Kingdom. The greatest will proved in Ireland was that of the 1st Earl of Iveagh (1847–1927), who left £13,486,146).

MOST MILLIONAIRES

The United States was estimated to have some 832,500 millionaire families in early 1985 with the million mark expected by December 1986. Most work 6 days a week for an average $121,000 (*£79,000*).

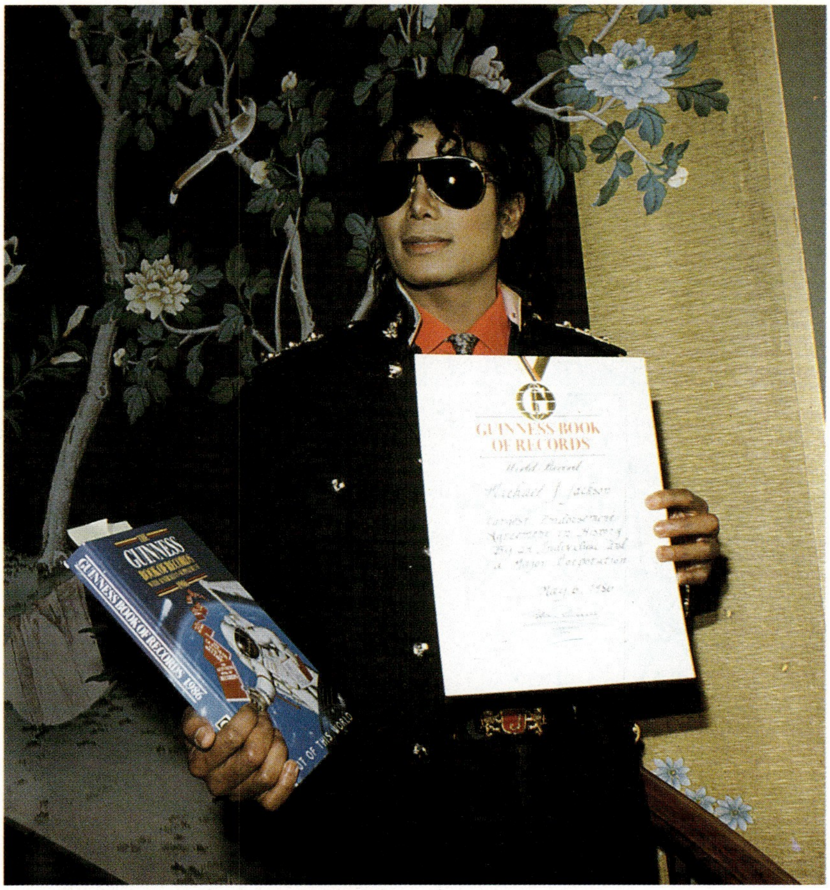

‘At a press conference in New York, USA, on 6 May 1986, it was announced that Michael Joseph Jackson had completed a transaction to endorse the soft drink Pepsi Cola. It has been indicated that the deal is worth over $50 million, the biggest individual endorsement agreement in history.’

GREATEST STOCK MARKET LOSS

The highest recorded personal paper losses on stock values have been those of Ray A. Kroc, Chairman of McDonald's Corporation with $64,901,718 (*then £27 million*) on 8 July 1974 and Edwin H. Land, President of Polaroid Corporation with $59,397,355 on 28–29 May 1974, when Polaroid stock closed $12.12 down at 43¼ on that day.

GREATEST BANKRUPTCY

Rajendra Sethia (b. 1950) was arrested in New Delhi on 2 Mar 1985 on charges including criminal conspiracy and forgery. He had been declared bankrupt by the High Court in London on 18 Jan 1985 when Esal Commodities was stated to be in debt for a record £170 million. His personal debts were estimated at £140 million.

‘John Lennon's Rolls Royce Phantom V, the most expensive used car at £1,768,000.’

PRECIOUS RECORDS

‘The world's largest artificial diamond of 1.2 carats produced in Japan by Sumitomo Denko Ltd in April 1982.’

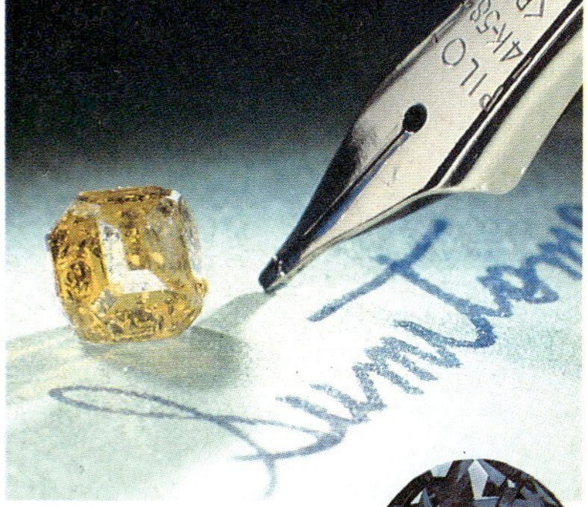

The world's most expensive gem – the 42.92 carat Terestchenko blue diamond auctioned for $4,580,000 (now £3.8 million).

DIAMOND RECORDS

The largest diamond is of 3106 metric carats (over 1¼ lb) – *The Cullinan*, found by Mr Gray on 25 Jan 1905 in the Premier Mine, Pretoria, South Africa. The first synthetic diamonds were produced by Prof. H. T. Hall at the General Electric Research Laboratories, USA on 16 Dec 1954. In Feb 1984 a Tass report from Leningrad, USSR announced that the institute of High Frequency Currents had produced an artificial diamond weighing 2,04 kg *4½ lb*.

The largest cut diamond stone is of 530.2 metric carats of 74 facets. Cleaved from *The Cullinan* in 1908, by Jak Asscher of Amsterdam and polished by Henri Koe known as *The Star of Africa* or Cullinan I and now in the Royal Sceptre. The Cullinan II is of 317.40 carats. Third on the list of the 55 diamonds of more than 100 carat is the Great Mogul of 280 old carats lost in the sack of Delhi in 1739 and arguably the most valuable object ever lost.

Diamond is the *hardest* known naturally occurring substance, with 5 times the indentation hardness of the next hardest mineral, corundum (Al_2O_3). The peak hardness value on the Knoop scale is 8400 compared with an average diamond of 7000. The rarest colour for diamond is blood red. The largest example is a flawless 5.05 carat stone found in Lichtenburg, South Africa in 1927 and now in a private collection in the US. The diamond per carat record price of $113,000 was set by the 41.3 carat ‘Polar Star’ bought in Geneva for £2,100,000 on 21 Nov 1980. The 42.92 carat Terestchenko blue diamond was auctioned at Christie's, Geneva on 14 Nov 1984 for $4,580,000. The largest blue diamond is the 45.85 carat Copenhagen Blue.

The largest star sapphire ever cut – the 733 carat Star of Queensland

SAPPHIRE RECORDS

The largest sapphire was a 2302 carat stone found at Anakie Queensland, Australia, in *c* 1935, now a 1318 carat head of President Abraham Lincoln (1809–65).

The largest cut sapphire is a 1444 carat black star stone carved from 2097 carats in 1953–5 into a bust of General Dwight David Eisenhower (1890–1969).

Both the sapphire busts are in the custody of the Kazanjian Foundation of Los Angeles, California, USA. Auction record for a single stone was set by a step-cut sapphire of 66.03 carats at £579,300 from the Rockefeller Collection at Sotheby's Zurich on 8 May 1980.

EMERALD RECORDS

The largest cut stone is a 86,136 carat natural beryl Gleim emerald. Found in Carnaiba, Brazil, Aug 1974. Carved by Richard Chan (Hong Kong). Appraised at $1,292,000 (*£178,000*) in 1982.

$520,000 (*then £305,000*) was paid for an 18.35 carat gem emerald ring sold at Sotheby Parke Bernet, New York, in Apr 1977.

RUBY RECORDS

The largest ruby was a 3421 carat broken stone reported found in July 1961 (largest piece 750 carats).

The largest cut ruby is a 1184 carat natural gem stone of Burmese origin. The largest star ruby is the 650 carat Vidyaraj ruby in Bangalore, India.

Since 1955 rubies have been the world's most precious gem attaining a price of up to £4000 per carat by 1969. A world record carat price of $100,639 (*then £46,600*) was set at Christie's sale in Geneva in Nov 1979 for a 4.12 carat caspian shaped ruby.

‘Since 1955 rubies have been the world's most precious gems.’

The 28¼ ton jade boulder discovered by Karl Ebner in Yukon, Canada in 1977.

The largest gold nugget ever found was one of 472½ lb in 1872.

The world's largest cut precious stone is the 21,327 carat topaz 'The Brazilian Princess'.

The largest ruby in the world is 'The Liberty Bell' of 8500 carats.

LARGEST PEARL

6,37 kg *14 lb 1 oz* 24 cm *9½ in* long by 14 cm *5½ in* in diameter – *Pearl of Laotze.*

Found: At Palawan, Philippines, 7 May 1934 in shell of giant clam.

Present location: The property of Wilburn Dowell Cobb from 1936 until his death, it was valued at $4,080,000 in July 1971. On 15 May 1980 it was bought at auction in San Francisco by Peter Hoffmann, a jeweller of Beverly Hills, California for $200,000 (*then £85,000*). An appraisal for the new owner Gina Diane Barbish in May 1982 by the San Francisco Gem Laboratory suggested a value of $32,640,000.

LARGEST TOPAZ

The 'Brazilian Princess' 21,327 carat 221 facets.

Present location: Exhibited by Smithsonian Institution, Nov 1978. Valued at $1,066,350 or $50 per carat. Cut from a 35,8 kg *79 lb* crystal. World's largest faceted stone.

BIGGEST GOLD NUGGET EVER FOUND

7560 oz (214,32 kg *472½ lb)* (reet gold*) Holtermann Nugget.*

Found: Beyers & Holtermann Star of Hope Gold Mining Co., Hill End, NSW, Australia, 19 Oct 1872.

The Holtermann Nugget contained some 99,8 kg *220 lb* of gold in a 285,7 kg *630 lb* slab of slate. The purest large nugget was the *Welcome Stranger*, found at Moliagul, Victoria, Australia, which yielded 62,92 kg *2248 troy oz* of pure gold from 70,92 kg *2280¼ oz.*

BIGGEST SILVER NUGGET EVER FOUND

2750 lb troy.

Found: Sonora, Mexico.

Present location: Appropriated by the Spanish Government before 1821.

ODDS-ON RECORDS

WORLD'S BIGGEST GAMBLING WIN

The world's biggest individual gambling win is $8,800,000 by Nicholas Jarich in the Pennsylvania state lottery on 23 July 1983.

THE BIGGEST LOSS

An unnamed Italian industrialist was reported to have lost £800,000 in 5 hr at roulette in Monte Carlo, Monaco on 6 Mar 1974. A Saudi Arabian prince was reported to have lost more than $1 million in a single session at the Metro Club, Las Vegas, USA in December 1974.

WORLD'S LARGEST CASINO

The largest casino in the world is the Resorts International Casino, Atlantic City, NJ, USA. It reported a record month in July 1983 with winnings of $29.3 million. The Casino comprises 5574 m² *60,000 ft²*, containing 127 gaming tables and 1640 slot machines. Attendances total over 35,000 daily at peak weekends.

BIGGEST BINGO BINGE

The largest 'house' in Bingo sessions was 15,756 at the Canadian National Exhibition, Toronto on 19 Aug 1983. Staged by the Variety Club of Ontario Tent No. 28, there was total prize money of $C250,000 with a record one-game payout of $C100,000.

FASTEST AND LONGEST 'FULL HOUSE' CALL

A 'Full House' call occurred on the 15th number by Norman A. Wilson at Guide Post Workingmen's Club, Bedlington, Northumberland on 22 June 1978, by Anne Wintle of Brynrethin, Mid Glamorgan, on a coach trip to Bath on 17 Aug 1982 and by Shirley Lord at Kahibah Bowling Club, New South Wales, Australia on 24 Oct 1983. 'House' was not called until the 86th number at the Hillsborough Working Men's Club, Sheffield, S. Yorkshire on 11 Jan 1982. There were 32 winners.

WORLD'S BIGGEST FOOTBALL POOLS WIN

Two unnamed punters won *c* £1.5 million each in November 1972 on the state run Italian pools. The winning dividend paid out by Littlewoods Pools in their first week in February 1923 was £2 12s 0d (*£2.60*). The record payout from the British Pools – which is also the biggest ever prize paid in any British competition – is £1,017,890 paid on 30 Apr 1986 to nursing sister Margaret Francis and ten colleagues from the Roundway Hospital, Devizes, Wiltshire, by Littlewoods Pools, making them the first ever Pools Millionaires. The largest amount won by a single person is £953,874.10 by brewery worker David Preston, 47, of Burton-on-Trent, Staffs, on 23 Feb 1980. This total comprised £804,573.35 from Littlewoods Pools and £149,300.75 from Vernons Pools.

HIGHEST EVER HORSE RACING ODDS

The highest secured odds were 1,099,299 to 1 by a backer from Otley, West Yorkshire on a seven horse accumulator on 10 May 1975. He won £10,992.99 for a 1p bet out of a total stake of £1.76 which in all netted him £12,878.14. Edward Hodson of Wolverhampton landed a 3,956,748 to 1 bet for a 55p stake on 11 Feb 1984, but his bookmaker had a £3000 payout limit. The world record odds on a 'double' are 31,793 to 1 paid by the New Zealand Totalisator Agency Board on a five shilling tote ticket on *Red Emperor* and *Maida Dillon* at Addington, Christchurch, in 1951.

HIGHEST HORSE RACING PAYOUT
Three punters each received $C735,403 for picking winners of six consecutive races at Exhibition Park, Vancouver, BC, Canada on 10 July 1982. The lowest price paid for a winning ticket was $4.

BIGGEST TOTE WIN
The best recorded tote win was one of £341 2s 6d to 2s (*£341.12½ to 10p*) representing odds of 3,410¼ to 1, by Catharine Unsworth of Blundellsands, Liverpool at Haydock Park on a race won by *Coole* on 30 Nov 1929. The highest odds in Irish tote history were £289.64 for 10p unit on *Gene's Rogue* at Limerick on 28 Dec 1981.

TOP TIPSTER
The only recorded instance of a racing correspondent forecasting ten out of ten winners on a race card was at Delaware Park, Wilmington, Delaware, USA on 28 July 1974 by Charles Lamb of the *Baltimore News American*.

ROULETTE RECORDS
The longest run on an ungaffed (i.e. true) wheel reliably recorded is six successive coups (in No. 10) at El San Juan Hotel, Puerto Rico on 9 July 1959. The odds with a double zero were 1 in 38^6 or 3,010,936,383 to 1.

The longest 'marathon' on record is one of 31 days from 10 Apr to 11 May 1970 at The Casino de Macao, to test the validity or invalidity of certain contentions in 20,000 spins.

BANDIT ROBBED!
The biggest beating handed to a 'one-armed bandit' was $2,478,716.15 by Rocco Dinubilo from Fresno, California at Harrah's Tahoe Casino, Nevada, USA on 31 Dec 1983.

‘A seven horse accumulator won £10,992.99 for a 1p bet in Otley, West Yorkshire on 10 May 1975.’

‘Below, the biggest British Pools payout – £1,017,890 in April 1986 to nursing sister Margaret Francis and ten colleagues from the Roundway Hospital, Devizes, Wilts, England.’

THE CRIMINAL RECORD

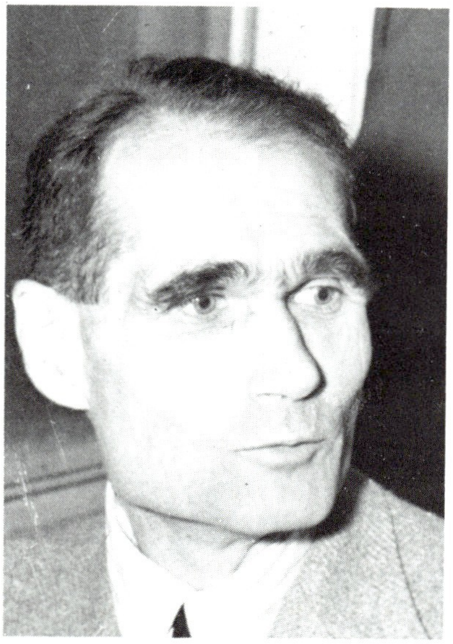

'Rudolph Hess was captured on 10 May 1941 and is now in his 45th year of imprisonment.'

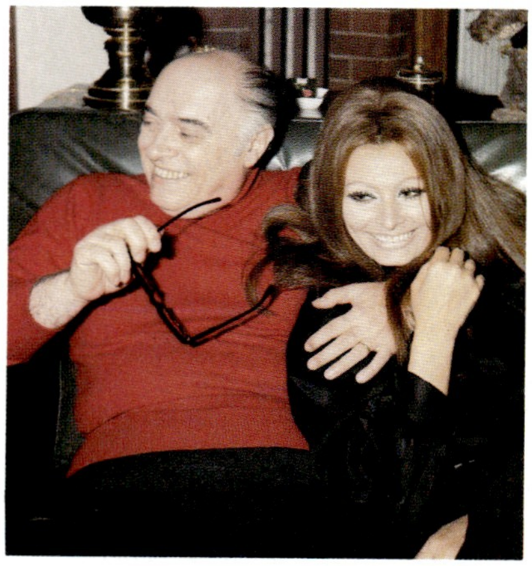

Carlo Ponti, husband of Sophia Loren was to have been fined the equivalent of $26.4 million in connection with claims for tax due but unpaid.

'Dudley Wayne Kyzer was sentenced to 10,000 years in prison for a triple murder (including his mother-in-law) in Tuscaloosa, Alabama on 4 Dec 1981.'

LARGEST OBJECT EVER STOLEN BY ONE PERSON

On a moonless night at dead calm high water on 5 June 1966 armed with only a sharp axe, N. William Kennedy slashed free the mooring lines at Wolfe's Cove, St Lawrence Seaway, Quebec, Canada, of the 10,639 dwt SS *Orient Trader* owned by Steel Factors Ltd of Ontario. The vessel drifted to a waiting blacked out tug thus escaping a ban on any shipping movements during a violent wild-cat waterfront strike. She sailed for Spain.

BIGGEST BANK FRAUD

The largest amount of money named in a defalcation case has been a gross £33,000,000 at the Lugano branch of Lloyd's Bank International Ltd in Switzerland on 2 Sept 1974. Mr Mark Colombo was arrested pending charges including falsification of foreign currency accounts and suppression of evidence.

RECORD COMPUTER FRAUD

Between 1964 and 1973, 64,000 fake insurance policies were created on the computer of the Equity Funding Corporation involving $2000 million.

Stanley Mark Rifkin (b. 1946) was arrested in Carlsbad, California by the FBI on 6 Nov 1978 charged with defrauding a Los Angeles bank of $10.2 million (*then £4.85 million*) by manipulation of a computer system. He was sentenced to 8 years in June 1980.

GREATEST RANSOMS

Historically the greatest ransom paid was that for Atahualpa by the Incas to Francisco Pizarro in 1532–3 at Cajamarca, Peru which constituted a hall full of gold and silver worth in modern money some $170 million (*£95 million*).

The greatest ransom ever reported is 1500 million pesos (*£25,300,000*) for the release of the brothers Jorge Born, 40 and Juan Born, 39, of Bunge and Born, paid to the left wing urban guerrilla group Montoneros in Buenos Aires, Argentina on 20 June 1975.

YOUNGEST KIDNAP VICTIM

The youngest person kidnapped has been Carolyn Wharton born at 12.46 p.m. on 19 March 1955 in the Baptist Hospital, Texas, USA and kidnapped, by a woman disguised as a nurse, at 1.15 p.m. aged 29 min.

WORLD'S LONGEST PRISON SENTENCE

A 10,000 year sentence was imposed on Dudley Wayne Kyzer, 40 on 4 Dec 1981 in Tuscaloosa, Alabama, USA for a triple murder (including his mother-in-law) in 1976. A sentence of 384,912 years was *demanded* at the prosecution of Gabriel March Grandos, 22, at Palma de Mallorca, Spain on 11 Mar 1972 for failing to deliver 42,768 letters or 9 years per letter.

Juan Corona, a Mexican-American, was sentenced to 25 consecutive life terms, for murdering 25 farm workers in 1970–71 around Feather River, Yuba City, California, at Fairfield on 5 Feb 1973. His 20th century record was surpassed by Dean Corll (27) in 1974 and John Wayne Gacy (33 victims) in 1980.

WORLD'S HEAVIEST FINE

It was reported in January 1979 that Carlo Ponti, husband of Sophia Loren, was to be fined the equivalent of $26.4 million by the Italian courts in connection with claims for tax alleged to be due but unpaid.

Tommaso Buschetta, probably the world's greatest 'supergrass' giving evidence in 1984 against the world's largest criminal organization – the Mafia.

LONGEST TIME IN PRISON

Paul Geidel (b. 21 Apr 1894) was convicted of second degree murder on 5 Sept 1911 as a 17 year old porter in a New York hotel. He was released from the Fishkill Correctional Facility, Beacon, New York aged 85 on 7 May 1980 having served 68 years 8 months and 2 days – the longest recorded term in US history. He first refused parole in 1974. Rudolf Hess was captured at Eaglesham on 10 May 1941 and in 1985 entered his 45th year in prison.

'Paul Geidel was released from Fishkill Correctional Facility, Beacon, New York having served 68 years, 8 months, 12 days. He was 85.'

THE ARRESTED RECORD

A record for arrests was set by Tommy Johns, 60, in Brisbane, Queensland, Australia on 9 Sept 1982 when he faced his 2000th conviction for drunkenness since 1957.

WORLD'S MOST EXPENSIVE PRISONER

Spandau Prison, Berlin, built 100 years ago for 600 prisoners is now used solely for the person widely and officially purported to be Nazi war criminal Rudolf Hess (b. 26 Apr 1894). The cost of maintenance of the staff of 105 has been estimated at $415,000 (*£245,000*) per annum.

BIGGEST BREAK-OUT

In February 1979 a retired US Army Colonel Arthur 'Bull' Simons led a band of 14 to break into Gasre prison, Tehran, Iran to rescue two fellow Americans. Some 11,000 other prisoners took advantage of this and the Islamic revolution in what became history's largest ever gaol break.

LAST FROM THE YARD-ARM

The last naval execution at the yard-arm was the hanging of Private John Dalliger, Royal Marines, aboard HMS *Leven* in Victoria Bay near Lu-ta, China, on 13 July 1860. Dalliger had been found guilty of two attempted murders.

'*Left:* Ruth Ellis, 28, the 14th and last woman executed in Britain this century. She was hanged for murder in 1955. *Centre:* SS Colonel Karl Adolf Eichmann hanged in Tel Aviv, Israel, in 1962. He was tried and found guilty of being the foremost organiser of Hitler's genocide of European Jewry in 1941–45. *Right:* George Blake (*né* Behar), whose treachery attracted a term of 42 years' imprisonment in 1961. This was the longest ever in British penal history.'

THE LAW'S LARGEST

The most expensive defamation trial in Great Britain has been the 87 day long case of *Gee v British Broadcasting Corporation* which ran before Rt Hon Lord Justice Croom-Johnson, P.C. D.S.C, from 22 Oct 1984 to 2 May 1985. Costs have been estimated at £1.5 million. Dr Sidney Gee was in the witness stand for 27 days and received a settlement of £100,007.

***Greatest Alimony Suit.* Belgian born Sheika Dena Al-Fassi, 23, filed the highest ever alimony claim of $3000 million (*then £1666 million*) against her former husband Sheik Mohammed Al-Fassi, 28, of the Saudi Arabia royal family in Los Angeles, California in February 1982. Mr Marvin Mitchelson explaining the size of the settlement claim alluded to the Sheik's wealth which included 14 homes in Florida alone and numerous private aircraft. On 14 June 1983 she was awarded $81 million (*then £52 million*) and declared she would be 'very, very happy' if she was able to collect.**

GREATEST DAMAGES *PERSONAL INJURY WORLD*

The greatest personal injury damages ever awarded were to a male child of undisclosed identity born in 1979 at the US Army's Le Herman General Hospital in a medical malpractice suit. If the child which had 'total cerebral palsy' lives out his expectation of life the potential US federal government payment will reach $70 million. Reports of 30 Sept 1983 did not disclose the name of the US Army doctor.

On 24 Nov 1983 a jury in Corpus Christi, Texas, USA awarded punitive damages of $106 million (*£75 million*) against the Ford Motor Co. for alleged design faults in the Ford Mustang II in which Bevary Durrill, 20 died in 1974. An appeal is pending.

GREAT BRITAIN

On 28 June 1985 Mrs Angela McCusker, 27, of Co. Fermanagh was awarded £500,000 in damages in Belfast High Court for severe brain damage and other injuries received in a car crash with a lorry. She sued her husband, who was driving and the lorry driver and lorry owners.

BREACH OF CONTRACT

The greatest damages ever awarded for a breach of contract were £610,392, awarded on 16 July 1930 to the Bank of Portugal against the printers Waterlow & Sons Ltd, of London, arising from their unauthorised printing of 580,000 five-hundred escudo notes in 1925. This award was upheld in the House of Lords on 28 Apr 1932. One of the perpetrators, Arthur Virgilio Alves Reis, served 16 years (1930–46) in gaol.

BREACH OF PROMISE

The largest sum involved in a breach of promise suit in the United Kingdom was £50,000, accepted in 1913 by Miss Daisy Markham, *alias* Mrs Annie Moss (d. 20 Aug 1962, aged 76), in settlement against the 6th Marquess of Northampton DSO (1885–1978).

DEFAMATION *World*

A sum of $16,800,000 (*£6,720,000*) was awarded to Dr John J. Wild, 58, at the Hennepin District Court, Minnesota, USA, on 30 Nov 1972 against The Minnesota Foundation and others for defamation, bad-faith termination of a contract, interference with professional business relationship and $10.8 million in punitive damages. The Supreme Court of Minnesota granted an option of a new trial or a $1.5 million *remittitur* to Dr Wild on 10 Jan 1975. The $39.6 million awarded in Columbus, Ohio on 1 Mar 1980 to Robert Guccione, publisher of *Penthouse*, for defamation against Lowry Flynt, publisher of *Hustler* was reduced by Judge Craig Wright to $4 million on 17 Apr 1980. The hearing ended in May 1982 with *Penthouse* being cleared of libel.

GREATEST COMPENSATION FOR WRONGFUL IMPRISONMENT

William De Palma (b. 1938) of Whitter, California, agreed to a $750,000 (*then £340,000*) settlement for 16 months wrongful imprisonment in McNeil Island Federal Prison, on 12 Aug 1975 after a 15 year sentence for armed robbery in Buena Park on forged fingerprint evidence in 1968.

GREATEST ALIMONY

The highest alimony awarded by a court has been $2,261,000 (*then £983,000*) against George Storer Sr, 74, in favour of his third wife Dorothy, 73, in Miami, Florida on 29 Oct 1974. Mr Storer, a broadcasting executive, was also ordered to pay his ex-wife's attorney $200,000 (*then £86,950*) in fees.

The world's greatest insurance claim of $1700 million *£890 million* resulted from the wreck of the *Amoco Cadiz*, 16 March 1978.

Since the Union of Parliaments in 1707 the only Scot to win an appeal in person before the House of Lords has been Mr Jack Malloch, an Aberdeen Schoolmaster. In 1971 he was restored to his employment with costs under the dormant but operative Teachers Act, 1882.

GREATEST DIVORCE SETTLEMENT

The highest High Court divorce award received was £700,000 on 13 Nov 1980 for 'Mrs P' after 23 years of marriage against her former husband from Jersey from whom she had been receiving £6000 per annum. In *Edgar* v *Edgar* in 1980, £750,000 was awarded but this was set aside on appeal when Mrs Edgar accepted a much lesser figure.

PATENT CASE

The greatest settlement ever made in a patent infringement suit is $55.8 million (*then £37.2 million*) in Pfizer Inc. v International Rectifier Corp. and Rochelle Laboratories over the antibiotic dioxycycline on 5 July 1983.

LARGEST SUIT

The highest amount of damages ever sought to date is $675,000,000,000,000 (then equivalent to 10 times the US national wealth) in a suit by Mr I. Walton Bader brought in the US District Court, New York City on 14 Apr 1971 against General Motors and others for polluting all 50 states.

HIGHEST COSTS

The trial judge in *R.* v *Sinclair and others* (the handless corpse murder) ordered the international drug trafficker Alexander James Sinclair, 36 of NZ (sentenced to a minimum term of 20 years for the murder of Marty Johnstone found in a quarry at Chorley, Lancashire) to pay £1 million for the Crown's costs.

Britain's most loquacious ever lawyer W. H. Upjohn KC. His concluding speech in the Globe and Phoenix Gold Mining case of 1916 went on for 45 days.

WORST IN THE WORLD

WORST IN THE WORLD

DATE		LOCATION	NUMBER KILLED	DISASTER
	1347–51	Eurasia: The Black Death (bubonic, pneumonia and septicaemic plague)	75,000,000	**Pandemic**
	1311–40	Mongol extermination of Chinese Peasantry	c 35,000,000	**Genocide**
April–Nov	1918	Worldwide: influenza	21,640,000	**Influenza**
	1969–71	Northern China (revealed May 1981)	c 20,000,000	**Famine**
12–13 Nov	1970	Ganges Delta Islands, Bangladesh	1,000,000	**Circular Storm**
Oct	1887	Hwang-ho River, China	900,00	**Flood**
23 Jan	1556	Shensi Province, China (duration 2 hours)	830,000	**Earthquake**
16 Dec	1920	Kansu Province, China	180,000	**Landslide**
6 Aug	1945	Hiroshima, Japan	141,000	**Atomic Bomb**
5–7 Apr	1815	Tambora Sumbawa, Indonesia	92,000	**Volcanic Eruption**
13–15 Feb	1945	Dresden, Germany	c 50,000	**Conventional bombing**
31 May	1970	Yungay, Huascarán, Peru	c 18,000	**Avalanches**
30 Jan	1945	*Wilhelm Gustloff* (25,484 tons) German liner torpedoed off Danzig by USSR submarine S-13	c 7700	**Marine** (single ship)
11 Aug	1979	Manchhu River Dam, Morvi, Gujarat, India	c 5000	**Dam Burst**
c 8 June	1941	Chungking (Zhong qing) China air raid shelter	c 4000	**Panic**
5–13 Dec	1951	London fog, England	2,850	**Smog**
	1931–35	Hawk's Nest hydroelectric tunnel, W Virginia, USA	c 2000	**Tunnelling** (Silicosis)
6 Dec	1917	Halifax, Nova Scotia, Canada	1963	**Explosion**
May	1845	The Theatre, Canton, China	1670	**Fire** (single building)
26 April	1942	Honkeiko Colliery, China (coal dust explosion)	1572	**Mining**
13–16 July	1942	New York City anti-conscription riots	c 1200	**Riot**
2 or 3 Nov	1982	Petrol tanker explosion inside Salang Tunnel, Afghanistan	c 1100	**Road**
18 Nov	1978	People's Temple cult by cyanide, Jonestown, Guyana	913	**Mass Suicide**
19–20 Feb	1945	Japanese soldiers, Ramree I., Burma (disputed)	c 900	**Crocodiles**
6 June	1981	Bagmati River, Bihir state, India	>800	**Railway**
16 May	1770	Dauphine's Wedding, Seine, Paris	>800	**Fireworks**
18 May	1925	South Central States, USA (3 hours)	689	**Tornado**
27 Mar	1977	KLM-Pan Am Boeing 747 ground crash, Tenerife	583	**Aircraft** (Civil)
	1907	Champawat district, India, tigress shot by Col. Jim Corbet (d. 1955)	436	**Man-eating animal**
April–May	1979	Novosibirsk B & CW plant, USSR	c 300	**Bacteriological & Chemical**
20 April	1888	Moradabad, Uttar Pradesh, India	246	**Hail**
23 Oct	1983	Lorry bomb, US Marine barracks, Beirut, Lebanon	243	**Terrorism**
27 Mar	1980	Alexander L. Kielland 'Flotel' (10,105 tons), North Sea	123	**Off-Shore Oil Plant**
18 Feb	1942	*Le Surcouf* rammed by US merchantman *Thomas Lykes* in Caribbean	130	**Submarine**
10 May	1977	Israeli military 'Sea Stallion', West Bank	54	**Helicopter**
9 May	1976	Cavalese resort, Northern Italy	42	**Ski Lift** (Cable car)
Dec	1952	USSR Expedition on Mount Everest	40	**Mountaineering**
27 Mar	1980	Vaal Reefs Gold mine lift fell 1,93 km *1.2 miles*	23	**Elevator (Lift)**
23 Dec	1975	Hut in Chinamasa Kraal nr Umtali, Zimbabwe (single bolt)	21	**Lightning**
13–15 Aug	1979	28th Fastnet Race – 23 boats sank or abandoned in Force 11 gale	19	**Yacht Racing**

Toxic cooking oil being destroyed following the world's worst mass poisoning. By May 1984 the death toll stood at 350. The two manufacturers await trial in Madrid.

CHAPTER 2

WELLIE-WANGING AND OTHER WONDERS

'John Stephenson who made the most northerly windsurf attempt at 76° N in the Arctic Circle seen here negotiating a Greenland iceberg.'

ZANY RECORDS

Rory Blackwell, the One-Man Band champion plays 24 instruments simultaneously.

WELLIE-WANGING (GUM BOOT THROWING)

The longest recorded distance (a Size 8 Challenger Dunlop Boot) for 'Wellie-wanging' is 52,73 m *173 ft* by Tony Rodgers of Warminster, Wilts on 9 Sept 1978. Rosemary Payne established the feminine record at Cannon Hill Park, Birmingham on 21 June 1975 with 39,60 m *129 ft 11 in*.

AUCTIONEERING

The longest one man auction on record is for 40 hr 7 min by Reg Coates in Gosport, Hampshire on 26–28 Apr 1985.

BAG-CARRYING

The greatest non-stop bag-carrying feat carrying 50,8 kg *1 cwt* of household coal in an open bag is 51,5 km *32 miles* by Brian Newton in 10 hr 18 min from Leicester to the Nottingham border on 27 May 1983.

The record for the 1012,5 m *1107.2 yd* course annual Gawthorpe, West Yorkshire race is 4 min 19 sec by Terry Lyons, 36 on 16 Apr 1979.

BAGPIPES

The longest duration pipe has been one of 100 hr by Neville Workman, Clive Higgins, Patrick Forth and Paul Harris, playing two at a time in shifts, of Churchill School Pipe Band, Harare, Zimbabwe on 9–13 July 1976.

BALANCING ON ONE FOOT

The longest recorded duration for balancing on one foot is 34 hr by Shri N. Ravi in Sathyamangalam City, Tamil Nadu, India on 17–18 Apr 1982. The disengaged foot may not be rested on the standing foot nor may any object be used for support or balance.

BALLOON FLIGHTS

The longest reported toy balloon flight is one of 16 090 km *10,000 miles* from Dobbs Ferry, New York, USA to Wagga Wagga, Australia. It was helium-filled and released by 11-year old Justin Fiore on 19 Apr 1982. The longest recorded hydrogen-filled balloon flight from the geographical British Isles is one of 9460 km *5880 miles* from Jersey which was returned from Camps Bay, Cape Province, South Africa on 28 Apr 1974, 43 days after release by Gerard Wankling.

BALLOON RELEASE

The largest mass balloon release ever achieved was one of 1,121,448 balloons at the Skyfest's One Million Balloon Salute at Anaheim, California, USA on 5 Dec 1985.

BAND MARATHONS

The longest recorded 'blow-in' is 100 hr 2 min by the Du Val Senior High School, Lanham, Maryland, USA on 13–17 May 1977. The minimum number of musicians is 10.

BAND ONE-MAN

Rory Blackwell, aided by his left-footed perpendicular percussion-pounder and his right-footed horizontal four pronged differential beater, played 24 (4 melody, 20 percussion) instruments in Plymouth, Devon on 2 May 1985. He also played in a single rendition 314 instruments in 1 min 23.07 sec in Dawlish, Devon on 27 May 1985. Dave Sheriff of Rugby, Warwickshire played his one-man band (which must include at least 3 instruments played simultaneously) for 100 hr 20 min on 24–28 Mar 1986 at the Hotel Leofric, Coventry, West Midlands. Micky Clarke of Chester, Cheshire created the women's record of the same time *at* the same time at the same place.

Barrow pushing. **The heaviest loaded one-wheeled barrow pushed for a minimum 60,96 m *200 level feet* is one loaded with bricks weighing a gross 3,51 tonnes *7750 lb* through 72,23 m *237 ft* by Gary Windebank at Romsey, Hampshire on 12 Oct 1985.**

BARREL JUMPING *ON ICE SKATES*
The official distance record is 8,99 m *29 ft 5 in* over 18 barrels by Yvon Jolin at Terrebonne, Quebec, Canada on 25 Jan 1981. The feminine record is 6,21 m *20 ft 4½ in* over 11 barrels by Janet Hainstock in Michigan, USA, on 15 Mar 1980.

BARREL ROLLING
The record for rolling a full 36 gallon metal beer barrel over a measured mile is 8 min 7.2 sec by Phillip Randle, Steve Hewitt, John Round, Trevor Bradley, Colin Barnes and Ray Glover of Haunchwood Collieries Institute and Social Club, Nuneaton, Warwickshire on 15 Aug 1982. A team of 10 rolled a 63,5 kg *140 lb* barrel 240,35 km *150 miles* in 30 hr 31 min in Chlumcany, Czechoslovakia on 27–28 Oct 1982.

BARROW RACING
The fastest time attained in a 1,609 km *1 mile* wheelbarrow race is 4 min 50.29 sec by John Coates and Brian Roades of Richmond, BC, Canada on 9 July 1983 at the Ladner Sports Festival, Delta, B.C. Brothers-in-law Malcolm Shipley and Adrian Freeburg pushed each other from John O'Groats to Land's End for charity in 30 days from 28 July to 26 Aug 1981.

BATH TUB RACING
The record for the annual international 57,9 km *36 miles* Nanaimo to Vancouver, British Columbia bath tub race is 1 hr 29 min 40 sec by Gary Deathbridge (Australia) on 30 July 1978. Tubs are limited to 1,90 m *75 in* and 6 hp motors. The greatest distance for paddling a hand propelled bath tub in 24 hr is 145,6 km *90.5 miles* by 13 members of Aldington Prison Officers Social Club, nr Ashford, Kent on 28–29 May 1983.

BATON TWIRLING
Victor Cerda, Sol Lozano, Harry Little III (leader) and Manuel Rodriguez, twirled batons for 122½ hours on 24–29 June 1984 in El Seveno, California.

BEARD OF BEES
The ultimate beard of bees was achieved by Max Bek, 21, of Arcola, Pennsylvania, USA with 70,000 bees weighing 9 kg *20 lb* reported in October 1985.

ZANY RECORDS

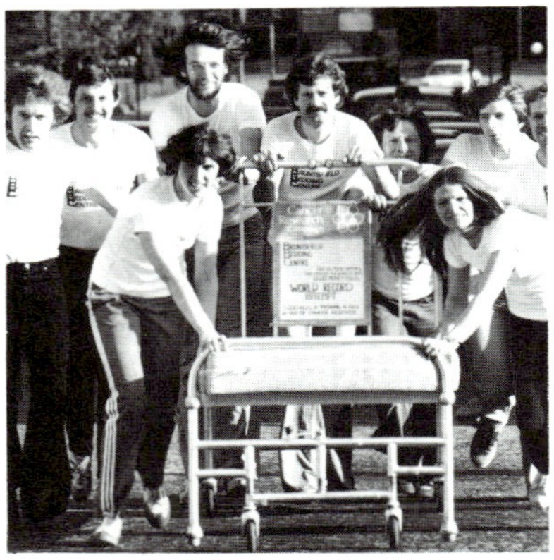

The longest recorded bed push of 5204 km on 21 June–26 July 1979.

'The farthest distance for a catapult shot is 415 m *1362 ft* by James M. Pfotenhauer on 10 Sept 1977.'

BEDMAKING

The record time set under the rigorous rules of the Australian Bedmaking Championships is 28.2 sec solo by Wendy Wall, 34, of Hebersham, Sydney, NSW on 30 Nov 1978. The British pair record with 1 blanket, 2 sheets, an undersheet, an uncased pillow, 1 counterpane and 'hospital' corners is 19.0 sec by Sisters Jill Bradbury and Chris Humpish of Hammersmith Hospital, London on 8 Oct 1985 on BBC TV *Record Breakers* programme.

BED OF NAILS

The duration record for lying on a bed of nails (sharp 15,2 cm *6 in*; 5 cm *2 in* apart) is 274 hr 2 min by Inge Widar Svingen ending on TV's 'Good Morning Norway' programme on 3 Nov 1984. Much longer durations are claimed by uninvigilated *fakirs* – the most extreme case being *Silki* who claimed 111 days in São Paulo, Brazil ending on 24 Aug 1969.

BED PUSHING

The longest recorded push of a normally sessile object is of 5204 km *3233 miles 1150 yd* in the case of a wheeled hospital bed by a team of 9 employees of Bruntsfield Bedding Centre, Edinburgh on 21 June–26 July 1979.

BED RACE

The record time for the annual Knaresborough Bed Race (established 1966) in North Yorkshire is 12 min 36 sec for the 3,27 km *2 mile 63 yd* course crossing the River Nidd by the Beavers' Team on 9 June 1984.

BEER LABEL COLLECTING

One of the greatest collections of different British Beer labels is 27,845 (to 1 Jan 1984) by Keith Osborne, Hon. Sec. of The Labologists Society (founded by Guinness Exports Ltd in 1958). His oldest is one from D. B. Walker & Co., Warrington of *c* 1846.

BEER STEIN CARRYING

Barmaid Rosie Schedelbauer covered 15 m *49 ft 2½ in* in 4.0 sec with 5 full steins in each hand in a televised contest at Königssee, West Germany on 29 June 1981.

BEST MAN

The world's champion 'best man' is Mr Wally Gant, a bachelor fishmonger from Wakefield, West Yorkshire, who officiated for the 50th time since 1931 in December 1964.

BICYCLE *MOST MOUNTING SIMULTANEOUSLY*

On 2 Apr 1984 at Mito, Ibaragi, Japan 16 members of the Mito-Itomi Unicycle Club mounted and rode a single bicycle a distance of 50 m *164 ft*.

BILLIARD TABLE JUMPING

Joe Darby (1861–1937) cleared a full-sized 3,65 m *12 ft* billiard table lengthwise, taking off from a 10 cm *4 in* high solid wooden block, at Wolverhampton, West Midlands on 5 Feb 1892.

BOOMERANG THROWING

World championships and codified rules were not established until 1970. The Boomerang Association of Australia's championship record for distance reached from the thrower before the boomerang returns is 111 m *364.1 ft* diameter by Bob Burwell in November 1981 at Albury. The longest unofficial out and return record on record is one of 114,3 m *375 ft* by Peter Ruhf (US) at Randwick, Sydney, NSW,

Australia on 28 June 1982. The longest flight duration (with self-catch) is one of 28.9 sec by Bob Burwell at Alberg, NSW on 7 Apr 1984. The greatest number of consecutive two handed catches on record is 653 by Bob Croll (Victoria) on the same occasion.

BRICK RACING

The record times recorded at the Annual NFBTE Young Builders Dry-brick championship in Leicester are 100 metres: 1 min 7.0 sec + 11 penalty points giving a gross 1 min 18.0 sec by Ian Jones on 3 June 1979, and 1 mile (team): 21 min 25 sec + 118 penalties giving an overall time of 23 min 23 sec by William Davis & Company (Leicester) Ltd, on 15 June 1980.

BRICK THROWING

The greatest reported distance for throwing a standard 2,268 kg *5 lb* building brick is 44,54 m *146 ft 1 in* by Geoff Capes at Braybrook School, Orton Goldhay, Cambridgeshire on 19 July 1978.

CAMPING OUT

The silent Indian *fakir* Mastram Bapu 'contented father' remained on the same spot by the roadside in the village of Chitra for 22 years 1960–82.

CANAL JUMPING

In the sport of Fierljeppen at Winsam, Friesland, Netherlands, the record is 18.61 m *61 ft 0¾ in* across the water with a 12.2 m *40 ft* aluminium pole set by Aarth de Wit in Aug 1983.

'Putting the finishing touches to the 24 tier, world's ultimate, wedding cake.'

16 members of the Mito Cycle Club travelled 50 m *164 ft* on one bicycle.

ZANY RECORDS

The tallest column of coins ever stacked on the edge of a coin is 205 Canadian 25 cent pieces on top of a Canadian Olympic commemorative coin by Bruce McConachy on 24 Feb 1985.

CARRIAGE DRIVING

The only man to drive 48 horses in a single hitch is Dick Sparrow of Zearing, Iowa, USA in 1972–77. The lead horses were on reins 41 m *135 ft* long.

CARD THROWING

Kevin St Onge threw a standard playing card 56,41 m *185 ft 1 in* at the Henry Ford Community College Campus, Dearborn, Michigan, USA on 12 June 1979.

CAR WRECKING

The greatest number of cars wrecked in a stunting career is 1847 to 1 June 1985 by Dick Sheppard of Gloucester, England.

CLAPPING

The duration record for continuous clapping (sustaining an average of 160 claps per min audible at 109,7 m *120 yd*) is 54 hr by V. Jeyaraman of Tamil Nadu, India, 13–15 Dec 1985.

CLUB SWINGING

Albert Rayner set a world record of 17,512 revolutions (4.9 per sec) in 60 min at Wakefield, W Yorkshire on 27 July 1981. M. Dobrilla swung continuously for 144 hr at Cobar, NSW finishing on 15 Sept 1913.

COIN BALANCING

The tallest column of coins ever stacked on the edge of a coin is 205 Canadian 25 cent pieces on top of a Canadian Olympic commemorative coin which was freestanding vertically on the base of a coin flat on the surface by Bruce McConachy (b. 1963) of West Vancouver, BC, for Fuji-TV in Tokyo, Japan on 24 Feb 1985. Alex Chervinsky (b. 22 Feb 1908) of Lock Haven, Pennsylvania, USA achieved a pyramid of 390 coins on his 75th birthday.

COIN SNATCHING

The greatest number of 10p pieces clean caught from being flipped from the back of a forearm into the same palm is 78 by Dean Gould of Felixstowe, Suffolk on 31 May 1985. *This category is now retired in favour of the international style in which the coins must be caught palm down in a single downward sweep.*

COMPETITION WINNINGS

The largest individual competition prize win on record is $307,500 *(then £109,821)* by Herbert J. Idle, 55, of Chicago in an encyclopaedia contest run by Unicorn Press Inc. on 20 Aug 1953. The highest value first prize offered in Britain has been a £50,000 new house in a £100,000 competition sponsored by Lever Brothers, British Gas, and the New Homes Marketing Board from Mar–Oct 1985.

COW CHIP TOSSING

The record distances in the country sport of throwing dried cow chips depends on whether or not the projectile may or may not be 'moulded into a spherical shape'. The greatest distance achieved under the 'non-sphericalization and 100% organic' rule (established in 1970) is 81,07 m *266 ft* by Steve Urner at the Mountain Festival, Tehachapi, California, USA on 14 Aug 1981.

CRAWLING

The longest continuous voluntary crawl (progression with one or other knee in unbroken contact with the ground) on record is 43,45 km *27 miles* by Chris Lock at Durdham Downs, Bristol, England on 18–19 Aug 1984. Over a space of 15 months ending on 9 Mar 1985 Jagdish Chander, 32, crawled 1400 km *870 miles* from Aligarh to Jamma, India to propitiate his favourite Hindu goddess Mata.

CROCHET

Mrs Barbara Jean Sonntag (b. 1938) of Craig, Colorado, USA crocheted 330 shells plus 5 stitches (equivalent to 4412 stitches) in 30 min at a rate of 147 stitches a minute on 13 Jan 1981. She also set a record for a crochet chain on 31 Oct 1981 with a strand measuring 56,16 km *34.9 miles*. Mrs Sybille Anthony bettered all knitting marathons in a 120 hr crochet marathon at Toombul Shopping-town, Queensland, Australia on 3–7 Oct 1977.

CUBISM

Minh Thai, 16, a Vietnamese refugee won the World Rubik Cube Championship held in Budapest, Hungary on 5 June 1982. His winning time after standardized dislocations was 22.95 sec. Ernö Rubik (Hungary) patented the device in 1975 with 43,252,003,274, 489,856,000 possible combinations.

CUSTARD PIE THROWING

The most times champion in the annual World Custard Pie Championships now at Ditton, Maidstone, Kent (instituted 1968) have been the 'The Birds' ('The Bashers') and the 'Coxheath Men' ('Custard Kings') each with 3 wins. The target (face) must be 2,53 m *8 ft $3\frac{7}{8}$ in* from the thrower who must throw a pie no more than 26,03 cm *$10\frac{1}{4}$ in* in diameter. Six points are scored for a square hit full in the face.

DANCING

LARGEST AND LONGEST DANCES

An estimated 25,000 attended a 'Moonlight Serenade' outdoor evening of dancing to the music of the Glen Miller Orchestra in Buffalo, New York, USA on 20 July 1984. An estimated total of 20,000 dancers took part in the National Square Dance Convention at Louisville, Kentucky, USA on 26 June 1983.

Marathon dancing must be distinguished from dancing mania, or tarantism, which is a pathological condition. The worst outbreak of this was at Aachen, Germany, in July 1374, when hordes of men and women broke into a frenzied and compulsive choreomania in the streets. It lasted for hours until injury or complete exhaustion ensued.

The most severe marathon dance staged as a public spectacle was one by Mike Ritof and Edith Boudreaux who logged 5148 hr $28\frac{1}{2}$ min to win $2000 at Chicago's Merry Garden Ballroom, Belmont and Sheffield, Illinois, USA from 29 Aug 1930 to 1 Apr 1931. Rest periods were progressively cut from 20 to 10 to 5 to nil minutes per hour with 10 inch steps and a maximum of 15 seconds for closure of eyes.

BALLET

In the *entrechat* (a vertical spring from the fifth position with the legs extended criss-crossing at the lower calf), the starting and finishing position each count as one such that in an *entrechat douze* there are *five* crossings and uncrossings. This was performed by Wayne Sleep for the BBC *Record Breakers* programme on 7 Jan 1973. He was in the air for 0.71 sec.

MOST TURNS

The greatest number of spins called for in classical ballet choreography is the 32 *fouettés rond de jambe en tournant* in 'Swan Lake' by Pyotr Ilyich Chaykovskiy (Tschaikovskiy) (1840–93). Miss Rowena Jackson (later Chatfield), MBE (b. Invercargill, NZ, 1925) achieved 121 such turns at her class in Melbourne, Victoria, Australia, in 1940.

'Mike Ritof and Edith Boudreaux danced for 5148 hr $28\frac{1}{2}$ min between 29 Aug 1930 and 1 Apr 1931.'

Un-stung hero – extraordinary sight of Max Beck covered by 70,000 bees. The bees are attracted by strapping boxes containing queen bees to parts of his body including his chin. (George Bilyk).

ZANY RECORDS

Eileen Foucher whose Belly Dance record of 106 hr took place at Rush Green Hospital, Romford Essex on 30 July–3 Aug 1984.

MOST CURTAIN CALLS

The greatest recorded number of curtain calls ever received by ballet dancers is 89 by Dame Margaret Evelyn Arias, DBE *née* Hookham (born Reigate, Surrey, 18 May 1919) *alias* Margot Fonteyn, and Rudolf Hametovich Nureyev (born on a train near Irkutsk, USSR, 17 Mar 1938) after a performance of 'Swan Lake' at the Vienna Staatsoper, Austria, in October 1964.

LARGEST CAST

The largest number of ballet dancers used in a production in Britain has been 2000 in the London Coster Ballet of 1962, directed by Lillian Rowley, at the Royal Albert Hall, London.

MARATHON

The individual continuous world record for ballroom dancing is 120 hr 30 min by Alain Dumas on 28 June–3 July 1983 at the Disco-Shop, Granby, Quebec, Canada. Nine girls worked shifts as his partner.

CHAMPIONS

The world's most successful professional ballroom dancing champions have been Bill Irvine, MBE and Bobbie Irvine, MBE who won 13 world titles between 1960 and 1972. The oldest competitive ballroom dancer is Albert J. Sylvester CBE, JP (b. 24 Nov 1889) of Corsham, Wiltshire. In 1977 he won the topmost amateur Alex Moore award for a 10 dance test with his partner Paula Smith in Bath on 26 Apr 1977. By 1981 he had won nearly 50 medals and trophies since he began dancing in 1964..

BELLY DANCING

The longest recorded example was one of 106 hr by Eileen Foucher at Rush Green Hospital, Romford, Essex on 30 July–3 Aug 1984.

CHARLESTON

The Charleston duration record is 110 hr 58 min by Sabra Starr of Lansdowne, Pennsylvania, USA on 15–20 Jan 1979.

CONGA

The longest recorded conga was one comprising a 'snake' of 8659 people from the South Eastern Region of the Camping and Caravanning Club of Great Britain and Ireland on 4 Sept 1982.

DISCO

The longest recorded disco dancing marathon is one of 371 hr by John Sharples of Preston, Lancashire on 18 Jan–3 Feb 1982.

FLAMENCO

The fastest flamenco dancer ever measured is Solero de Jerez aged 17 who in Brisbane, Australia in September 1967 in an electrifying routine attained 16 heel taps.

HIGH KICKING

The world record for high kicks (heel to ear level) is 10,376 in 6 hr 5 min 55 sec by Alagarajah Srikandarajah at Aubigney, France on 22 July 1984. Tara Hobbs, 13, set a speed record of 95 kicks in 1 min on BBC TV's *The Record Breakers* on 2 Sept 1984. Veronica Evans set a speed record for 50 in Manchester on 24 Dec 1931 with 25.0 sec.

JIVING

The duration record for non-stop jiving is 97 hr 42 min by Richard Rimmer (with a relay of partners) of Caterham, Surrey on 11–16 Nov 1979. Under the strict rules of the European Rock n' Roll Association the duration pair record is 22 hr by Mirco and Manuela Catalono in Munich on 6–7 Feb 1981.

TAP
The fastest *rate* ever measured for any tap dancer has been 1440 taps per min (24 per sec) by Roy Castle on the BBC TV *Record Breakers* programme on 14 Jan 1973. The greatest ever assemblage of tap dancers in a single routine is 3450 organised outside Macy's Store in New York City, USA on 19 Aug 1984.

LIMBO
The lowest height for a bar (flaming) under which a limbo dancer has passed is 15,5 cm *6⅛ in* off the floor by Marlene Raymond, 15 at the Port of Spain Pavilion, Toronto, Canada on 24 June 1973. Strictly no part of the body other than the sole or side of the foot should touch the ground though the brushing of a shoulder blade does not in practice usually result in disqualification. The record on roller skates is 13,33 cm *5¼ in* by Tracey O'Callaghan on 2 June 1984 and Sandra Siviour on 30 Mar 1985 both at Bexley North, NSW, Australia to equal Denise Culp of Rock Hill, South Carolina, USA on 22 Jan 1984.

SQUARE DANCE CALLING
Alan Covacic called continuously for 24 hr 2 min for the Wheelers and Dealers SDC at St John's Hospital, Stone, Buckinghamshire on 23–24 Nov 1984.

The house that got the chop by the Black Leopard Karate team of Alberta, Canada using only hands and feet in 3 hr 18 min.

DEBATING *MOST PROTRACTED*
The Literary and Debating Society of University College, Galway, Ireland, debated the motion 'That Ireland is Green' for 153 hr 20 min on 21–27 Feb 1985. The 188 formal and 120 other participants used words of 17 languages.

DEMOLITION WORK
Fifteen members of the Black Leopard Karate Club demolished a 7-room wooden farmhouse west of Elnora, Alberta, Canada in 3 hr 18 min by foot and empty hand on 13 June 1982.

DOMINO TOPPLING
The greatest number of dominoes (set up single handed) toppled is 281,581 out of 320,236 set up by Klaus Friedrich, 22, in Bayern, West Germany, on 27 Jan 1984. The dominoes fell within 12 min 57.3 sec having taken 31 days (10 hours daily) to set up.

The record for a team (maximum people) is 518,242 by Nihon University, Yokohama, Japan on 26 Mar 1985.

DRUMMING
The world's duration drumming record is 42 days 1 hr 6 min 20 sec by Laurent Rebboah of Cupertino, California, USA, on 22 Sept–3 Nov 1983.

DUCKS AND DRAKES
The best accepted ducks and drakes (stone-skipping) record is 29 skips (14 plinkers and 15 pitty-pats) by Arthur Ring, 69, on 4 Aug 1984. Forty skips are alleged to be possible with 2 inch wide artificial discs with central dimples.

EGG DROPPING
The greatest height from which fresh eggs have been dropped (to earth) and remained intact is 198 m *650 ft* by David S. Donoghue from a helicopter on 2 Oct 1979 on a Tokyo Golf Course.

EGG AND SPOON RACING
Chris Riggio of San Francisco, California, USA completed a 45,86 km *28.5 mile* fresh egg and dessert spoon marathon in 4 hr 34 min on 7 Oct 1979.

'Fire-eater Jean Leggett holds the women's record with 6607 torches.'

ZANY RECORDS

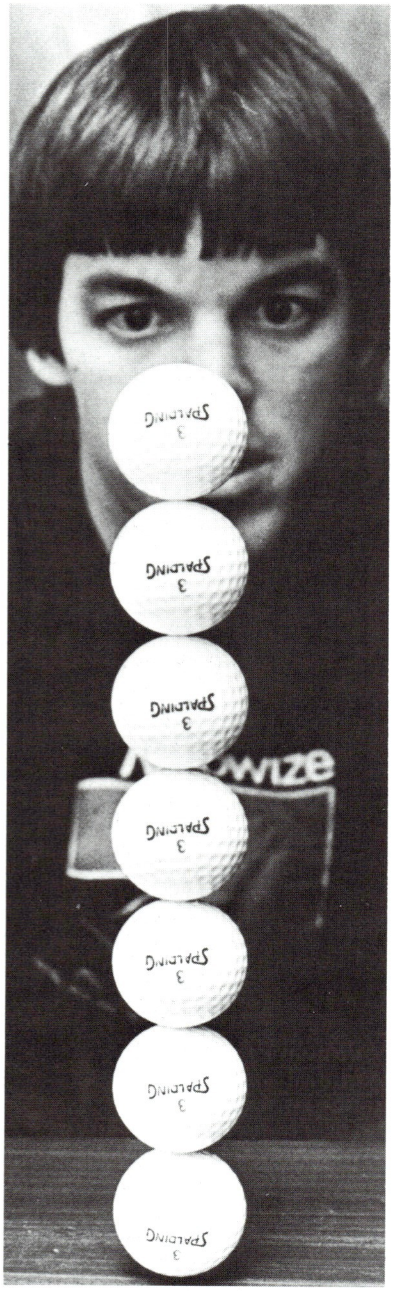

Lang Martin balanced 7 golf balls vertically without adhesive at Charlotte, North Carolina, USA on 9 Feb 1980.

FLUTE MARATHON
The longest recorded marathon by a flautist is 48 hr by Joe Silmon in HMS *Grampus* in Gosport, Hampshire on 19–20 Feb 1977.

FOOTBAG
The world record for keeping a footbag airborne is 17,872 consecutive kicks or hacks by Andy Linder (USA) in Portland, Oregon on 16 Aug 1983 and 6184 consecutive kicks by Tricia Sullivan, 22, (USA) at the BBC TV Centre, London on the *Record Breakers* on 21 Oct 1984. The sport originated in Oregon, USA in 1972 and was invented by John Stalberger (USA).

GOLF BALL BALANCING
Lang Martin balanced 7 golf balls vertically without adhesive at Charlotte, North Carolina, USA on 9 Feb 1980.

GUITAR PLAYING
The longest recorded solo guitar playing marathon is one of 253 hr 20 min by Ray Rogers on 16–27 July 1979 in Mansfield, Ohio, USA in aid of The March of Dimes.

HAIR-DRESSING
Hugo Vanpe cut, set and styled hair continuously for 366 hr on 8–23 June 1984 in Kensington, Johannesburg, South Africa.

HAIR SPLITTING
The greatest reported achievement in hair splitting has been that of the former champion cyclist and craftsman Alfred West (1901–1985) who has succeeded in splitting a human hair 17 times into 18 parts on eight occasions.

HANDBELL RINGING
The longest recorded handbell ringing recital has been one of 56 hr 9 min by the 12 Handbell Ringers of Ecclesfield School, Sheffield on 21–23 July 1985.

HANDSHAKING
A world record for handshaking was set up by Theodore Roosevelt (1858–1919), President of the USA, when he shook hands with 8513 people at a New Year's Day, White House Presentation in Washington, DC, USA on 1 Jan 1907. Gary Squires of the Leigh Round Table, Lancs shook 9313 different hands on 29 March 1986. *Many record claims have been rendered meaningless because aspirants merely tend to arrange circular queues or wittingly or unwittingly shake the same hands repetitively.*

HIGH DIVING
The highest regularly performed head first dives are those of professional divers from La Quebrada ('the break in the rocks') at Acapulco, Mexico, a height of 26,7 m *87½ ft*. The leader of the 27 divers in the exclusive Club de Calvadistas is Raul Garcia (b. 1928) with more than 35,000 dives. The first feminine accomplishment was by Barbara Winters (b. 12 Nov 1953), *née* Mayer, on 7 Dec 1976. The base rocks, 6,40 m *21 ft* out from the take-off, necessitate a leap of 8,22 m *27 ft* out. The water is 3,65 m *12 ft* deep.

The world record high dive is 53,23 m *174 ft 8 in* by Randal Dickison (USA) at Ocean Park, Hong Kong on 6 Apr 1985. The feminine record is 36,57 m *120 ft* by Lucy Wardle (USA) at the same exhibition. The highest witnessed in Britain is one of 32,9 m *108 ft* into 2,43 m *8 ft* of

Judy Leden's successful attempt on the women's world hang gliding record for distance travelled in a straight line taken at 5486 m *18,000 ft*, over Boundary Peak on the California-Nevada border.

High DIVING *cont.*

water at the Aqua show at Earl's Court, London on 22 Feb 1946 by Roy Fransen, (1915–85).

On 8 May 1885, Sarah Ann Henley, aged 24, jumped from the Clifton Suspension Bridge, which crosses the Avon, England. Her 76 m *250 ft* fall was slightly cushioned by her voluminous dress and petticoat acting as a parachute. She landed, bruised and bedraggled, in the mud on the north bank and was carried to hospital by four policemen. On 11 Feb 1968 Jeffrey Kramer, 24, leapt off the George Washington Bridge 76 m *250 ft* above the Hudson River, New York City, NY and survived. Of the 696 (to 1 Jan 1980) identified people who have made 73 m *240 ft* suicide dives from the Golden Gate Bridge, San Francisco, California, USA since 1937, twelve survived of whom Todd Sharratt, 17, was the only one who managed to swim ashore unaided.

Col Harry A Froboess (Switzerland) jumped 110 m *360 ft* into the Bodensee from the airship *Graf Hindenburg* on 22 June 1936.

The greatest height reported for a dive into an air bag is 99,36 m *326 ft* by the stuntman Dan Koko from the top of Vegas World Hotel and Casino into a 6,1 × 12,2 × 4,2 m *20 × 40 × 14 ft*, target on 13 Aug 1984. His impact speed was 141 km/h *88 mph*. Kitty O'Neill dived 54,8 m *180 ft* from a helicopter over Northridge, California on 9 Sept 1979 on to an air cushion measuring 9,14 × 18,28 m *30 × 60 ft* for a TV film stunt.

***High-kicking.* The world high-kicking champion is a male – Alagarajah Srikandarajah whose ankle surpassed his ear 10,376 times in 6 hr 5 min 55 sec.**

ZANY RECORDS

Kym Coberly the Texan who raised her hula hoop record from 59 to 72 hours by never letting it drop. (*D. Kalm*)

'*Hoop rolling.* In 1968 it was reported that Zolilio Diaz (Spain) had rolled a hoop 965 km *600 miles* from Mieres to Madrid and back in 18 days.'

Jane Wyman (the one-time Mrs Ronald Reagan) with Regis Toomey whose 185 second screen kiss was a war-time sensation. (*Ronald Grant*)

HIGHEST SHALLOW DIVE

Henri La Mothe (b. 1904) set a record diving 8,53 m *28 ft* into 31,43 cm *12⅜ in* of water in a child's paddling pool in Northridge, California, on 7 Apr 1979. He struck the water chest first at a speed of 45,7 km/h *28.4 mph*.

HULA HOOPING

The highest claim for sustaining gyrating hoops between shoulders and hips is 81 by William Kleeman 'Chico' Johnson (b. 8 July 1939) on BBC TV *Record Breakers* on 18 Sept 1983. Three complete gyrations are mandatory. The feminine record is 65 by Melody Howe (USA) on BBC TV *Pebble Mill* in March 1985. The longest recorded marathon for a single hoop is 72 hr by Kym Coberly in Denton, Texas, USA on 17–20 Oct 1984.

HUMAN CANNONBALL

The first human cannonball was Amilio Onra *né* Maitrejean at Cirque, D'Hiver, Paris on 21 Nov 1875. The record distance for firing a human from a cannon is 53,5 m *175 ft* in the case of Emanuel Zacchini, son of the pioneer Hugo Zacchini of 1928 in the Ringling Bros and Barnum & Bailey Circus, Madison Square Gardens, New York City, USA, in 1940. His muzzle velocity has been estimated at 86,9 km/h *54 mph*. On his retirement the management were fortunate in finding that his daughter Florinda was of the same calibre. An experiment on Yorkshire TV on 17 Aug 1978 showed that when Miss Sue Evans, 17 was fired she was 9.5 mm *⅜ in* shorter on landing.

HUMAN FLY

The longest climb achieved on the vertical face of a building occurred on 25 May 1981 when Daniel Goodwin, 25, scaled the outside of the 443 m *1454 ft* Sears Tower, Chicago in 7 hr 25 min at the rate of 99 cm/min *3.2 ft/min* using 'T' clamps and suction cups. The name of the masked 'human fly', who has ridden at 380 km/h *240 mph* atop a DC-8 jetliner in April 1977 has not been disclosed. It is however believed unlikely that he is a member of the jet set. Lead climber Jean-Claude Droyer (b. 8 May 1946) of Paris and Pierre Puiseux (b. 2 Dec 1953) of Pau, France climbed up the outside of the Eiffel Tower to a height of 300 m *984 ft* with no dynamic mechanical assistance on 21 July 1980. Jean-Claude took 2 hr 18 min 15 sec to complete the climb.

Jaromir Wagner (b. Czechoslovakia 1941) became the first man to fly the Atlantic standing on the wing of an aircraft. He took off from Aberdeen, Scotland on 28 Sept 1980.

JOKE CRACKING

T. R. (Tim) Benker of Chicago told jokes unremittingly for 48 hr at the Mt Prospect Saugerry, Illinois on 27–29 Dec 1984. The duo record is 52 hr by Wayne Malton and Mike Hamilton at the Howard Johnson Motor Hotel, Toronto airport, Ontario, Canada on 13–16 Nov 1975.

JUMBLE SALE

Britain's largest Jumble Sale was 'Jumbly '79' sponsored by *Woman's Own* at Alexandra Palace, London on 5–7 May 1979 in aid of Save The Children Fund. The attendance was 60,000 and the gross takings in excess of £60,000. The Winnetka Congregational Church, Illinois, USA raised $145,161.86 (*then £120,968*) in their 3rd one-day rummage sale on 19 May 1985.

The Cleveland Convention Center, Ohio, White Elephant Sale (inst. 1933) of 28–29 Oct 1981 raised $382,270.19 (*then £212,370*). The 2500 volunteers took $120,000 (*then £66,660*) from more than 10,000 rummagers in the first 2 hours from 19 323 m² *208,000 ft²* of stalls.

Daniel Goodwin holds the Human Fly record, having scaled the outside of the Sears Tower, Chicago – the world's tallest building.

The longest kite ever flown (*above*), a 650 m long Thai snake. This flew in the Netherlands in 1984 three years before the largest (*below*) ever flown in the same country, weighing in at 230 kg and with 550 square metres of surface area.

KISSING

The most prolonged osculatory marathon in cinematic history is one of 185 sec by Regis Toomey and Jane Wyman (later Mrs Ronald Reagan) in *You're In the Army Now* released in 1940. Eddie Leven and Delphine Crha celebrated the breaking of the record for the longest ever kiss of 17 days 9 hr in Chicago, USA on 24 Sept 1985 with a kiss. John McPherson kissed 4444 women in 8 hr in Eldon Square, Newcastle-upon-Tyne on 8 Mar 1985, a rate of 1 each 6.48 sec.

Underwater

The most protracted kiss underwater was one of 2 min 18 sec by Toshiaki Shirai and Yukiko Nagata on Channel 8, Fuji TV in Tokyo, Japan on 2 Apr 1980.

ZANY RECORDS

'Steve McPeak (USA), the world's highest high wire walker or funambulist climbing the funicular cable on the Sugar Loaf, Rio de Janeiro, Brazil *(Franklin Berger)*. The greatest height above street level of any high wire performance has been from a 42,6 m *140 ft* wire between the 411 m *1350 ft* twin towers of the World Trade Center, New York City by Philippe Petit, 24, of Nemours, France on 7 Aug 1974. He was charged with criminal trespass after a 75 min display of at least 7 crossings. The police psychiatrist opined 'Anyone who does this 110 storeys up can't be entirely right.''

KITE FLYING *GREATEST NUMBER*

The most kites flown on a single line is 5,581 by Kazuhiko Asaba, 60 at Kamakura, Japan on 8 Nov 1983.

KITE FLYING *ALTITUDE*

The classic record is 9740 m *31,955 ft* by a chain of 8 kites over Lindenberg, East Germany on 1 Aug 1919. The record for a single kite is 6860 m (min)–8530 m (max) *22,500–28,000 ft* by Prof. Philip R. and Jay P. Kunz of Laramie, Wyoming, USA on 21 Nov 1967. *Kite Lines* magazine of Baltimore, Maryland, USA does not accept triangulation by line angle and length but only range-finder sightings or radar.

KITE FLYING *DURATION*

The longest recorded flight is one of 180 hr 17 min by the Edmonds Community College team at Long Beach, Washington, USA on 21–29 Aug 1982. Managing the flight of the J-25 parafoil was Harry N. Osborne.

KNITTING

The world's most prolific hand-knitter of all time has been Mrs Gwen Matthewman of Featherstone, West Yorkshire. She had attained a speed of 111 stitches per min in a test at Phildar's Wool Shop, Central Street, Leeds on 29 Sept 1980. Her technique has been filmed by the world's only Professor of Knitting – a Japanese.

KNOT-TYING

The fastest recorded time for tying the six Boy Scout Handbook Knots (square knot, sheet bend, sheep shank, clove hitch, round turn and two half hitches and bowline) on individual ropes is 8.1 sec by Clinton R. Bailey Sr, 52, of Pacific City, Oregon, USA, on 13 Apr 1977.

LEAP FROGGING

Fourteen members of the Phi Gamma Delta Club at the University of Washington, Seattle, USA, covered 968,8 km *602 miles* in 114 hr 46 min on 20–25 Mar 1983. (Total leaps 108,463 – one every 9.77 yd.)

LIGHTNING MOST TIMES STRUCK

The only man in the world to be struck by lightning 7 times is ex-Park Ranger Roy C. Sullivan (USA) the human lightning conductor of Virginia. His attraction for lightning began in 1942 (lost big toe nail), and was resumed in July 1969 (lost eyebrows), in July 1970 (left shoulder seared), on 16 Apr 1972 (hair set on fire), on 7 Aug 1973 (new hair refired and legs seared), on 5 June 1976 ankle injured, and sent to Waynesboro Hospital with chest and stomach burns on 25 June 1977 after being struck while fishing. In Sept 1983 he was reported to have died by his own hand having been rejected in love.

LION-TAMING

The greatest number of lions mastered and fed in a cage by an unaided lion-tamer was 40, by 'Captain' Alfred Schneider in 1925. Clyde Raymond Beatty handled more than 40 'cats' (mixed lions and tigers) simultaneously. Beatty (b. Bainbridge, Ohio, 10 June 1903, d. Ventura, California, USA, 19 July 1965) was the featured attraction at every show he appeared with for more than 40 years. He insisted upon being called a lion-trainer. More than 20 lion-tamers have died of injuries since 1900.

LOG ROLLING

The record number of International Championships is 10 by Jubiel Wickheim (of Shawnigan Lake, British Columbia, Canada) between 1956 and 1969. At Albany, Oregon on 4 July 1956 Wickheim rolled on a 35,5 cm *14 in* log against Chuck Harris of Kelso, Washington, USA for 2 hr 40 min before losing.

MERRY GO ROUND

The longest merry go round marathon on record is one of 312 hr 43 min by Gary Mandau. Chris Lyons and Dana Dover in Portland, Oregon, USA on 20 Aug–2 Sept 1976.

MESSAGE IN A BOTTLE

The longest recorded interval between drop and pick-up is 72 years in the case of a message thrown from the *SS Arawatta* out of Cairns, Queensland on 9 June 1910 in a lotion bottle and reported to be found on Moreton Island on 6 June 1983.

MILK BOTTLE BALANCING

The greatest distance walked by a person continuously balancing a full pint milk bottle on the head is 38,6 km *24 miles* by Ashrita Furman of Jamaica, NY, USA on 10 July 1983.

MUSICAL CHAIRS

The largest game on record was one starting with 5151 participants and ending with Bill Bronson, 18, on the last chair at University of Notre Dame, Indiana, USA on 6 Sept 1985.

NEEDLE THREADING

The record number of times a strand of cotton can be threaded through a number 13 needle (eye 12,7 mm × 1,6 mm $\frac{1}{2}$ *in* × $\frac{1}{16}$ *in*) in 2 hr is 3795 by Miss Brenda Robinson of the College of Further Education, Chippenham, Wiltshire on 20 Mar 1971.

Ashrita Furman who walked 24 miles continuously balancing a bottle of milk on 10 July 1983.

'The greatest number of storeys achieved in building freestanding houses of standard playing cards is 61 in the case of a tower using 3650 cards to a height of 3,53 m *11 ft 7 in* built by James Warnock at Cantley, Quebec, Canada, on 8 Sept 1978.'

ZANY RECORDS

'The longest recorded electric organ playing is by Angie Thompson whose first and last chords were separated by 110 hours.'

'The British record for a human pyramid is 29 performing a balancing act on the pedestal of a single London post box. *(Sunday Times)*'

NOODLE MAKING
Mark Pi of the China Gate Restaurant, Columbus, Ohio, USA made 2048 noodle strings (over 1,52 m *5 ft*) in 34.5 sec on 12 Feb 1983.

OMELETTE MAKING
The greatest number of two-egg omelettes made in 30 min is 315 by John Elkhay at the City Lights Restaurant in Providence, Rhode Island, USA on 29 June 1985.

ONION PEELING
The record for peeling 22,67 kg *50 lb* of onions is 3 min 18 sec by Alain St John in Plainfield, Connecticut, USA on 6 July 1980. Under revised rules stipulating a minimum of 50 onions, Alfonso Salvo of York, Pennsylvania, USA peeled 22,67 kg *50 lb* of onions (52 onions) in 5 min 23 sec on 28 Oct 1980.

ORGAN
The longest recorded electric organ marathon is one of 411 hr by Vince Bull at the Comet Hotel, Scunthorpe, South Humberside on 2–19 June 1977. The longest church organ recital ever sustained has been 110 hr by Angie Thompson at St Stephen's Church, Newport, Brough, Humberside on 16–20 Apr 1985.

PADDLE BOATING
The longest recorded voyage in a paddle boat is 3582 km *2226 miles* in 103 days by the foot power of Mick Sigrist and Brad Rud down the Mississippi River from the headwaters in Minnesota to the Gulf of Mexico on 4 Aug–11 Nov 1979.

PIANO PLAYING
The longest piano-playing marathon has been one of 1218 hr (50 days 18 hr) playing 22 hr every day (with 5 min intervals each playing hour) from 7 May to 27 June 1982 by David Scott at Wagga Wagga Leagues Football Club, NSW, Australia.

In the now discontinued non-stop category the longest on record was 176¾ hr (7 days 8¾ hr) by Jim Montecino in the Trocadero Ball Room, Auckland, New Zealand in 1951.

PIPE SMOKING
The duration record for keeping a pipe (3,3 g *0.1 oz* of tobacco) continuously alight with only an initial match under IAPSC (International Association of Pipe Smokers Clubs) rules is 126 min 39 sec by the five-time champion William Vargo of Swartz Creek, Michigan at the 27th World Championships in 1975. The only other 5-time champion is Paul T. Spaniola (USA) (1951–66–70–73–77). Longer durations have been recorded in less rigorously invigilated contests in which the foul practices of 'tamping' and 'gardening' are not unknown.

PLATE SPINNING
The greatest number of plates spun simultaneously is 72 by Shukuni Sasaki of Takamatsu, Japan at Nio Town Taiyo Exhibition, Kagawa, on 16 July 1981. The British record is 54 set by Holley Gray set during BBC *Record Breakers* on 6 May 1980.

PARACHUTING RECORDS

Category	Name		Place	Date	
First from Tower[1]	Louis-Sébastian Lenormand (1757–1839)	quasi-parachute	Montpellier France		1783
First from Balloon	André-Jacques Garnerin (1769–1823)	680 m *2230 ft*	Monceau Park, Paris	22 Oct	1797
Earliest Mid-air Rescue	Miss Dolly Shepherd brought down Miss Louie May on her single chute	from balloon at 3350 m *11,000 ft*)	Longton, Staffordshire	9 June	1908
First from Aircraft					
(man)	'Captain' Albert Berry	Aerial exhibitionist	St Louis, Missouri	1 Mar	1912
(woman)	Mrs Georgina 'Tiny' Broadwick (b. 1893)		Griffith Park, Los Angeles	21 June	1913
Lowest Escape	S/Ldr Terence Spencer, DFC, RAF	9–12 m *30–40 ft*	Wismar Bay, Baltic	19 Apr	1945
Longest Duration Fall	Lt Col Wm H. Rankin, USMC	40 min due to thermals	North Carolina	26 July	1956
Highest Escape	Flt-Lt J. de Salis and Fg Off P. Lowe, RAF	17 068 m *56,000 ft*	Monyash, Derby	9 April	1958
Longest Delayed Drop					
(man)	Capt Joseph W. Kittinger[2]	25 816 m *84,700 ft*, 16.04 miles from balloon at 31 333 m *102,800 ft*	Tularosa, New Mexico	16 Aug	1960
(woman)	O. Kommissarova (USSR)	14 100 m *46,250 ft*	over USSR	21 Sept	1965
(civilian, over UK)	P. Halfacre, R. O'Brien, R. James	8321 m *27,300 ft* from 9144 m *30,000 ft*	Sibson, Peterborough	27 Aug	1983
(civilian, world)	R. W. K. Beckett (GB), Harry Ferguson (GB)	9144 m *30,000 ft* from 9754 m *32,000 ft*	D. F. Malan Airport, Cape Town	23 Nov	1969
(group, UK)	S/Ldr J. Thirtle, AFC; F/Sgt A. K. Kidd, AFM; Sgt L. Hicks (d. 1971); Sgt P. P. Keane, AFM BEM; Sgt K. J. Teesdale, AFM	11 943 m *39,183 ft* from 12 613 m *41,383 ft*	Boscombe Down, Wiltshire	16 June	1967
Longest Base Jump[3]	Carl Ronald Boenische; Jean K. Campbell Boenische	1763 m *5784 ft*	Trollveggan Spire, Romsdal, Norway	4 July	1984
Most Southerly	T/Sgt Richard J. Patton (d. 1973)	Operation Deep Freeze	South Pole	25 Nov	1956
Most Northerly	Dr Jack Wheeler (USA); pilot Capt Rocky Parsons	−31,6 °C *−25 °F*	In Lat 90° 00′ N	15 Apr	1981
Cross Channel					
(Lateral fall)	Sgt Bob Walters with 3 soldiers and 2 Royal Marines	35,4 km *22 miles* from 7600 m *25,000 ft*	Dover to Sangatte, France	31 Aug	1980
Career total					
(man)	Yuri Baranov and Anatolyi Osipov (USSR)	10,000	over USSR	to Sept	1980
(woman)	Valentine Zakoretskaya (USSR)	8000	over USSR	1964–Sept	1980
Highest Landing	Ten USSR parachutists[4]	7133 m *23,405 ft*	Lenina Peak	May	1969
Heaviest Load	US Space Shuttle *Columbia* external rocket retrieval	80 ton capacity, triple array, each 36,5 m *120 ft* diameter	Atlantic off Cape Canaveral, Florida	12 Apr	1981
Highest from Bridge	Donald R. Boyles	320 m *1053 ft*	Royal Gorge, Colorado	7 Sept	1970
Highest Tower Jump	Herbert Leo Schmidtz (USA)	KTUL-TV Mast 604 m *1984 ft*	Tulsa, Oklahoma	4 Oct	1970
Biggest Star (3.4 sec hold)	72 man team	Formation held 3.4 sec. (US Parachuting Assoc rules	De Land, Florida	3 Apr	1983
Highest Column					
(world)	22 Chinese team		China	Mar	1984
(Great Britain)	17 Royal Marine Team		Netheravon, Wiltshire	18 Apr	1984
Lowest Indoor Jump	Andy Smith and Phil Smith	58,5 m *192 ft*	Houston Astrodome, Texas	16–17 Jan	1982
Most travelled	Kevin Seaman from a Cessna Skylane (pilot Charles E. Merritt)	19 611 km *12,186 miles*	Jumps in all 50 US States	26 July–15 Oct	1972
Oldest Man	Edwin C. Townsend	85 years 1 day	Riverview, Florida, USA	6 Feb	1982
Oldest Woman	Mrs Stella Davenport (GB)	75 years 8 months	Bridlington Aerodrome, Humberside	27 June	1981
24 Hour Total	David Huber (USA)	250	Issaquah, Washington, USA	3–4 July	1985

[1] *The king of Ayutthaya, Siam in 1687 was reported to have been diverted by an ingenious athlete parachuting with two large umbrellas. Faustus Verancsis is reputed to have descended in Hungary with a framed canopy in 1617.*
[2] *Maximum speed in rarefied air was 1006 km/h* 625.2 mph *at 27 430 m* 90,000 ft *– marginally supersonic.*
[3] *'Base' is an acronym for jumping from fixed objects – Building, Antenna, Span and Earth, Carl Boenische was killed on 7 July 1984.*
[4] *Four were killed.*

POGO STICK JUMPING

The greatest number of jumps achieved is 130,077 by Guy Stewart in Reading, Ohio, USA on 8–9 Mar 1985.

PARACHUTING *LONGEST FALL WITHOUT*

It is estimated that the human body reaches 99 per cent of its low level terminal velocity after falling 573 m *1880 ft* which takes 13–14 sec. This is 188–201 km/h *117–125 mph* at normal atmospheric pressure in a random posture, but up to 298 km/h *185 mph* in a head down position.

The British record is 5485 m *18,000 ft* by Flt-Sgt Nicholas Stephen Alkemade, aged 21, who jumped from a blazing RAF Lancaster bomber over Germany on 23 Mar 1944. His headlong fall was broken by a fir tree near Oberkürchen and he landed without a broken bone in a snow bank 45 cm *18 in* deep.

'Vesna Vulovic, then 23, a Jugoslavenski Aerotransport hostess, survived when her DC-9 blew up at 10 160 m *33,330 ft* over the Czechoslovak village of Serbska Kamenice on 26 Jan 1972. She was in hospital for 16 months after emerging from a 27 day coma and having many bones broken.'

ZANY RECORDS

'The world's greatest collection of tap dancers, 3,450 assembled at Macy's Department Store in New York City.'

POLE-SQUATTING

Modern records do not, in fact, compare with that of St Simeon the Younger (*c* AD 521–597), called Stylites (Greek, *stylos*=pillar) a monk who spent his last 45 years up a stone pillar on The Hill of Wonders, near Antioch, Syria. This is probably the longest lasting example of record setting.

There being no international rules, the 'standards of living' atop poles vary widely. The pre-existing record of 440 days was surpassed by Mark Sutton for the Paraplegic Association in Victoria, B.C., Canada, who descended on 1 July 1985 after 488 days.

Robin S. Colley stayed in a barrel (max. capacity 108 gallons) atop a pole (9,14 m *30 ft*) in Plymouth, Devon for 34 days 1 hr on 4 Aug–7 Sept 1982. This authentic achievement was only notified subsequent to the 33 days 1 hr 6 min by Robert 'Rob' C. Roy (b. 1961) outside The Black Horse, Darlaston, Staffordshire on 28 July–30 Aug 1984.

QUIZZES

The highest number of participants was 80,977 in the All Japan High School Quiz Championship televised by NTV on 31 Dec 1983. The most protracted contest was that lasting 100 hr 7 min in Shrewsbury, Shropshire on 19–24 Apr 1984. The two teams correctly answered 16,978 of the 25,135 questions.

ROCKING CHAIR

The longest recorded 'Rockathon' is 444 hr by Linda Kennedy at the IKEA store, Calgary, Alberta, Canada on 16 Jan–3 Feb 1984.

ROLLER LIMBO

Denise Culp of Rock Hill, South Carolina, USA went under a 13,33 cm *5¼ in* bar on roller skates on 22 Jan 1984.

ROLLING PIN

The record distance for a woman to throw a 907 g *2 lb* rolling pin is 53,4 m *175 ft 5 in* by Lori La Deane Adams, 21 at Iowa State Fair, Iowa, USA, on 21 Aug 1979.

SEE-SAW

George Partridge and Tamara Marquez of Auburn High School, Washington, USA on a suspension see-saw completed 1101 hr 40 min (indoor) on 28 Mar–13 May 1977. Georgia Chaffin and Tammy Adams of Goodhope Jr High School, Cullman, Alabama, USA completed 730 hr 30 min (outdoor) on 25 June–25 July 1975.

SERMON

The longest sermon on record was delivered by the Rev. Ronald Gallagher at the Baptist Temple, Lynchburg, Virginia, USA for 120 hr on 26 June–1 July 1983. From 31 May to 10 June 1969 the 14th Dalai Lama (b. 6 July 1934 as Tenzin Gyalto) the exiled ruler of Tibet, completed a sermon on Tantric Buddhism for 5–7 hr per day to total 60 hr in India.

SHAVING

The fastest demon barber on record is Gerry Harley, who shaved 987 men in 60 min with a safety razor in Gillingham, Kent on 28 Apr 1983 taking a perfunctory 3.64 sec per volunteer. On 13 Aug 1984 he shaved 235 even braver volunteers with a cut throat razor in a less perfunctory 15.3 sec per face. He drew blood only once.

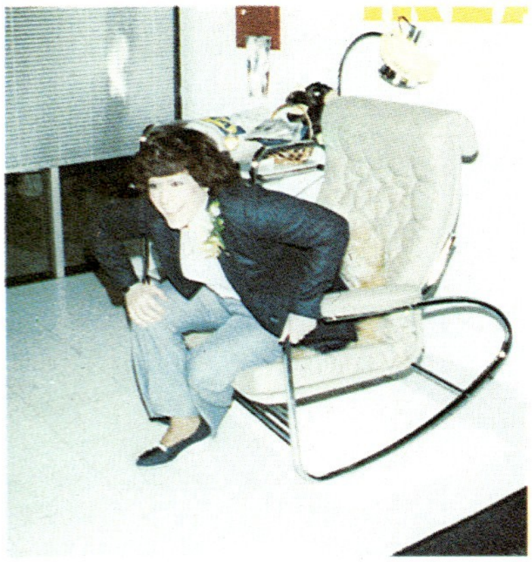

Linda Kennedy who rocked on for 444 hr.

SHORTHAND FASTEST

The highest recorded speeds ever attained under championship conditions are: 300 words per min (99.64 per cent accuracy) for 5 min and 350 wpm (99.72 per cent accuracy, that is, two insignificant errors) for 2 min by Nathan Behrin (USA) in tests in New York in December 1922. Behrin (b 1887) used the Pitman system invented in 1837. Morris I. Kligman, official court reporter of the US Court House, New York has taken 50,000 words in 5 hr (a sustained rate of 166.6 wpm). Rates are much dependent upon the nature, complexity and syllabic density of the material. Mr G. W. Bunbury of Dublin, Ireland held the unique distinction of writing at 250 wpm for 10 min on 23 Jan 1984.

Mr Arnold Bradley achieved a speed of 309 wpm without error using the Sloan-Duployan system with 1545 words in 5 min in a test in Walsall, West Midlands on 9 Nov 1920.

Sara Denu setting her unrivalled record of 1350 downward circles known as muscle grinds in a gym in Wisconsin, USA on 21 May 1983.

SHOUTING

The greatest number of wins in the national town criers' contest is 11 by Ben Johnson of Fowey, Cornwall, who won in 1939, 1949–55, 1966, 1969 and 1973. The first national feminine champion has been Mrs Henrietta Sargent, town crier, of The Three Horse Shoes, Cricklade, Wiltshire in 1980. On being told she had beaten the other 31 contestants she said 'I'm speechless.'

SHOWERING

The most prolonged continuous shower bath on record is one of 340 hr 40 min by Kevin McCartney of State University College, at Buffalo, New York, USA, on 29 Mar to 12 Apr 1985. The feminine record is 121 hr 1 min by Lisa D'Amato on 5–10 Nov 1981 at Harpur College, Binghampton, New York, USA. Desquamation can be a positive danger.

SINGING

The longest recorded solo singing marathon is one of 200 hr 20 min by Jorge Antonio Midalgo Chamorro at the Piano Bar, Barcelona, Spain, on 7–11 Nov 1985. The marathon record for a choir has been 72 hr 2 min by the combined choir of Girls' High School and Prince Edward School, Salisbury (now Harare), Zimbabwe on 7–10 Sept 1979. Acharya Prem Bhikuji started chanting the Akhand Rama-Dhoon since 31 July 1964 and devotees have continued these devotions which were still in progress in 23 Dec 1985.

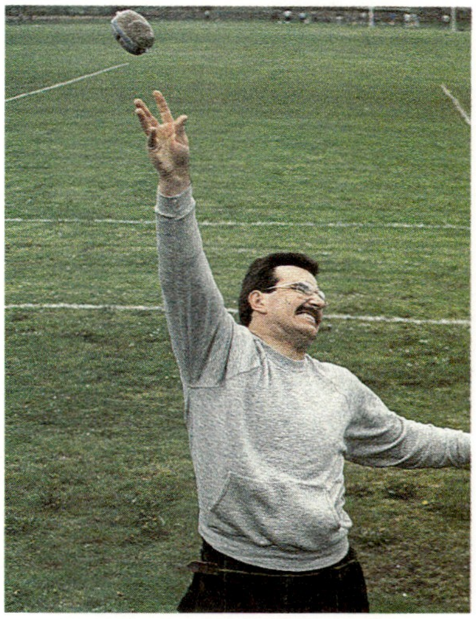

Alan Pettigrew holds the world's haggis hurling record of 55,11 m *180 ft 10 in*.

SKATE BOARDING

'World' championships have been staged intermittently since 1966. David Frank, 25 covered 441,1 km *275.98 miles* in 36 hr 43 min 40 sec in Toronto, Canada on 11–12 Aug 1985.

The highest speed recorded on a skate board under USSA rules is 115,53 km/h *71.79 mph* on a course at Mt Baldy, California in a prone position by Richard K. Brown, 33, on 17 June 1979. The stand-up record is 86,01 km/h *53.45 mph* by John Hutson, 23 at Signal Hill, Long Beach, California on 11 June 1978. The high jump record is 1,67 m *5 ft 5.7 in* by Trevor Baxter (b. 1 Oct 1962) of Burgess Hill, Sussex at Grendole, France on 14 Sept 1982. At the 4th US Skateboard Association championship, at Signal Hill on 25 Sept 1977, Tony Alva, 19, jumped 17 barrels (5,18 m *17 ft*).

STAMP LICKING

Mrs Kaye Kane (using the GPO London rules) licked and affixed 144 definitive stamps in 4 minutes at Launceston, Tasmania on 21 Apr 1985.

ZANY RECORDS

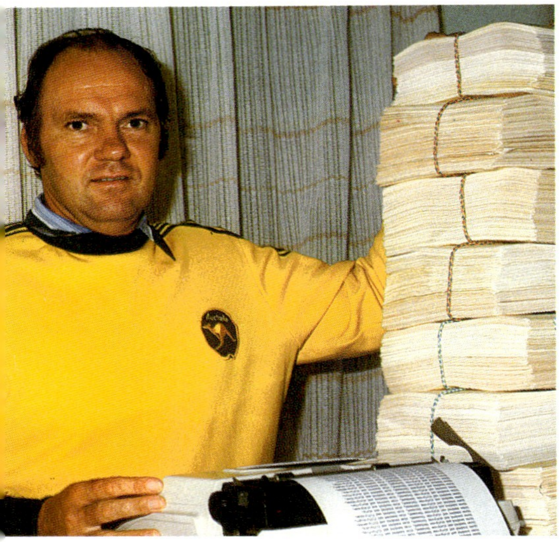

Les Stewart of Queensland, Australia has typed the numbers 1–417,000 in words on 8230 quarto sheets as of 26 February 1986

TEETH-PULLING

The man with 'the strongest teeth in the world' is 'Hercules' John Massis (b. Wilfried Oscar Morbée, 4 June 1940) of Oostakker, Belgium, who raised a weight of 233 kg *513⅝ lb* 15 cm *6 in* from the ground with a teeth bit at Evrey, France on 19 Mar 1977. Massis prevented a helicopter from taking off using only a tooth-bit harness in Los Angeles, California, USA on 7 Apr 1979 for a *Guinness Spectacular* TV Show.

TIGHTROPE WALKING

The greatest 19th century tightrope walker was Jean François Gravelet, *alias* Charles Blondin (1824–97), of France, who made the earliest crossing of the Niagara Falls on a 76 mm *3 in* rope, 335 m *110 ft* long, 48,75 m *160 ft* above the Falls on 30 June 1859. He also made a crossing with Harry Colcord, pick-a-back on 15 Sept 1860. Though other artists still find it difficult to believe, Colcord was his agent. The oldest wirewalker was 'Professor' William Ivy Baldwin (1866–1953), who crossed the South Boulder Canyon, Colorado, USA on a 97,5 m *320 ft* wire with a 38,1 m *125 ft* drop on his 82nd birthday on 31 July 1948.

TIGHTROPE WALKING *ENDURANCE*

The world tightrope endurance record is 185 days by Henri Rochetain (b. 1926) of France on a wire 120 m *394 ft* long, 25 m *82 ft* above a supermarket in Saint Etienne, France, on 28 Mar–29 Sept 1973. His ability to sleep on the wire has left doctors puzzled. Steven G. Wallenda, 33, walked 3,81 km *2.36 miles* on a wire 76,2 m *250 ft* long 9,75 m *32 ft* high at North Port, Florida, USA on 26 Mar 1983 in 3 hr 31 min.

TIGHTROPE WALKING *HIGHEST AND STEEPEST*

Steve McPeak (b. 21 Apr 1945) of Las Vegas, Nevada, USA ascended the 46,6 mm *1.83 in* diameter Zugspitzbahn cable for a vertical height of 705 m *2313 ft* in 3 stints aggregating 5 hr 4 min on 24/25/28 June 1981. The maximum gradient over the stretch of 2282 m *7485 ft* was above 30 degrees. Earlier on 28 June 1981 he had walked on a thinner stayed cable 181 steps across a gorge at the top of the 2963 m *9721 ft* mountain with a sheer drop of 960 m *3150 ft* below him.

The first crossing of the River Thames was achieved by Charles Elleano (b. 1911) of Strasbourg, France on a 320 m *1050 ft* wire 18,2 m *60 ft* above the river in 25 min on 22 Sept 1951.

TREE-CLIMBING

The fastest speed climb up a 30,4 m *100 ft* fir spar pole and return to the ground is one of 27.16 sec by Ed Johnson of Victoria, BC, Canada in July 1982 at the Lumberjack World Championships in Hayward, Wisconsin.

The fastest time up a 9 m *29.5 ft* coconut tree barefoot is 4.88 sec by Fuatai Solo, 17, in Sukuna Park, Fiji on 22 Aug 1980.

The greatest number of motor tyres supported in a free-standing 'lift' is 96 by Gary Windebank of Romsey, Hants on Feb 1984.

TYRE SUPPORTING

The greatest number of motor tyres supported in a free-standing 'lift' is 96 by Gary Windebank of Romsey, Hants on Feb 1984. The total weight was 653 kg *1440 lb*. The tyres used were Michelin XZX 155×13.

TYPEWRITING *FASTEST*

The highest recorded speeds attained with a ten-word penalty per error on a manual machine are:

Five min: 176 wpm net Mrs Carole Forristall Waldschlager Bechen at Dixon, Illinois on 2 Apr 1959.

One hour: 147 words (net rate per min) Albert Tangora (USA) (Underwood Standard), 22 Oct 1923.
The official hour record on an electric machine is 9316 words (40 errors) on an IBM machine, giving a net rate of 149 words per min, by Margaret Hamma, now Mrs Dilmore (USA), in Brooklyn, New York City, NY, USA on 20 June 1941. Mary Ann Morel (South Africa) set a numerical record at the CABEX '85 Exhibition in Johannesburg, South Africa on 6 Feb 1985 by typing spaced numbers from 1 to 781 in 5 mins. Mrs Barbara Blackburn of Everett, Washington State, can maintain 150 wpm for 50 min (37,500 key strokes) and attain speeds of 170 wpm using the Dvorak Simplified Keyboard (DSK) system.

In an official test in 1946 Stella Pajunas, now Mrs Garnard, atttained a rate of 216 words in a minute on an IBM machine.

TYPEWRITING *LONGEST*

The world duration record for typewriting on an electric machine is 264 hr by Violet Gibson Burns at The Royal Easter Show, Sydney, Australia on 29 Mar–9 Apr 1985.

Mary Ann Morel soaks her weary fingers after typing spaced numbers from 1 to 781 in 5 minutes. Quite a speedy type!

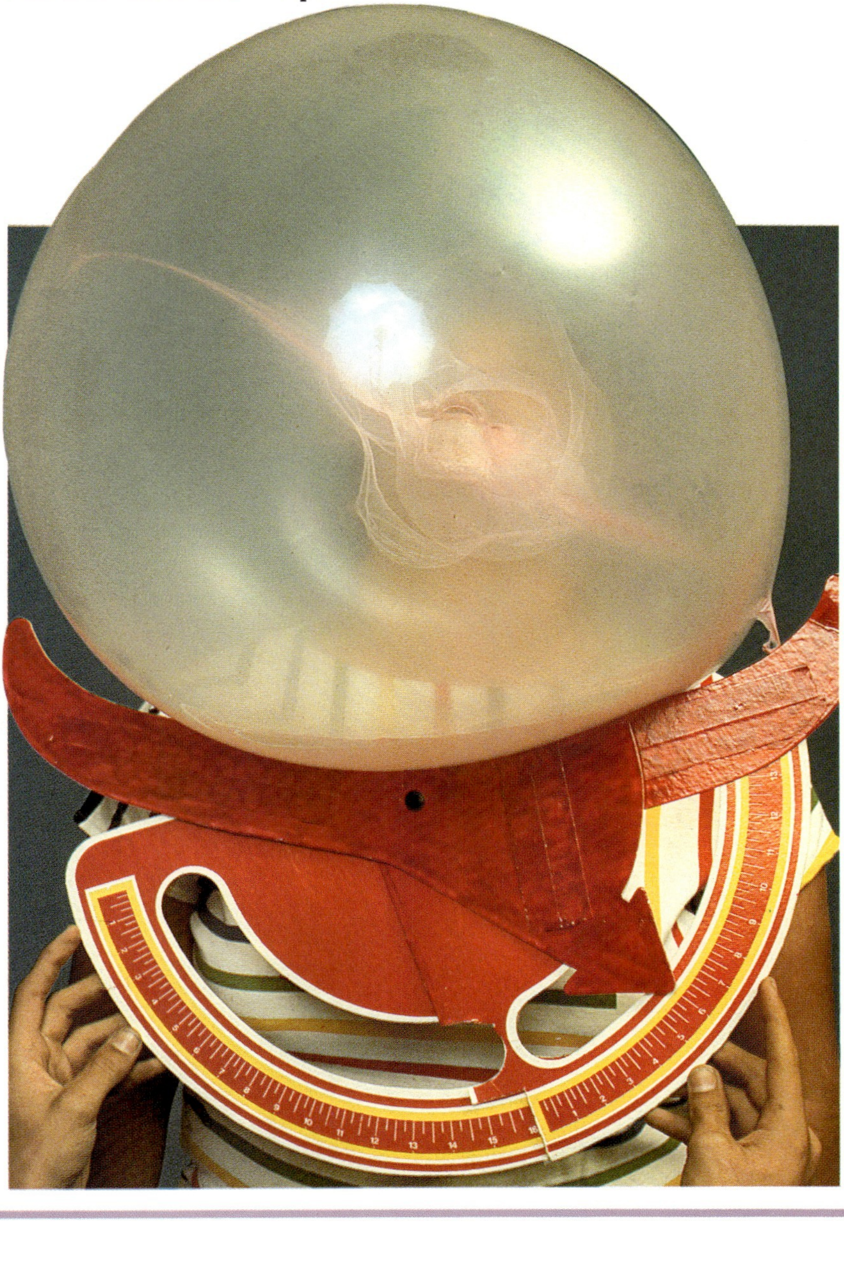

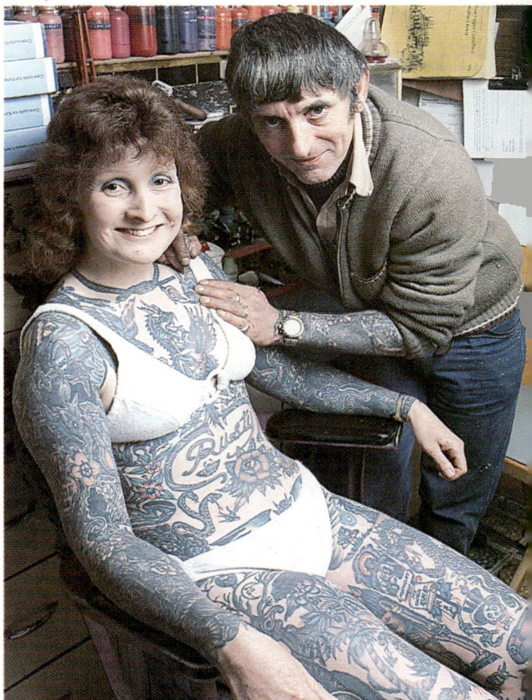

2500 decorate the world's most tattooed lady – Rusty Field.

'The greatest reported diameter for a bubble gum is 55,8 cm *22 in* by Susan Montgomery Williams of Fresno, Calif, USA.'

ZANY RECORDS

'*Whistling (Loudest and Longest).* Roy Lomas achieved 122.5 decibels at 2½ metres in the Deadroom at the BBC Manchester Studios on 19 Dec 1983. The whistling marathon record is by David 'Harpo' Hall of Berkeley, California, USA, who completed 25 hr non-stop on the AM San Francisco TV Show on 1 April 1983.'

'In April 1983 Tsutomi Ishii of Tokyo demonstrated the ability to write the names of 44 countries (148 letters) on a single grain of rice.'

High speed yodeller Canadian Donn Reynolds whose leather larynx can emit 157 tone changes for men.

WALL OF DEATH

The greatest endurance feat on a wall of death was 6 hr 7 min 38 sec by Hugo Dabbert (b. Hildesheim, 24 Sept 1938) at Rüsselsheim, West Germany on 14 Aug 1980. He rode 6841 laps on the 10 m *32.8 ft* diameter wall on a Honda CM 400T averaging 35,2 km/h *21.8 mph* for the 214,8 km *133.4 miles*

WRITING MINUSCULE

In 1926 an account was published of Alfred McEwen's pantograph record in which the 56 word version of the Lord's Prayer was written by diamond point on glass in the space of 0,04×0,02 mm *0.0016×0.0008 in.* Frank C. Watts of Felmingham, Norfolk demonstrated for photographers on 24 Jan 1968, his ability, without mechanical or optical aid, to write the Lord's Prayer 34 times (9452 letters) within the size of a definitive UK postage stamp, viz. 21,33×18,03 mm *0.84×0.71 in.* Tsutomu Ishii of Tokyo demonstrated the ability to write the names of 44 countries (184 letters) on a single grain of rice and TOKYO JAPAN in Japanese on a human hair in April 1983. In Dec 1980 Michael Isaacson, Associate Professor of the School of Applied and Engineering Physics, Cornell University, Ithaca, New York, succeeded in etching the 16 letters in 'molecular devices' on a sodium chloride crystal with a 100,000 volt, electron beam. The 'writing' was 2 nanometers wide.

WRITING UNDER HANDICAP

The ultimate feat in 'funny writing' would appear to be the ability to write extemporaneously and decipherably backwards, upside down, laterally inverted (mirror-style) while blindfolded with both hands simultaneously. Three claims to this ability with both hands and feet simultaneously, by Mrs Carolyn Webb of Thirlmere, NSW, Australia, Mrs Judy Hall of Chesterfield, Virginia, USA, and Robert Gray of Toronto, Ontario, Canada are outstanding but have not been witnessed in the act by our staff.

YODELLING

The most protracted yodel on record was that of Errol Bird for 26 hr in Lisburn, Northern Ireland on 27–28 Sept 1984. Yodelling has been defined as 'repeated rapid changes from the chest-voice to falsetto and back again'. The most rapid recorded is 5 tones (3 falsetto) in 1.9 sec by Donn Reynolds of Canada on 25 July 1984.

YO-YO

The Yo-yo originates from a Filipino jungle fighting weapon recorded in the 16th century weighing 1,81 kg *4 lb* with a 6 m *20 ft* thong. The word means 'come-come'. Though illustrated in a book in 1891 as a bandalore the craze did not begin until it was started by Donald F. Duncan of Chicago, USA in 1926. The most difficult modern yo-yo trick is the 'Whirlwind' incorporating both inside and outside horizontal loop-the-loops. The individual continuous endurance record is 120 hr by John Winslow of Gloucester, Virginia, USA on 23–28 Nov 1977. Dr Allen Bussey in Waco, Texas, USA on 23 Apr 1977 completed 20,302 loops in 3 hr (including 6886 in a single 60 min period). He used a Duncan Imperial with a 87,6 cm *34½ in* nylon string.

The largest yo-yo ever constructed was one by Dr Tom Kuhn weighing 116,11 kg *256 lb* test launched from a 52,2 m *150 ft* crane in San Francisco, California, USA, on 13 Oct 1979.

THE HUGEST HAGGIS & OTHER FOODIE FEATS

The highest restaurant is in Chacaltaya Ski resort, Bolivia at 5340 m *17,519 ft*.

MOSTEST ENTRÉE

The largest menu item in the world is roasted camel, prepared occasionally for Bedouin wedding feasts. Cooked eggs are stuffed in fish, the fish stuffed in cooked chickens, the chickens stuffed into a roasted sheep carcass and the sheep stuffed into a whole camel.

MOST EXPENSIVE FOOD

The most expensively priced food (as opposed to spice) is First Choice Black Périord truffle (*Tuber melanosporum*) retailed at £8.50 per 12,5 g *0.44 oz* tin.

LONGEST BANANA SPLIT

The longest banana split ever made was one of 2594 m *8510 ft* (over 1.6 miles) in length embracing 15,912 bananas, 4319 litres *950 gal* of ice cream, 416,8 kg *919 lb* chocolate syrup, 1353,5 litres *297¾ gal* of topping, 125 kg *276 lb* of nuts and 8910 cherries by the Junior Class of Millburn High School, Millburn, New Jersey on 22 May 1983.

LARGEST BARBECUE

On 31 Jan 1981, 46,386 chicken halves supplied by Ernie Morgado were barbecued for 15,000 people at Iolani School, Honolulu, Hawaii. At the 1982 holding of the annual Fancy Farm Picnic, Kentucky (est. 1880) on 6 August the consumption of mutton, pork and chicken meat reached 6,80 tonnes *15,000 lb*. The cook was Harold Carrico.

LARGEST BEEFBURGER

The largest beefburger on record is one of 2001 kg *4411.41 lb* made on 26 Mar 1983 by the 'Slager 2001' butchers of Ukkel, Brussels, Belgium. The burger had a surface area of 36 m² *387.5 ft²* and was cut into 7440 portions after grilling.

LARGEST ICED LOLLIPOP

The world's largest iced lollipop was one of 2608 kg *5750 lb* constructed for the Westside Assembly of God Church, Davenport, Iowa, USA on 7 Sept 1975. The largest 'regular' lollipop was one of 181,4 kg *400 lb* (220 lb of sugar and 180 lb of corn syrup) made by American Candy Co., Selma, Alabama for the World's Fair, Knoxville, Tennessee, USA on 28 Apr 1982.

The world's tallest cake stood 13.8 m *45 ft 5 in*. It was built by the staff of the Hyatt Central Plaza Bangkok Hotel, Thailand on 12 September 1985.

THE HUGEST HAGGIS & OTHER FOODIE FEATS

The world's largest cake weighed 40.82 tonnes *90,000 lb* was baked in 32 hours at Austin, Texas on 20 February 1986.

'The largest pan-baked loaf weighing 101,6 kg *2 cwt* from San Lameer, Natal, South Africa 26 May 1984.'

'Too many cooks spoil the broth but it took this number in Spain to cook the world's largest paella.'

The smallest bar in the world in The Huddersfield Hotel, West Yorkshire.

STRAWBERRY BOWL
The largest bowl of strawberries with a net weight of 204,57 kg *451 lb* was weighed on 25 June 1983 at Guildhall, Worcester.

TABLE *LONGEST*
A buffet table 1007,3 m *3304 ft* long was set up for the 400th anniversary of Hudiksvall, Sweden on 19 June 1982. Some 4000 people including HM The King of Sweden were seated.

LARGEST YORKSHIRE PUDDING
The largest Yorkshire pudding on record is one measuring 5,63×1,19 m *18 ft 6 in×3 ft 11 in* baked for $4\frac{3}{4}$ hr at the Swan's Nest Hotel, Stratford-upon-Avon, Warwickshire by Bob Wyatt and Kevin Fernley on 28 Nov 1981.

TOP SELLING SWEET
The world's top selling sweets are Life Savers with 29,651,840,000 rolls between 1913 and 30 June 1980. A tunnel formed by the holes in the middle placed end to end would stretch to the moon and back 3 times. Thomas Syta of Van Nuys, California, USA made one last 7 hr 10 min (with hole intact) on 15 Jan 1983.

LARGEST CAKE
The largest cake ever created was a Stars and Stripes cake of 37,18 tonnes *81,982 lb* including 13,96 tonnes *30,786 lb* of icing baked in $14\frac{1}{2}$ hours by Chef Franz Eichenauer at the Convention Hall, Atlantic City, New Jersey, USA on 4 July 1982. The tallest recorded free-standing wedding cake is one of over 40 tiers, 11,58 m *38 ft* tall. It was made by Roy Butterworth and M. Olaizola on 7 May 1983 in Quebec, Canada.

HEAVIEST AND LARGEST EASTER EGGS
The heaviest Easter egg ever made was one weighing 3430 kg *7561 lb* $13\frac{1}{2}$ *oz*, measuring 3,04 m *10 ft* high, by Siegfried Berndt at 'Macopa' Patisserie, Leicester, England and completed on 7 Apr 1982. An egg 5,42 m *17 ft* $9\frac{3}{8}$ *in* tall weighing 2323 kg *5121 lb* was exhibited by Patisserie Eueen Lauwers at Schelle, Belgium on 19 Mar 1983.

LARGEST HAGGIS
The largest haggis (encased in 7 ox stomach linings) on record was one weighing 245,6 kg $541\frac{1}{2}$ *lb* made for the CWS Hypermarket of Glasgow, Scotland by David A. Hall Ltd of Broxburn, Lothian, Scotland in January 1980. The cooking time was 12 hr.

LONGEST LOAF
The longest one-piece loaf ever baked was one of 428,29 m *1405 ft* $1\frac{3}{4}$ *in* baked by the First Bellair School Scout Group, South Africa on 10–12 June 1983.

LARGEST APPLE PIE
The largest apple pie ever baked was that by the ITV Chef Glynn Christian in a 12 m×7 m *40 ft×23 ft* dish at Hewitts Farm, Chelsfield, Kent on 25–27 Aug 1982. Over 600 bushels of apples were included in the pie which weighed 13,66 tonnes *30,115 lb*. It was cut by Rear Admiral Sir John Woodward.

LARGEST MEAT PIE
The largest meat pie ever baked weighed $5\frac{3}{4}$ tons, measuring 5,48×1,83×0,45 m *18×6 ft×18 in deep*, the eighth in the series of Denby Dale, West Yorkshire pies, to mark four royal births, baked on 5 Sept 1964. The first was in 1788 to celebrate King George III's return to sanity, but the fourth (Queen Victoria's Jubilee, 1887) went a bit 'off' and had to be buried in quick-lime.

APPLE PEELING
The longest single unbroken apple peel on record is one of 52,51 m *172 ft 4 in* peeled by Kathy Wafler, of Wolcott, NY, USA in 11 hr 30 min at Long Ridge Mall, Rochester, NY on 16 Oct 1976. The apple weighed 567 g *20 oz*.

This record Yorkshire Pudding measured over 7.6×1.2 m *25×4 ft*.

The world's largest fish and chip shop is Harry Ramsden's at White Cross, Guiseley, West Yorkshire.

'The world's most expensive cheese in its home market is Le Leruns made from Ewes milk at 90 francs per kilo (*now £3.40 per lb*). Cheese made to the Liederkranz formula in Van Wert, Ohio, USA retails for $2.25 per 4 oz; equivalent to $9.00 (*£6.40*) per lb.'

THE HUGEST HAGGIS & OTHER FOODIE FEATS

'The greatest number of storeys achieved from a champagne fountain is 44 using 10,404 long-stemmed glasses by Pascal Leclerc at Los Angeles on 18 June 1984.'

POTATO PEELING

The greatest amount of potatoes peeled by 5 people to an institutional cookery standard with standard kitchen knives in 45 min is 266,5 kg *587 lb 8 oz* by J. Mills, M. McDonald, P. Jennings, E. Gardiner and V. McNulty at Bourke Street Hall, Melbourne, Vic, Australia on 17 Mar 1981.

CHICKEN PLUCKING

Ernest Hausen (1877–1955) of Fort Atkinson, Wisconsin, USA, died undefeated after 33 years as a champion. On 19 Jan 1939 he was timed at 4.4 sec and reputedly twice did 3.5 sec a few years later.

The record time for plucking 121 chickens clean by a team of 4 women at the annual Chicken Plucking Championship at Masaryktown, Florida, USA is 32.9 sec set on 9 Oct 1976 by Doreena Cary, Diana Grieb, Kathy Roads and Dorothy McCarthy.

CUCUMBER SLICING

Norman Johnson of Blackpool College of Art and Technology set a record of 13.4 sec for slicing a 30,48 cm *12 in* cucumber 3,81 cm *1½ in* diameter at 22 slices to the inch (total 244 slices) on West Deutscher Rundunk in Cologne on 3 Apr 1983.

TURKEY PLUCKING

Vincent Pilkington of Cootehill, County Cavan, Ireland killed and plucked 100 turkeys in 7 hr 32 min on 15 Dec 1978. His record for a single turkey is 1 min 30 sec on RTE Television in Dublin on 17 Nov 1980.

On 23 May 1983 Joe Glaub (USA) killed 7300 turkeys in a 'working' day.

EGG DROPPING

The greatest height from which fresh eggs have been dropped (to earth) and remained intact is 198 m *650 ft* by David S. Donoghue from a helicopter on 2 Oct 1979 on a Tokyo Golf Course.

EGG SHELLING

Two kitchen hands, Harold Witcomb and Gerald Harding shelled 1050 dozen eggs in a 7¼ hr shift at Bowyers, Trowbridge, Wiltshire on 23 Apr 1971. Both were blind.

EGG THROWING

The longest authenticated distance for throwing a fresh hen's egg without breaking is 96,90 m *317 ft 10 in* by Risto Antikainen to Jyrki Korhonen at Siilinjarvi, Finland on 6 Sept 1982.

GRAPE CATCHING

The greatest distance at which a grape thrown from level ground has been caught in the mouth is 82,4 m *270 ft 4 in* by Paul J. Tavilla at Dedham, Massachusetts on 9 Aug 1979. On 16 May 1982 he caught a grape thrown 97,9 m *321 ft 5 in* off a 31 storey building in Fort Lauderdale, Florida. A claim for 107,9 m *354 ft* is now under investigation from Denver, Colorado.

CHAMPAGNE FOUNTAIN

The tallest successfully filled column of champagne glasses is one 23 high filled from the top by Carl Groves and Peter Sellars on the 'Daryl Somers show', Channel 9 TV, Richmond, Victoria, Australia on 19 Apr 1983.

GUZZLERS FOR GLORY

While no healthy person has been reported to have succumbed in any contest for eating non-toxic food or drinking non-alcoholic drinks, such attempts, from a medical point of view must be regarded as *extremely* inadvisable, particularly among young people. Gluttony record attempts should aim at improving the *rate* of consumption rather than volume. Guinness Superlatives will not list any records involving the consumption of more than 2 litres *3.52 Imperial pints* of beer nor any at all involving spirits. Nor will records for such potentially dangerous categories as live ants, chewing gum, marsh mallow or raw eggs with shells be published. The ultimate in stupidity – the eating of a bicycle – has however been recorded since it is unlikely to attract competition.

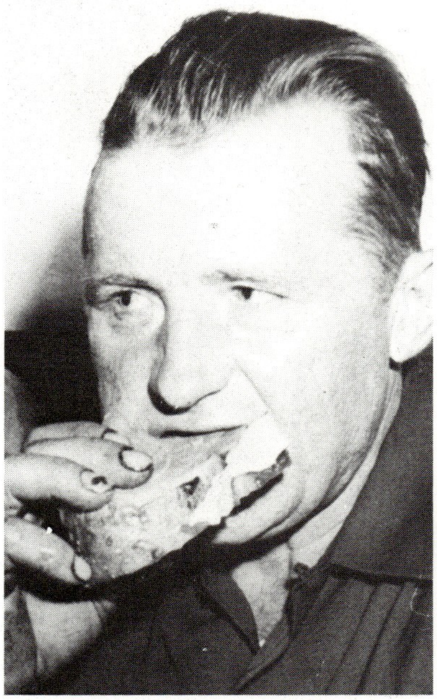

Hamburger King, Philip Yazdzik, the famous Chicago trencherman from the 'bad old days'. On 25 Apr 1955, he demolished 77 hamburgers 'at a sitting'. Today's 'Gluttony Records' are sensibly recorded only over much more abbreviated times.

Records for eating and drinking by trenchermen do not match those suffering from the rare disease of bulimia (morbid desire to eat) and polydipsia (pathological thirst). Some bulimics exceed 20,000 calories a day and others eat all their waking hours. An extreme consumption of 174,236 kg *384 lb 2 oz* of food in six days by Matthew Daking, aged 12 (known as Mortimer's case) was reported in 1743. Fannie Meyer of Johannesburg, after a skull fracture, was stated in 1974 to be unsatisfied by less than 160 pints of water a day. By October 1978 he was down to 52 pints. Miss Helge Andersson (b. 1908) of Lindesberg, Sweden was reported in January 1971 to have been drinking 22,73 litres *40 pints* of water a day since 1922 – a total of 3982 hectolitres *87,600 gal.*

The world's greatest trencherman has been Edward Abraham ('Bozo') Miller (b. 1909) of Oakland, California, USA. He consumes up to 25,000 calories a day or more than 11 times that recommended. He stands 1,71 m *5 ft 7½ in* tall but weighs from 127 to 139 kg *20–21½ st* with a 144 cm *57 in* waist. He had been undefeated in eating contests since 1931 (see below). He ate 27 (907 g *2 lb*) pullets at a sitting in Trader Vic's, San Francisco in 1963. Phillip Yadzik (b. 1912) of Chicago in 1955 ate 77 large hamburgers in 2 hours and in 1957 101 bananas in 15 min. The bargees on the Rhine are reputed to be the world's heaviest eaters with 5200 calories a day. However the New Zealand Sports Federation of Medicine reported in December 1972 that a long-distance road runner consumed 14,321 calories in 24 hr.

Specific records have been claimed as follows:

Liquidising, processing or puréeing foodstuffs is not permitted. However drinking during attempts is permissible.

BAKED BEANS

2780 cold baked beans one by one with a cocktail stick in 30 min by Karen Stevenson of Wallasey, Merseyside on 4 Apr 1981.

BANANAS

17 (edible weight minimum 128 g *4½ oz* each) in 2 min by Dr Ronald L. Alkana at the University of California, Irvine on 7 Dec 1973.

BEER

Steven Petrosino drank 1 litre of beer in 1.13 sec on 22 June 1977 at 'The Gingerbreadman', Carlisle, Pennsylvania.

Peter G. Dowdeswell (b. London 29 July 1940) of Earls Barton, Northants holds the following records:

2 pints – 2.3 sec Zetters Social Club, Wolverton, Bucks, 11 June 1975.

2 litres – 6.0 sec Carriage Horse Hotel, Higham Ferrers, Northants, 7 Feb 1975.

YARDS OF ALE

2½ pints – 5.0 sec RAF Upper Heyford, Oxfordshire, 4 May 1975.

3 pints – 5.0 sec Royal Oak, Bishop's Cleeve, Gloucestershire, 6 July 1985.

Karen Stevenson picking her way through 2780 cold baked beans with a cocktail stick in 30 min.

GUZZLERS FOR GLORY

'Lynda Kuerth who consumed 23 frankfurters weighing a total of 2 lb 14 oz in 3 min 10 sec *(Neil Benson)*'

YARDS OF ALE *cont.*
3½ pints – 5.44 sec Easby Street, Nottingham, 5 July 1985.
UPSIDE DOWN
2 pints – 6.4 sec Top Rank Club, Northants, 25 May 1975.

CHAMPAGNE
1000 bottles per annum by Bobby Acland of the Black Raven, Bishopgate, City of London.

CHEESE
453 g *16 oz* of Cheddar in 1 min 13 sec by Peter Dowdeswell in Earls Barton, Northants on 14 July 1978.

CHICKEN
2,1 kg *4 lb 10 oz* in 10 min 37 sec by Valentin Florentino Muñoz Muñoz at Kortezubi, Vizcaya, Spain on 27 Apr 1986.

CLAMS
424 (Littlenecks) in 8 min by Dave Barnes at Port Townsend Bay, Washington, USA on 3 May 1975.

COCKLES
113,5 centilitres *2 pints* in 60.8 sec by Tony Dowdeswell at Kilmarnock, Ayrshire on 1 June 1984.

DOUGHNUTS
12¾ (1,445 kg *51 oz*) in 5 min 46 sec by James Wirth, and 13 (1,474 kg *52 oz*) in 6 min 1.5 sec by John Haight, both at the Sheraton Inn, Canandaigua, New York on 3 Mar 1981.

EELS
453 g *1 lb* of elvers in 13.7 sec by Peter Dowdeswell at Reeves Club, Bristol on 20 Oct 1978.

EGGS
(Hard Boiled) 14 in 58 sec by Peter Dowdeswell at the Stardust Social Club, Corby, Northants on 18 Feb 1977.
(Soft Boiled) 38 in 75 sec by Peter Dowdeswell in Kilmarnock, Ayrshire on 28 May 1984.
(Raw) 13 in 1.0 sec by Peter Dowdeswell at Kilmarnock, Ayrshire on 16 May 1984.

FRANKFURTERS
23 (56,6 kg *2 oz*) in 3 min 10 sec by Lynda Kuerth, 21 at the Veterans Stadium, Philadelphia, on 12 July 1977.

GHERKINS
453 g *1 lb* in 43.6 sec by Rex Barker of Elkhorn, Nebraska, USA on 30 Oct 1975.
453 g *1 lb* (liquidized) in 35.2 sec by Peter L. Citron on TV in San Francisco, USA on 1 Apr 1983. *This category has now been retired.*

GRAPES
3 lb 1 oz of grapes in 34.6 secs by Jim Ellis of Montrose, Michigan, USA on 30 May 1976.

HAGGIS
737 g *26 oz* in 49 sec by Peter Dowdeswell at The Grand Hotel, Hartlepool on 21 Feb 1983.

HAMBURGERS
21 hamburgers (each weighing 100 g *3½ oz* totalling 2,07 kg of meat) and buns in 9 min 42 sec by Peter Dowdeswell at Cockshut Hill School, Yardley, Birmingham on 30 June 1984.

ICE CREAM
1,530 kg *3 lb 6 oz* in 50.04 sec by Tony Dowdeswell at the Cardinal Wolsey Hotel, East Molesey, Surrey on 26 Jan 1984. The ice cream must be unmelted.

JELLY
56,8 centilitres *20 fl oz* in 13.11 sec by Peter Dowdeswell at Stoke Mandeville, Buckinghamshire on 27 June 1984. The jelly must be gelatinous.

KIPPERS
27 (self-filleted) in 60 min by Karen Stevenson of Wallasey, Merseyside on 5 March 1982.
LEMONS
12 quarters (3 lemons) whole (including skin and pips) in 15.3 sec by Bobby Kempf of Roanoke, Virginia, USA on 2 May 1979.
MEAT
One whole roast ox in 42 days by Johann Ketzler of Munich, Germany in 1880.
MEAT PIES
22 (each weighing 156 g *5½ oz*) in 18 min 13 sec by Peter Dowdeswell of Earls Barton, Northants on 5 Oct 1978.
MILK
2 pt (113,5 centilitres *or 1 Imperial quart*) in 3.2 sec by Peter Dowdeswell at Dudley Top Rank Club, West Midlands on 31 May 1975.
OYSTERS (*Eating, Opening*)
2,72 kg *6 lb* (edible mass of 288) in 1 min 33 sec by Tommy Greene at Annapolis, Maryland on 6 July 1985. The record for opening oysters is 100 in 2 min 45.5 sec by W. Heath Jnr at Babson Park, Florida, USA on 28 Oct 1983.
PANCAKES
(15,2 cm *6 inch* diameter buttered and with syrup) 62 in 6 min 58.5 sec by Peter Dowdeswell at The Drapery, Northampton on 9 Feb 1977.
PEANUTS
100 (whole unshelled) singly in 46 sec by Jim Kornitzer, 21 at Brighton, Sussex on 1 Aug 1979.
PEAS
7175 petis pois one by one in 60 min using chopsticks by Mrs Janet Harris, Seal Hotel, Selsey, West Sussex on 16 Aug 1984.
PICKLED ONIONS
91 pickled onions (total weight 850 g *30 oz*) in 1 min 8 sec by Pat Donahue in Victoria, British Columbia on 9 Mar 1978.
POTATOES
1,36 kg *3 lb* in 1 min 22 sec by Peter Dowdeswell in Earls Barton, Northants on 25 Aug 1978.
POTATO CRISPS
Thirty 56,6 g *2 oz* bags in in 24 min 33.6 sec, without a drink, by Paul G. Tully of Brisbane University in May 1969. Charles Chip Inc. of Mountville, Pennsylvania produced crisps 10×17,5 cm *4×7 in* from outsize potatoes in February 1977.
PRUNES
144 in 34 sec by Peter Dowdeswell at Easy Street Nightclub, Nottingham on 26 Apr 1985.
RAVIOLI
2,25 g *5 lb* (170 squares) in 5 min 34 sec by Peter Dowdeswell at Pleasurewood Hills American Theme Park, Lowestoft, Suffolk on 25 Sept 1983.
SANDWICHES
40 in 17 min 53.9 sec (jam 'butties' 15,2×9,5×1,2 cm *6×3¾×½ in*) by Peter Dowdeswell on 17 Oct 1977 at The Donut Shop, Reedley, California, USA.
SAUSAGE MEAT
96 pieces totalling 5 lb 12¾ oz by Peter Dowdeswell on Fuji TV, Tokyo, Japan on 24 Feb 1985. No 'Hot Dog' contest results have been remotely comparable.
SHRIMPS
1,36 kg *3 lb* in 4 min 8 sec by Peter Dowdeswell of Earls Barton, Northants on 25 May 1978.

Peter Dowdeswell, champion stuffer of cheese, elvers, eggs, haggis, hamburgers, jelly, meat pies, pancakes, potatoes, prunes, ravioli, sandwiches, sausage meat, shrimps, snails, spaghetti, strawberries and champion quaffer of beer, yards of ale, and milk.

GUZZLERS FOR GLORY

Valentin Florentino Muñoz Muñoz ate a world-beating 5,64 kg *4 lb 10 oz* of chicken in 10 min 37 sec. on 27 Apr 1986.

'New Yorker Donna Maiello guzzling her way through a plate of spaghetti, she found her long fingernails helped to scoop up 91,44 m *100 yd* in 27.75 sec on 22 May 1982.'

SNAILS
1,1 kg *38.8 oz* in 1 min 5.6 sec by Andoni Basterrechea Dominguez at Kortezuli, Vizcaya, Spain on 27 Apr 1986.

SPAGHETTI
91.44 m *100 yd* in 21.7 sec by Peter Dowdeswell at The Globe Hotel, Weedon, Northants on 25 Feb 1983.

STRAWBERRIES
907 g *2 lb* in 12.95 sec by Peter Dowdeswell at Easby Street, Nottingham on 5 July 1985.

SUSHI
680 g *1½ lb* of nigiri-sushi in 1 min 13.5 sec in Tokyo, Japan on 22 Feb 1985.

TORTILLA
74 (total weight 1,85 kg *4 lb 1½ oz*) in 30 min by Tom Nall in the 2nd World Championship at Mariano's Mexican Restaurant, Dallas, Texas, USA on 16 Oct 1973.

TREE
3,35 m *11 ft* Birch (12 cm *4.7 in* diameter trunk) in 89 hr by Jay Gwaltney, 19 on WKQX's 'Outrageous Contest', Chicago, 11–15 Sept 1980.

WHELKS
100 (unshelled) in 5 min 17 sec by John Fletcher at The Apples and Pears Public House, Liverpool Street Station, London on 18 Aug 1983.

WINKLING
50 shells picked (with a straight pin) in 3 min 15 sec by Mrs B. Charles at Eastbourne, East Sussex on 4 Aug 1982.

GREATEST OMNIVORE
Michel Lotito (b. 15 June 1950) of Grenoble, France, known as Monsieur Mangetout, has been eating metal and glass since 1959. Gastroenterologists have X-rayed his stomach and have described his ability to consume 900 g *2 lb* of metal per day as unique. His diet since 1966 has included 10 bicycles, a supermarket trolley in 4½ days, 7 TV sets, 6 chandeliers and a low calorie Cessna light aircraft which he ate in Caracas, Venezuela. He is said to have provided the only example in history of where a coffin (handles and all) ended up inside a man.

CHAPTER 3

ANIMAL SUPERLATIVES

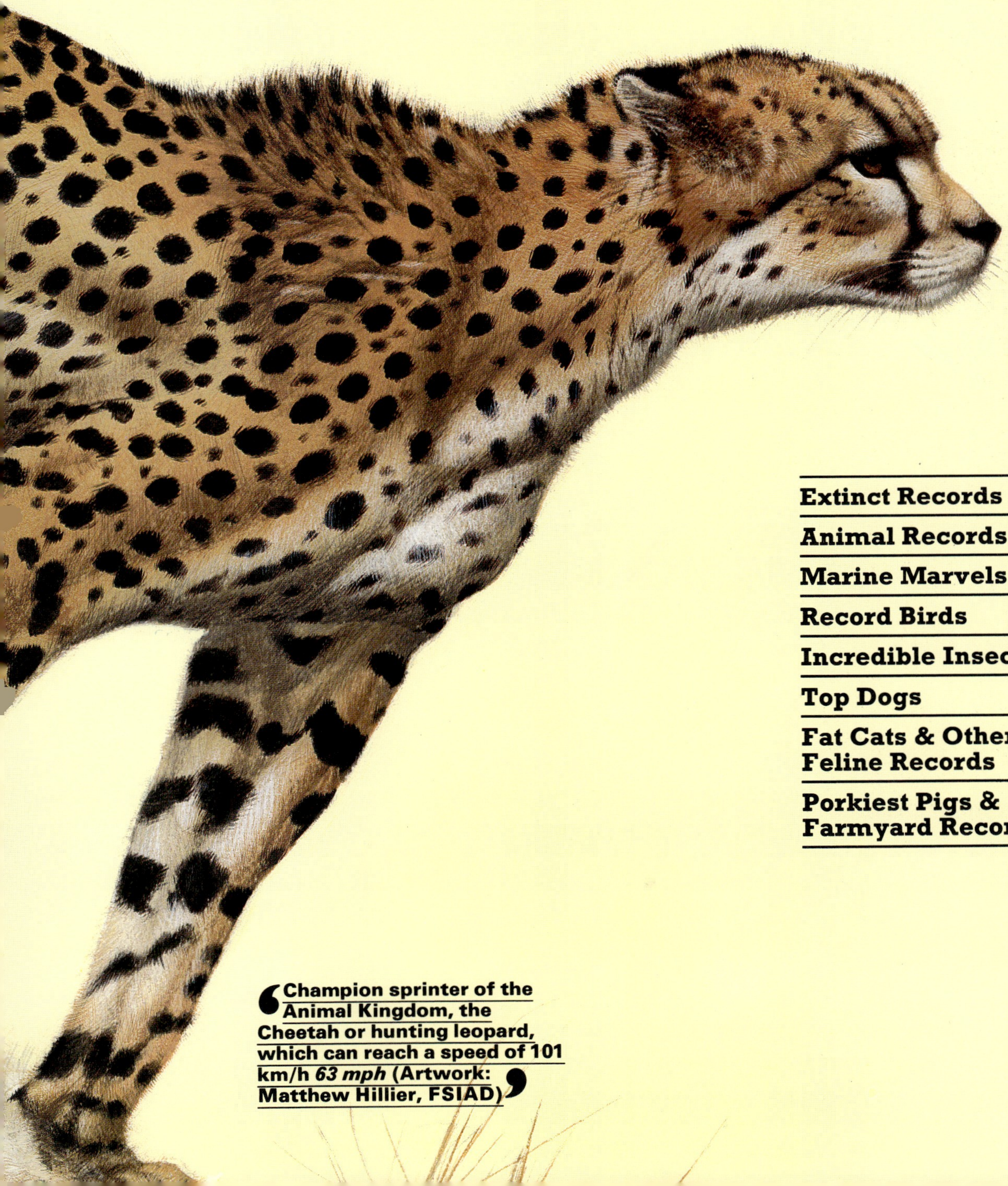

'Champion sprinter of the Animal Kingdom, the Cheetah or hunting leopard, which can reach a speed of 101 km/h *63 mph* (Artwork: Matthew Hillier, FSIAD)'

EXTINCT RECORDS

‘The Cretaceous Age’s answer to the Harrier Jump Jet (wing span 7,70 m *25¼ ft*) – the pterosaur had a wing span of 11 m *36 ft*. (*Artwork Matthew Hillier*)’

LONGEST DINOSAUR

A huge diplodocid scapula-coracoid bone measuring 2,69 m *8 ft 10 in* in length was found in the Dry Mesa Quarry in western Colorado, USA in 1979. This presupposes a diplodicus from the Middle to Late Jurassic (135–160 million years ago) with an overall length of 45–50 m *147–164 ft* and a weight of 50–55 tonnes *49–54 tons*. It was dubbed the ‘ultrasaurus’. The remains of an Ultrasaurus-type brachiosaurid of comparable size has since been discovered in Korea. Rebbachisaurus with a back vertebrae measuring up to 1,52 m *5 ft* from Morocco and Tunisia was probably equally large.

HEAVIEST DINOSAUR

The heaviest land vertebrates of all time were the massive brachiosaurids (‘arm lizards’) of the Late Jurassic (135–165 million years ago) of East Africa, the Sahara, Portugal and the south-western USA. A complete skeleton excavated by a German expedition at the famous Tendaguru site, southern Tanganyika (Tanzania) between 1909 and 1911 and now mounted in the Humboldt Museum für Naturkunde, East Berlin measures 22,7 m *74 ft 6 in* in total length (height at shoulder 6,4 m *21 ft*) and has a raised head height of 11,8 m *39 ft*. *Brachiosaurus brancai*, as it was named, weighed a computed 78,26 tonnes *77 tons* in life, but the museum also possesses bones from other individuals collected at the same site which are up to one-third as big again.

LONGEST AND HEAVIEST *Britain*

Britain’s longest (and heaviest) land vertebrate was the Sauropod (‘whale lizard’), which roamed across southern England about 150 million years ago. It measured up to 20,88 m *68 ft 6 in* in total length and weighed about 25 tonnes *24.5 tons*.

MOST FEROCIOUS DINOSAUR

The largest of the flesh-eating dinosaurs was probably the 5,7 tonne *5.6 ton Tyrannosaurus rex* (‘king tyrant lizard’) which stalked over what are now the states of Montana and Wyoming in the USA about 75,000,000 years ago. No complete single skeleton of this dinosaur has ever been discovered, but a composite skeleton in the American Museum of Natural History, New York City has a height of 5,5 m *18 ft* when standing on its hind legs. It has been estimated that the overall length was about 12 m *40 ft*. *Tarbosaurus efremovi* (‘alarming lizard’), its Mongolian counterpart, measured up to 14 m *46 ft* in length but had a longer tail and was less heavily built. An upper jaw bone (maxilla) of another *T. rex* preserved at the University of California, Berkeley is nearly 30% more massive than that in New York and must have belonged to a tyrannosaurid weighing closer to 12 tonnes/*tons*.

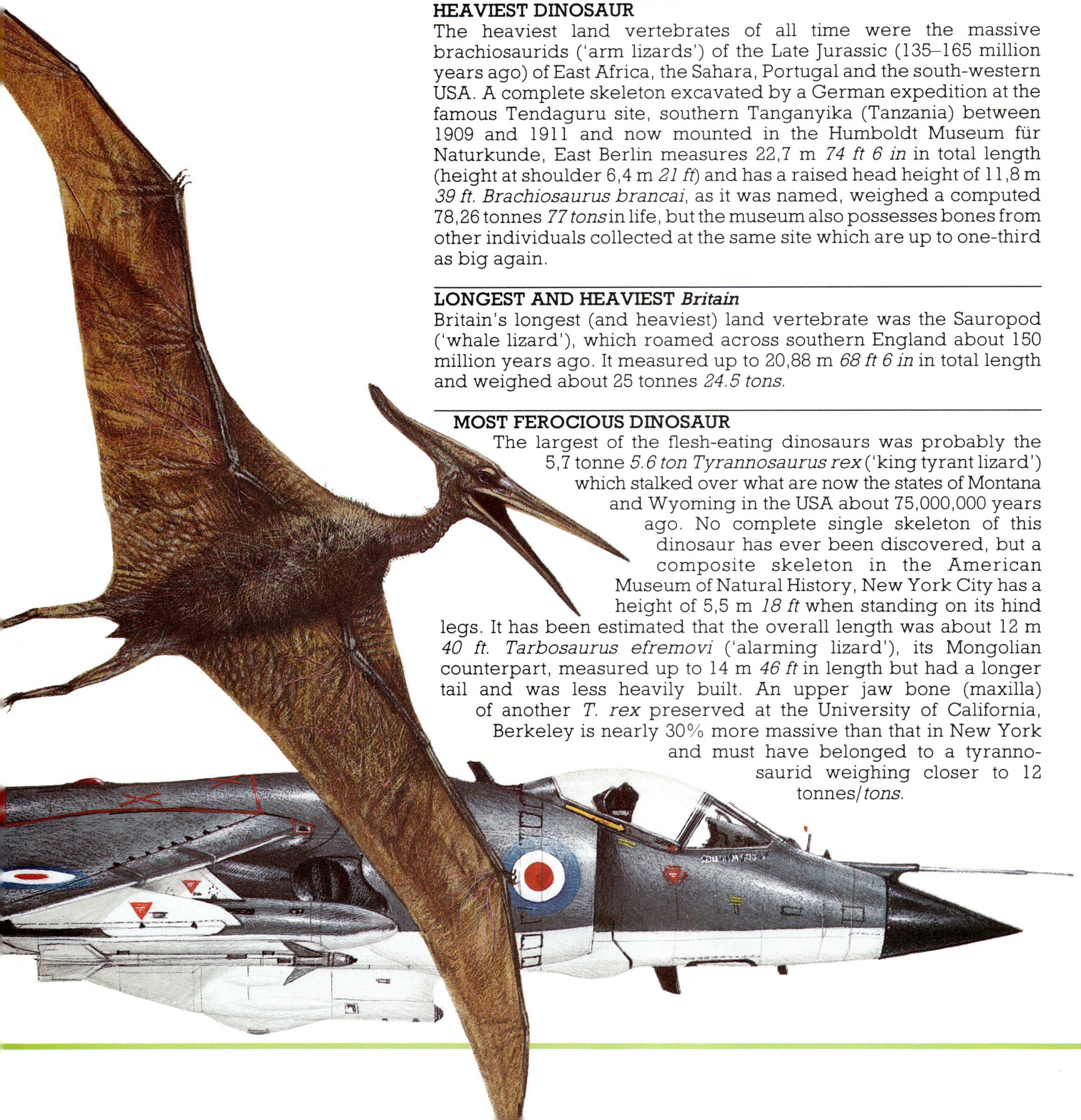

'Dimmest dinosaur. **The *Stegosaurus* ('plated reptile'), which measured up to 9 m *30 ft* in total length had a walnut-sized brain weighing only 70 g $2\frac{1}{2}$ *oz*, which represented 0.004 of 1% of its computed body weight of $1\frac{3}{4}$ tonnes/*tons* (cf. 0.074 of 1% for an elephant and 1.88% for a human). It roamed widely across the Northern Hemisphere about 150,000,000 years ago.'**

LARGEST PREHISTORIC 'BIRD'

The largest flying creature was the Pterosaur which glided over what is now the state of Texas, USA about 65 million years ago. Partial remains discovered in Big Bend National Park, West Texas in 1971 indicate that this reptile must have had a wing span of 11–12 m *36–39 ft* and weighed about 86 kg *190 lb*.

LONGEST PREHISTORIC SNAKE

The longest prehistoric snake was the python-like *Gigantophis garstini*, which inhabited what is now Egypt about 55,000,000 years ago. Parts of a spinal column and a small piece of jaw discovered at Fayum in the Western Desert indicate a length of *c* 11 m *37 ft*. Another fossil giant snake, *Madtsoia bai* from Patagonia, S America, measured *c* 10 m *33 ft* in length, comparable with the longest constrictors living today.

LARGEST PREHISTORIC FISH

No prehistoric fish larger than living species has yet been discovered. The claim that the Great shark, which abounded in Miocene seas some 15,000,000 years ago, measured 24 m *80 ft* in length, based on ratios from fossil teeth has now been shown to be in error. The modern estimate is that this shark did not exceed 13,1 m *43 ft*.

LARGEST MAMMOTH

The largest prehistoric elephant was the Steppe mammoth, which roamed over what is now central Europe a million years ago. A fragmentary skeleton found in Mosbach, West Germany indicates a shoulder height of 4,5 m *14 ft 9 in*.

LARGEST DINOSAUR EGGS

The largest known dinosaur eggs are those of *Hypselosaurus priscus*, ('high ridge lizard'), a 12,19 m *40 ft* long titanosaurid which lived about 80,000,000 years ago. Some examples found in the valley of the Durance near Aix-en-Provence, southern France in October 1961 would have had, uncrushed, a length of 300 mm *12 in* and a diameter of 255 mm *10 in* (capacity 3,3 litres *5.8 pints*).

LARGEST PREHISTORIC CROCODILE

The largest known crocodile was *Deinosuchus riograndensis*, which lived in the lakes and swamps of what is now the state of Texas, USA about 75,000,000 years ago. Fragmentary remains discovered in Big Bend National Park, West Texas, indicate a hypothetical length of 16 m *52 ft 6 in*, compared with the 12–14 m *39.3–45.9 ft* of the *Sarcosuchus imperator* of Niger. The huge gavial *Rhamphosuchus*, which lived in what is now northern India about 2,000,000 years ago, was even longer reaching 18,3 m *60 ft*, but it was not so heavily built.

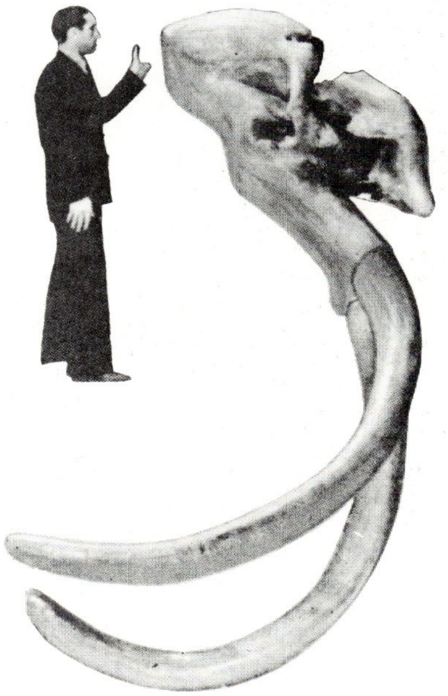

The heaviest recorded fossil tusks are a pair belonging to a 4,06 m *13 ft 4 in* tall Columbian mammoth (*Mammuthus columbi*) in the State Museum, Lincoln, Nebraska, USA which have a combined weight of 226 kg *498 lb* and measure 4,21 m *13 ft 9 in* and 4,14 m *13 ft 7 in* respectively. They were found near Campbell, Nebraska in April 1915.

ANIMAL RECORDS

'A life sized artist's drawing of the Golden-dart poison frog which harbours enough venom to kill 2200 humans.'

African Bush Elephant: largest living mammal

LARGEST AND HEAVIEST

The largest and heaviest animal in the world is the female Blue or Sulphur-bottom whale, also called Sibbald's rorqual. The longest specimen ever recorded was a female landed at the Compania Argentina de Pesca, Grytviken, South Georgia some time in the period 1904–20 which measured 107 Norwegian fot 33,58 m *110 ft 2½ in* in length. A nursing cow whale may generate up to 590 kg *1300 lb* of milk per day. The tongue and heart of the 190 tonne *187 ton* female taken by the *Slava* whaling fleet in the Southern Ocean on 20 Mar 1947 weighed 4,29 tonnes *4.22 tons* and 698,5 kg *1540 lb* respectively.

Britain's largest frog is a captive African bull frog which weighs 1.89 kg *4 lb 3 oz*.

HEAVIEST BRAIN

The Sperm whale has the heaviest brain of any living animal. The brain of a 14,93 m *49 ft* bull processed in the Japanese factory ship *Nissin Maru No. 1* in the Antarctic on 11 Dec 1949 weighed 9,2 kg *20.24 lb* compared with 6,9 kg *15.38 lb* for a 27 m *90 ft* Blue whale. The heaviest brain recorded for an elephant was an exceptional 7,5 kg *16.5 lb* in the case of a 1957 kg *1.94 ton* Asiatic cow. The brain of the adult bull African elephant is normally 4,2–5,4 kg *9¼–12 lb*.

LARGEST EYE

The giant squid has the largest eye of any living animal. The ocular diameter may exceed 38 cm *15 in* (cf. 30 cm *11.81 in* for a 33⅓ long-playing record).

LARGEST EGG

The largest egg of any living animal is that of the Whale shark. One egg case measuring 30 × 14 × 9 cm *12 in by 5.5 in by 3.5 in* was picked up on 29 June 1953 at a depth of 31 fathoms (56,6 m *186 ft*) in the Gulf of Mexico 209 km *130 miles* south of Port Isabel, Texas, USA. The egg contained a perfect embryo of a Whale shark 35 cm *13.78 in* long.

THE HUNGRIEST

The most phenomenal eating machine in nature is the larva of the Polyphemus moth of North America which, in the first 48 hours of its life, consumes an amount equal to 86,000 times its own birthweight. In human terms, this would be equivalent to a 3,17 kg *7 lb* baby taking in 273 tonnes *269 tons* of nourishment!

ANIMAL RECORDS

LARGEST LAND CARNIVORE
The largest living terrestrial carnivore is the Kodiak bear, which is found on Kodiak Island and the adjacent Afognak and Shuyak islands in the Gulf of Alaska, USA. The average adult male has a nose to tail length of 2,4 m *8 ft* (tail about 10 cm *4 in*), stands 132 cm *52 in* at the shoulder and weighs between 476 and 533 kg *1050–1175 lb*. In 1894 a weight of 751 kg *1656 lb* was recorded for a male shot at English Bay, Kodiak Island, whose *stretched* skin measured 4,11 m *13 ft 6 in* from the tip of the nose to the root of the tail. This weight was exceeded by a 'cage-fat' male in the Cheyenne Mountain Zoological Park, Colorado Springs, Colorado, USA which scaled 757 kg *1670 lb* at the time of its death on 22 Sept 1955. In 1981 an unconfirmed weight of over 907 kg *2000 lb* was reported for a Peninsula giant bear on exhibition at the Space Farms Zoological Park at Beemerville, New Jersey, USA.

WORLD'S FASTEST ANIMAL
A Peregrine falcon reached 350 km/h *(217 mph)* during a 'stoop' (dive) in Germany in 1963.

FASTEST ANIMAL ON LAND
The fastest of all land animals over a short distance (i.e. up to 549 m *600 yd*) is the Cheetah or Hunting leopard of the open plains of East Africa, Iran, Turkmenia and Afghanistan, with a probable maximum speed of 96–101 km/h *60–63 mph* over suitably level ground. Speeds of 114, 135 and even 145 km/h *71, 84 and 90 mph*, have been claimed for this animal, but these figures must be considered exaggerated. Tests in London in 1937 showed that on an oval greyhound track over 316 m *345 yd* a female cheetah's average speed over three runs was 69,8 km/h *43.4 mph* (cf. 69,6 km/h *43.26 mph* for the fastest racehorse), but this specimen was not running flat out and had great difficulty negotiating the bends. The fastest land animal over a sustained distance (i.e. 914 m *1000 yd* or more) is the Pronghorn antelope of the western United States. Specimens have been observed to travel at 56 km/h for 6 km *35 mph for 4 miles*, 67 km/h for 1,6 km *42 mph for 1 mile* and 88,5 km/h for 0,8 km *55 mph for half a mile*.

THE RAREST
A number of mammals are known only from a single (holotype) specimen. An example is Garrido's hutia known only from a single specimen collected on the islet of Cayo Maja, off southern Cuba in April 1967. In 1979 zoologists uncovered the first evidence that the Bali leopard still existed on the island. On 19 Jan 1984 the Wild Life Service in Tasmania announced that a Tasmanian wolf had been sighted in October 1982.

FASTEST GROWING
The fastest growth in the Animal Kingdom is that of the Blue whale calf. A barely visible ovum weighing a fraction of a milligramme (*0.000035 oz*) grows to a weight of *c* 26 tonnes *26 tons* in 22¾ months, made up of 10¾ months gestation and the first 12 months of life. This is equivalent to an increase of 30,000 million-fold.

A stoop dive in which the Peregrine Falcon (top right) achieves speeds of 217 mph.

The skin of the Reticulated python, the world's longest snake, can reach 10 m *32 ft 9 in* in length.

ANIMAL WORLD RECORDS

	Largest/Heaviest	Longest/Tallest	Smallest/Lightest	Fastest	Longest Lived	Commonest	Rarest
WHOLE ANIMAL KINGDOM	190 tonnes Blue whale (*Balaenoptera musculus*); female 27,6 m *90½ ft* long caught by Soviet ship *Slava* in Antarctica, 1947	55 m *180 ft* Bootlace worm (*Lineus longissimus*); St Andrews, Fife, Scotland, 1864	0,2 mm *0.008 in* long Hairy-winged beetles (family *Ptiliidae*) and battledore-wing fairy flies (family *Myrmaridae*)	350 km/h *217 mph* Peregrine falcon (*Falco peregrinus*) during stoop. Germany 1963–7	*c.* 220 years Ocean quahog (*Arctica islandica*). Example with 220 annual growth rings reported from mid-Atlantic, 1982	Nematodes sea worms. Est. population 4×10^{25} *cf.* Est. total of all living things on Earth of 3×10^{33}	A member of species known only from a single specimen or holotype
MAMMALS	Land Mammal; est. 12,24 tonnes African bush elephant (*Loxodonta africana*) Angola, 1974	6,09 m *20 ft* Giraffe (*Giraffa camelopardalis tippelskirchi*) from Kenya. 'George' d. Chester Zoo, 22 July 1969	1,75–2,0 g *0.062–0.071 oz* Kitti's hog-nosed bat (*Craseonycteris thonglongyai*), Thailand	96–101 km/h *60–63 mph* Cheetah (*Acionyx jubatus*)	120 years Man (see p 11) *Homo sapiens* 1865–*fl.* 1985	House mouse (*Mus musculus*): distribution embraces all continents	Single Tasmanian wolf or thylacine (*Thyalacine cynocephalus*) positively identified after a 46 year void, Tasmania, July 1982 by a wildlife ranger. Last captured specimen d. 7 Sept. 1936.
BIRDS	156,5 kg *345 lb* Ostrich (*Struthio c. camelus*). Up to 2,7 m *9 ft* tall North Africa	Largest wing span 3,63 m *11 ft 11 in* Wandering albatross (*Diomedea exulans*) Tasman Sea, 18 Sept 1965	1,6 g *0.056 oz* male Bee hummingbird (*Mellisuga helanae*) Cuba, Caribbean. Overall length 57 mm *2¼ in*	Level flight (*air speed*): 171 km/h *106.2 mph* White throated spinetail swift (*Hirundapus caudacutus*) USSR, 1942	80+ years male Greater sulphur-crested cockatoo (*Cacatua galerita*) London Zoo 1925–82. Fully mature when acquired.	In the wild; 10,000 million Red-billed quelea (*Quelea quelea*) sub-Saharan Africa	Yellow-fronted bowerbird (*Amblyornis flavifrons*) one male sighting from 1895 to 1981
REPTILES	>2 tonnes, 8,63 m *28 ft 4 in* Norman River, Australia, July 1957, Salt-water crocodile (*Crocodylus porosus*)	10 m *32 ft 9 in* Reticulated python (*Phython reticulatus*) Celebes, 1912	18 mm *0.7 in* Gecko (*Sphaerodactylus parthenopion*) British Virgin Islands, 1964	On land: 29 km/h *18 mph* Six-lined racerunner (*Cnemidophorus sexlineatus*) South Carolina, 1941	152+ years male Marion's tortoise (*Geochelone sumeiriei*); Mauritius d. 1918	Sea snake (*Astrotia stokesii*) found *en masse* from Arabian Sea to south western Pacific	Holotype—Dwarf chameleon (*Evoluticanda tuberculata*), Madagascar
SNAKES	Nearly 227 kg *500 lb* Anaconda (*Eunectes murinus*) girth 111 cm *44 in*, length 8,45 m *27 ft 9 in* Brazil, *c.* 1960	Of venomous species 5,71 m *18 ft 9 in* King Cobra (*Ophiophagus hannah*) or Hamadryad, Malaya 1937 (d. London Zoo)	11,9 cm *4.7 in* Thread snake (*Leptotyphlops bilineata*), West Indies	11 km/h *7 mph* Black mamba (*Dendroaspis polylepsis*) Tanzania April 1906	40 years 3 months, Common Boa (*Boa c. constrictor*) named 'Popeye', Philadelphia Zoo, USA, d. April 1977	(see above) in May 1929 a coiled mass of these sea snakes in the Malacca Straits measured 96 km *60 miles*	Keel-scaled boa (*Casarea dussumieri*) of Round Island, western Indian Ocean has total population of 58 (1982)
AMPHIBIANS	65 kg *143 lb* Chinese giant salamander (*Andrias davidianus*) Hunan Province	180 cm *5 ft 11 in* length (see left)	8,5–12,4 mm *0.33–0.48 in* Arrow-poison frog (*Smithnillus limbatus*) Cuba	*c.* 29 km/h *18 mph* take-off speed by champions in frog leaping contests	*c.* 55 years Japanese giant salamander (*Andrias japonicus*) 1826–1881, Amsterdam Zoo, Netherlands	Marine toad (*Bufo marinus*) world-wide distribution. Female may ovulate 35,000 eggs in a year	Israel painted frog (*Discoglossus nigriventer*) Lake Huleh – 5 since 1940
FISHES	43 tonnes *42.4 tons* Whale shark (*Rhincodon typus*) Koh Chik, Gulf of Siam 1919. Length 18,5 m *60¾ ft*	(Of freshwater fish) 327 kg *720 lb* European catfish (*Siluris glanis*) 4,6 m *15 ft*, Dnelper River, USSR, *c.* 1856	4 mg *0.00014 oz* Dwarf pygmy goby (*Pandaka pygmaea*) Luzon, Philippines. Males 7,5–9,9 mm *0.28–0.38 in* long. Up to 7150 per oz	Est. *109 km/h* 68 mph Sailfish *Istiophorus platypterus*, Long Key, Florida	82 years Lake sturgeon (*Acipenser fulvescens*) based on annuli; Lake Winnebago, Wisconsin, USA, 1951–54	Deep-sea bristlemouth (*Cyclothone elongata*) 76 mm *3 in* long; world-wide	Holotypes (see above)
ARACHNIDS	'Nearly 85 g *3 oz*' *Lasiodora klugi*; Manaos, Brazil 1945	270 mm *10.6 in* legspan. *Lasiodora sp.*; Puraque, W. Brazil 1973	0,43 mm *0.016 in* male *Patu marplesi*; Western Samoa, 1956	*c.* 16 km/h *10 mph*, Sun spiders genus solpuga. Middle East and African deserts	*c.* 28 years female *Mygalomorphae* (tarantula) Mexico *c.* 1923–1951	Crab spiders (family *Thomisidae*) are common with worldwide distribution	Trapdoor spider (genus *Liphistius*) south-east Asia
CRUSTACEANS	20,14 kg *44 lb 6 oz* North Atlantic lobster (*Homarus americanus*) overall length 1,06 m *3½ ft* Nova Scotia, 11 Feb 1977	>3,65 m *12 ft* claw span Giant spider crab (*Macrocheira kaempferi*) Eastern Japan	0.25 mm *0.01 in*, Water flea (genus *Alonella*) northern Europe	28 km/h *18 mph* Lobsters *H. vulgaris* and *Polinurus vulgaris* when leaping backwards	*c.* 50 years North American lobster (see left)	650 million tonnes krill (*Euphausia superba*) of the southern oceans. A 10 million tonne swarm was tracked in March 1981	Holotypes (see above)
INSECTS	100 g *3.5 oz* Goliath beetle (*Goliathus giganteus*) equatorial Africa	330 mm *13 in* female Giant stick insect (*Pharnacia serratipes*) Indonesia	See above: Smallest in Whole Animal Kingdom	58 km/h *36 mph* Deer bot-fly (*Cephenemyla pratti*)	47 years Splendour beetle (*Buprestidae aurulenta*) Prittlewell, Essex 1936–83	Springtails (Order Collembola) attain densities of 54 000/m^2 or *5000 per* ft^2	(Butterfly) Only 2 specimens of the eight spotted skipper (*Dalla octomaculata*) of Costa Rica, found since 1900. Many holotypes exist
MOLLUSCS	2 tonnes/*tons* Atlantic Giant squid (*Architeuthis dux*) Thimble Tickle Bay, Newfoundland, 2 Nov 1878	17,37 m *57 ft* Giant squid (*Architeuthis longimanus*) Tentacle 14,93 m *49 ft*, New Zealand, 1887	0,5 mm *0.02 in* diameter univalve shell *Ammonicera rota*; British waters	(Of snails) 50,3 m *55 yd* per hour. Common garden snail *Helix aspersa*. Some species 58 cm *23 in* per hour	See above: Longest lived Whole Animal Kingdom	Sea hare (*Tethys californicus*) can lay a million eggs in a day	Prices up to $12,000 have been offered by conchologists for examples of *Conus cypraea*

RECORD LITTER

The greatest number of young born to a *wild* mammal at a single birth is 31 (30 of which survived) in the case of the Tail-less tenrec found in Madagascar and the Comoro Islands. The normal litter size is 12–15, although females can suckle up to 24.

ANIMAL RECORDS

A life-size comparison of the leg of the biggest of all rodents, the 113 kg *$17\frac{1}{2}$ stone* Capybara with Britain's Old World harvest mouse weighing 7 g *$\frac{1}{4}$ oz*.

SLOWEST GROWING
The slowest growth is that of the deep-sea clam of the North Atlantic, which takes *c* 100 years to reach a length of 8 mm *0.31 in.*

THE SLOWEST AND SLEEPIEST
The slowest moving land mammal is the Ai or Three-toed sloth of tropical America. The average ground speed is 1,83–2,44 m *6–8 ft* a minute (0,109–0,158 km/h *0.068–0.098 mph*), but in the trees it can 'accelerate' to 4,57 m *15 ft* a minute (0,272 km/h *0.17 mph*) (cf. these figures with the 0,05 km/h *0.03 mph* of the common garden snail and the 0,27 km/h *0.17 mph* of the giant tortoise). The slowest swimming marine mammal is the Sea Otter which has a top speed of *c* 9,6 km/h *6 mph*. Some armadillos and opossums sleep more than two-thirds of their life.

THE LONGEST LIVED
No other mammal can match the extreme proven 120 years attained by Man (*Homo sapiens*) (see p. 12). It is probable that the closest approach is made by the Asiatic elephant (*Elephas maximus*). The greatest age that has been verified with absolute certainty is 81 years in the case of Nepal's royal elephant 'Prem Prased', who died in Katmandu on 27 Feb 1985. The longest lived marine mammal is Baird's beaked whale (*Berardius bairdii*) which has a maximum life-span of *c* 70 years.

SMALLEST LAND ANIMAL
The endangered Kitti's hog-nosed bat or Bumblebee bat, is now restricted to a few caves near the forestry station at Ban Sai Yoke on the Kwae Noi River, Kanchanaburi, Thailand. Mature specimens (both sexes) have a wing span of *c* 160 mm *6.29 in* and weigh 1,75–2 g *0.062–0.071 oz*. The smallest mammal found in the British Isles is the European pygmy shrew. Mature specimens have a head and body length of 43–64 mm *1.69–2.5 in*, a tail length of 31–46 mm *1.22–1.81 in* and weigh between 2,4 and 6,1 g *0.084 and 0.213 oz*.

‘The world's largest species of monkey, the Mandrill of West Africa can attain a weight of 54 kg *119 lb*.’

SMALLEST MARINE MAMMAL
The smallest totally marine mammal in terms of weight is probably Commerson's dolphin also known as Le Jacobite, found off the southern tip of South America. In six adult specimens the weights ranged from 23 kg *50.7 lb* to 35 kg *77.1 lb*. The Sea otter of the north Pacific is of comparable size (25–38,5 kg *55–81.4 lb*).

LARGEST LAND CARNIVORE
The largest living terrestrial carnivore is the Kodiak bear, which is found on Kodiak Island and the adjacent Afognak and Shuyak islands in the Gulf of Alaska, USA. The average adult male has a nose to tail length of 2,4 m *8 ft* (tail about 10 cm *4 in*), stands 132 cm *52 in* at the shoulder and weighs between 476 and 533 kg *1050–1175 lb*. In 1894 a weight of 751 kg *1656 lb* was recorded for a male shot at English Bay, Kodiak Island, whose *stretched* skin measured 4,11 m *13 ft 6 in* from the tip of the nose to the root of the tail. This weight was exceeded by a 'cage-fat' male in the Cheyenne Mountain Zoological Park, Colorado Springs, Colorado, USA which scaled 757 kg *1670 lb* at the time of its death on 22 Sept 1955. In 1981 an unconfirmed weight of over 907 kg *2000 lb* was reported for a Peninsula giant bear on exhibition at the Space Farms Zoological Park at Beemerville, New Jersey, USA.

LARGEST MARINE CARNIVORE
The largest toothed mammal ever recorded is the Sperm whale also called the Cachalot. The average adult bull measures 14,3 m *47 ft* in length and weighs about 33,5 tonnes *33 tons*. The largest accurately measured specimen on record was a 20,7 m *67 ft 11 in* bull captured off the Kurile Islands, north-west Pacific, by a USSR whaling fleet in the summer of 1950.

The European Catfish can measure up to 4,57 m *15 ft* compared with the Pike which grows to 0,914 m *3 ft.*

MARINE MARVELS

WORLD'S LARGEST SEA FISH *AGNATHA, GNATHOSTOMATA*

The largest fish in the world is the rare plankton-feeding Whale shark (*Rhincodon typus*), which is found in the warmer areas of the Atlantic, Pacific and Indian Oceans. It is not, however, the largest marine animal, since it is smaller than the larger species of whales (mammals). The largest carnivorous fish (excluding plankton eaters) is the comparatively rare Great white shark (*Carcharodon carcharias*), also called the 'Maneater', which ranges from the tropics to temperate zone waters. Females are larger than males. A 6,4 m *21 ft* female caught off Castillo de Cojimar, Cuba in May 1945 weighed 3312 kg *7302 lb.* A 6,5 m *21 ft 4 in* female was caught near Hobart, Tasmania in June 1983 but weighed 2040 kg *4500 lb.*

LARGEST FRESHWATER FISH

The largest fish which spends its whole life in fresh or brackish water is the European catfish or Wels (in the 19th century lengths up to 4,57 m *15 ft* and weights up to 336,3 kg *720 lb* were reported for Russian specimens), but today anything over 1,83 m *6 ft* and 91 kg *200 lb* is considered large. The Arapaima, also called the Pirarucu, found in the Amazon and other South American rivers and often claimed to be the largest freshwater fish, averaged 2 m *6½ ft* and 68 kg *150 lb.* The largest 'authentically recorded' measured 2,48 m *8 ft 1½ in* in length and weighed 147 kg *325 lb.* It was caught in the Rio Negro, Brazil in 1836. In September 1978, a Nile perch weighing 188,6 kg *416 lb* was netted in the eastern part of Lake Victoria, Kenya.

FASTEST FISH

The Cosmopolitan sailfish is generally considered to be the fastest species of fish, although the practical difficulties of measurement make data extremely difficult to secure. A figure of 109,7 km/h *68.1 mph* (91 m *100 yd* in 3 sec) has been cited for one off Florida, USA. The swordfish has also been credited with very high speeds, but the evidence is based mainly on bills that have been found deeply embedded in ships' timbers. A speed of 50 knots (92,7 km/h *57.6 mph*) has been calculated from a penetration of 56 cm *22 in* by a bill into a piece of timber, but 30–35 knots (56–64 km/h *35–40 mph*) is the most conceded by some experts. A Wahoo, 1,1 m *43 in* in length is capable of attaining a speed of 77 km/h *47.8 mph.*

THE LARGEST SEAL

The largest of the 34 known species of pinniped is the Southern elephant seal, which inhabits the sub-Antarctic islands. Adult bulls average 5 m *16½ ft* in length (tip of inflated snout to the extremities of the outstretched tail flippers), 3,7 m *12 ft* in maximum bodily girth and weigh about 2268 kg (*5000 lb 2.18 tons*). The largest accurately measured specimen on record was a bull killed in Possession Bay, South Georgia on 28 Feb 1913 which measured 6,5 m *21 ft 4 in* after flensing (original length about 6,85 m *22½ ft*) and probably weighed at least 4 tonnes/*tons*. There are old records of bulls measuring 7,62–9,14 m *25–30 ft* and even 10,66 m *35 ft* but these figures must be considered exaggerated.

An adult bull Southern Elephant Seal, of the sub-Antarctic the largest known pinniped which can weigh up to 4 tons and measure over 6,7 m *22 ft* in length.

LONGEST LIVED FISH

Aquaria are of too recent origin to be able to establish with certainty which species of fish can be regarded as being the longest lived. Early indications are, however, that the Lake sturgeon of North America can live to about 82 years. In July 1974 a growth ring count of 228 years was reported for a female Koi fish, a form of fancy carp, named 'Hanako' living in a pond in Higashi Shirakawa, Gifu Prefecture, Japan, but the greatest authoritatively accepted age for this species is 'more than 50 years'. In 1948 the death was reported of an 88-year-old female European eel named 'Putte' in the aquarium at Halsingborg Museum, southern Sweden. She was allegedly born in the Sargasso Sea, North Atlantic in 1860, and was caught in a river as a three-year-old elver.

MOST POISONOUS FISH

The most venomous fish in the world are the Stonefish of the tropical waters of the Indo-Pacific, and in particular *Synanceja horrida* which has the largest venom glands of any known fish. Direct contact with the spines of its fins, which contain a strong nerve-attacking poison, often proves fatal.

MOST ELECTRIC

The most powerful electric fish is the Electric eel which is found in the rivers of Brazil, Colombia, Venezuela and Peru. An average sized specimen can discharge 400 volts at 1 ampere, but measurements up to 650 volts have been recorded.

‘The largest mammal, the Blue Whale, can achieve a length of 33,5 m *110 ft* and weigh up to 174 tons.’

MARINE MARVELS

'The greatest depth from which a fish has been recovered is 8300 m *27,230 ft* in the Puerto Rico, Trench in April 1970. The fish, a 16.5 cm *6½ in* long *Bassogigas profundissimus* was caught by the US research vessel *John Elliott*.'

DEEPEST DIVING

The greatest *recorded* depth to which a whale has dived is 620 fathoms (1134 m *3720 ft*) by a 14,32 m *47 ft* bull Sperm whale found with its jaw entangled with a submarine cable running between Santa Elena, Ecuador and Chorillos, Peru, on 14 Oct 1955. At this depth the whale withstood a pressure of 118 kg f/cm² *1680 lb/in²* of body surface. On 25 Aug 1969 another bull Sperm whale was killed 160 km *100 miles* south of Durban after it had surfaced from a dive lasting 1 hr 52 min, and inside its stomach were found two small sharks which had been swallowed about an hour earlier. These were later identified as *Scymnodon* sp, a species found only on the sea floor. At this point from land the depth of water is in excess of 3193 m *10,476 ft 1646 fathoms*) for a radius of 48–64 km *30–40 miles*, which now suggests that the Sperm whale sometimes descends to a depth of over 3000 m *10,000 ft* when seeking food and is limited by pressure of time rather than by pressure of pressure.

MOST VALUABLE FISH

The world's most valuable fish is the Russian sturgeon (*Huso huso*). One 1227 kg *2706 lb* female caught in the Tikhaya Sosna River in 1924 yielded 245 kg *541 lb* of best quality caviare which would be worth £123,000 on today's market.

OLDEST GOLDFISH

Goldfish have been reported to live for over 40 years in China. The British record is held by a specimen named 'Fred' owned by Mr A. R. Wilson of Worthing, Sussex, which died on 1 Aug 1980, aged 41 years.

LARGEST CRAB

The largest of all crustaceans (although not the heaviest) is the Sanschouo or Giant spider crab, also called the Stilt crab, which is found in deep waters off the south-eastern coast of Japan.

LARGEST OCTOPUS

The largest octopus known to science is *Octopus appollyon* of the coastal waters of the North Pacific which regularly exceeds 3,7 m *12 ft* in radial spread and 25 kg *55 lb* in weight. One huge individual caught single-handed by skin-diver Donald E. Hagen in Lower Hoods Canal, Puget Sound, Washington, USA on 18 Feb 1973 had a spread of 7,01 m *23 ft* and weighed 53,8 kg *118 lb 10 oz*. In November 1896 the remains of an unknown animal weighing an estimated 6–7 tonnes/*tons* were found on a beach near St Augustine, Florida, USA. Tissue samples were later sent to the US National Museum in Washington, DC, and in 1970 they were *positively* identified as belonging to a giant form of octopus. Some experts, however, do not agree with this assessment because there was no evidence of tentacles or a beak and believe the decomposing carcase was more probably that of a large whale or shark.

'*Largest Shell.* The largest of all existing shells is the marine Giant clam, which is found on the Indo-Pacific coral reefs. A specimen measuring 110 cm *43.3 in* across and weighing 333 kg *734 lb* was collected near Ishigaki Island, Okinawa, Japan, found in 1956 but not formally measured until Aug 1984.'

RECORD BIRDS

LARGEST FLYING BIRD

The heaviest flying bird or carinate is the Kori bustard or Paauw of East and South Africa. Weights up to 18 kg *40 lb* have been reliably reported for cock birds shot in South Africa. The Mute swan which is resident in Britain, can also reach 18 kg *40 lb* on occasion, and there is a record from Poland of a cob weighing 22,5 kg *49.5 lb* which could not fly.

BIGGEST BIRD OF PREY

The heaviest bird of prey is the Andean condor, adult males averaging 9,09–11,3 kg *20–25 lb*. A weight of 14,1 kg *31 lb* has been claimed for a California condor (average weight 9kg *20 lb*) now preserved in the California Academy of Sciences, Los Angeles.

WORLD'S SMALLEST BIRD

The smallest bird in the world is the male Bee hummingbird of Cuba and the Isle of Pines. The smallest bird of prey is the 35 g *1.23 oz* White-fronted falconet of NW Borneo which is sparrow-sized. The smallest sea bird is the Least storm petrel, which breeds on many of the small islands in the Gulf of California, NW Mexico. Adult specimens average 140 mm *5½ in* total length and weigh *c* 28 g *1 oz.*

WORLD'S RAREST BIRD

Because of the practical difficulties involved in assessing bird populations in the wild, it is virtually impossible to establish the identity of the world's rarest living bird. The strongest contenders must be the Ooaa of Kauai, Hawaiian Islands, which was down to a single pair in 1980 and the protected Dusty seaside sparrow of Titus Marshes, Florida, USA with only 4 males known in 1984. The world's rarest bird of prey is the Madagascar fish eagle now down to *c* 10 pairs.

RECORD WING SPAN

The Wandering albatross of the southern oceans has the largest wing span of any living bird. The only other bird reliably credited with a wingspread in excess of 3,35 m *11 ft* is the vulture-like Marabou stork of Africa. In the 1940s an extreme measurement of 4,06 m *13 ft 4 in* was reported for a male shot in Central Africa, but this species rarely exceeds 2,43 m *9 ft*.

MOST ABUNDANT WILD SPECIES

The most abundant species of wild bird is the Red-billed quelea. The most abundant sea bird is probably Wilson's storm-petrel of the Antarctic. No population estimates have been published, but the number must run into hundreds of millions. Britain's most abundant sea bird is the Common guillemot with an estimated 577,000 breeding pairs in 1969–70.

FASTEST AND SLOWEST FLIERS

The fastest flying bird in *level* flight (compared to *diving* flight – see 'Fastest animal', p. 82) is the White-throated spine-tailed swift. The slowest flying bird is the American woodcock which has been timed at 8 km/h *5 mph* without sinking.

LONGEST-LIVING BIRDS

The greatest irrefutable age reported for any bird is 72+ years. Other records which are regarded as *probably* reliable included 73 years (1818–91) for a Greater sulphur-crested cockatoo; 72 years (1797–1869) for an African grey parrot; 70 years (1770–1840) for a Mute swan and 69 years for a raven.

'The contrast between the largest and smallest living birds. The Bee hummingbird shown actual size compared to the eye of an ostrich. The ostrich is 97,000 times bigger. *(Artwork Matthew Hillier)*'

'Largest bird in the world. **The largest living bird is the North African ostrich which is found in reduced numbers south of the Atlas Mountains from Upper Senegal and Niger across to the Sudan and central Ethiopia.'**

RECORD BIRDS

The Red-billed Quelea is the world's commonest bird, but also probably the most destructive of crops.

THE 40-MINUTE EGG

The largest egg produced by any living bird is that of the ostrich. The average example measures 15–20 cm *6–8 in* in length, 10–15 cm *4–6 in* in diameter and weighs 1,65–1,78 kg *3.63–3.88 lb* (equal to the volume of two dozen hen's eggs). It requires about 40 min for boiling. The shell though 1,5 mm *1/16 in* thick can support the weight of a 127 kg *20 st* man.

'PRUDLE' – THE WORLD'S MOST TALKATIVE PARROT

The world's most talkative bird is a male African grey parrot named 'Prudle', owned by Mrs Lyn Logue of Golders Green, London, which won the 'Best talking parrot-like bird' title at the National Cage and Aviary Bird Show held in London each December for 12 consecutive years (1965–76). Prudle, who has a vocabulary of nearly 800 words, was taken from a nest at Jinja, Uganda in 1958. He retired undefeated.

INCREDIBLE INSECTS AND SPIDERS

BLONDI – THE BIRD-EATING SPIDER

The world's largest known spiders in terms of leg span are the bulky theraphosid spiders of the genera *Lasiodora* and *Grammostola* of Brazil, and *Theraphosa* (see illustration of *Theraphosa blondi*, actual size) of NE South America, all of which have been credited with leg spans in excess of 250 mm *10 in*.

MOST POISONOUS SPIDER

The most venomous spiders in the world are the Brazilian wandering spiders of the genus *Phoneutria*, and particularly *P. fera*, which has the most active venom of any living spider. These large and highly aggressive creatures frequently enter human dwellings and hide in clothing or shoes. When disturbed they bite furiously several times, and hundreds of accidents involving these species are reported annually. Fortunately an effective antidote is available, and when deaths do occur they are usually children under the age of seven.

SIX TIMES FASTER THAN THE FASTEST SPRINTER

The highest speed recorded for a spider on a level surface is by *Tenegaria gigantea*. This is 33 times her body length per sec compared with the human record of 5½ times.

INCREDIBLE INSECTS AND SPIDERS

'The smallest known spider is *Patu marplesi* of Western Samoa at 0,43 mm *0.016 in.*'

'Britain's and the world's most senior beetle. It was found on the staircase at the home of Mr W. Euston of Southend, Essex after 47 years as a larva.'

***Theraphosa blondi*, the 'bird-eating' spider of South America, shown actual size.**

LARGEST WEBS
The largest webs are the aerial ones spun by the tropical orb weavers of the genus *Nephila*, which have been measured up to 573 cm *18 ft 9¾ in* in circumference. The smallest webs are spun by spiders like *Glyphesis cottonae*, etc. which are about the size of a postage stamp, which cover about 480 mm² *0.75 in²*.

WORLD'S LARGEST FLEA
The largest known flea is *Hystrichopsylla schefferi*, which was described from a single specimen taken from the nest of a Mountain beaver at Puyallup, Washington, USA in 1913. Females measure up to 8 mm *0.31 in* in length which is the diameter of a pencil.

WORLD'S LONGEST INSECT
The longest insect in the world is the giant stick-insect of Indonesia. The longest known beetles (excluding antennae) are the Hercules beetles of Central and South America, which have been measured up to 190 mm *7.48 in* and 180 mm *7.08 in* respectively More than half the length, however, is taken up by the prothoracic horn.

BEE HIVE RECORD
The greatest reported amount of wild honey ever extracted from a single hive is 249,02 kg *549 lb* recorded by A. D. Wilkes of Cairns, Queensland, Australia in the 11 months Feb–Dec 1983.

WORLD'S HEAVIEST INSECT
The heaviest insects in the world are the Goliath beetles of equatorial Africa. The largest members of the group are *Goliathus regius* and *Goliathus goliathus* (=*giganteus*) and weigh in at 100 g *3.5 oz.*

LARGEST BUTTERFLIES AND MOTHS
The largest known butterfly is the protected Queen Alexandra's birdwing which is restricted to the Popondetta Plain in Papua, New Guinea. Females may have a wing span exceeding 280 mm *11.02 in* and weigh over 5 g *0.176 oz.* The largest moth in the world (although not the heaviest) is the Hercules moth of tropical Australia and New Guinea. A wing area of up to 263,2 cm² *40.8 in²* and a wing span of 280 mm *11 in* have been recorded. In 1948 an unconfirmed measurement of 360 mm *14.17 in* was reported for a female captured near the post office at the coastal town of Innisfail, Queensland, Australia. The rare Owlet moth of Brazil has been measured up to 308 mm *12.16 in* wing span, and the Philippine atlas moth up to 260 mm *11.02 in*, but both these species are lighter than the Hercules moth.

FASTEST FLYING INSECT
Experiments have proved that the widely publicised claim in 1926 that the Deer bot-fly could attain a speed of 1316 km/h *818 mph* (*sic*) was widely exaggerated. If true it would have generated a supersonic 'pop'! Acceptable modern experiments have now established that the highest maintainable airspeed of any insect is 39 km/h *24 mph*, rising to a maximum of 58 km/h *36 mph* for short bursts.

TOP DOGS

'Bluey' wearing his over-large commemorative collar for being the oldest dog (26 years) in Victoria, Australia, he died three years later on 14 Nov 1939.

LARGEST LITTER

The largest recorded litter of puppies is one of 23 thrown on 19 June 1944 by 'Lena', a foxhound bitch owned by Commander W. N. Ely of Ambler, Pennsylvania, USA. On 6–7 Feb 1975 'Careless Ann', a St Bernard, owned by Robert and Alice Rodden of Lebanon, Missouri, USA also produced a litter of 23, 14 of which survived. The British record is held by 'Settrina Baroness Medina' (d. 1983), an Irish red setter owned by Mgr M. J. Buckley, Director of the Wood Hall Centre, Wetherby, West Yorkshire. The bitch gave birth to 22 puppies, 15 of which survived, on 10 Jan 1974.

WORLD'S LARGEST DOG

The heaviest breed of domestic dog is the St Bernard. The heaviest recorded example is 'Benedictine Schwarzwald Hof', owned by Thomas and Ann Irwin of Grand Rapids, Michigan, USA. He was whelped in 1982 and weighed 140,6 kg *22 st 2 lb* on 3 Dec 1984 (height at shoulder 99 cm *39 in*). The heaviest dog ever recorded in Britain is 'Heidan Dark Blue' (whelped 23 Apr 1978) also called 'Jason', a St Bernard owned by Nicol Plummer of Skeffington, Leics. In December 1981 he reached a peak 138,23 kg *21 st 10¾ lb* (shoulder height 86,3 cm *34 in*) but by January 1983 he was down to 95,25 kg *15 st* after being put on a diet and shortly before his death on 4 Nov 1983 he scaled 93,4 kg *14 st 10 lb*.

MOST IMPRESSIVE DOG FUNERAL

The largest dog funeral on record was for the mongrel dog 'Lazaras' belonging to the eccentric Emperor Norton I of the United States, Protector of Mexico, held in San Francisco, in 1862 which was attended by an estimated 10,000 people.

TOP RATTER

The greatest ratter of all time was a 11,8 kg *26 lb* 'bull and terrier' dog named 'Billy'. During the five-year period 1820–24 he despatched 4000 rats in 17 hr in matches, a remarkable feat considering that he was blind in one eye. His most notable feat was the killing of 100 rats in 5 min 30 sec at the cockpit in Tufton St, Westminster, London on 23 Apr 1825. He died at 23 Feb 1829 aged 13 yrs. James Searle's famous 'bull and terrier' bitch 'Jenny Lind' was another outstanding ratter. On 12 July 1853 she was backed to kill 500 rats in under 3 hr at 'The Beehive' in Old Crosshall Street, Liverpool, and completed the job in 1 hr 36 min.

The world's rarest dog is the Chinook, which was developed in the USA in the early years of the century as a sled dog. There are now 76, all in the USA.

OLDEST DOG

Authentic records of dogs living over 20 years are rare, but even 34 years has been accepted by one authority. The greatest reliable age recorded for a dog is 29 years 5 months for a Queensland 'heeler' named 'Bluey', owned by Mr Les Hall of Rochester, Victoria, Australia. The dog was obtained as a puppy in 1910 and worked among cattle and sheep for nearly 20 years. He was put to sleep on 14 Nov 1939.

SMALLEST DOG

The world's smallest breeds of dog are the Yorkshire terrier, the Chihuahua and the Toy poodle, *miniature* versions of which have been known to weigh less than 453 g *16 oz* when adult.
The smallest mature dog on record was a matchbox-sized Yorkshire terrier owned by Mr Arthur F. Marples of Blackburn, Lancs, a former editor of the magazine *Our Dogs*. This tiny atom, which died in 1945 aged nearly 2 years, stood 6,3 cm *2½ in* at the shoulder and measured 9,5 cm *3¾ in* from the tip of its nose to the root of its tail. Its weight was an incredible 113 g *4 oz*!

CHAMPION DOG DAD

The greatest sire of all time was the champion greyhound 'Low Pressure', nicknamed 'Timmy', whelped in September 1957 and owned by Mrs Bruna Amhurst of Regent's Park, London. From December 1961 until his death on 27 Nov 1969 he fathered 2414 registered puppies, with at least 600 others unregistered.

'Max of Pangoula, a German shepherd, holds the high-jump record at 3.48 m *11 ft 5⅛ in.*'

STRONGEST DOG

The greatest load ever shifted by a dog was 2905 kg *6400½ lb* of railroad steel pulled by a 80 kg *176 lb* St Bernard named 'Ryettes Brandy Bear' at Bothell, Washington, USA on 21 July 1978. The 4-year-old dog, owned by Douglas Alexander of Monroe, Washington, pulled the weight on a four-wheeled carrier across a concrete surface for a distance of 4,57 m *15 ft* in less than 90 sec. The strongest dog in the world in terms of most proportionate weight hauled is 'Barbara-Allen's Dark Hans', a 44 kg *97 lb* Newfoundland, who pulled 2289 kg *5054½ lb* (=23,5 kg *52 lb* per 0,45 kg *per lb* body weight) across a cement surface at Bothell on 20 July 1979. The dog, owned by Miss Terri Dickinson of Kenmore, Washington, was only 12 months old when he made the attempt. The record time for the annual 1688 km *1049 mile* sled race from Anchorage to Nome, Alaska (inaugurated 1973) is 11 days 15 hr 6 min by Susan Butchers's team of dogs in the 1986 race.

WORLD'S TOP SHOW DOG

The greatest number of Challenge Certificates won by a dog is the 78 compiled by the famous chow chow 'Ch. U'Kwong King Solomon' (whelped 21 June 1968). Owned and bred by Mrs Joan Egerton of Bramhall, Cheshire, 'Solly' won his first CC at the Cheshire Agricultural Society Championship Show on 4 June 1969, and his 78th CC was awarded at the City of Birmingham Championship Show on 4 Sept 1976. He died on 3 Apr 1978. The greatest number of 'Best-in-Show' awards won by any dog in all-breed shows is the 158 compiled by the Scottish terrier bitch 'Ch. Braeburn's Close Encounter' (whelped 22 Oct 1978) up to the end of Oct 1984. She is owned by Sonnie Novick of Plantation Acres, Florida, USA.

'The tallest dog ever recorded 'Shamgret Danzas' with his owner Peter Comley of Milton Keynes. Whelped in 1975 and measures 105,4 cm *41½ in* and stands 205,7 cm *6 ft 9 in* tall on his hind legs.' *(David Hoy)*

MOST VALUABLE DOGS

In 1907 Mrs Clarice Ashton Cross of Ascot, Berkshire turned down an offer of £32,000 (equivalent to £865,000 today!) from the American financier and industrialist J. Pierpont Morgan for her famous Pekingese 'Ch. Ch'êrh of Alderbourne' (1904-*fl.* 1914). Mr Morgan then came back with an 'open' cheque, but again she turned him down.

The largest legacy devoted to a dog was by Miss Ella Wendel of New York who 'left' her standard poodle named 'Toby' £15 million in 1931.

WORLD'S TOP POLICE DOG

The greatest drug-sniffing dog on record was a golden retriever named 'Trep' (whelped 1969), owned by former policeman Tom Kazo of Dade County, Miami, Florida, USA. During the 5-year period 1973–77 'Agent K9–3', as he was also known, sniffed out $63 million (*then £36 million*) worth of narcotics. His owner said he would retire his pet, who could detect 16 different drugs, when he reached the magic $100 million (*then £57 million*) mark, but it is not known whether Trep achieved this target. The only drug-sniffing dog with a 100% arrest record was a German shepherd of the US Army called 'General'. During the period April 1974 to March 1976 this canine detective and his handler, SP4 Michael R. Harris of the 591st Military Police Company in Fort Bliss, Texas, carried out 220 searches for narcotics, arrested 220 people for possession and uncovered 330 caches of drugs.

FAT CATS & OTHER FELINE RECORDS

'A cat called 'Mincho' lived up a forty foot tree for six years during which time she produced three litters of kittens.'

OLDEST RECORDED CATS

Cats are generally longer-lived than dogs. Information on this subject is often obscured by two or more cats bearing the same nickname in succession. The oldest cat ever recorded was probably the tabby 'Puss', owned by Mrs T. Holway of Clayhidon, Devon who celebrated his 36th birthday on 28 Nov 1939 and died the next day. A more recent and better-documented case was that of the female tabby 'Ma', owned by Mrs Alice St George Moore of Drewsteignton, Devon. This cat was put to sleep on 5 Nov 1957 aged 34.

RECORD CAT – MOTHER

A cat named 'Dusty', aged 17, living in Bonham, Texas, USA, gave birth to her 420th kitten on 12 June 1952. A 21-year-old cat 'Tippy' living in Kingston-upon-Hull, Humberside gave birth to her 343rd kitten in June 1933.

WORLD'S RICHEST CAT

When Mrs Grace Alma Patterson of Joplin, Missouri, USA died in January 1978 she left her entire estate worth $250,000 (*then £131,000*) to her 8,16 kg *18 lb* white alley cat 'Charlie Chan'. When the cat dies the estate, which includes a three-bedroom house, a 2,9 ha *7 acre* pet cemetery and a collection of valuable antiques, will be auctioned off and the proceeds donated to local and national humane societies.

CAT LITTER

The largest litter ever recorded was one of 19 kittens (4 stillborn) delivered by Caesarean section to 'Tarawood Antigone', a 4-year-old brown Burmese, on 7 Aug 1970. Her owner, Mrs Valerie Gane of Church Westcote, Kingham, Oxfordshire, said the result was a mis-mating with a half-Siamese. Of the 15 survivors, 14 were males and one female.

The largest live litter (all of which survived) was one of 14 kittens born in December 1974 to a Persian cat named 'Bluebell', owned by Mrs Elenore Dawson of Wellington, Cape Province, South Africa.

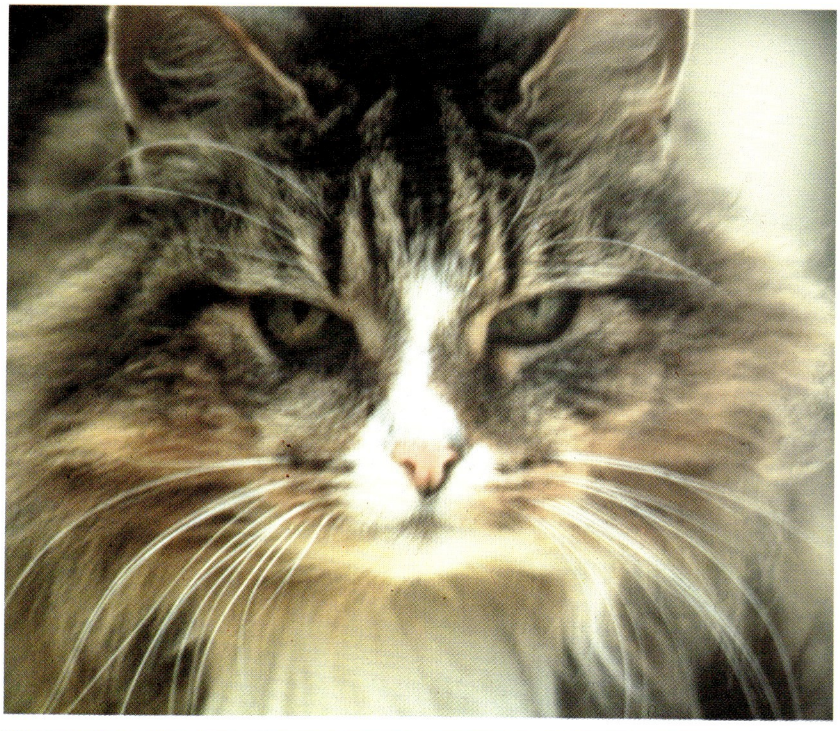

Towser, who has caught over 23,000 mice whilst prowling the Glenturret Distillery near Crieff in Tayside, Scotland.

FAT CAT RECORD

The heaviest domestic cat on record is an 8-year-old neutered male tabby named 'Himmy' owned by Thomas Vyse of Redlynch, Cairns, Queensland, Australia. On 12 Jan 1985 he weighed 21,3 kg *46 lb 15¼ oz* (neck 38,1 cm *15 in*, waist 83,8 cm *33 in*, length 96,52 cm *38 in*). The heaviest cat ever recorded in Britain is an 11-year-old male tabby called 'Poppa' owned by Miss Gwladys Cooper of Newport, Gwent, S Wales. He scaled 20,19 kg *44½ lb* in Nov 1984. The largest of the 330 breeds of cat is the ragdoll with males weighing 6,8–9,07 kg *15–20 lb*.

CRAZIEST CAT RECORD

The most eccentric cat on record was a black female named 'Mincho', who ran up a 12 m, *40 ft* high tree in Buenos Aires, Argentina, and never came down again! The local people used to push food up to her on a pole and a milkman delivered daily. In 1954 the cat was still going strong after spending six years aloft, and had even managed to produce three litters of kittens during her marathon tree squat!

MOST SHIPWRECKED CAT

The only cat known to have survived three major shipwrecks was a one-year-old male tabby named 'Oscar', who started his adventures on the high seas aboard the mighty battleship *Bismarck*. When the pride of the German navy was sunk 1100 km *660 miles* west of Brest, France, on 27 May 1941 the bedraggled cat was picked up by the British destroyer HMS *Cossack*, but his stay aboard the 'enemy' ship was also short-lived. On 10 November the same year the destroyer was torpedoed in the Atlantic and sent to the bottom. This time Oscar was rescued and transferred to the HMS *Ark Royal*, but three days later he found himself in the water again when the aircraft carrier was torpedoed by a German submarine in the Mediterranean. Luckily he was sighted on a floating plank three hours after the tragedy occurred and was taken by destroyer to Gibraltar. Two weeks later, with only six lives left, he was shipped to a sailors' rest home in Northern Ireland, where the peaceful surroundings were more to his liking.

WORLD'S MOST VALUABLE CAT

In 1967 Miss Elspeth Sellar of Grafham, Surrey turned down an offer of 2000 guineas (£2100) from an American breeder for her champion copper-eyed white Persian tom 'Coylum Marcus' (b. 28 Mar 1965) who died on 14 Apr 1978.

TOWSER THE MOUSER

The greatest mouser on record is a female tortoiseshell named 'Towser' (b. 21 Apr 1963) owned by Glenturret Distillery Ltd near Crieff, Tayside, Scotland who notched up her 24,621st kill by her 22nd birthday. She averages 3 mice per day.

SMALLEST DOMESTIC CATS

The smallest breed of domestic cat is the Singapura or 'Drain Cat' of Singapore. Adult males average 2,72 kg *6 lb* in weight and adult females 1,81 kg *4 lb*. A male Siamese cross named 'Ebony-Eb-Honey Cat' owned by Miss Angelina Johnstone of Boise, Idaho, USA tipped the scales at only 0,79 kg *1 lb 12 oz* in February 1984 when aged 23 months.

The heaviest domestic cat on record 'Himmy'. According to his owner he is a moderate eater, a normal meal consists of meat, kidney, hearts or fish yet he still weights in at a mere 21,3 kg *46 lb 15¼ oz*.

PORKIEST PIGS & FARMYARD RECORDS

‘Field to Loaf Record. The fastest time for producing loaves from growing wheat is 40 min 44 sec at O. S. North's Bakery at Heydon, near Royston, Hertfordshire on 10 Sept 1983.’

HEAVIEST COWS

Of heavyweight cattle the heaviest on record was a Holstein-Durham cross named ‘Mount Katahdin’ exhibited by A. S. Rand of Maine, USA in 1906–10 and frequently weighed at an even 2267 kg *5000 lb*. He was 1,88 m *6 ft 2 in* at the shoulder with a 3,96 m *13 ft* girth and died in a barn fire *c* 1923. The British record is the 2032 kg *4480 lb* of ‘The Bradwell Ox’ owned by William Spurgin of Bradwell, Essex. He was 4,57 m *15 ft* from nose to tail and had a girth of 3,35 m *11 ft* when 6 years old in 1830. The largest breed of heavyweight cattle is the Chianini, brought to Italy from the Middle East in pre-Roman times. Mature bulls average 1,73 m *5 ft 8 in* at the forequarters and weigh 1300 kg *2865 lb*. The Airedale Heifer of East Riddlesdon, near Keighley, South Yorkshire *c* 1820 was 3,62 m *11 ft 10.6 in* long and weighed 1197,5 kg *2640 lb*.

The highest recorded birthweight for a calf is 102 kg *225 lb* from a British Friesian cow at Rockhouse Farm, Bishopston, Swansea, West Glamorgan, in 1961.

FATTEST PIGS

The heaviest hog recorded was the Poland-China hog ‘Big Bill’ of 1157,5 kg *2552 lb (22¾ cwt)* measuring 2,75 m *9 ft* long with a belly on the ground, owned by Burford Butler of Jackson, Tennessee, USA and chloroformed in 1933. Raised by W. J. Chappall he was mounted and displayed in Weekly County, Tennessee until 1946. The British record is a hog of 639,5 kg *12 cwt 66 lb* bred by Joseph Lawton of Astbury, Cheshire. In 1774 it stood 1,43 m *4 ft 8½ in* in height and was 2,94 m *9 ft 8 in* long. The highest recorded weight for a piglet at weaning (8 weeks) is 36,7 kg *81 lb* for a boar, one of nine piglets farrowed on 6 July 1962 by the Landrace gilt ‘Manorport Ballerina 53rd’, *alias* ‘Mary’, and sired by a Large White named ‘Johnny’ at Kettle Lane Farm, West Ashton, Trowbridge, Wiltshire.

BOUNCIEST LAMB

The highest recorded birthweight for a lamb in the world is 17,2 kg *38 lb* at Clearwater, Sedgwick County, Kansas, USA in 1975, but neither this lamb nor the ewe survived.

Depicted in front of the Lamb and Flag, Little Haywood, Staffs. Britain's heaviest hog weighed in at 639,5 kg *12 cwt 66 lb*. (John D. Lacey)

HIGHEST PRICED *BULL*

The highest price ever paid for a bull is $2,500,000 (*then £1,087,000*) for the beefalo ($1\frac{3}{8}$ bison, $\frac{3}{8}$ charolais, $\frac{1}{4}$ Hereford) 'Joe's Pride' sold by D. C. Basalo of Burlingame, California to the Beefalo Cattle Co. of Canada, of Calgary, Alberta, Canada on 9 Sept 1974. The young 14-month-old Canadian Holstein bull 'Pickland Elevation B. ET' was bought by Premier Breeders of Stamfordham, Northumberland for £233,000.

The highest price ever paid for a bull in Britain is 60,000 guineas (£63,000), paid on 5 Feb 1963 at Perth, Scotland, by James R. Dick (1928–74) co-manager of Black Watch Farms, for 'Lindertis Evulse', an Aberdeen-Angus owned by Sir Torquil and Lady Munro of Lindertis, Kirriemuir, Tayside, Scotland. This bull failed a fertility test in August 1963, thus becoming the world's most expensive piece of beef.

The heaviest hog ever recorded – 'Big Bill' who weighed in at 1157,5 kg *2552 lb.*

COW

The highest price ever paid for a cow is $1,025,000 (*then £640,625*) for the Holstein Allendairy Glamorous Ivy by Albert Cormier of Georgetown, Ontario, Canada at Doeberiener dispersal sale at Jamestown, Pennsylvania on 20 Nov 1982. The British record is £33,600 for 'Ullswater Beatexus 8th', a British Friesian sold to The British Livestock Embryo Syndicate of Royston, Hertfordshire by Sir Keith and Lady Showering of West Horrington, Wells, Somerset on 9 May 1981 (auctioneers: Hobsons).

SHEEP SHEARING

The highest recorded speed for sheep shearing in a working day was that of John Fagan who machine-sheared 804 lambs (average 89.3 per hour) in 9 hr at Hautora Rd, Pio Pio, New Zealand on 8 Dec 1980. Peter Casserly of Christchurch, New Zealand, achieved a solo blade (i.e. hand-shearing) record of 353 lambs in 9 hours on 13 Feb 1976. In a shearing marathon, four men machine-sheared 2519 sheep in 29 hr at Stewarts Trust, Waikia, Southland, New Zealand on 11 Feb 1982.

PIG

The highest price ever paid for a pig is $56,000 (then *£38,356*) for a cross-breed barrow named 'Bud' owned by Jeffrey Roemisch of Hermleigh, Texas and sold on 5 March 1983. The UK record is 3300 guineas (£3465), paid by Malvern Farms for the Swedish Landrace gilt 'Bluegate Ally 33rd' owned by Davidson Trust in a draft sale at Reading, Berkshire on 2 Mar 1955.

HORSE

The highest price for a draught horse is $47,500 (£9970) paid for the 7-year-old Belgian stallion 'Farceur' by E. G. Good at Cedar Falls, Iowa, USA on 16 Oct 1917. A Welsh mountain pony stallion 'Coed Cock Bari' was sold to an Australian builder in Wales in September 1978 for 21,000 guineas (*then £22,050*).

'*SHEEP*. The highest price ever paid for a ram is $A79,000 (*£49,500*) by the Gnowangerup Animal Breeding Centre, Western Australia for a Merino ram from the Colinsvale Stud, South Australia at the Royal Adelaide Show on 10 Sept 1981.'

DONKEY

Perhaps the lowest ever price for livestock was at a sale at Kuruman, Cape Province, South Africa in 1934 where donkeys were sold for less than 2p each.

PORKIEST PIGS & FARMYARD RECORDS

THE YOLKIEST EGG
The highest claim for the number of yolks in a chicken's egg is 9 reported by Mrs Diane Hainsworth of Hainsworth Poultry Farms, Mount Morris, New York, USA in July 1971 and also from a hen in Kirghizia, USSR in Aug 1977.

THE MILKIEST COWS
The highest recorded world lifetime yield of milk is 211 025 kg *465,224 lb* (*207.68 tons*) by the unglamorously named cow No 289 owned by M. G. Maciel & Son of Hanford, California, USA to 1 May 1984. The greatest yield of any British cow was that given by Winton Pel Eva 2 owned by John Waring of Glebe House, Kilnwick near Pocklington with 165 tonnes. The greatest recorded yield for one lactation (maximum 365 days) is 25 247 kg *55,661 lb* by the Holstein 'Beecher Arlinda Ellen' owned by Mr and Mrs Harold L. Beecher of Rochester, Indiana, USA in 1975. The British lactation record (305 days) was set by Michaelwood Holm Emoselle 25 (b. 1 Aug 1973), a Friesian, owned by Mr & Mrs M. T. Holder of Aylesmore Farm, Newent, Gloucestershire 19 400 kg *42,769 lb* in 1984–5. The highest reported milk yield in a day is 109,3 kg *241 lb* by 'Urbe Blanca' in Cuba on or about 23 June 1982.

THE CHAMPION EGG-LAYER
The highest authenticated rate of egg-laying is by a white leghorn chicken hen, no 2988 at the College of Agriculture, University of Missouri, USA, with 371 eggs in 364 days in an official test conducted by Professor Harold V. Biellier ending on 29 Aug 1979. The UK record is 353 eggs in 365 days in a National Laying Test at Milford, Surrey in 1957 by a Rhode Island Red owned by W. Lawson of Welham Grange, Retford, Nottinghamshire.

THE HEAVIEST CHICKEN EGG
The heaviest egg reported is one of 454 g *16 oz*, with double yolk and double shell, laid by a white Leghorn at Vineland, New Jersey, USA, on 25 Feb 1956. The largest recorded was one of 'nearly 12 oz' for a 5 yolked egg 31 cm *12¼ in* around the long axis and 22,8 cm *9 in* around the shorter axis laid by a Black Minorca at Mr Stafford's Damsteads Farm, Mellor, Lancashire in 1896.

The biggest bovine reunion – Isabelle the Limousin cow at St Ives, Cambridge inspecting her 19 calves. When they were embryos they were implanted into host mothers.

CHAPTER 4

THE NATURAL WORLD

'The northwest face of Half Dome, Yosemite, California, USA is the world's steepest – 670 m *2200 ft* never varying more than 7 degrees from the vertical. It was first climbed by an American three-man team in July 1957'

SPACE RECORDS

'The remotest star visible to the naked eye is 12,500,000,000,000,000,000 miles away and moving our way.'

THE LARGEST PLANET

The nine major planets (including the Earth) are bodies within the Solar System and which revolve round the Sun in definite orbits. The search for Planet X continues. Jupiter, with an equatorial diameter of 142 984 km *88,846 miles* and a polar diameter of 133 708 km *83,082 miles* is the largest of the nine major planets, with a mass 317.83 times, and a volume 1321.4 times that of the Earth. It also has the shortest period of rotation resulting in a Jovian day of only 9 hr 50 min 30.003 sec in the equatorial zone.

THE SMALLEST PLANET

The smallest and coldest planet is Pluto, with its partner Charon, announced on 22 June 1978 which have an estimated surface temperature of −220 °C *−360 °F* (53 deg C *100 deg F* above absolute zero). Their mean distance from the Sun is 5 913 514 000 km *3,674,488,000 miles* and their period of revolution is 248.54 years. The diameter is *c* 3000 km *1860 miles* and the mass is about 1/400th of that of the Earth. Pluto was first recorded by Clyde William Tombaugh (b. 4 Feb 1906) at Lowell Observatory, Flagstaff, Arizona, USA, on 18 Feb 1930 from photographs taken on 23 and 29 Jan and announced on 13 Mar. Because of its orbital eccentricity Pluto moved closer to the Sun than Neptune between 23 Jan 1979 and 15 Mar 1999.

THE HOTTEST PLANET

For Venus a surface temperature of 462 °C *864 °F* has been estimated from measurements made from the USSR *Venera* and US Pioneer *Cytherean* surface probes. Venus has a canyon 6,4 km *4 miles* and 402 km *250 miles* long 1609 km *1000 miles* south of Venusian equator.

THE LARGEST STAR

The most massive known star is the faint-blue R 136a, 179,000 light years distant in the Tarantula Nebula (or 30 Doradus), an appendage of the Large Magellanic Cloud and assessed in February 1983 to have a mass 2100 times greater than our own Sun and a diameter 50 times greater. However, Betelgeux (top left star of Orion) has a diameter of 700 million km *400 million miles* or about 500 times greater than the Sun. In 1978 it was found to be surrounded by a tenuous 'shell' of potassium $1,6 \times 10^{12}$ km or *11 000 astronomical units* in diameter. The light left Betelgeux in AD 1680.

'The most spectacular solar flare ever recorded, spanning more than 588,000 km *365,000 miles* photographed on 19 Dec 1973 during the third and final manned Skylab mission.' *(NASA)*

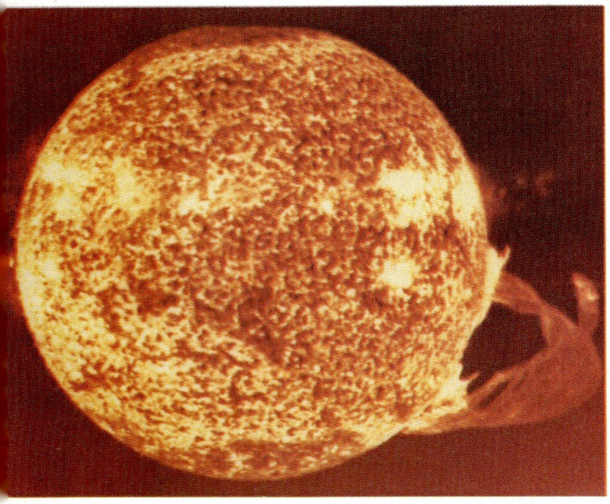

THE BRIGHTEST STAR

Sirius A (*Alpha Canis Majoris*), also known as the Dog Star, is apparently the brightest star of the 5776 stars of naked eye visibility in the heavens, with an apparent magnitude of −1.46. It is in the constellation *Canis Major* and is visible in the winter months of the northern hemisphere, being due south at midnight on the last day of the year. The Sirius system is 8.64 light-years distant and has a luminosity 26 times as much as that of the Sun. It has a diameter of 2,33 million km *1,450,000 miles* and a mass of $4,26 \times 10^{27}$ tonnes *4.20×10^{27} tons*. The faint white dwarf companion Sirius B has a diameter of only 10 000 km *6000 miles* but is 350,000 times heavier than the Earth. Sirius will reach a maximum of −1.67 in *c* AD 61,000.

THE MOON'S HIGHEST MOUNTAIN

In the absence of a sea level, lunar altitudes are measured relative to an adopted reference sphere of radius 1738,000 m *1079.943 miles*. Thus the greatest elevation attained on this basis by any of the 12 US astronauts has been 7830 m *25,688 ft* on the Descartes Highlands by Capt John Watts Young USN and Major Charles M. Duke Jr on 27 Apr 1972.

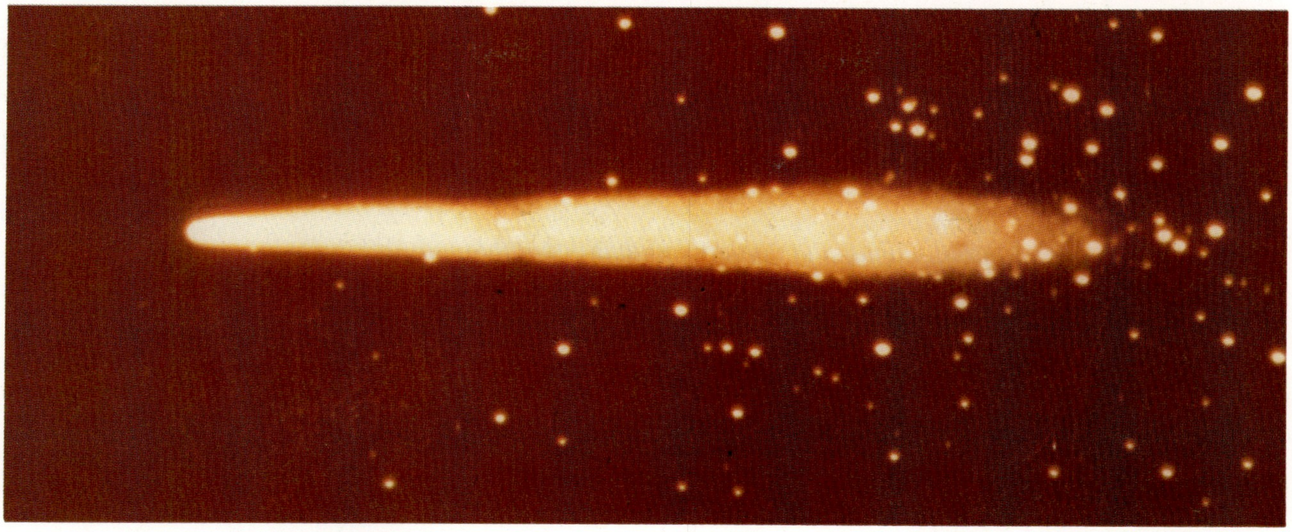

THE STAR WITH THE LONGEST NAME

The longest name for any star is *Shurnarkabtishashutu*, the Arabic for 'under the southern horn of the bull'.

THE FARTHEST VISIBLE OBJECT

The remotest heavenly body visible with the *naked eye* is the Great Galaxy in *Andromeda* (Mag. 3.47), known as Messier 31. This is a rotating nebula in spiral form, and its distance from the Earth is about 2,120,000 light-years, or about 20×10^{18} km *12,500,000,000,000,000,000 miles* and is moving towards us.

THE MOON'S BIGGEST CRATER

Only 59 per cent of the Moon's surface is directly visible from the Earth because it is in 'captured rotation', *i.e.* the period of rotation is equal to the period of orbit. The largest wholly visible crater is the walled plain Bailly, towards the Moon's South Pole, which is 295 km *183 miles* across, with walls rising to 4250 m *14,000 ft*. The Orientale Basin, partly on the averted side, measures more than 965 km *600 miles* in diameter. The deepest crater is the Newton crater, with a floor estimated to be between 7000–8850 m *23,000 and 29,000 ft* below its rim and 2250 m *14,000 ft* below the level of the plain outside. The brightest directly visible spot on the Moon is *Aristarchus*.

THE LARGEST AND OLDEST METEORITES

When a meteoroid penetrates to the Earth's surface, the remnant is described as a meteorite. This occurs about 150 times per year over the whole land surface of the Earth. Although the chances of being struck are deemed negligible, the most anxious time of day for meteorophobes is 3 p.m. The largest known meteorite is one found in 1920 at Hoba West, near Grootfontein in south-west Africa. This is a block 2,75 m *9 ft* long by 2,43 m *8 ft* broad, estimated to be 132,000 lb (59 tonnes/*tons*). The largest meteorite exhibited by any museum is the 'Tent' meteorite, weighing 68,085 lb (30 882 kg *30.39 tons*) found in 1897 near Cape York, on the west coast of Greenland, by the expedition of Commander (later Rear-Admiral) Robert Edwin Peary (1856–1920).

The oldest dated meteorites are from the Allende fall in Chihuahua, Mexico on 8 Feb 1969 dating back to 4610 million years. It was reported in August 1978 that dust grains in the Murchison meteorite which fell in Australia in September 1969 also pre-date the formation of the Solar System 4600 million years ago.

'On 13–14 March 1986, the European Satellite Giotto penetrated to within 540 km *335 miles* of the nucleus of Halley's Comet.'

The largest known meteorite estimated to weigh 59 tonnes/ton and was found in 1920 at Hoba West, south west Africa.

KING CLONE & OTHER PLANT RECORDS

WORLD'S OLDEST PLANT
'King Clone', the oldest known clone of the creosote plant (*Larrea tridentata*) found in south west California, was estimated in February 1980 by Prof. Frank C. Vasek to be 11,700 years old. It is possible that crustose lichens in excess of 500 mm *19.6 in* in diameter may be as old. In 1981 it was estimated that Antarctic lichens of more than 100 mm *3.9 in* in diameter are at least 10,000 years old. The oldest pot-plant is the succulent *Fockea crispa* potted by Baron Jacquin (1728–1817) at the Schönbrunn gardens, Vienna *c* 1801.

ALL-TIME TALLEST TREE
The tallest tree ever measured by any governmental forester was recently re-discovered in a report by William Ferguson, Inspector of Victoria State Forests. He reported in February 1872 a fallen Mountain ash 5,48 m *18 ft* in diameter at 1,52 m *5 ft* above ground level and 132,5 m *435 ft* in length.

WORLD'S OLDEST TREE
The oldest recorded tree was a bristlecone pine designated WPN-114, which grew at 3275 m *10,750 ft* above sea-level on the north-east face of the Wheeler Ridge on the Sierra Nevada, California, USA. During studies in 1963 and 1964 it was found to be about 4900 years old but was cut down with a chain saw. The oldest known *living* tree is the bristlecone pine named *Methuselah* at 3050 m *10,000 ft* in the California side of the White Mountains confirmed as 4600 years old. In March 1974 it was reported that this tree had produced 48 live seedlings. Dendrochronologists estimate the *potential* life-span of a bristlecone pine at nearly 5500 years, but that of a California Big Tree at perhaps 6000 years. No single cell lives more than 30 years. A report in March 1976 stated that some enormous specimens of Japanese cedar had been dated by carbon-14 to 5200 BC.

MOST EXPENSIVE TREE
The highest price ever paid for a tree is $51,000 (*then £18,214*) for a single Starkspur Golden Delicious apple tree from near Yakima, Washington, USA, bought by a nursery in Missouri in 1959.

WORLD'S LARGEST TREE
The most massive living thing on Earth is the biggest known Giant Sequoia named the 'General Sherman', standing 83,02 m *272.4 ft* tall, in the Sequoia National Park, California, USA. It has a true girth of 24,32 m *79.8 ft* (1980) (at 1,52 m *5 ft* above the ground). The 'General Sherman' has been estimated to contain the equivalent of 600,120 board feet of timber, sufficient to make 5,000,000,000 matches. The foliage is blue-green, and the red-brown tan bark may be up to 61 cm *24 in* thick in parts. Estimates (1981) place its weight, including its root system, at 6100 tonnes *6000 long tons*. The largest known petrified tree is one of this species with a 89,9 m *295 ft* trunk near Coaldale, Nevada, USA.

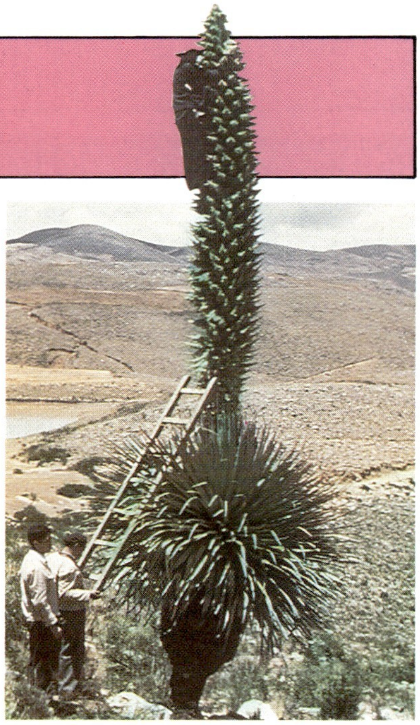

The world's largest and slowest flowering herb is the Bolivian *Puya raimondii*. Its panicle can be 10.7 m *35 ft* high and emerges only after about 150 years.

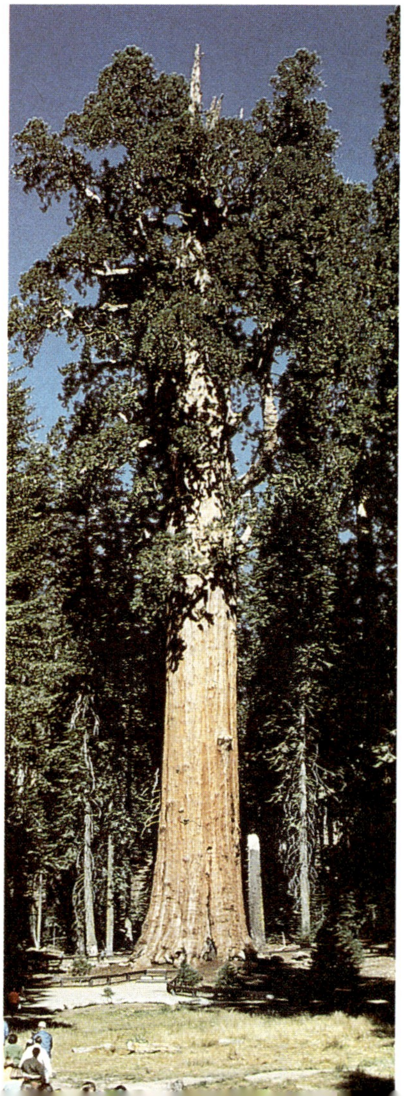

The most massive living thing on earth, the tree named 'General Sherman' situated as a tourist attraction in California, USA.

RIVER DEEP, MOUNTAIN HIGH

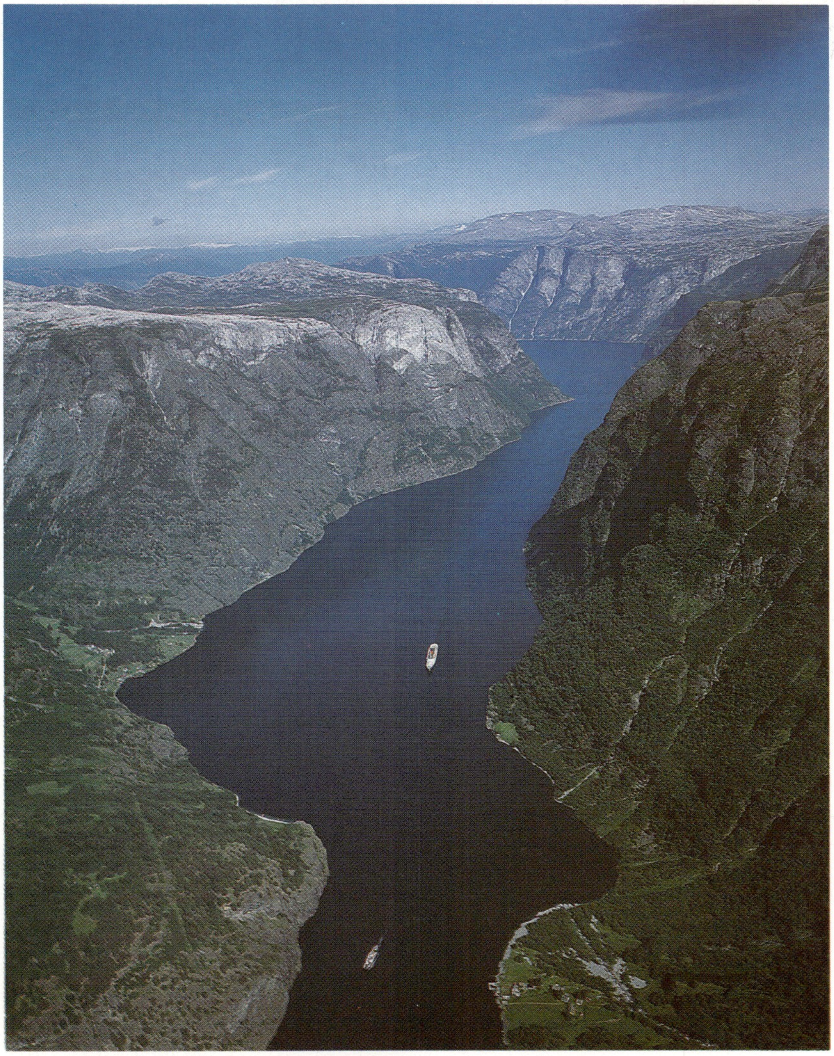

The longest of the Norwegian fjords is the Sogne Fjord. Along its 183 km *113.7 mile* length it averages only 4.75 km *3 miles* in width and has a deepest point of 1245 m *4085 ft*.

WORLD'S HIGHEST MOUNTAIN

An eastern Himalayan peak of 8848 m *29,028 ft* above sea-level on the Tibet–Nepal border (in an area first designated Chu-mu-lang-ma on a map of 1717) was discovered to be the world's highest mountain in 1852 by the Survey Department of the Government of India, from theodolite readings taken in 1849 and 1850. In 1860 its height was computed to be 8840 m *29,002 ft*. On 25 July 1973 the Chinese announced a height of 8848,1 m *29,029 ft 3 in*. In practice the altitude can only be justified as a mean 8848 m *29,028 ft ±25 ft*. The 8,85 km *5½ mile* high peak was named Mount Everest after Col Sir George Everest, CB (1790–1866), formerly Surveyor-General of India. Other names for Everest are: Sagarmatha (Nepalese), Qomolongma (Chinese) and Mi-ti Gu-ti Cha-pu Long-na (Tibetan). After a total loss of 11 lives since the first reconnaissance in 1921, Everest was finally conquered at 11.30 a.m. on 29 May 1953. The mountain whose summit is farthest from the Earth's centre is the Andean peak of Chimborazo (6267 m *20,561 ft*), 158 km *98 miles* south of the equator in Ecuador, South America. Its summit is 2150 m *7057 ft* further from the Earth's centre than the summit of Mt Everest. The highest mountain on the equator is Volcán Cayambe (5878 m *19,285 ft*), Ecuador, in Long. 77° 58′ W. A mountaineer atop the summit would be moving at 1671 km/h *1038 mph* relative to the Earth's centre due to the Earth's rotation.

‘The highest undersea mountain, Seamount, is almost as high as Mount Everest. It was discovered in 1953 in the Tonga Trench of the Pacific between Samoa and New Zealand and rises 8690 m *28,500 ft* from the sea bed. Its summit is 365 m *1200 ft* below the sea's surface.’

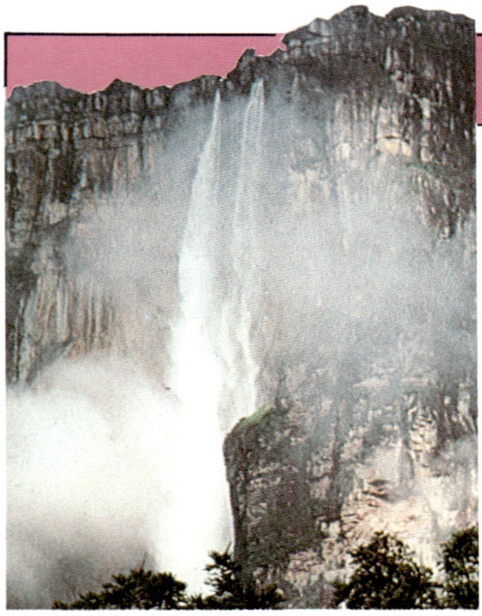

RIVER DEEP, MOUNTAIN HIGH

HIGHEST UNCLIMBED MOUNTAIN
The highest unclimbed mountain is now only the 31st highest – Zemu Gap Peak (7780 m *25,526 ft*) in the Sikkim Himalaya.

THE LARGEST SECRET RIVER
In August 1958 a river was tracked by radio isotopes flowing under the Nile. It has six times more water than the Nile – 500 000 m² *20,000,000 ft²* of water flows each year.

WORLD'S LONGEST RIVERS
The two longest rivers in the world are the Amazon, flowing into the South Atlantic, and the Nile flowing into the Mediterranean. Which is the longer is more a matter of definition than simple measurement. The true source of the Amazon was discovered in 1953 to be a stream named Huarco, rising near the summit of Cerro Huagra (5238 m *17,188 ft*) in Peru. This stream progressively becomes the Toto then the Santiago then the Apurimac, which in turn is known as the Ene and then the Tambo before its confluence with the Amazon prime tributary the Ucayali. The length of the Amazon from this source to the South Atlantic via the Canal do Norte was measured in 1969 to be 6448 km *4007 miles* (usually quoted to the rounded off figure of 6437 km *4000 miles*).

The length of the Nile watercourse, as surveyed by M. Devroey (Belgium) before the loss of a few miles of meanders due to the formation of Lake Nasser, behind the Aswan High Dam, was 6670 km *4145 miles*. This course is the more acceptable one from the source in Burundi of the Luvironza branch of the Kagera feeder of the Victoria Nyanza via the White Nile (*Bahrel-Jebel*) to the delta.

'*World's highest waterfall.* **The highest waterfall in the world is the Salto Angel in Venezuela, on a branch of the River Carrao, an upper tributary of the Caroni with a total drop of 979 m *3212 ft* – the longest single drop is 807 m *2648 ft*. They were named for the United States pilot James (Jimmy) Angel (died 8 Dec 1956), who had crashed near by on 9 Oct 1937. The falls, known by the Indians as Cherun-Meru, were first reported by Ernesto Sanchez La Cruz in 1910.**'

'**The world's largest cavern surveyed by the 1980 British-Malaysian Mulu Expedition. Its length is 700 m *2300 ft*.**'

Sarawak Chamber
LOBANG NASIP BAGUS
Gunung Mulu National Park, Sarawak

▲▲ main floor slope

200 metres

Wembley Stadium for scale

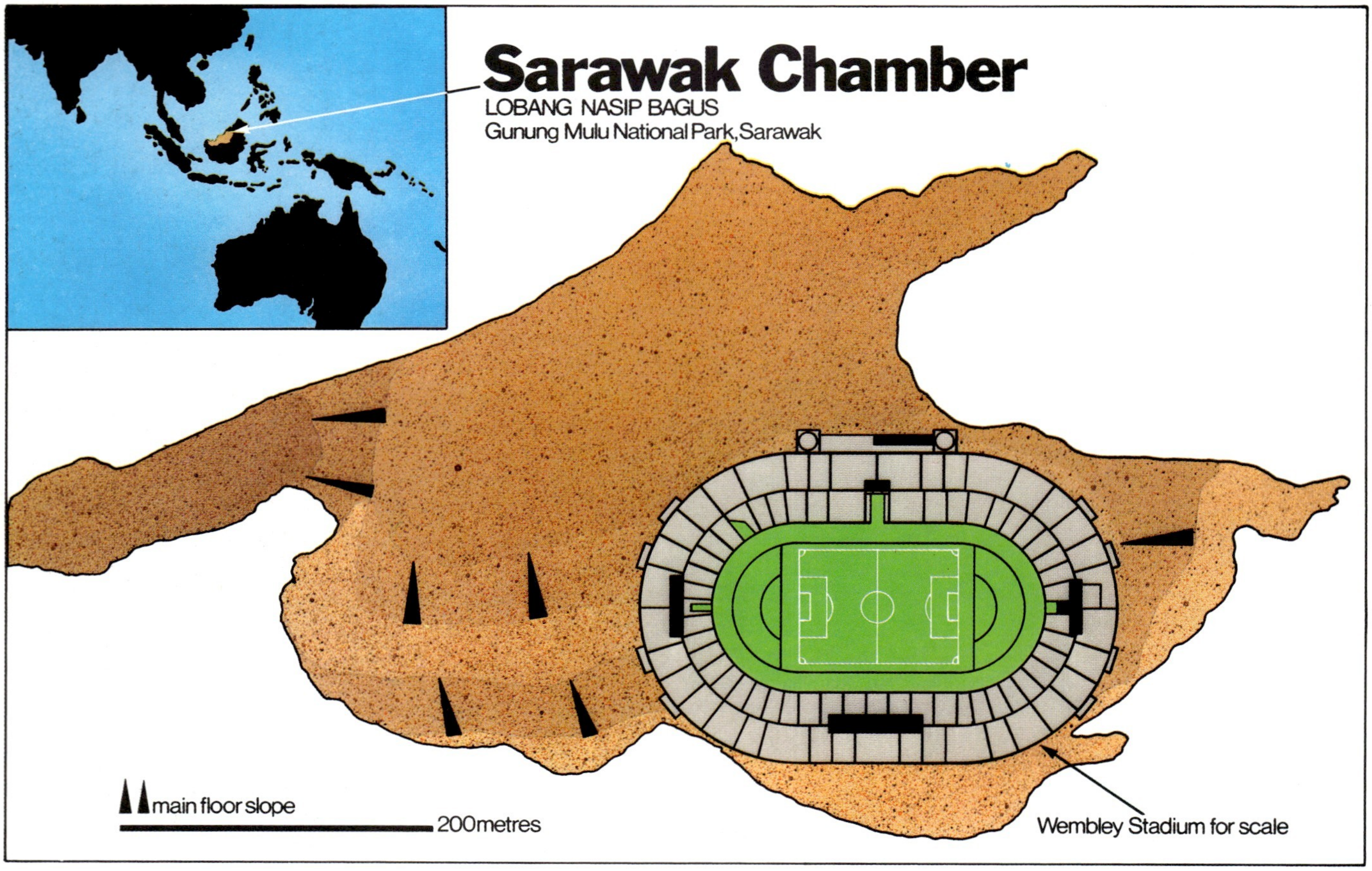

DEEPEST CAVES BY COUNTRIES

These depths are subject to continuous revisions.

Depth m	ft		
1535	*5036*	Réseau de Foillis (Gouffre Jean Bernard)	France
1470	*4824*	Snieznaja Piezcziera	USSR
1338	*4390*	Puerta de Illamina	Spain
1246	*4088*	Sistema Huautia	Mexico
1219	*3999*	Schwersystem	Austria
1208	*3964*	Complesso Fighiera Carchia	Italy
975	*3199*	Anou Ifflis	Algeria
878	*2880*	Holloch	Switzerland
876	*2875*	Brezno pri Gamsovo Glavici	Yugoslavia
768	*2520*	Jaskinia Sniezna	Poland
751	*2464*	Ghar Parau, Zagros	Iran
308	*1010*	Ogof Ffynnon Ddu	Wales
214	*702*	Giant's Hole System	England
179	*587*	Reyfad Pot	N Ireland
140	*459*	Carrowmore Cavern	Rep. of Ireland

WORLD'S DEEPEST LAKE

The deepest lake in the world is Ozero (Lake) Baykal in central Siberia, USSR. It is 620 km *385 miles* long and between 32 and 74 km *20–46 miles* wide. In 1957 the lake's Olkhon Crevice was measured to be 1940 m *6365 ft* deep and hence 1485 m *4872 ft* below sea-level.

THE ICEBERG RECORDS

The largest iceberg on record was an Antarctic tabular 'berg of over 31 000 km^2 *12,000 miles^2* (335 km *208 miles* long and 97 km *60 miles* wide and thus larger than Belgium) sighted 240 km *150 miles* west of Scott Island, in the South Pacific Ocean, by the USS *Glacier* on 12 Nov 1956. The 61 m *200 ft* thick Arctic ice island T.1 (360 km^2 *140 miles^2*) (discovered in 1946) was tracked for 17 years. The tallest iceberg measured was one of 167 m *550 ft* reported off western Greenland by the US icebreaker *East Wind* in 1958.

WORLD'S DEEPEST GORGE

The deepest canyon is El Cañón de Colca, Peru reported in 1929 which is 3223 m *10,574 ft* deep. It was first traversed by the Polish Expedition CANOADES '79 Kayak team 12 May–14 June 1981. A stretch of the Kai River in central Nepal flows 5485 m *18,000 ft* below its flanking summits of the Dhaulagiri and Annapurna groups. The deepest submarine canyon yet discovered is one 40 km *25 miles* south of Esperance, Western Australia, which is 1800 m *6,000 ft* deep and 32 km *20 miles* wide.

El Canon de Colca, Peru reported to be world's only 2 mile deep gorge and was unknown to the rest of the world until 1929.

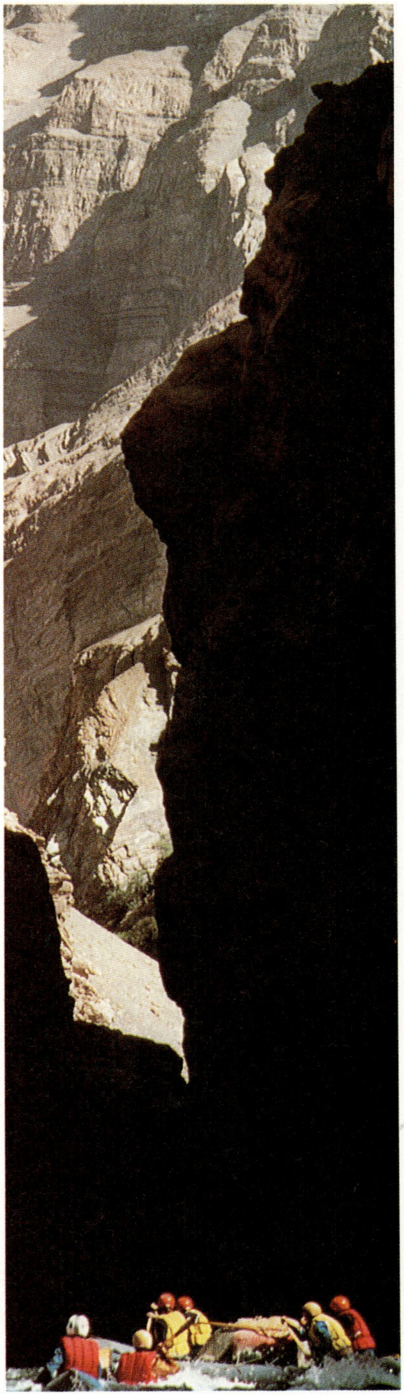

Lake Baykal, the world's deepest lake in central Siberia, USSR. It is 385 miles long and approx 46 miles wide. (*Novosti*)

FREEZES, DROUGHTS & WEATHER RECORDS

The Atacama Desert in Chile where it did not rain for 400 years.

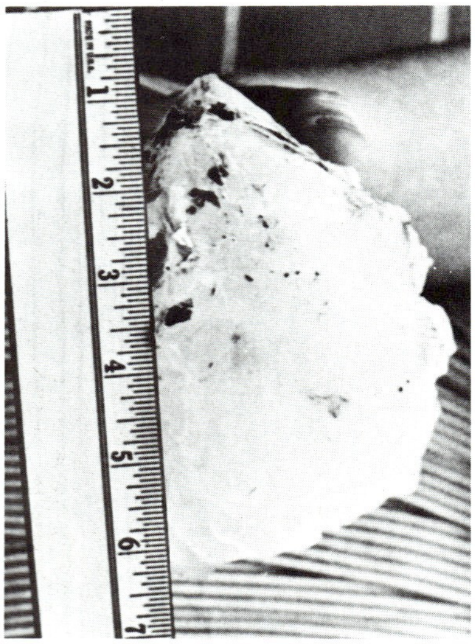

The largest authenticated single hailstone fell in the USA at Coffeyville Kansas on 3 Sept 1970 and it could have been as big as 200 mm *8 in* when first picked.

THICKEST ICE RECORD

The greatest recorded thickness of ice is 4776 m *15,670 ft (2.97 miles)* measured by radio echo soundings from a US Antarctic Research aircraft at 69° 9′ 38″ S 135° 20′ 25″ E 400 km *250 miles* from the coast in Wilkes Land on 4 Jan 1975.

WORLD RECORD RAINFALL

1. GREATEST RAINFALL (24 hours): *World* 1870 mm *73.62 in*, Cilaos, La Réunion, Indian Ocean, 15–16 March 1952. *UK & Ireland* 279 mm *11.00 in*, Martinstown, Dorset, 18–19 July 1955.

2. GREATEST RAINFALL (Calendar Month): *World* 9299 mm *366.14 in*, Cherrapunji, Meghalaya, India, July 1861. *UK & Ireland* 1436 mm *56.54 in*, Llyn Llydau, Snowdon, Gwynedd, October 1909.

3. GREATEST RAINFALL (12 months): *World* 26 461 mm *1041.78 in*, Cherrapunji, Meghalaya, 1 Aug 1860–31 July 1861. *UK & Ireland* 6527 mm *257 in*, Sprinkling Tarn, Cumbria, in 1954.

WORLD'S WETTEST PLACES

(Annual mean): *World* Cherrapunji, India (alt. 1313 m *4308 ft*) 11477,4 mm *451.8 in* (av. 1851–1960). In 1948 15 773 mm *621 in. UK & Ireland* Styhead Tarn (487 m *1600 ft*), Cumbria, 4391 mm *172.9 in.*

WORLD'S HOTTEST PLACES

HIGHEST SHADE TEMPERATURE: *World* 58 °C *136.4 °F* al'Azīzīyah, Libya (alt. 111 m *367 ft*) 13 Sept 1922. *UK & Ireland* 36.77 °C *98.2 °F* Raunds, Northants; Epsom, Surrey and Canterbury, Kent 9 Aug 1911.

PROGRESSIVE RECORDINGS OF EXTREME HIGH TEMPERATURES WORLD WIDE

53,0 °C	*127.4 °F*	Ouargla, Algeria	27 Aug 1884
54,4 °C	*130 °F*	Amos, California, USA	17 Aug 1885
54,4 °C	*130 °F*	Mammoth Tank, California, USA	17 Aug 1885
56,7 °C	*134 °F*	Death Valley, California, USA	10 July 1913
58,0 °C	*136.4 °F*	Al'Aziziyah (el-Azizia), Libya	13 Sept 1922

PROGRESSIVE RECORDINGS OF EXTREME LOW TEMPERATURES WORLD WIDE

−58,3 °C	*−73 °F*	Floeberg Bay, Ellesmere I., Canada	1852
−68 °C	*−90.4 °F*	Verkhoyansk, Siberia, USSR	3 Jan 1885
−68 °C	*−90.4 °F*	Verkhoyansk, Siberia, USSR	5 & 7 Feb 1892
−68 °C	*−90.4 °F*	Oymyakon, Siberia, USSR	6 Feb 1933
−73,5 °C	*−100.4 °F*	South Pole, Antarctica	11 May 1957
−74,5 °C	*−102.1 °F*	South Pole, Antarctica	17 Sept 1957
−78,34 °C	*−109.1 °F*	Sovietskaya, Antarctica	2 May 1958
−80,7 °C	*−113.3 °F*	Vostok, Antarctica	15 June 1958
−81,2 °C	*−114.1 °F*	Sovietskaya, Antarctica	19 June 1958
−83,0 °C	*−117.4 °F*	Sovietskaya, Antarctica	25 June 1958
−85,7 °C	*−122.4 °F*	Vostok, Antarctica	7–8 Aug 1958
−86,7 °C	*−124.1 °F*	Sovietskaya, Antarctica	9 Aug 1958
−87,4 °C	*−125.3 °F*	Vostok, Antarctica	25 Aug 1958
−88,3 °C	*−126.9 °F*	Vostok, Antarctica	24 Aug 1960
−89,2 °C	*−128.6 °F*	Vostok, Antarctica	21 July 1983

EARTHQUAKES AND VOLCANOES

WORLD'S GREATEST EARTHQUAKES

It is estimated that each year there are some 500,000 detectable seismic or micro-seismic disturbances of which 100,000 can be felt and 1000 cause damage. The deepest recorded hypocentres are of 720 km *447 miles* in Indonesia in 1933, 1934 and 1943.

PROGRESSIVE LIST OF THE WORLD'S STRONGEST INSTRUMENTALLY RECORDED EARTHQUAKES

Kanamori Scale Magnitudes	Gutenberg–Richter Scale			
8.8	8.6	Colombia coast	31 Jan	1906
(8.6)	8.6	Assam, India	15 Aug	1950
9.0	(8¼)	Kamchatka, USSR	4 Nov	1952
9.1	(8.3)	Andreanol, Aleutian Islands, USA	9 Mar	1957
9.5	(8.3)	Lebu, Chile	22 May	1960

MOST DEADLY EARTHQUAKES

The greatest loss of life occurred in the earthquake (*ti chen*) in the Shensi, Shansi and Honan provinces of China, of 2 Feb 1556, when an estimated 830,000 people were killed. The highest death roll in modern times has been in the Tangshan 'quake (Mag. 8.2) in Eastern China on 27 July 1976 (local time was 3 a.m. 28 July). A first figure published on 4 Jan 1977 revealed 655,237 killed, later adjusted to 750,000. On 22 Nov 1979 the New China News Agency unaccountably reduced the death toll to 242,000. The site of the city was still a prohibited area 5½ years later in Jan 1982. The greatest material damage was in the 'quake on the Kwanto plain, Japan, of 1 Sept 1923 (Mag. 8.2). In Sagami Bay the sea-bottom in one area sank 400 m *1310 ft*. The official total of persons killed and missing in the *Shinsai* or great 'quake and the resultant fires was 142,807. In Tokyo and Yokohama 575,000 dwellings were destroyed. The cost of the damage was estimated at £1000 million (*now more than £4000 million*). It has however been estimated that a 7.5 magnitude shock (G-R scale) 48 km *30 miles* north of Los Angeles would result in damage estimated at $75,000 million.

The world's largest active volcano is Mauna Loa in Hawaii at 6060 m *19,882 ft*. It erupted last in April 1984.

EARTHQUAKES AND VOLCANOES

VOLCANOES

The total number of known active volcanoes in the world is 850 of which many are submarine. The greatest active concentration is in Indonesia, where 77 of its 167 volcanoes have erupted within historic times. The name volcanoes derives from the now dormant Vulcano Island (from the God of fire Vulcanus) in the Mediterranean.

GREATEST ERUPTION

The total volume of matter discharged in the eruption of Tambora, a volcano on the island of Sumbawa, in Indonesia, 5–7 Apr 1815, was 150–180 km^3. The energy of this 2245 km/h *1395 mph* eruption, which lowered the height of the island by 1250 m *4100 ft* from 4100 m *13,450 ft* to 2850 m *9350 ft*, was 8.4×10^{19} joules. A crater 11 km *7 miles* in diameter was formed. Some 90,000 were killed or died of famine. This compares with a probable 60–65 km^3 ejected by Santorini and 20 km^3 ejected by Krakatoa (see below). The internal pressure at Tambora has been estimated at 3270 kg/cm^2 or *20.76 tons/in^2*.

GREATEST EXPLOSION

The greatest explosion (possibly since Santorini in the Aegean Sea *c.* 1626 BC) occurred at *c.* 10 a.m. (local time), or 3.00 a.m. GMT, on 27 Aug 1883, with an eruption of Krakatoa, an island (then 47 km^2 *18 miles^2*) in the Sunda Strait, between Sumatra and Java, in Indonesia. A total of 163 villages were wiped out, and 36,380 people killed by the wave it caused. Rocks were thrown 55 km *34 miles* high and dust fell 5330 km *3313 miles* away 10 days later. The explosion was recorded four hours later on the island of Rodrigues, 4776 km *2968 miles* away, as 'the roar of heavy guns' and was heard over 1/13th part of the surface of the globe. This explosion estimated to have had about 26 times the power of the greatest H-bomb test (by the USSR) was still only a fifth part of the Santorini cataclysm.

LARGEST AND HIGHEST *ACTIVE*

The highest volcano regarded as active is Volcán Antofalla (6450 m *21,162 ft*), in Argentina, though a more definite claim is made for Volcán Guayatiri or Guallatiri (6060 m *19,882 ft*), in Chile, which erupted in 1959. The world's largest active volcano is Mauna Loa (4168 m *13,677 ft*), Hawaii which erupted in 1975 and in April 1984.

Mount St Helena during eruption.

CHAPTER 5

BUILDING BIG

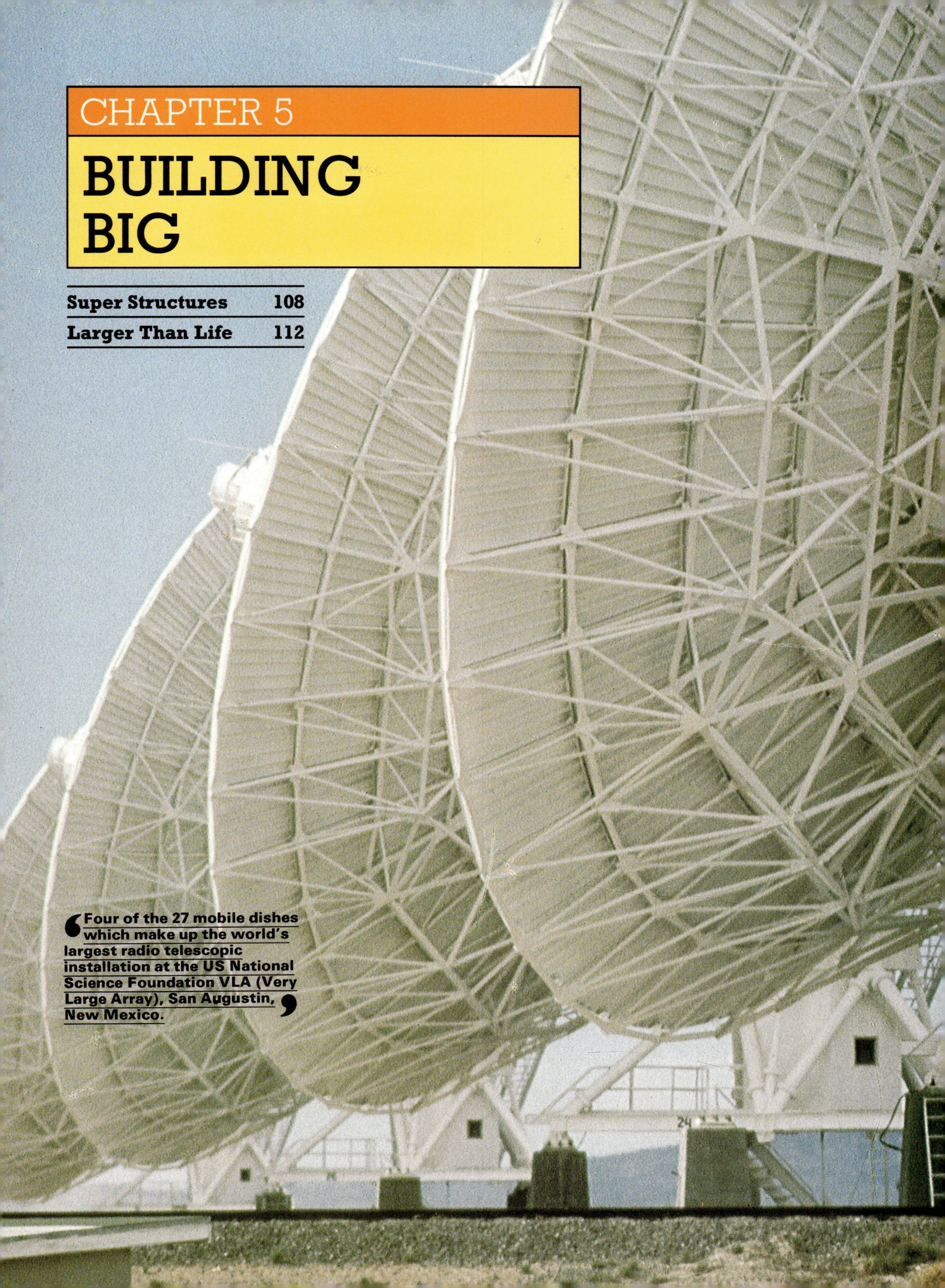

‘Four of the 27 mobile dishes which make up the world’s largest radio telescopic installation at the US National Science Foundation VLA (Very Large Array), San Augustin, New Mexico.’

The tallest office block. Sears Tower Chicago.

SUPER STRUCTURES

WORLD'S TALLEST STRUCTURE

The tallest structure in the world is the guyed Warszawa Radio mast at Konstantynow near Gabin and Plock 96 km *60 miles* north-west of the capital of Poland. It is 646,38 m *2120 ft 8 in* tall or more than four tenths of a mile. The mast was completed on 18 July 1974 and put into operation on 22 July 1974. It was designed by Jan Polak and weighs 550 tonnes/*tons*. The mast is so high that anyone falling off the top would reach their terminal velocity and hence cease to be accelerating before hitting the ground. Work was begun in July 1970 on this tubular steel construction, with its 15 steel guy ropes. It recaptured for Europe a record held in the USA since the Chrysler Building surpassed the Eiffel Tower in 1929.

WORLD'S TALLEST BUILDING

The tallest office building in the world is the Sears Tower, the national headquarters of Sears, Roebuck & Co. in Wacker Drive, Chicago, Illinois with 110 storeys rising to 443 m *1454 ft* and begun in August 1970. Its gross area is 4,400,000 ft^2 (40,8 ha *101.0 acres*). It was 'topped out' on 4 May 1973. It surpassed the World Trade Center in New York City in height at 2.35 p.m. on 6 Mar 1973 with the first steel column reaching to the 104th storey. The addition of two TV antennae brought the total height to 475,18 m *1559 ft*. The building's population is 16,770 served by 103 elevators and 18 escalators. It has 16,000 windows. Tentative plans for a 169 storey 701 m *2300 ft* tall building, projected to cost $1250 million, for the Chicago Loop, Illinois, USA were published on 27 Oct 1981. Plans for a 150 storey 509 m *1670 ft* tower, entitled Television City, in New York City were unveiled by Donald Trump on 18 Nov 1985.

BRITAIN'S TALLEST BUILDING

The tallest office block in Britain and the tallest cantilevered building in the world is the £72 million National Westminster tower block in Bishopsgate, City of London completed in 1979. It has 49 storeys and 3 basement levels, serviced by 21 lifts, and is 183 m *600 ft 4 in* tall. The gross floor area is 59,121 m^2 *636,373 ft^2* (5,9 ha *14.6 acres*).

WORLD'S LARGEST PUB

The largest beer-selling establishment in the world is the Mathäser, Bayerstrasse 5, München (Munich), West Germany, where the daily sale reaches 48 000 litres *84,470 pints*. It was established in 1829, was demolished in the Second World War and rebuilt by 1955 and now seats 5500 people. The through-put at the Dube beer halls in the Bantu township of Soweto, Johannesburg, South Africa may, however, be higher on some Saturdays when the average consumption of 27 280 litres (*6000 gal, 48,000 pints*) is far exceeded.

'The world's oldest building is the Wooden Pagoda at Nera, Japan. It celebrates its 1271st birthday this year.'

WORLD'S LARGEST BUILDINGS

INDUSTRIAL

The largest industrial plant in the world is the Nizhniy Tagil Railroad Car and Tank Plant, 136 km *85 miles* north-west of Sverdlovsk, USSR which has 827 000 m^2 or *204.3 acres* of floor space. It has an annual capacity to produce 2500 T-72 tanks.

COMMERCIAL

The greatest ground area covered by any building in the world under one roof is the auction building of the Co-operative VBA (Verenigde Bloemnveilingen Aalsmeer), which measures 808,75× 375 m *884.4×410.1 yd* with a floor surface of 303,282 m^2 *74.94 acres*. The first section of this site of the world's largest flower auction at Aalsmeer, Netherlands was completed in February 1972. The building with the largest cubic capacity in the world is the Boeing Company's main assembly plant at Everett, Washington State, USA completed in 1968 with a capacity of 5,6 million m^3 *200 million ft^3*.

WORLD'S TALLEST CHIMNEY STACKS

The world's tallest chimney is the $5.5 million International Nickel Company's stack 379,6 m *1245 ft 8 in* tall at Copper Cliff, Sudbury, Ontario, Canada, completed in 1970. It was built by Canadian Kellogg Ltd, in 60 days and the diameter tapers from 35,4 m *116.4 ft* at the base to 15,8 m *51.8 ft* at the top. It weighs 39 006 tonnes *38,390 tons* and became operational in 1971. The world's most massive chimney is one of 350 m *1148 ft* at Puentes, Spain, built by M. W. Kellogg Co. It contains 15 750 m³ *20,600 yd³* of concrete and 1315 tonnes *2.9 million lb* of steel and has an internal volume of 189 720 m³ *6.7 million ft³*. Europe's tallest chimney serves the Zasavje thermo-power plant in Trboulje, Yugoslavia completed to 350 metres *1181 ft* on 1 June 1976.

WORLD'S LARGEST HOTEL

The hotel with most rooms in the world is the 12 storey Hotel Rossiya in Moscow, USSR, with 3200 rooms providing accommodation for 6000 guests, opened in 1967. It would thus require more than 8½ years to spend one night in each room. In addition there is a 21 storey 'Presidential' tower in the central courtyard. The hotel employs about 3000 people, and has 93 lifts. The ballroom is reputed to be the world's largest. Muscovites are not permitted as residents while foreigners are charged 16 times more than the very low rate charged to USSR officials. The Izmailovo Hotel complex, opened in July 1980 for the XXII Olympic Games in Moscow, was designed to accommodate 9500 people.

WORLD'S LARGEST HOUSE

The largest private house in the world is the 250-room Biltmore House in Asheville, North Carolina, USA. It is owned by George and William Cecil, grandsons of George Washington Vanderbilt II (1862–1914). The house was built between 1890 and 1895 in an estate of 48 160 ha *119,000 acres*, at a cost of $4,100,000 (then *£1,708,333*) and now valued at $55,000,000 with 4856 ha *12,000 acres*. The most expensive private house ever built is the Hearst Ranch at San Simeon, California, USA. It was built in 1922–39 for William Randolph Hearst (1863–1951), at a total cost of more than $30,000,000 (*then £6,120,000*). It has more than 100 rooms, a 32 m *104 ft* long heated swimming pool, a 25 m *83 ft* long assembly hall and a garage for 25 limousines. The house required 60 servants to maintain it.

RESTAURANT RECORDS

The earliest restaurant was opend in 1725 in Calle de Cuchilleros 17, Madrid. Goya, the painter, was a dishwasher there in 1765 when he was 19. The Paris restaurant now serving most 'covers' per day is La Cupole with 2000. The highest restaurant in the world is at the Chacaltaya ski resort, Bolivia at 5340 m *17,519 ft*. The highest in Great Britain is the Ptarmigan Observation Restaurant at 1112 m *3650 ft* above sea-level on Cairngorm (1244 m *4084 ft*) near Aviemore, Highland, Scotland.

‘*World's longest bridge span.* The world's longest bridge span is the main span of the Humber Estuary Bridge, England at 1410 m *4626 ft*.’

‘The world's largest commercial building under one roof is the flower auction market at Aalsmeer, Netherlands. It has a floor surface of 368,477 m² *91.05* acres.’

SUPER STRUCTURES

'The world's longest dam – part of the Yacyreta-Apipe dam on the Parana river, which stretches 72 km *44.7 miles* along the borders of Paraguay and Argentina.'

WORLD'S LONGEST CANAL

The longest canalised system in the world is the Volga–Baltic Canal opened in April 1965. It runs 2300 km *1850 miles* from Astrakhan up the Volga, via Kuybyshev, Gor'kiy and Lake Ladoga, to Leningrad, USSR. The longest canal of the ancient world has been the Grand Canal of China from Peking to Hangchou. It was begun in 540 BC and not completed until 1327 by which time it extended (including canalised river sections) for 1781 km *1107 miles*. The estimated work force *c* AD 600 reached 5,000,000 on the Pien section. Having been allowed by 1950 to silt up to the point that it was, in no place, more than 1,8 m *6 ft* deep, it is now, however, plied by ships of up to 2000 tonnes/*tons*.

WORLD'S LONGEST RAILWAY BRIDGE

The longest railway bridge in the world is the Huey P. Long Bridge, Metairie, Louisiana, USA with a railway section 7009 m *22,996 ft* (7 km *4.35 miles*) long. It was completed on 16 Dec 1935 with a longest span of 241 m *790 ft*. The Yangtse River Bridge, completed in 1968 in Nanking, China is the world's longest combined highway and railway bridge. The rail deck is 6772 m *4.20 miles* and the road deck is 4589 m *2.85 miles*.

HIGHEST DAM IN THE WORLD

The highest dam in the world is the Grande Dixence in Switzerland, completed in September 1961 at a cost of 1600 million Swiss francs (*then £151,000,000*). It is 285 m *935 ft* from base to rim, 700 m *2296 ft* long and the total volume of concrete in the dam is 5 957 000 m^3 *7,792,000* yd^3. The Rogunsky earth-fill dam will have a final height of 325 m *1066 ft* across the Vakhsh River, Tadzhikistan, USSR with a crest length of only 660 m *2165 ft*. Building since 1973, completion date is still unconfirmed.

LONGEST RAILWAY TUNNEL IN THE WORLD

The world's longest main-line rail tunnel is the 22,3 km *13 miles 1397 yd* long Oshimizu Tunnel (Daishimizu) on the Tokyo–Niigata Joetsu line in central Honshu under the Tanigawa mountain which was holed through on 25 Jan 1979. The cost of the whole project reached £3150 million by March 1981. Fatalities in 7 years have been 13.

The longest covered bridge is the Trans-Canada Highway Bridge at Hartland, New Brunswick, Canada. It was completed in 1899 and measures 390.8 m *1282 ft*.

DEEPEST MAN-MADE HOLE

Man's deepest penetration into the Earth's crust is a geological exploratory drilling near Zapolarny, Kola peninsula, USSR begun in 1970. On 28 Dec 1983 12 000 m *39,370 ft* or *7.45 miles* was reached. Progress has understandably greatly slowed to 500 m *1640 ft* per annum as the eventual target of 15 000 m *49,212 ft*, in 1989–90 is neared. The drill bit is mounted on a turbine driven by a mud pump. The temperature at 11 km *6.83 miles* was already 200 °C *392 °F*.

FASTEST LIFTS

The fastest domestic passenger lifts in the world are the express lifts to the 60th floor of the 240 m *787.4 ft* tall 'Sunshine 60' building, Ikebukuro, Tokyo, Japan completed 5 Apr 1978. They were built by Mitsubishi Corp. and operate at a speed of 609,6 m/min *2000 ft/min or* 36,56 km/h *22.72 mph*. Much higher speeds are achieved in the winding cages of mine shafts. A hoisting shaft 2072 m *6800 ft* deep, owned by Western Deep Levels Ltd in South Africa, winds at speeds of up to 65,8 km/h *40.9 mph* (1095 m *3595 ft* per min). Otitis-media (popping of the ears) presents problems much above even 16 km/h *10 mph*.

The largest scientific building in the world with the base of the 5 engined Stage 1 end of the Saturn V launcher. The Vehicle Assembly Building at the John F. Kennedy Space Center, Cape Canaveral, USA and the rocket which gulps 13,6 tonnes of liquid oxygen and kerosine per second. (*Kenneth A. Brookes*)

LARGER THAN LIFE

The tallest fountain in Great Britain, the Emperor at Chatsworth, Derbyshire. It has reached a height of 79 m 260 ft. (The Duchess of Devonshire)

WORLD'S LARGEST MAZE

The oldest dateable representation of a labyrinth is that on a clay tablet from Pylos, Greece from *c* 1200 BC.

The world's largest hedge maze is that at Longleat, nr Warminster, Wilts, with 2,59 km *1.61 miles* of paths flanked by 16,180 yew trees. It was opened on 6 June 1978 and measures 115,8 × 53,34 m *380 × 175 ft*. 'Il Labirinto' at Villa Pisani, Stra, Italy in which Napoleon was 'lost' in 1807 had 6,4 km *4 miles* of pathways.

LONGEST STAIRCASE IN THE WORLD

The world's longest stairway is the service staircase for the Niesenbahn funicular which rises to 2365 m *7758 ft* near Spiez, Switzerland. It has 11,674 steps and a banister. The stone cut T'ai Chan temple stairs of 6600 steps in the Shantung Mountains, China ascend 1428 m in 8 km *4700 feet in 5 miles*. The longest spiral staircase is one 336,2 m *1103 ft* deep with 1520 steps installed in the Mapco-White County Coal Mine, Carmi, Illinois, USA by Systems Control Inc. in May 1981.

LARGEST CLOCK

The world's most massive clock is the Astronomical Clock in the Cathedral of St Pierre, Beauvais, France, constructed between 1865 and 1868. It contains 90,000 parts and measures 21,1 m *40 ft* high, 6,09 m *20 ft* wide and 2,7 m *9 ft* deep. The Su Sung clock, built in China at K'aifeng in 1088–92, had a 20,3 tonnes *20 ton* bronze armillary sphere for 1,52 tonnes, *1½ tons* of water. It was removed to Peking in 1126 and was last known to be working in its 12,1 m *40 ft* high tower in 1136.

The world's largest clock face is that of the floral clock at Tokachigaoka Park, Otofuke, Hokkaido, Japan, completed on 1 Aug 1982 with a diameter of 18 m *59 ft 0⅝ in.*

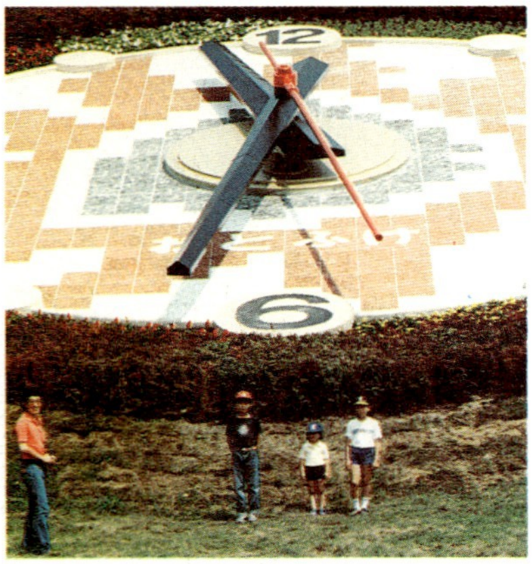

The world's largest clock face – the floral clock at Tokachigaoka Park, Japan. It measures 18 m 59 ft ⅝ in in diameter.

THE GIANT BED

In Bruges, Belgium, Philip, Duke of Burgundy had a bed 3,81 × 5,79 m *12½ wide and 19 ft long* erected for the perfunctory *coucher officiel* ceremony with Princess Isabella of Portugal in 1430. The largest bed in Great Britain is the Great Bed of Ware, dating from *c* 1580, from the Crown Inn, Ware, Hertfordshire, now preserved in the Victoria and Albert Museum, London. It is 3,26 × 3,37 × 2,66 m *10 ft 8½ wide, 11 ft 1 in long and 8 ft 9 in tall.*

THE GIANT BLANKET

The largest blanket ever made measured 20,7 × 30,48 m *68 × 100 ft* weighing 272 kg *600 lb*. It was knitted in 20,160 squares in 10 months (October 1977–July 1978) by *Woman's Weekly* readers for Action Research for The Crippled Child. It was shown on BBC TV *Record Breakers* in October 1978.

THE GIANT CHAIR

The world's largest chair is the 907 kg *2000 lb* 10,08 m *33 ft 1 in* tall, 5,96 m *19 ft 7 in* wide chair constructed by Anniston Steel & Plumbing Co. Inc. for Miller Office Furniture in Anniston, Alabama, USA and completed in May 1981.

TABLECLOTH

The world's largest tablecloth is one 200 m *219 yd* long by 1,8 m *2 yd* wide double damask made by John S. Brown & Sons Ltd of Belfast in 1972 and shipped to a royal palace in the Middle East. There was also an order for matching napkins for 450 places.

The world's largest office building is the Pentagon at Arlington, Virginia. This, the home of the US Defense Department has over 149 acres of floor space. 29,000 people work in the building and there are 44,000 telephones.

WORLD'S LARGEST NUTS
The largest nuts ever made weigh 5,3 tonnes *104.3 cwt* each and have an outside diameter of 132 cm *52 in* and a 63, 5 cm *25 in* thread. Known as 'Pilgrim Nuts', they are manufactured by Doncasters Moorside Ltd of Oldham, Lancashire for use on the columns of a large forging press.

THE GIANT CHANDELIER
The world's largest chandelier was built in Murano, Italy in 1953 for the Casino Knokke, Belgium. It measures 8 m *26 ft 3 in* in circumference and 7 m *23 ft* in height and weighs 37 tonnes/*tons*.

THE GIANT CHRISTMAS CRACKER
The largest functional cracker ever constructed was one 17,24 m *56 ft 7 in* in length and 2,9 m *9½ ft* in diameter built for British Rail Hull Paragon Station and pulled on 21 Nov 1980.

THE GIANT VASE
The largest vase on record is one 2,78 m *8 ft* in height, weighing 294,8 kg *650 lb*, thrown by Sebastiano Maglio at Haeger Potteries of Dundee, Illinois, USA (founded 1872) during August 1976.

THE GIANT CURTAIN
The largest curtain ever built has been the bright orange-red 4064 kg *4 ton* 56 m *185 ft* high curtain suspended 411 m *1350 ft* across the Rifle Gap, Grand Hogback, Colorado, USA by the Bulgarian-born sculptor Christo (*né* Javacheff) on 10 Aug 1971. It blew apart in a 80 km/h *50 mph* gust 27 hr later. The total cost involved in displaying this work of art was $750,000 (*then £312,500*).

The world's largest functional curtain is one 167,6×19,8 m *550 ft long×45 ft* high in the Brabazon hangar at British Aerospace Filton, Bristol used to enclose aircraft in the paint spraying bay. It is electrically drawn.

THE GIANT CANDLE
A candle 24,38 m *80 ft* high and 2,59 m *8½ ft* in diameter was exhibited at the 1897 Stockholm Exhibition by the firm of Lindahls. The overall height was 38,70 m *127 ft*.

The world's largest snow construction was the Ice Palace built in St Paul, Minnesota, USA during the Winter Carnival, January 1986. Its 30,000 ice blocks reached to a height of 36.5 m *120 ft*.

LARGER THAN LIFE

'The world's longest outdoor escalator at Ocean Park, Hong Kong. It has an overall length of 227 m *745 ft* and a total vertical rise of 115 m *377 ft* above sea level. It was built by Otis and can carry 4000 people in either direction.'

THE GIANT CARPET

Of ancient carpets the largest on record was the gold-enriched silk carpet of Hashim (dated AD 743) of the Abbasid caliphate in Baghdad, Iraq. It is reputed to have measured 54,86 × 91,44 m *180 by 300 ft.* A 4851 m² *52,225 ft²* or 1.23 acre 28 ton red carpet was laid on 13 Feb 1982, by the Allied Corporation, from Radio City Music Hall to the New York Hilton along the Avenue of the Americas.

THE GIANT CIGAR

The largest cigar ever made measures 5,095 m *16 ft 8½ in* in length and weighs 262 kg *577 lb 9 oz* (over ¼ ton) taking 243 hours and using 3330 full tobacco leaves. It was made by Tinus Vinke and Jan Veijmer in February 1983 and is in the Tobacco Museum in Kampen, Holland. The largest marketed cigar in the world is the 35,5 cm *14 in* Valdez Emperado by San Andres Cigars.

THE LARGEST PIECE OF FURNITURE IN THE WORLD

The largest item of furniture in the world is the wooden bench in Green Park, Obihiro, Hokkaido, Japan which seats 1282 people and measures 400 m *1312 ft 4 in* long. It was completed by a team of 770 on 19 July 1981.

ALL-TIME DEMOLITION RECORD

The largest building demolished by explosives has been the 21 storey Traymore Hotel, Atlantic City, New Jersey, USA, on 26 May 1972 by Controlled Demolition Inc. of Towson, Maryland. This 600 room hotel had a cubic capacity of 181 340 m³ *6,495,500 ft³*. The tallest chimney ever demolished by explosives was the Matla Power Station chimney, Kriel, South Africa on 19 July 1981. It stood 275 m *902 ft* and was brought down by The Santon (Steeplejack) Co. Ltd of Manchester, England.

WORLD'S LARGEST GARBAGE DUMP

Reclamation Plant No. 1, Fresh Kills, Staten Island, opened in March 1974, is the world's largest sanitary landfill. In its first 4 months 457 000 tonnes *450,000 tons* of refuse from New York City was dumped on the site by 700 barges.

PYRAMID OLDEST

The oldest known pyramid is the Djoster step pyramid at Saqqâra, Egypt constructed by Imhotep to a height of 62 m *204 ft* originally with a Tura limestone casing in *c.* 2650 BC. The largest known single block comes from the Third Pyramid (the pyramid of Mycerinus) and weighs 290 tonnes *285 tons*. The oldest New World pyramid is that on the island of La Venta in south-eastern Mexico built by the Olmec people *c.* 800 BC. It stands 30 m *100 ft* tall with a base dimension of 128 m *420 ft*.

'The port of New York and New Jersey, USA is physically the world's largest with a navigable waterfront of 1215 km *755 miles*.'

CHAPTER 6

THAT'S ENTERTAINMENT

'Dolly Parton, the world's highest paid live entertainer.'

MOVIE MOSTS

Rita Moreno whose trophies include all 4 of the major show business awards – Oscars (motion pictures, founded in 1928), Tony (theatre, 1947), Emmy (TV, 1948) and Grammy (recording, 1957).

MOST EXPENSIVE FILM

The highest ever budgeted film has been *Star Trek* which received its world première in Washington, DC on 6 Dec 1979. Paramount Studios stated that the cost of this space epic directed by Robert Wise and produced by Gene Roddenberry, was $46 million (*then £21 million*). A figure of $60 million has been attributed to *Superman II* but never substantiated.

LEAST EXPENSIVE FILM

Cecil Hepworth's highly successful release of 1905 *Rescued by Rover* cost £7 13s 9d (then *$37.40*).

HIGHEST EARNINGS *BY AN ACTOR*

The highest rate of pay in cinema history is that paid to Sylvester Stallone (b. New York City, 6 July 1946) with $12 million for *Rocky IV* plus a, as yet uncompleted, share of box office. In January 1986 Hollywood sources predicted that his salary plus profit share from *Rambo* would reach $20 million. The highest paid actress in 1985 was Meryl Streep (b. Summit, N.J., 1949) with $3 million for her role in *Out of Africa*.

Marlon Brando – highest paid actor in the film *Superman*.

The late Walt Disney who amassed a record 32 Oscar awards with his greatest cartoon character Mickey Mouse.

MOST EXPENSIVE FILM RIGHTS

The highest price ever paid for film rights is $9,500,000 (*then £4,950,000*) announced on 20 Jan 1978 by Columbia for *Annie*, the Broadway musical by Charles Strouse starring Andrea McCardle, Dorothy Loudon and Reid Shelton.

LARGEST LOSS

On 13 May 1981 Steven Bach was fired by United Artists after the loss (shooting, studio overheads and distribution) on *Heaven's Gate* reached $57 million.

HIGHEST BOX-OFFICE EARNERS

The box office gross championships for films is highly vulnerable to inflated ticket prices. Calculations based on the 1983 value of the dollar shows that *Gone With the Wind* with Clark Gable (1901–60) and Vivien Leigh (1913–67) released in 1939 is unsurpassed at $312 million. The highest numerical (as opposed to value) dollar champion is Steven Speilberg's *ET: The Extra-Terrestrial*, released on 11 June 1982, and which by 2 Jan 1983 had grossed $322 million (*then £208 million*). On 29 May 1983 *The Return of the Jedi* (20th Century-Fox) grossed $8,440,105 (*£5,445,200*) for a single day record, and a record $6,219,929 (*£4,013,000*) for its opening day on 25 May 1983.

Heaven's Gate
From Michael Cimino, director of "The Deer Hunter," comes an epic saga of the days when America was young.

The biggest flop in cinema history, *Heaven's Gate*, cost United Artists $57 million (£29 million).

MOST OSCARS

Walter (Walt) Elias Disney (1901–66) won more 'Oscars' – the awards of the United States Academy of Motion Picture Arts and Sciences, instituted on 16 May 1929 for 1927–8 – than any other person. The physical count comprises 20 statuettes, and 112 other plaques and certificates including posthumous awards. The only person to win four Oscars in a starring role has been Miss Katharine Hepburn, formerly Mrs Ludlow Ogden Smith (b. Hartford, Conn., 9 Nov 1909) in *Morning Glory* (1932–3), *Guess Who's Coming to Dinner* (1967), *The Lion in Winter* (1968) and *On Golden Pond* (1981). She was 12 times nominated. Only 4 actors have won two Oscars in starring roles – Fredric March (1897–1975) in 1931/32 and 1946, Spencer Tracy in 1937 and 1938, Gary Cooper in 1941 and 1952, and Marlon Brando in 1954 and 1972. Edith Head (Mrs Wiard B. Ihnen) (d. 1981) won 8 individual awards for costume design. Oscars are named after Mr Oscar Pierce of Texas, USA. The films with most awards have been *Ben Hur* (1959) with 11, followed by *Gone With the Wind* (1939) with 10 and *West Side Story* (1961) with 10. The film with the highest number of nominations was *All About Eve* (1950) with 14. It won 6. The youngest ever winner was Shirley Temple (b. 24 Apr 1928) aged 5 with her honorary Oscar, and the oldest George Burns (b. 20 Jan 1896) aged 80 for *The Sunshine Boys* in 1976.

MOST ACTED CHARACTER

The character most frequently recurring on the screen is Sherlock Holmes, created by Sir Arthur Conan Doyle (1859–1930). Sixty-eight actors portrayed him in 186 films between 1900 and 1986.

MOST SEQUELS

Japan's *Tora-San* films have now stretched from *Tora-San I* in August 1968 to *Tora-San XXXII* in 1983 with Kiyoshi Atsumi (b. 1929) starring in each for Schochiku Co.

LARGEST CINEMA IN THE WORLD

The largest cinema in the world is the Radio City Music Hall, New York City, opened on 27 Dec 1932 with 5945 (now 5882) seats. The Roxy, opened in New York City on 11 March 1927 had 6214 (later 5869) seats but was closed on 29 Mar 1960. Cineplex, opened at the Toronto Eaton Centre, Canada on 19 Apr 1979 has 18 separate theatres with an aggregate capacity of 1700.

CHAMPION FILM-GOER

Albert E. Van Schmus (b. 1921) saw 16,945 films in 32 years (1949–1982) as a rater for Motion Picture Association of America Inc.

Japan's best-known face – that of Kiyoshi Atsumi who has starred in *Tora San* for more than 15 years.

The Imax Theatre, Taman Mini Park, Indonesia contains the world's largest cinema screen 28,28 × 21,48 m *92 ft × 9 in × 70 ft 6 in*, opened in March 1984.

The biggest cinema screen in the world is in the Imax Theatre, Taman Mini Park, Jakarta, Indonesia.

Dame Anna Neagle, DBE, who died on 3 June 1986, held the record-breaking total of 2062 performances of *Charlie Girl*.

TV TOPS

Bamber Gascoigne who has served as quizmaster on *University Challenge* for 24 years.

Aaron Spelling, the most prolific TV producer of all time. Up to 1985 he had produced 2237 hours of broadcasting.

James Coburn is reputed to have received $500,000 (*then £250,000*) for uttering two words on a series of Schlitz beer commercials.

HIGHEST PAID TV PERFORMERS

Carroll O'Connor, star of *Archie Bunker's Place*, received $275,000 (*£182,500*) for each of 22 episodes in the 1982/83 season totalling $6,050,000 (*£4 million*). Peter Falk (b. 16 Sept 1927), the disarmingly persistent detective *Columbo*, was paid from $300,000 to $350,000 for a single episode of his series of six. Singer Kenny Rogers was reported in February 1983 to have been paid $2 million (*then £1,280,000*) for a single taping of a concert for HBO (Home Box Office) TV Channel. The highest paid newscaster and journalist is Dan Ruther of the CBS Nightly News reported in Feb 1986 to be paid $2,500,000 (*then* £1,785,000) per annum.

LONGEST-RUNNING SHOWS *WORLD*

The world's most durable TV show is NBC's *Meet the Press* first transmitted on 6 Nov 1947 and weekly since 12 Sept 1948, originated by Lawrence E. Spivak, who appeared weekly as either moderator or panel member until 1975. On 11 Dec 1980 Mike Douglas presented the 4754th version of his show started in 1960.

BRITAIN

Andy Pandy was first transmitted on 11 July 1950 but consisted of repeats of a cycle of 26 shows until 1970. *Come Dancing* was first transmitted on 29 Sept 1950 but is seasonal. *Sooty* was first presented on BBC by its deviser Harry Corbett (born 1918) from 1952 to 1967 and is continued by his son Matthew on ITV. *The Good Old Days* light entertainment ran from 20 July 1953 to 31 Dec 1983. Barney Colehan produced all 244 programmes. The *BBC News* was inaugurated in vision on 5 July 1954. Richard Baker OBE read the news from 1954 to Christmas 1982. Of current affairs programmes the weekly BBC *Panorama* was first transmitted on 11 Nov 1953 but has summer breaks, whereas Granada's *What The Papers Say* has been transmitted weekly since 5 Nov 1956. The monthly *Sky at Night* has been presented by Patrick Moore OBE without a break or a miss since 26 Apr 1957. The longest serving TV quizmaster is Bamber Gascoigne of Granada's *University Challenge* which has run since 21 Sept 1962. The longest running domestic drama serial is Granada's *Coronation Street* which has run twice weekly since 9 Dec 1960. William Roache has played Ken Barlow without a break since the outset.

SQUAREST EYE

In July 1978 it was estimated that the *average* American child by his or her 18th birthday has watched 710 solid days (17,040 hours) of TV, seen more than 350,600 commercials and more than 15,000 TV murders. In 1983 it was estimated that the US national average watching per household reached a record 7 hr 2 min per day in 83.3 million TV households. There are 571 TV sets per 1000 people in the USA compared with 348 in Sweden and 330 in Britain.

MOST EXPENSIVE PRODUCTION

The Winds of War, a seven part Paramount World War II saga, aired by ABC was the most expensive ever TV production costing $42 million over 14 months shooting. The final episode on 13 Feb 1983 attracted a rating of 41% (% of total number of viewers), and a share of 56% (% of total sets turned on that were tuned in).

BIGGEST VIEWING AUDIENCE

The greatest projected number of viewers worldwide for a televised event is 2,500 million for the live and recorded transmissions of the XXIIIrd Olympic Games in Los Angeles, California from 27 July to 13 Aug 1984. The American Broadcasting Co. airing schedule comprised 187½ hours of coverage on 56 cameras. The estimated viewership for the 'Live Aid' concerts organised by Bob Geldof and Bill Graham, via a record 12 satellites, was 1.6 billion or one third of the world's population. See also chapter 11.

The programme which attracted the highest ever viewership was the *Goodbye, Farewell and Amen* final episode of M*A*S*H (the acronym for Mobile Army Surgical Hospital 4077) transmitted by CBS on 28 Feb 1983 to 60.3% of all households in the United States. It was estimated that some 125 million people tuned in, taking a 77% share of all viewing. The UK record is 39 million for the wedding of TRH the Prince and Princess of Wales in London on 29 July 1981.

HIGHEST TV ADVERTISING RATES

The highest TV advertising rate has been $550,000 per ½ min (*then £91,666 per sec*) for ABC network prime time during the transmission of Super Bowl XIX on 19 Jan 1985. In Great Britain the peak time weekday 60 sec spot rate (5.40–10.40 p.m.) for Thames Television is £43,400+VAT (April 1985). The longest run was 7 min 10 sec by Great Universal Stores on *Good Morning Britain* for £100,000 on 20 Jan 1985.

HIGHEST-PAID ACTORS IN COMMERCIALS

In 1977 James Coburn of Beverly Hills, California was reputed to have been paid $500,000 (*then £250,000*) for uttering two words on a series of Schlitz beer commercials. The words 'Schlitz Light' were thus at a quarter of a million dollars per syllable. Brooke Shields (b. 31 May 1965) was reportedly paid $250,000 (*then £125,000*) for one minute of film by a Japanese TV commercial film maker in 1979. Faye Dunaway was reported in May 1979 to have been paid $900,000 (*then £450,000*) for uttering 6 words for a Japanese department store TV commercial. Britain's most durable TV commercial has been the Brooke Bond chimpanzee commercial first transmitted on 21 Nov 1971.

'*Bat Out of Hell* by Meatloaf stayed in the UK album charts for a record 384 weeks. (London Features International.)'

Alan Alda with the other members from the cast of M*A*S*H which attracted the highest ever viewership on its final episode when shown in the USA.

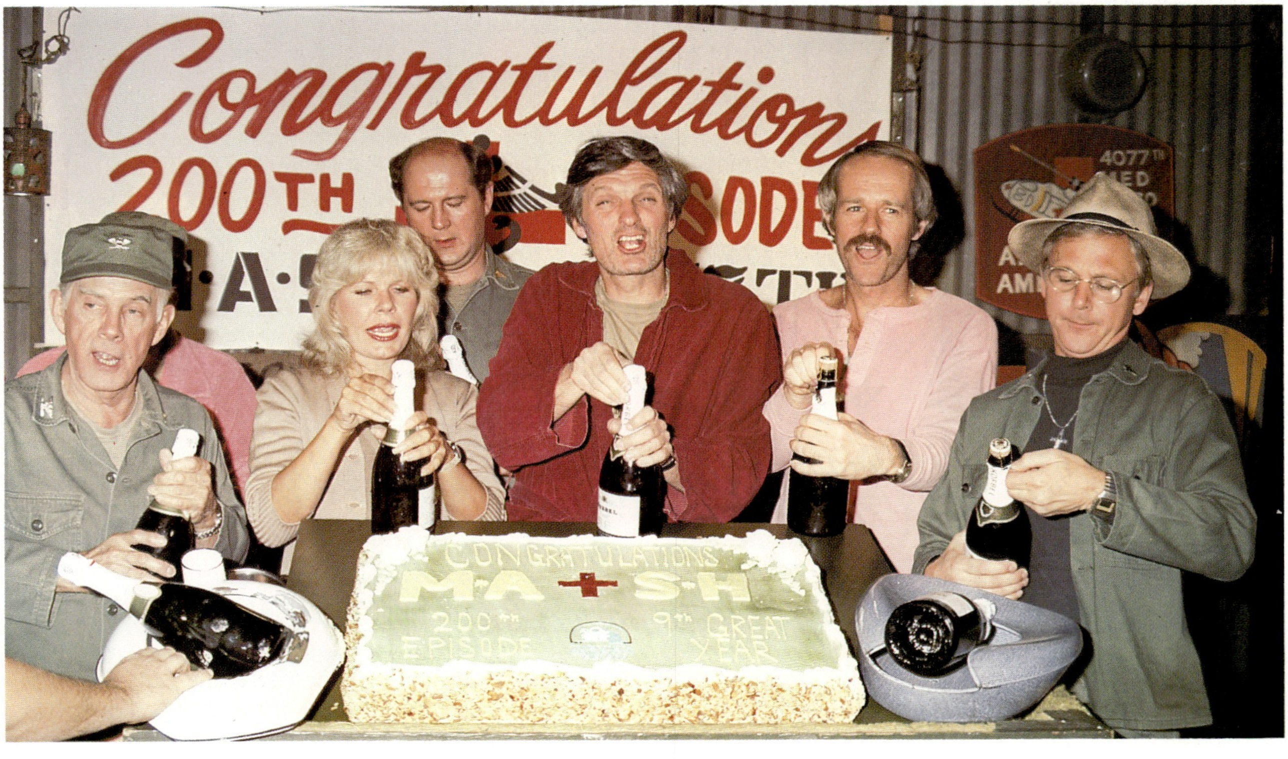

ROCK, POP & OTHER RECORDS

Michael Jackson's album *Thriller* in April 1984, was the first ever to surpass 35 million sales. *(London Features International)*

Wladziu Valentino Liberace is the world's highest paid pianist.

Jean-Michel Jarre composed the score for the outdoor performance at Downtown Houston, Texas which was seen by a world record live audience of 1.3 million on 5 April 1986.

BEST-PAID SINGERS

Of great fortunes earned by singers, the highest on record are those of Enrico Caruso (1873–1921), the Italian tenor, whose estate was about $9,000,000 (*then £1,875,000*) and the Italian-Spanish coloratura soprano Amelita Galli-Curci (1889–1963), who received about $3,000,000 (*£750,000*). In 1850, up to $653 was paid for a single seat at the concerts given in the United States by Johanna ('Jenny') Maria Lind, later Mrs Otto Goldschmidt (1820–87), the 'Swedish Nightingale'. She had a range from g to e^{111} of which the middle register is still regarded as unrivalled. The tenor Count John Francis McCormack (1884–1945) of Ireland gave up to 10 concerts to capacity audiences in a single season in New York City.

David Bowie drew a fee of $1.5 million (*then £960,000*) for a single show at the US Festival in Glen Helen Regional Park, San Bernardino County, California on 26 May 1983. The 4-man Van Halen rock band attracted a matching fee.

MOST SUCCESSFUL GROUP

The singers with the greatest sales of any group have been the Beatles. This group from Liverpool, Merseyside, comprised George Harrison, MBE (b. 25 Feb 1943), John Ono (formerly John Winston) Lennon, MBE (b. 9 Oct 1940–k. 8 Dec 1980), James Paul McCartney, MBE (b. 18 June 1942) and Richard Starkey, MBE *alias* Ringo Starr (b. 7 July 1940). The all-time Beatles sales by May 1985 have been estimated by EMI at over 1000 million discs and tapes.

All 4 ex-Beatles sold many million further records as solo artists. Since their break-up in 1970, it is estimated that the most successful group in the world in terms of record sales is the Swedish foursome ABBA with a total of 215 million discs and tapes by April 1985.

FASTEST SELLING RECORD OF ALL TIME

The fastest selling record of all time is *John Fitzgerald Kennedy – A Memorial Album* (Premium Records), recorded on 22 Nov 1963, the day of Mr Kennedy's assassination, which sold 4,000,000 copies at 99 cents (*then 35p*) in six days (7–12 Dec 1963), thus ironically beating the previous speed record set by the satirical LP *The First Family* in 1962–3. The fastest selling British record is the Beatles' double album *The Beatles* (Apple) with 'nearly 2 million' in its first week in November 1968.

Richard Clayderman (b. Philippe Pages, 1954) of France is reputed to have sold 25 million LPs in the 3 years to Jan 1983 for which he collected 127 gold and 23 platinum records.

MOST GOLD DISCS WINNERS

The only *audited* measure of gold, platinum and multiplatinum singles and albums within the United States, is certification by the Recording Industry Association of America introduced 14 Mar 1958. Out of the 2,582 RIAA awards made to 1 Jan 1985, The Beatles with 44 (plus one with Billy Preston) have most for a group. McCartney has 23 more awards outside the group and with Wings (including one with Stevie Wonder and one with Michael Jackson). The most awards to an individual is 45 to Elvis Presley (1935–77) spanning 1958 to 1 Jan 1985. Globally however Presley's total of million-selling singles has been authoritatively put at 'approaching 80'.

On the 20 July 1985 Live Aid's 60 rock music acts in London and Philadelphia raised a record-breaking £35 million in two weeks for African famine relief.

MOST SUCCESSFUL SONGWRITER

In terms of single records, the most successful of all songwriters has been Paul McCartney, formerly of the Beatles and now of Wings. Between 1962 and 1 Jan 1978 he wrote jointly or solo 43 songs which sold a million or more.

ALL-TIME BEST-SELLING ALBUMS

The best-selling album of all time is *Thriller* by Michael Joseph Jackson (b. Gary, Indiana, 29 Aug 1958) with global sales in excess of 38 million copies by August 1985. The best-selling album by British performers is considered to be *Dark Side Of The Moon* recorded by Pink Floyd (Dave Gilmour, Nick Mason, Roger Waters, and Rick Wright), in June 1972–January 1973 in London, with sales of over 17 million by April 1985.

ALL-TIME BEST-SELLING SINGLES

The greatest seller of any gramophone record to date is *White Christmas* by Irving Berlin (b Israel Bailin, at Tyumen, Russia, 11 May 1888) with 25,000,000 for the Crosby single (recorded 29 May 1942) and more than 100,000,000 in other versions. The highest claim for any 'pop' record is an unaudited 25,000,000 for *Rock Around the Clock*, copyrighted in 1953 by James E. Myers under the name Jimmy DeKnight and the late Max C. Freedmann and recorded on 12 Apr 1954 by Bill Haley (1927–1981) and the Comets. The top-selling British record of all time is *I Want to Hold Your Hand* by the Beatles, released in 1963, with world sales of over 13,000,000. The top-selling single of all time in the United Kingdom is *Feed The World – Do They Know It's Christmas* written and produced by Bob Geldof and Midge Ure with 3·6 million by May 1985 with a further 3¾ million world wide. The profits (about £60 million) were in aid of Ethiopian Famine Relief Fund.

'***Fastest concert sell-out.*** **The fastest sell-out in Broadway history occurred when seats for 'Barry Manilow In Concert' for 12 nights (21 Feb–5 Mar 1983) was sold out for $782,160 (*then £500,000*) in 4 hours at the 1983 seat Uris Theatre.**'

ROCK, POP & OTHER RECORDS

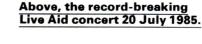

Elton John who drew an estimated audience of 400,000 to Central Park, New York City concert in 1980. (*Pictorial Press*)

Above, the record-breaking Live Aid concert 20 July 1985.

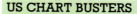

US CHART BUSTERS

SINGLES

Singles record charts were first published by *Billboard* on 20 July 1940 when the No. 1 was *I'll Never Smile Again* by Tommy Dorsey (b. 19 Nov 1905, d. 26 Nov 1956). Three discs have stayed top for a record 13 consecutive weeks – *Frenesi* by Artie Shaw from December 1940; *I've Heard that Song Before* by Harry James from February 1943 and *Goodnight Irene* by Gordon Jenkins and the Weavers from August 1950. *Tainted Love* by Soft Cell stayed on the chart for 43 consecutive weeks from January 1982. The Beatles have had most No.1 records (20) and Elvis Presley has had most hit singles on Billboard's Hot 100 – 149 from 1956 to May 1986.

ALBUMS

Billboard first published an album chart on 15 Mar 1945 when the No. 1 was *King Cole Trio* featuring Nat 'King' Cole (b. 17 Mar 1919, d. 15 Feb 1965). *South Pacific* was No. 1 for 69 weeks (non-consecutive) from May 1949. *Dark Side of The Moon* by Pink Floyd enjoyed its 621 weeks on the *Billboard* charts in May 1986. The Beatles had most No. 1s (15) and Presley most hit albums (93 from 1956 to May 1986).

The Who on 31 May 1976 set the record for the loudest rock group using a total power of 76,000 watts from eight 800 W Crown DEC 300A amplifiers at an outside concert held at Charlton Athletic Football Ground, London.

The Beatles are the most successful group of all time, with sales estimated of 1000 million records and tapes.

UK CHART BUSTERS

SINGLES

Singles record charts were first published in Britain on 14 Nov 1952 by *New Musical Express. I Believe* by Frankie Laine (b. 30 Mar 1913) held No. 1 position for 18 weeks (non-consecutive) from April 1953, with *Rose Marie* by Slim Whitman (b. 20 Jan 1924) the consecutive record holder with 11 weeks from July 1955. The longest stay has been the 163 weeks of *My Way* by Francis Albert Sinatra (b. 12 Dec 1917) in 10 separate runs from 2 Apr 1969 into 1984. The record for an uninterrupted stay is 56 weeks for Englebert Humperdinck's *Release Me* from 26 Jan 1967. The Beatles and Presley hold the record for most No. 1 hits with 17 each, with Presley having an overall record of 106 hits in the UK singles chart from 1956 to May 1985.

ALBUMS

The first British album chart was published on 8 Nov 1958 by *Melody Maker*. The first No. 1 LP was the film soundtrack *South Pacific* which held the position for a record 70 consecutive weeks and eventually accumulated a record 115 weeks at No. 1. The album with the most total weeks on chart was the soundtrack to *The Sound of Music* with 381 weeks. The Beatles have had most No. 1 albums – 12; and Elvis Presley the most hit albums – 90.

LOUDEST ROCK GROUP

The amplification at *The Who* concert at Charlton Athletic Football Ground, London on 31 May 1976 provided by a Tasco PA System had a total power of 76,000 watts from eighty 800 W Crown DEC 300 A Amplifiers and twenty 600 W Phase Linear 200s. The readings at 50 m *164 ft* from the front of the sound system were 120 db. Sound engineer Rob Cowlyn with Duran Duran claimed that the audience's level of anticipatory screaming in Australia in November 1983 exceeded 120 dB *before* the group came on stage. The US group Manowar, a heavy metal rock band, claim to have measured a reading of 160 dB in October 1984 is unsupportable. *Exposure to high noise levels is known to cause PSH – Permanent Shift of Hearing or partial up to total instant deafness.*

'David Bowie (born David Robert Jones in London on 8 Jan 1947) who attracted history's highest ever fee of $1.5 million for a single show in California on the 'Serious Moonlight Tour' in May 1983. *(Pictorial Press)*'

ART RECORDS

“*The world's most expensive painting.* The highest price ever bid at a public auction for any painting is £7,500,000 for *The Adoration of the Magi* by Andrea Mantegna (1431–1506), sold for the Marquess of Northampton at Christie's, London on 18 Apr 1985 and bought by the J. Paul Getty Museum of Malibu, California. With an 8% buyer's premium, this amounts to £8,100,000.”

THE MOST EXPENSIVE DRAWING

The highest price ever paid for any drawing is £3,546,000 for a study of an apostle's head and hand for the Transfiguration in the Vatican by Raphael (Raffaello Santi 1483–1520) and sold for the 11th Duke of Devonshire (b. 1920) at Christie's, London on 3 July 1984.

THE MOST PROLIFIC PAINTER

Picasso was the most prolific of all painters in a career which lasted 78 years. It has been estimated that Picasso produced about 13,500 paintings or designs, 100,000 prints or engravings, 34,000 book illustrations and 300 sculptures or ceramics. His lifetime *œuvre* has been valued at £500 million. Morris Katz (b. 1932) of Greenwich Village, New York City is the most prolific painter of saleable portraits in the world. His sales total as of 21 Apr 1982 was 110,600. Described as the 'King of Schlock Art', he sells his paintings 'cheap and often'.

THE MOST REPETITIOUS PAINTER

Antonio Bin of Paris has painted the *Mona Lisa* on some 300 occasions. These sell for up to £1000 apiece.

THE LARGEST MURAL

The world's largest mural was unveiled in 44 colours on the 30 storey Villa Regina condominium, Biscayne Bay, Miami, Florida on 14 Mar 1984 covering 27 870 m^2 *300,000* ft^2. The longest recorded continuous mural was one stretching 302 m *990 ft* on the History of Nechells, completed by 6 artists in Birmingham, England on 5 Dec 1984.

The artist Christo's flaming pink plastic borders to 11 islands off Florida, USA in 1983 claims to be the world's largest 'work of art'.

THE LARGEST ART GALLERY

The world's largest art gallery is the Winter Palace and the neighbouring Hermitage in Leningrad, USSR. One has to walk 24 km *15 miles* to visit each of the 322 galleries, which house nearly 3,000,000 works of art and objects of archaeological interest. The world's largest modern art museum is the Georges Pompidou National Centre for Art and Culture, Beauborg, opened in Paris in 1977 with 17 700 m² *183,000 ft²* of floor space. The most heavily endowed is the J. Paul Getty Museum, Malibu, California with an initial £700,000,000 in January 1974 and now £104 million p.a. for acquisitions. It has 38 galleries.

'The largest mobile weighs 8 tons and was installed at the Federal Reserve Bank of Philadelphia, Pennsylvania, USA on 24–25 May 1976.'

THE LARGEST MOSAIC

The world's largest mosaic is on the walls of the central library of the Universidad Nacional Autónoma de Mexico, Mexico City. There are four walls, the two largest measuring 1203 m² *12,949 ft²* each representing the pre-Hispanic past. The largest Roman mosaic in Britain is the Woodchester Pavement, Gloucestershire of *c* AD 325, excavated in 1793, now re-covered with protective earth. It measures 14,3 m *47 ft* square comprising $1\frac{1}{2}$ million terrerae. A brilliant total reconstruction was carried out by Robert and John Woodward in 1973–82.

THE FINEST PAINTBRUSH IN THE WORLD

The finest standard brush sold is the 000 in Series 7 by Winsor and Newton known as a 'triple goose'. It is made of 150–200 Kolinsky sable hairs weighing 15 mg *0.000520 oz.*

THE LARGEST PIECE OF SCULPTURE

The world's largest sculptures are the mounted figures of Jefferson Davis (1808–89), Gen. Robert Edward Lee (1806–70) and Gen. Thomas Jonathan ('Stonewall') Jackson (1824–63), covering 0,5 ha *1.33 acres* on the face for Stone Mountain, near Atlanta, Georgia. They are 27,4 m *90 ft* high. Roy Faulkner was on the mountain face for 8 years 174 days with a thermo-jet torch working with the sculptor Walker Kirtland Hancock and other helpers from 12 Sept 1963 to 3 Mar 1972. If completed the world's largest sculpture will be that of the Indian chief Tashunca-Uitco (*c* 1849–77), known as Crazy Horse, of the Oglala tribe of the Dakota or Nadowessious (Sioux) group. The sculpture was begun on 3 June 1948 near Mount Rushmore, South Dakota, USA. A projected 171,6 m *563 ft* high and 195 m *641 ft* long, it was the uncompleted life work of one man, Korczak Ziólkowski (1908–82). The horse's nostril is 15,2 m *50 ft* deep and 10,7 m *35 ft* in diameter. In 1984 another 200,000 tons of granite blasted off the mountain face brought the total to 7.8 million tons.

(*Above*) Korczak Ziolkowski who devoted his life to rock blasting a 563 ft high sculpture of 'Crazy Horse'.

HILL FIGURES

In August 1968, a 100 m *330 ft* tall figure was found on a hill above Tarapacá, Chile.

The largest human hill carving in Britain is the 'Long Man' of Wilmington, East Sussex, 68 m *226 ft* in length. The oldest of all White Horses in Britain is the Uffington White Horse in Oxfordshire, dating from the late Iron Age (*c* 150 BC) and measuring 114 m *374 ft* from nose to tail and 36 m *120 ft* high.

MOST MASSIVE MOBILE

The most massive mobile is *White Cascade* weighing 8 tonnes/*tons* and measuring 30,48 m *100 ft* from top to bottom installed on 24–25 May 1976 at the Federal Reserve Bank of Philadelphia, Pennsylvania, USA. It was designed by Alexander Calder (1898–1976), whose first mobiles were exhibited in Paris in 1932 and whose *Big Crinkley* sold for a record £555,572 at Sotheby's, New York on 10 May 1984.

MUSICAL RECORDS OF NOTE

An environmental rendition of Handel's Water Music by the world's first underwater violinist, Mark Gottlieb.

THE RECORD-BREAKING TUBA

The largest recorded brass instrument is a tuba standing 2,28 m *7½ ft* tall, with 11,8 m *39 ft* of tubing and a bell 1 m *3 ft 4 in* across. This contrabrass tuba was constructed for a world tour by the band of John Philip Sousa (1854–1932), the United States composer, in *c* 1896–8, and is still in use. The instrument is now owned by a circus promoter in South Africa.

THE LARGEST DOUBLE BASS

The largest double bass ever constructed was one 4,26 m *14 ft* tall, built in 1924 in Ironia, New Jersey, USA by Arthur K. Ferris, allegedly on orders from the Archangel Gabriel. It weighed 590 kg *11.6 cwt* with a sound box 2,43 m *8 ft* across, and had leathern strings totalling 31,7 m *104 ft*. Its low notes could be felt rather than heard. On 27 June 1984 members of 'Bass Ten' from Bournemouth, Dorset bowed and 6-fingered a double bass simultaneously in a rendition of Monti's *Czardas* at Hever Castle, Kent.

THE WORLD'S BIGGEST ORGAN

The largest and loudest musical instrument ever constructed is the now only partially functional Auditorium Organ in Atlantic City, New Jersey, USA. Completed in 1930, this heroic instrument had two consoles (one with seven manuals and another movable one with five), 1477 stop controls and 33,112 pipes ranging in tone from 4,7 mm *3/16 of an inch* to the 19 m *64 ft* tone. It had the volume of 25 brass bands, with a range of seven octaves.

THE MOST MASSIVE ORCHESTRA

The largest orchestra ever assembled was one of 20,100 at the Ullevaal Stadium, Oslo, of Norges Musikkorps Forbund bands from all Norway on 28 June 1964. On 17 June 1872, Johann Strauss the younger (1825–99) conducted an orchestra of 987 pieces supported by a choir of 20,000 at the World Peace Jubilee in Boston, Massachusetts, USA. The number of first violinists was 400.

THE WORLD'S BIGGEST OPERA HOUSE

The largest opera house in the world is the Metropolitan Opera House, Lincoln Center, New York City, NY, USA, completed in September 1966 at a cost of $45,700,000 (*then £16,320,000*). It has a capacity of 3800 seats in an auditorium 137 m *451 ft* deep. The stage is 71 m *234 ft* wide and 44,5 m *146 ft* deep. The tallest opera house is one housed in a 42-storey building on Wacker Drive in Chicago, Illinois, USA.

The largest functional organ in the world is the Grand Court in the Wanamaker Store in Philadelphia, USA. It has 30,000 pipes and a six-tiered keyboard.

THE GRANDEST PIANO
The grandest grand piano built was one of $1\frac{1}{4}$ tonnes/*tons* 3,55 m *11 ft 8 in* in length made by Chas H. Challen & Son Ltd of London in 1935. The longest bass string measured 3,02 m *9 ft 11 in* with a tensile strength of 30 tonnes/*tons*.

THE LARGEST DRUM
The largest drum ever constructed was one 3,65 m *12 ft* in diameter weighing 272 kg *600 lb* for the Boston World Peace Jubilee of 1872.

THE MOST EXPENSIVE PIANO
The highest price ever paid for a piano is $390,000 (*then £177,273*) at Sotheby Parke Bernet, New York City on 26 Mar 1980 for a Steinway grand of *c* 1888 sold by the Martin Beck Theatre and bought by a non-pianist.

THE MOST VALUABLE VIOLIN
The highest ever price paid at auction for a violin or any musical instrument is £396,000 for La Cathédrale Stradivari dated 1707 at Sotheby's, London on 22 Nov 1984. Some 700 of the 1116 violins by Stradivarius (1644–1737) have survived. His Alarol violin was confirmed by Jacques Francais to have been sold by private treaty by W. E. Hill for $1.2 million (*then £600,000*) to a Singaporean.

THE MOST VALUABLE CELLO
The highest ever auction price for a violoncello is £145,000 at Sotheby's London on 8 Nov 1978 for a Stradivari made in Cremona, Italy in 1710.

THE WETTEST WATER MUSIC
The pioneer violinist to surmount the problems of playing the violin underwater was Mark Gottlieb. Submerged in Evergreen State College swimming bath in Olympia, Washington, USA in March 1975 he gave a submarine rendition of Handel's Water Music. His most intractable problem was his underwater *détaché*. On 7 Oct 1979 the first underwater quartet performed in the *Challenge the Guinness* TV show on Channel 7 in Tokyo, Japan.

THE LONGEST SYMPHONY
The longest of all single classical symphonies is the orchestral symphony No. 3 in D minor by Gustav Mahler (1860–1911) of Austria. This work, composed in 1896, requires a contralto, a women's and boys' choir in addition to a full orchestra. A full performance requires 1 hr 40 min, of which the first movement alone takes between 30 and 36 min.

THE SHORTEST OPERA
The shortest opera published was *The Deliverance of Theseus* by Darius Milhaud (b. 4 Sept 1892) first performed in 1928 which lasts for 7 min 27 sec.

'The largest and presumably also the loudest playable guitar in the world is one 4,35 m *14 ft $3\frac{1}{4}$ in* tall, and 140 kg *309 lb* in weight, built by Joe Kovacic of Lado Musical Inc., Scarborough, Ontario, Canada. The most expensive standard sized guitar is the German chittara battente by Jacob Stadler, dated 1624, which was sold for £10,500 at Christie's, London on 12 June 1974.'

The highest price ever paid for a musical instrument. The violin known as 'La Cathedrale' made in 1707 by Stradivari sold for £396,000. *(Sotheby's London)*

The world's longest alphorn. Sound takes 70.6 milliseconds to travel from mouthpiece to bowl.

WORD RECORDS

Wa Chih-hui (1865–1953) who formulated in 1913, *zhùyīn fùhào*, the Northern Chinese world's most used alphabet of 37 letters. (*Below*) The earliest known writings of man – the 7000-year-old Chinese markings now decoded to mean the numbers 'five', 'seven', and 'eight'.

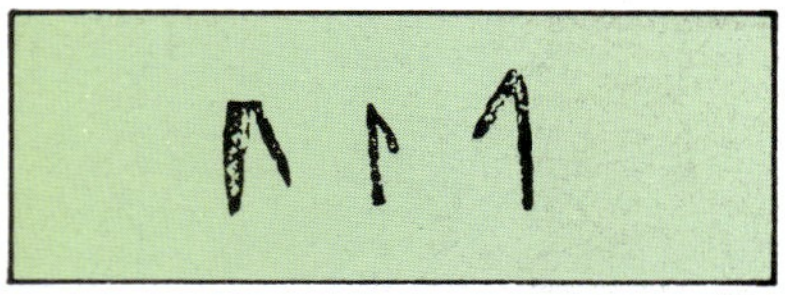

THE OLDEST WRITING

The written language with the longest continuous history is Chinese extending over more than 6000 years from the Yangshao culture to the present day.

THE OLDEST ENGLISH WORDS

It was first suggested in 1979 that languages ancestral to English and to Latvian (both Indo-European) split *c* 3500 BC. Research shortly to be published will indicate some words of a pre-Indo-European substrate survive in English – apple (apal), bad (bad), gold (gol) and tin (tin).

THE WORLD'S MOST POPULAR LANGUAGE

The language spoken by more people than any other is Northern Chinese, or Mandarin.

THE MOST COMPLICATED LANGUAGE

The following extremes of complexity have been noted: Chippewa, the North American Indian language of Minnesota, USA, has the most verb forms with up to 6000; Tillamook, the North American Indian language of Oregon, USA, has the most prefixes with 30; Tabassaran, a language in Daghestan, USSR, uses the most noun cases with 35, while Eskimo use 62 forms of the present tense and simple nouns have as many as 252 inflections. In Chinese the 40 volume *Chung-wén Tà Tz'u-tiĕn* dictionary lists 49,905 characters. *The Dictionary of Chinese Characters* in eight volumes will contain 20 million characters when completed in 1989. The written language provides 92 different characters of 'i^4'. The most complex written character in Chinese is that representing *xiè* consisting of 64 strokes meaning 'talkative'. The most complex in current use is *yù* with 32 strokes meaning to urge or implore.

THE RICHEST LANGUAGE

The English language contains about 490,000 words plus another 300,000 technical terms, the most in any language, but it is doubtful if any individual uses more than 60,000. Those in Great Britain who have undergone a full 16 years of education use perhaps 5000 words in speech and up to 10,000 words in written communications. The membership of the International Society for Philosophical Enquiry (no admission for IQs below 148) have an average vocabulary of 36,250 words.

THE LONGEST AND SHORTEST ALPHABETS

The language with most letters is Cambodian with 72 (including useless ones) and Rotokas in central Bougainville Island has least with 11 (just a, b, e, g, i, k, o, p, ř, t and u).

LARGEST LETTERS

The largest permanent letters in the world are the giant 183 m *600 ft* letters spelling READYMIX on the ground in the Nullarbor near East Balladonia, Western Australia. This was constructed in December 1971.

SMALLEST LETTERS

The 16 letters MOLECULAR DEVICES have been etched into a salt crystal by an electron beam so that the strokes were only 2 to 3 nm (10^{-9}) wide – the width of 20 hydrogen atoms. This was done by Michael Isaacson at Cornell University, Ithaca, NY, USA in Feb 1982.

The English language contains some 790,000 words (including technical terms) but it is doubtful if any individual uses more than 60,000.

THE WORLD'S GREATEST LINGUIST

The most multi-lingual living person in the world is Georges Henri Schmidt (b. Strasbourg, France, 28 Dec 1914), the Chief of the UN Terminology Section in 1965–71. The 1975 edition of *Who's Who in the United Nations*, listed 'only' 19 languages because he was then unable to find time to 'revive' his former fluency in 12 others. Powell Alexander Janulus (b. 1939) has worked with 41 languages in Provincial Court of British Columbia, Vancouver, Canada. Britain's greatest linguist is George Campbell (b. 9 Aug 1912), who is retired from the BBC Overseas Service where he *worked* with 54 languages.

George Campbell, Britain's greatest linguist who worked with 54 languages during his time with the BBC Overseas Service.

THE WORLD'S LONGEST WORD

Lengthy concatenations and some compound or agglutinative words or nonce words are or have been written in the closed up style of a single word, e.g. the 182 letter fricassee of 17 sweet and sour ingredients in Aristophanes' comedy *The Ecclesiazusae* in the 4th century BC. A compound 'word' of 195 Sanskrit characters (which transliterates into 428 letters in the Roman alphabet) describing the region near Kanci, Tamil Nadu, India appears in a 16th-century work by Tirumalāmbā, Queen of Vijayanagara.

THE LONGEST WORD IN ENGLISH

The longest word in the *Oxford English Dictionary* is floccipaucinihilipilification (alternatively spelt in hyphenated form with 'n' in seventh place), with 29 letters, meaning 'the action of estimating as worthless', first used in 1741, and later by Sir Walter Scott (1771–1832). *Webster's Third International Dictionary* lists among its 450,000 entries: pneumonoultramicroscopicsilicovolcanoconiosises (47 letters) the plural of a lung disease contracted by some miners.

COMMONEST ENGLISH WORDS AND LETTERS

In written English the most frequently used words are in order: the, of, and, to, a, in, that, is, I, it, for *and* as. The most used in conversation is I. The commonest letter is 'e' and the commonest initial letter is 'T'.

WORLD'S LONGEST WORDS

Japanese[1]	Chi-n-chi-ku-ri-n (12 letters) —a very short person (slang)
Spanish	Suberextraordinarịsimo (22 letters) —extraordinary
French	Anticonstitutionnellement (25 letters) —anticonstitutionally. Anthropoclimatologiquement[2] (26 letters) —anthropoclimatologically
Croatian	Prijestolonasljednikovica (25 letters) —wife of an heir apparent.
Italian	Precipitevolissimevolmente (26 letters) —as fast as possible.
Portuguese	inconstitucionalissimamente (27 letters) —with the highest degree of unconstitutionality.
Icelandic	Hæstaréttarmálaflutningsmaôur (29 letters) —supreme court barrister
Russian	ryentgyenoelyektrokardiografichyeskogo (33 Cyrillic letters, transliterating as 38) —of the radioelectrocardiographic.
Hungarian	Megszentségtelenithetetlenségeskedéseitekért (44 letters) —for your unprofaneable actions.
Turkish[5]	Cekoslovakyalilastiramadiklarimizdanmiymissiniz (47 letters) —'are you not of that group of persons that we were said to be unable to Czecholslovakianise?'
Dutch[5]	Kindercarnavalsoptochtvoorbereidingswerkzaamheden (49 letters) —preparation activities for a children's carnival procession
Mohawk[3]	tkanuhstasrihsranuhwe'tsraaksahsrakaratattsrayeri' (50 letters) —the praising of the evil of the liking of the finding of the house is right.
German[4,5]	Donaudampfschiffahrtselectrizitaetenhaupt betriebswerkbauunterbeamtengesellschaft (81 letters) —The club for subordinate officials of the head office management of the Danube steamboat electrical services (Name of a pre-war club in Vienna).
Swedish[5]	Spårvagnsaktiebolags skensmutsskjutarefack föreningspersonal beklädnadsmagasins förrådsförvaltaren (94 letters) —Manager of the depot for the supply of uniforms to the personel of the track cleaners' union of the tramway company.

[1] Patent applications sometimes harbour long compound 'words'. An extreme example is one of 13 kana which transliterates to the 40 letter Kyukitsûrohekimenfuchakunenryŏsekisanryŏ meaning 'the accumulated amount of fuel condensed on the wall face of the air intake passage'.

[2] Not accepted by *savants* to be an acceptable French word.

[3] Lengthy concatenations are a feature of Mohawk. Above is an example.

[4] The longest dictionary word in every day usage is Kraftfahrzeugreparaturwerkstätten (33 letters or 34 if the ä is written as ae) meaning motor vehicle repair shops (or service garages).

[5] Agglutinative words not found in standard dictionaries.

THE RECORD BOOK

"*Top selling.* It was announced on 13 Mar 1953 that 672,058,000 copies of the works of Generalissimo Stalin (born Yózef Vissarionovich Dzhugashvili) (1879–1953), had been sold or distributed in 101 languages. If true, the all-time best-selling author."

The late Agatha Christie (1890–1976) who was one of our top selling lady crime writers. *(Popperfoto)*

THE WORLD'S ALL-TIME BEST SELLER

Excluding versions of the Bible, the world's all-time best *selling* copyright book is the *Guinness Book of Records* first published from 107 Fleet Street, London EC4 in September 1955 by the Guinness Brewery to settle arguments in Britain's 81,400 pubs and edited by Norris Dewar McWhirter (b. 12 Aug 1925) and his twin brother Alan Ross McWhirter (k. 27 Nov 1975). Its cumulative sale in 26 languages to mid-1985 was in excess of 54 million copies and increasing by some 50,000 per week.

THE LARGEST BOOK IN THE WORLD

The largest book in the world is the *Super Book* measuring 2,74 × 3,07 m *9 ft × 10 ft $2\frac{1}{8}$ in* weighing 252,6 kg *557 lb* consisting of 300 pages published in Denver, Colorado, USA in 1976.

THE SMALLEST BOOK IN THE WORLD

The smallest marketed bound printed book with cursive material is one printed on 22 gsm paper measuring 1 × 1 mm *$\frac{1}{25}$ × $\frac{1}{25}$ in*, comprising the children's story *Old King Cole!* and published in 85 copies in March 1985 by The Gleniffer Press of Paisley, Scotland. The pages can only be turned (with care) by the use of a needle.

BEST-SELLING NOVELS

The novel with the highest sales has been *Valley of the Dolls* (first published March 1966) by Jacqueline Susann (Mrs Irving Mansfield) (1921–74) with a world-wide total of 27,465,000 to 1 May 1985. In the first 6 months Bantam sold 6.8 million. In the United Kingdom the highest print order has been 3,000,000 by Penguin Books Ltd, for their paperback edition of *Lady Chatterley's Lover*, by D. H. (David Herbert) Lawrence (1885–1930). The total sales to May 1986 were 4,685,000. Alistair Stuart MacLean (b. Scotland, April 1922) between 1955 and 1986 wrote 29 books of which the sales of 19 have exceeded a million copies and 13 have been filmed. *The Cruel Sea* by Nicholas Monsarrat (1910–79) published in 1951 by Cassell, reached sales of 1,200,000 in its *original* edition.

The most expensive work of art ever, *The Gospel Book of Henry the Lion, Duke of Saxony* which realised £8,140,000 on 6 Dec 1983 at Sotheby's, London.

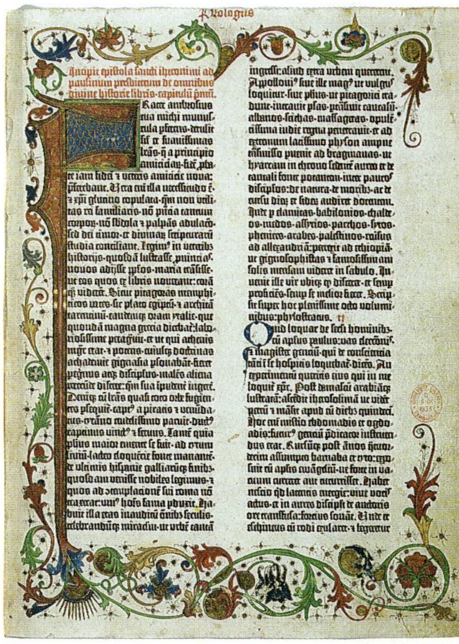

The Gutenburg Bible. Only 21 copies exist, and one was sold for $2,400,000 (then *£1,265,000*) in 1978, making it the most expensive book in history.

THE MOST EXPENSIVE BOOK OF ALL TIME

The highest price paid for any book or any work of art was £8,140,000 for the 226 leaf *The Gospel Book of Henry the Lion, Duke of Saxony* at Sotheby's, London on 6 Dec 1983. The book, 34,3 × 25,4 cm *13½ × 10 in*, was illuminated by the monk Herimann in *c* 1170 at Helmershansen Abbey with 41 full page illustrations, and was bought by Hans Kraus for the Hermann Abs consortium.

NOVEL-WRITING RECORD HOLDER

The greatest number of novels published by an authoress is 904 by Kathleen Lindsay (Mrs Mary Faulkner) (1903–73) of Somerset West, Cape Province, South Africa. She wrote under two other married names and 8 pen names. Baboorao Arnalkar (b. 9 June 1907) of Maharashtra State, India between 1936 and 1984 has published 1092 short mystery stories in book form and several non-fiction books.

After receiving a probable record 743 rejection slips the British novelist John Creasey, MBE (1908–73), under his own name and 25 *noms de plume* had 564 books totalling more than 40,000,000 words published from 1932 to his death on 9 June 1973. The British authoress with the greatest total of full-length titles is Miss Ursula Harvey Bloom (Mrs A. C. G. Robinson, formerly Mrs Denham-Cookes 1892–1984), who reached 560 in 1976, starting in 1924 with *The Great Beginning* and including the best sellers *The Ring Tree* (novel) and *The Rose of Norfolk* (non-fiction). Enid Mary Blyton (1898–1968) (Mrs Darrell Waters) completed 600 titles of children's stories, many of them brief, with 59 in the single year 1955. She was translated into a record 128 languages.

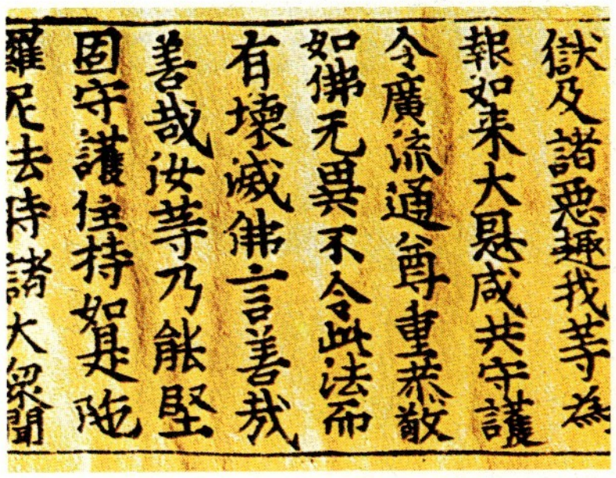

'The oldest surviving printed work – the Dharani Scroll from Korea dating from no later than AD 704. *(Sherwood Press, London)*'

BEST-PAID WRITER

In 1958 Mrs Deborah Schneider of Minneapolis, Minnesota, USA, wrote 25 words to complete a sentence in a competition for the best blurb for Plymouth cars. She won from about 1,400,000 entrants the prize of $500 (*then £178*) every month for life. On normal life expectations she would have collected $12,000 (*£4,285*) per word.

THE MOST REJECTED AUTHOR

The greatest recorded number of publisher's rejections for a manuscript is 223 for his 130,000 word manuscript *World Government Crusade* written in 1966 by Gilbert Young (b. 1906) of Bath, England. The record for rejections before publication (and wide acclaim) is 69 from 55 publishers by Prof. Steven Goldberg's *The Inevitability of Patriarchy*.

THE MOST OVERDUE LIBRARY BOOK

The most overdue book taken out by a known borrower was one reported on 7 Dec 1968, checked out in 1823 from the University of Cincinnati Medical Library on Febrile Diseases (London, 1805 by Dr J. Currie). This was returned by the borrower's great-grandson Richard Dodd. The fine calculated to be $2264 (*then £1102 10s*) was waived.

LARGEST ADVANCE PAYMENT

The greatest advances paid for any book is $5,000,000 (*then £3,430,000*) for *Whirlwind* by James Clavell at auction in New York City on 11 Jan 1986 to William Morrow & Co. and Avon Books.

Frederick Forsyth's *The Fourth Protocol* earned him over £3 million in advances against royalties.

RECORDS BY POST

'Baseball star Hank Aaron received 900,000 letters in one year. 300,000 of them were hate letters because he had broken 'Babe' Ruth's career record for 'home runs'.'

THE LONGEST LETTER EVER WRITTEN
The longest personal letter based on a word count is one of 1,402,344 started on 3 Jan 1982 by Alan Foreman of Erith, Kent, and posted to his wife Janet on 25 Jan 1984.

THE BRIEFEST CORRESPONDENCE
The shortest correspondence on record was that between Victor Marie Hugo (1802–85) and his publisher Hurst & Blackett in 1862. The author was on holiday and anxious to know how his new novel *Les Misérables* was selling. He wrote '?'. The reply was '!'.

THE WORLD'S MOST WRITTEN-TO PERSON
The highest confirmed mail received by any private citizen in a year is 900,000 letters by the baseball star Hank Aaron reported by the US Postal Department in June 1974. About a third were letters of hate engendered by his bettering of 'Babe' Ruth's career record for 'home runs' set in 1927.

PEN PALS *MOST DURABLE*
The longest sustained correspondence on record is one of 75 years from 11 Nov 1904 between Mrs Ida McDougall of Tasmania, Australia and Miss R. Norton of Sevenoaks, Kent until Mrs McDougall's death on 24 Dec 1979.

BIRTHDAY CARD – MOST PARSIMONIOUS
Mrs Amelia Finch (b. 18 Apr 1912) of Lakehurst, New Jersey, USA and Mr Paul E. Warburgh (b. 1 Feb 1902) of Huntington, New York have been exchanging the same card since 1 Feb 1927.

CHRISTMAS CARDS
The greatest number of personal Christmas cards sent out is believed to be 62,824 by Mrs Werner Erhard of San Francisco, California in December 1975. The earliest known Christmas card was sent out by Sir Henry Cole (1808–82) in 1843 but did not become an annual ritual until 1862.

THE MOST EXPENSIVE LETTER
The highest price ever paid on the open market for a single autograph letter signed is $100,000 (*then £45,000*), paid on 18 Oct 1979 at a Charles Hamilton auction in New York City for a brief receipt signed by the Gloucestershire-born Button Gwinnett (1732–77), one of the 56 signatories of the United States' Declaration of Independence of 1776.
The highest price paid for a signed autograph letter of a living person is $12,500 (*then £5430*) at the Hamilton Galleries on 22 Jan 1981 for a letter from President Ronald Reagan praising Frank Sinatra.

CHAPTER 7

TRANSPORT RECORDS

‘Kenneth Eriksson of Appelbo, Sweden exhibiting a fine sense of economy in his Opel Kadett which used only two tyres for nearly 20 km’ *12½ miles.*

SPEED RECORDS

THE FASTEST MAN

The fastest speed at which humans have travelled is 39 897 km/h *24,791 mph* when the Command Module of Apollo X carrying Col (*now* Brig. Gen.) Thomas Patten Stafford, USAF (b. Weatherford, Okla, 17 Sept 1930), and Cdr Eugene Andrew Cernan (b. Chicago, 14 Mar 1934) and Cdr (*now* Capt.) John Watts Young, USN (b. San Francisco, 24 Sept 1930), reached this maximum value at the 121,9 km *400,000 ft* altitude interface on its trans-Earth return flight on 26 May 1969.

THE FASTEST WOMAN

The highest speed ever attained by a woman is 28 115 km/h *17,470 mph* by Jnr Lt (now Lt-Col) Valentina Vladimirovna Tereshkova-Nikolayev (b. 6 Mar 1937) of the USSR in *Vostok 6* on 16 June 1963. The highest speed ever achieved by a woman aircraft pilot is 2687,42 km/h *1669.89 mph* by Svetlana Savitskaya (USSR) reported on 2 June 1975.

OFFICIAL AIR SPEED RECORD

The official air speed record is 3529,56 km/h *2193.167 mph* by Capt. Eldon W. Joersz and Maj. George T. Morgan, Jr, in a Lockheed SR-71A near Beale Air Force Base, California, USA over a 15 to 25 km course on 28 July 1976.

Richard Noble (GB) alongside his Rolls Royce Avon Jet *Thrust 2* – official holder of the world land speed record since October 1983. (*Chris Marks*)

PROGRESSIVE SPEED RECORDS

Speed Km/h	mph	Person and Vehicle	Place	Date
40	*25*	Sledging	Heinola, Finland	*c.* 6500 BC
55	*35*	Horse-riding	Anatolia, Turkey	*c.* 1400 BC
70	*45*	Mountain Sledging	Island of Hawaii (now USA)	*ante* AD 1500
80	*50*	Ice Yachts (earliest patent)	Netherlands	AD 1600
95	*56.75*	Grand Junction Railway 2–2–2: *Lucifer*	Madeley Banks, Staffs, England	13 Nov 1830
141,3	*87.8*	Tommy Todd, downhill skier	La Porte, California, USA	Mar 1873
144,8	*90*	Midland Railway 4–2–2 2,36 m *7 ft 9 in* single	Ampthill, Bedford, England	Mar 1897
210,2	*130.61*	Siemens and Halske electric engine	Marienfeld-Zossen, near Berlin	27 Oct 1903
c. 257,5	*c. 150*	Frederick H. Marriott (fl. 1957) Stanley Steamer *Wogglebug*	Ormond Beach, Florida, USA	26 Jan 1907
339	*210.64*	Sadi Lecointe (France) Nieuport-Delage 29	Villesauvage, France	25 Sept 1921
668,2	*415.2*	Flt Lt (Later Wing Cdr) George Hedley Stainforth AFC *Supermarine S.6B*	Lee-on-Solent, England	29 Sept 1931
1004	*623.85*	Flugkapitan Heinz Dittmar *Me. 163V–1*	Peenemunde, Germany	2 Oct 1941
1078	*670*	Capt Charles Elwood Yeager, USAF *Bell XS-1*	Muroc Dry Lake, California, USA	14 Oct 1947
1556	*967*	Capt Charles Elwood Yeager, USAF *Bell XS-1*	Muroc Dry Lake, California, USA	26 Mar 1948
4675,1	*2905*	Major Robert M. White, North American *X-15*	Muroc Dry Lake, California, USA	7 Mar 1961
c. 28 260	*c. 17,560*	Flt Maj Yuriy Alekseyevich Gagarin, *Vostok 1*	Earth orbit	12 Apr 1961
38 988	*24,226*	Col Frank Borman, USAF, Capt James Arthur Lovell, Jr, USN, Major William A. Anders, USAF *Apollo VIII*	Trans-lunar injection	21 Dec 1968
39 897	*24,790.8*	Cdrs Eugene Andrew Cernan and John Watts Young, USN and Col Thomas P. Stafford, USAF *Apollo X*	Re-entry after lunar orbit	26 May 1969

LAND SPEED *MAN*
The highest reputed speed on land is 1190,377 km/h *739.666 mph* or Mach 1.0106 by Stan Barrett (US) in *The Budweiser Rocket*, a rocket-engined 3-wheeled car at Edwards Air Force Base, California on 17 Dec 1979.

The *official* one mile land speed record is 1019,467 km/h *633.468 mph* set by Richard Noble, OBE (b. 1946) on 4 Oct 1983 over the Black Rock Desert, north Nevada, USA in his 17,000 lb thrust Rolls Royce Avon 302 jet powered *Thrust 2*, designed by John Ackroyd.

LAND SPEED *WOMEN*
The highest land speed recorded by a woman is 843,323 km/h *524.016 mph* by Mrs Kitty Hambleton *née* O'Neil (US) in the 48,000 hp rocket-powered 3-wheeled S.M.1 *Motivator* over the Alvard Desert, Oregon, USA on 6 Dec 1976. Her official two-way record was 825 126 km/h *512.710 mph* and she probably touched 965 km/h *600 mph* momentarily.

WATER SPEED *MAN*
The highest speed ever achieved on water is an estimated 300 knots (556 km/h *345 mph*) by Kenneth Peter Warby, MBE, (b. 9 May 1939) on the Blowering Dam Lake, NSW, Australia on 20 Nov 1977 in his unlimited hydroplane *Spirit of Australia*. The official world water speed record is 277.57 knots (514,389 km/h *319.627 mph*) set on 8 Oct 1978 by Warby on Blowering Dam Lake.

WATER SPEED *WOMAN*
The fastest woman on water is Mary Rife (USA), who has driven her drag boat *Proud Mary* at more than 305 km/h *190 mph*.

WATER SPEED *PROPELLER DRIVEN*
The highest officially recorded speed for propeller-driven craft is 368,54 km/h *229 mph* by Eddie Hill in his supercharged hydroplane *The Texan* at Chowchilla, California, USA.

Sir Malcolm Campbell's *Bluebird* which first bettered 482 km/h *300 mph* in 1935 at Bonneville Salt Flats, Utah, USA.

The late Gary Gabelich's *Blue Flame* which first exceeded 1000 km/h *621.37 mph* in 1970 at Bonneville.

The first penetration of the sound barrier by a wheeled vehicle – the *Budweiser Rocket* an unofficial 1190 km/h *739 mph* at Edwards Air Base, California in 1979.

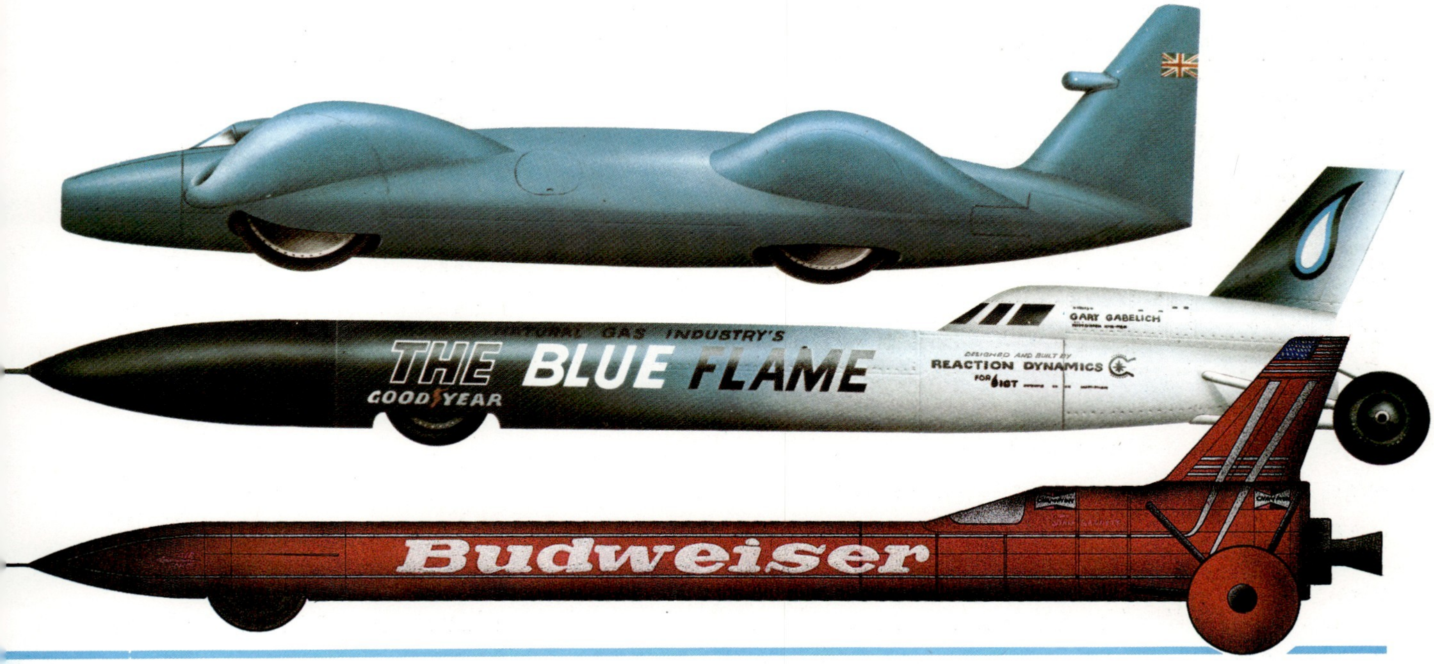

FOUR-WHEEL WONDERS

FASTEST CARS

CATEGORY	KM/H	*MPH*	CAR	DRIVER	PLACE	DATE
Jet Engined (*official*)	1019,4	*633.468*	Thrust 2	Richard Noble (GB)	Black Rock Desert, Nevada, USA	4 Oct 1983
Rocket Engined (*official*)	1001,473	*622.287*	Blue Flame	Gary Gabelich (US)	Bonneville, Utah, USA	23 Oct 1970
Wheel Driven (*turbine*)	690,909	*429.311*	Bluebird	Donald Campbell (UK)	Lake Eyre, Australia	17 July 1964
Wheel Driven (*multi piston engines*)	673,516	*418.504*	Goldenrod	Robert Summers (US)	Bonneville, Utah, USA	12 Nov 1965
Wheel Driven (*single piston engine*)	575,149	*357.391*	Herda-Knapp-Milodon	Bob Herda	Bonneville, Utah, USA	2 Nov 1967
Rocket Engined (*unofficial*)*	1190,377	*739.666*	Budweiser Rocket	Stan Barrett (US)	Edwards Air Force Base, California, USA	17 Dec 1979

*This published speed of Mach 1.0106 is *not* officially sanctioned by the USAF whose Digital Instrumented Radar was not calibrated or certified. The radar information was *not* generated by the vehicle directly but by an operator aiming the dish by means of a TV screen. A claim to 6 significant figures appears unjustifiable.

FAST CARS *ROAD CARS*

Various detuned track cars have been licensed for road use but are not purchasable production models. Manufacturers of very fast and very expensive models understandably limit speed tests to stipulated engine revs. The fastest current manufacturer's *claim* (as opposed to independently road-tested) for any road cars is the Vector W2A custom order car from Vector Cars, Venice, California with a 'terminal velocity' in excess of 321,8 kmh *200 mph*. The claimed speed at 7000 rpm by the 1984 Ferrari 308 GTO is 304,9 kmh *189.5 mph*. Aston Martin announced on 1 Mar 1985 the production of 50 Vantage-Zagatos with 432 bhp engines and a speed of 300 kmh *186.4 mph* costing £87,000. The highest ever *tested* speed is 289,5 kmh *179.9 mph* for the Lamborghini Countach LP 500 S in March 1984. The car was kept out of the 'red sector' i.e. at below 7000 rpm. The highest road-tested acceleration reported is 0–96,5 kmh *0–60 mph* in 4.1 sec for an MG Metro 6R4 International Rally Car in 1986.

DIESEL ENGINED

The prototype 230 hp *3 litre* Mercedes C 111/3 attained 327,3 kmh *203.3 mph* in tests on the Nardo Circuit, Southern Italy on 5–15 Oct 1978, and in April 1978 averaged 314,462 kmh *195.398 mph* for 12 hours, so covering a world record 3773,55 km *2399.76 miles*.

ROCKET POWERED SLEDS

The highest speed recorded on ice is 399,00 kmh *247.93 mph* by *Oxygen* driven by Sammy Miller (b.15 Apr 1945) on Lake George, NY, USA on 15 Feb 1981.

'The world's longest car – the 10-wheeled Ultra Limo Fifty Footer built in 1985 by Vini Bergeman and Kraig Kavanagh of Ultra Limo, La Palma, California USA. There is a 3,65 m *12 ft* swimming bath at one end. *(Franklin Berger)*'

ONE OWNER, LOW MILEAGE

The highest recorded mileage for a car was 1 906 879 authenticated kilometres *1,184,880 miles* by August 1978 for a 1957 Mercedes 180 D owned by Robert O'Reilly of Olympia, Washington State, USA. Its subsequent fate is unknown. R. L. Bender of Madison, Wisconsin claimed 1 643 206 km *1,021,041 miles* for his car on 9 June 1984.

MORE MILES TO THE GALLON

The greatest distance driven without refuelling on a tank full of fuel (88,12 l *19.41 galls*) is 1851,2 km *1150.3 miles* by an Audi 100 turbo diesel driven by Stuart Bladon with his son Bruce (navigator) and Bob Proctor (RAC observer) from Land's End to John O'Groats and back to West Falkirk in 22 hrs 28 min in July 1984. The average speed was 82,33 km/h *51.17 mph* giving 4.77 l/100 km *59.27 mpg*.

129.9 MILES ON TWO WHEELS

The longest recorded distance for driving on 2 wheels is 209,2 km *129.9 miles* in an Opel Kadett by Michael Signoret at the Paul Ricard circuit in Provence, France on 14 Mar 1985.

'The lowest car on the road, Andy Saunder's 86,4 cm *34 inch* high custom-made Mini.'

'Jay Ohrberg's 16-wheeled 'American Dream', the ultimate in long limousines at 18,3 m *60 ft*. One of the many luxurious features is the hot tub. Others include a swimming pool, helipad, satellite dish and a crystal chandelier.'

FOUR-WHEEL WONDERS

3340 MILES BACKWARDS WITHOUT STOPPING

Charles Creighton (1908–70) and James Hargis of Maplewood, Missouri, USA, drove their Ford Model A 1929 roadster in reverse from New York City 5375 km *3340 miles* to Los Angeles, California on 26 July–13 Aug 1930 without once stopping the engine. They arrived back in New York in reverse on 5 Sept so completing the 11 555 km *7180 miles* in 42 days. The highest average speed attained in any non-stop reverse drive exceeding 800 km *500 miles* was achieved by Gerald Hoagland who drove a 1969 Chevrolet Impala 806,2 km *501 miles* in 17 hr 38 min at Chemung Speed Drome, New York, USA on 9–10 July 1976 to average 45,72 kmh *28.41 mph*.

WORLD'S OLDEST DRIVER

Roy M. Rawlins (b. 10 July 1870) of Stockton, California, USA, was warned for driving at 152 kmh *95 mph* in a 88,5 kmh *55 mph* zone in June 1974. On 25 Aug 1974 he was awarded a California State licence valid until 1978 by Mr John Burrafato, but Mr Rawlins died on 9 July 1975, one day short of his 105th birthday.

THE LONGEST TOW

The longest tow on record was one of 7658 km *4759 miles* from Halifax, Nova Scotia to Canada's Pacific Coast, when Frank J. Elliott and George A. Scott of Amherst, Nova Scotia, persuaded 168 passing motorists in 89 days to tow their Model T Ford (in fact engineless) to win a $1000 bet on 15 Oct 1927.

‘The longest load transported in the UK was this gas storage vessel completing its 0,8 km ½ *mile* journey on 10 July 1985.’

‘The car and instructor Rick Chattaway, responsible for the fastest driving test failure. At 1 second and 18 inches – this unenviable record was set in the Australian town of Modbury, Adelaide on 19 Nov 1984.’

‘On 19 Aug 1985 Robert E. Barber broke the 79-year-old record for a steam car driving No 744 *‘Steamin' Demon*, built by the Barber-Nichols Engineering Co, 234,33 kmh *145.607 mph* at Bonneville Salt Flats, Utah, USA.’

TWO-WHEEL WONDERS

LONGEST TANDEM
The longest true tandem bicycle ever built (i.e. without a third stabilizing wheel) is one of 20,40 m *66 ft 11 in* for 35 riders built by the Pedaalstompers Westmalle of Belgium. They rode *c* 60 m *195 ft* in practice on 20 Apr 1979. The machine weighs 1100 kg *2425 lb.*

UNDERWATER CYCLING RECORD
Thirty-two certified Scuba divers in 60 hours on 27–29 Nov 1981 rode a submarine tricycle 104,54 km *64.96 miles* on the bottom of Amphi High School pool, Tucson, Arizona, USA, in a scheme devised by Lucian Spataro to raise money for the Casa De Los Ninos Nursery.

UNICYCLE RECORDS
The tallest unicycle ever mastered is one 31,01 m *101 ft 9 in* tall ridden by Steve McPeak (with a safety wire or mechanic suspended to an overhead crane) for a distance of 114,6 m *376 ft* in Las Vegas in October 1980. The freestyle riding of ever taller unicycles (that is without any safety harness) must inevitably lead to serious injury or fatality. Deepak Lele of Maharashtra, India unicycled 6378 km *3963 miles* from New York to Los Angeles on 6 June to 25 Sept 1984. Brian Davis, 33 of Tillicoultry, Clackmannan, Scotland rode 1450 km *901 miles* from Land's End to John O'Groats on 16 May to 4 June 1980 in 19 days 1 hr 45 min. Takayuki Koike of Kanagawa, Japan set a record for 160,9 km *100 miles* in 7 hr 49 min 12 sec on 16 Sept 1985. The sprint record from a standing start over 100 metres is 14.89 sec by Floyd Grandall of Pontiac, Michigan, USA, in Tokyo, Japan on 24 Mar 1980.

'WHEELIE' RECORDS
Doug Domokos on the Alabama International Speedway, Talladega, USA on 27 June 1984 covered 233,34 km *145 miles* non-stop on the rear wheel of his Honda XR 500. He stopped only when the gas ran out. The first recorded case of bettering 160,9 km/h *100 mph* on one wheel was by Ottis Lance at Penwell Raceway Park, Texas, USA on 21 May 1983 with 180,2 km/h *112 mph* over 402 m *440 yds* on a Suzuki GS-1000.

TWO WHEEL DRIVING
The longest recorded distance for driving a car on 2 wheels is 209,2 km *129.9 miles* in an Opel Kadett by Michael Signoret at the Paul Ricard circuit in Provence, France on 14 Mar 1985.

FASTEST MOTORBIKES
Road machine The 115 bhp Japanese Honda V65 Magna with a liquid-cooled, in-line V-4, 16 valve DoHC engine of 1098 cc capacity has a design speed of 278,4 km/h *173 mph.*
Racing machine There is no satisfactory answer to the identity of the fastest track machine other than to say that the current Kawasaki, Suzuki and Yamaha machines have all been geared to attain speeds marginally in excess of 300 km/h *186.4 mph* under race conditions.

MOTORBIKE ENDURANCE RECORD
The longest time a solo motorcycle has been kept in nonstop motion is 500 hr by Owen Fitzgerald, Richard Kennett and Don Mitchell who covered 13 570 km *8432 miles* in Western Australia on 10–31 July 1977.

'The two-seater double-decker tandem built by Kesaichiro Tagawa, Osaka, Japan. It measures 5 m *16.4 ft* in length and is 3,4 m *11.1 ft* to the upper storey handlebars.'

'The world's smallest wheeled rideable bicycle is one with 3,5 cm *1.37 in* wheels weighing 700 g *24.6 oz* built and ridden by Jacques Puyoou of Pau, Pyrénées-Atlantiques, France in 1983. He has also built a tandem 36 cm *14.1 in* long to accommodate Madame Puyoou.'

AIR RECORDS

'Fred Finn evidently believes in travelling in the best of British – in the sky or on the road. As a supersonic passenger he has no peers having just recorded his 604th *Concorde* flight.'

'The largest landplane ever to fly, the Lockheed C-5A Galaxy has a take-off weight of over 340 tons. *(K. J. A. Brookes)*'

'*Quickest Paris–London.* The fastest time to travel the 344 km *214 miles* from central Paris to central London (BBC TV centre) is 38 min 58 sec by David Boyce on 24 Sept 1983 by motorcycle–helicopter to Le Bourget; Hawker Hunter jet (pilot Michael Carlton) to Biggin Hill, Kent; helicopter to the TV centre car park.'

FASTEST AIRCRAFT IN THE WORLD

The fastest fixed-wing aircraft in the world was the US North American Aviation X-15A-2, which flew for the first time (after modification from X-15A) on 25 June 1964 powered by a liquid oxygen and ammonia rocket propulsion system. Ablative materials on the airframe once enabled a temperature of 3000 °F to be withstood. The landing speed was 210 knots (389,1 km/h *242 mph*) momentarily. The highest speed attained was 7274 km/h *4520 mph* (Mach 6.7) when piloted by Maj William J. Knight, USAF (b. 1930), on 3 Oct 1967.

QUICKEST LONDON–NEW YORK

The record for central London to downtown New York City by helicopter and Concorde is 3 hr 59 min 44 sec and the return in 3 hr 40 min 40 sec both by David J. Springbett, 1981 Salesman of the Year, and David Boyce of Stewart Wrightson (Aviation) Ltd on 8 and 9 Feb 1982.

WORLD'S FASTEST AIRLINER

The supersonic BAC/Aerospatiale *Concorde*, first flown on 2 Mar 1969, with a capacity of 128 passengers, cruises at up to Mach 2.2 (*2333 km/h* 1450 mph). It flew at Mach 1.05 on 10 Oct 1969, exceeded Mach 2 for the first time on 4 Nov 1970 and became the first supersonic airliner used on passenger services on 21 Jan 1976 when Air France and British Airways opened services simultaneously between, respectively, Paris–Rio de Janeiro and London–Bahrain. Services between London and New York and Paris and New York began on 22 Nov 1977. The New York–London record is 2 hr 56 min 35 sec set on 1 Jan 1983.

LARGEST WING-SPAN EVER

The aircraft with the largest wing span ever constructed is the $40 million Hughes H.4 *Hercules* flying-boat ('Spruce Goose'), which was raised 21,3 m *70 ft* into the air in a test run of 914 m *1000 yd*, piloted by Howard Hughes (1905–76), off Long Beach Harbor, California, USA, on 2 Nov 1947. The eight-engined 193 tonnes *190 ton* aircraft had a wing span of 97,51 m *319 ft 11 in* and a length of 66,64 m *218 ft 8 in* and never flew again. In a brilliant engineering feat she was moved bodily by Goldcoast Corp aided by the US Navy barge crane YD-171 on 22 Feb 1982 to her final resting place 9,6 km *6 miles* across the harbour under a 213,4 m *700 ft* diameter dome.

(*Left*) 'The Battle of the "B's"'. Donald R. Stits' *Baby Bird* with a length of 3,35 m *11 ft* and a wing span of 1,91 m *6 ft 3 in* vying for the title 'Smallest Plane' with Robert H. Starr's *Bumble Bee*, (*below*), length 2,84 m *9 ft 4 in* – wing span 1,98 m *6 ft 6 in*.

Wing Commander Kenneth H. Wallis in his WA-116F autogyro in which he broke the straight-line distance record of 874,32 km *543.27 miles*. *(K. J. A. Brookes)*

WORLD ALTITUDE RECORD

The official world altitude record by an aircraft taking off from the ground under its own power is 123,524 ft (37 650 m *23.39 miles*) by Aleksandr Fedotov (USSR) in a Mikoyan E.266M, (MiG-25) aircraft, powered by two 14 000 kg *30,865 lb* thrust turbojet engines, on 31 Aug 1977.

LONGEST SCHEDULED FLIGHT

The longest distance scheduled non-stop flight is the weekly Pan-Am Sydney–San Francisco non-stop 13 hr 25 min Flight 816, in a Boeing 747 SP, opened in December 1976, over 12 030 km *7475 statute miles*. The longest delivery flight by a commercial jet is 16 560 km *8936 nautical miles* or *10,290 statute miles* from Seattle, Washington, USA to Cape Town, South Africa by the South African Airway's Boeing 747 SP (Special performance) 'Matroosberg' with 178 400 kg *175.5 tons* of pre-cooled fuel in 17 hr 22½ min on 23–24 Mar 1976.

The world's largest helicopter – the Soviet Union's Mil Mi-12, weighing over 100 tons it has lifted a payload of over 39¼ tons to a height of almost 2400 m *8000 ft*. *(K. J. A. Brookes)*

AIR RECORDS

'The flight duration record for a paper aircraft is 16.89 sec by Ken Blackburn at N. Carolina State University, USA on 29 November 1983.'

SMALLEST AEROPLANE EVER BUILT

The smallest aeroplane ever flown is the 'Baby Bird', designed and built by Donald R. Stits. It is 3,35 m *11 ft* long, with a wing span of 1,91 m *6 ft 3 in* and weighs 114,3 kg *252 lb* empty. It is powered by a 55 hp 2 cylinder Hirth engine, giving a top speed of 177 km/h *110 mph.* It was first flown on 4 Aug 1984 at Camarillo, California. The smallest jet is the 450 km/h *280 mph Silver Bullet* weighing 196 kg *432 lb* with a 5.18 m *17 ft* wing span built by Bob Bishop (USA).

WORLD'S LARGEST AIRLINER

The highest capacity jet airliner is the Boeing 747 'Jumbo Jet', first flown on 9 Feb 1969 and has a capacity of from 385 to more than 500 passengers with a maximum speed of 969 km/h *602 mph.* Its wing span is 59,64 m *195.7 ft* and its length 70,7 m *231.8 ft.* It entered service on 22 Jan 1970. The Boeing 747-300 with a lengthened upper deck, which allows an extra 37 passengers, entered service in March 1983.

SHORTEST SCHEDULED FLIGHT

The shortest scheduled flight in the world is that by Loganair between the Orkney Islands of Westray and Papa Westray which has been flown with Britten-Norman Islander twin-engined 10-seat transports since September 1967. Though scheduled for 2 min, in favourable wind conditions it has been accomplished in 58 sec by Capt Andrew D. Alsop.

BUSIEST AIRPORT IN THE WORLD

The world's busiest airport is the Chicago International Airport, O'Hare Field, Illinois, USA with a total of 746,376 movements and 49,954,362 passengers in the year 1985. This represents a take-off or landing every 42.25 sec round the clock. Heathrow Airport, London handles more *international* traffic than any other. The busiest landing area ever has been Bien Hoa Air Base, south Vietnam, which handled more than 1,000,000 take-offs and landings in 1970. The world's largest 'helipad' was An Khe, south Vietnam.

Spruce Goose, Howard Hughes H.4 *Hercules*, the flying boat with the largest wing span ever constructed.

RAIL RECORDS

The LNER 4–6–2 *Mallard* which in 1938 set a world record for a steam engine with 201 km/h *125 mph*. (*Pat Gibbon*)

FASTEST TRAIN EVER
The world's fastest rail speed with passengers is 517 km/h *321.2 mph* by a Maglev (magnetic levitation) test train over the 7 km *4.3 mile* long JNR experimental track at Miyazaki, Japan in December 1979. The highest speed recorded on any national rail system is 380 km/h *236 mph* by the French SNCF high speed train TGV-PSE on trial near Tonnerre on 26 Feb 1981. The TGV (Train à Grande Vitesse) inaugurated on 27 Sept 1981 by Sept 1983 reduced its scheduled time for the Paris–Lyon run of 425 km *264 miles* to 2 hr exactly, so averaging 212,5 km/h *132 mph*. The peak speed attained is 270 km/h *168 mph*.

'The longest train ever was a 500 wagon, four mile long, coal train which weighed 42,000 tons.'

FASTEST STEAM TRAIN
The highest speed ever ratified for a steam locomotive was 201 km/h *125 mph* over 402 m *440 yd* by the LNER 4–6–2 No. 4468 *Mallard* (later numbered 60022), which hauled seven coaches weighing 243 tonnes *240 tons* gross, down Stoke Bank, near Essendine, between Grantham, Lincolnshire, and Peterborough, Cambridgeshire, on 3 July 1938. Driver Joseph Duddington was at the controls with Fireman Thomas Bray. The engine suffered some damage. On 12 June 1905 a speed of 204,48 km/h *127.06 mph* was claimed for the 'Pennsylvania Special' near Elida, Ohio, USA but has never been accepted by leading experts.

LONGEST TRAM JOURNEY
The longest tramway journey now possible is from Krefeld St Tönis to Witten Annen Nord, W. Germany. With luck at the 8 interconnections the 105,5 km *65.5 mile* trip can be achieved in 5½ hr. By late 1977 there were still some 315 tramway systems surviving of which the longest is that of Leningrad, USSR with 2500 cars on 53 routes. The last in Britain is at Blackpool, Lancashire.

WORLD'S STEEPEST TRACK
The world's steepest standard gauge gradient by adhesion is 1:11 between Chedde and Servoz on the metre gauge SNCF Chamonix line, France.

WORLD'S LONGEST LINE
The world's longest run is one of 9438 km *5864½ miles* on the Trans Siberian line from Moscow to Nakhodka, USSR, in the Soviet Far East. There are 97 stops in the journey which takes 8 days 4 hr 25 min. The Baykal-Amur northern main line (BAM), begun with forced labour in 1938, was scheduled for completion on 24 Oct 1984. A total of 283 million m^3 *10,000 million* ft^3 of earth had to be moved and 1987 bridges built in this £8000 million project.

LARGEST STATION
The world's largest railway station is Grand Central Terminal, Park Avenue and 43rd Street, New York City, NY, USA, built 1903–13. It covers 19 ha *48 acres* on two levels with 41 tracks on the upper level and 26 on the lower. On average more than 550 trains and 180,000 people per day use it, with a peak of 252,288 on 3 July 1947.

The TGV (*Train à Grande Vitesse*) inaugurated on 27 Sept 1981, reduced its scheduled time in Sept 1983 for the Paris–Lyon run to 2 hr exactly. The peak speed attained was 270 km/h *168 mph*.

SEA-GOING RECORDS

The largest sailing vessel ever built was the *France II* (5806 gross tons), launched at Bordeaux in 1911. The *France II* was a steel-hulled, five-masted barque (square-rigged on four masts and fore and aft rigged on the aftermost mast). Her hull measured 127,4 m *418 ft* overall. Although principally designed as a sailing vessel with a stump topgallant rig, she was also fitted with two steam engines. She was wrecked off New Caledonia on 13 July 1922. The only seven-masted sailing schooner ever built was the 114,4 m *375.6 ft* long *Thomas W. Lawson* (5218 gross tons) built at Quincy, Massachusetts, USA in 1902 and lost in the English Channel on 15 Dec 1907.

LARGEST EVER WRECK

The largest ship ever wrecked has been the 312,186 dwt VLCC (Very Large Crude Carrier) *Energy Determination* which blew up and broke in two in the Straits of Hormuz on 12 Dec 1979. Her full value was $58 million (*then £26.3 million*).

MOST COLOSSAL COLLISION

The closest approach to an irresistible force striking an immovable object occurred on 16 Dec 1977, 35 km *22 miles* off the coast of Southern Africa when the tanker *Venoil* (330,954 dwt) struck her sister ship *Venpet* (330,869 dwt).

RECORD SIZE AIRCRAFT CARRIER

The warships with the largest full load displacement in the world are the US Navy aircraft carriers *Dwight D. Eisenhower, Theodore Roosevelt* and *Carl Vinson* at 91,487 tons. They are 322,9 m *1092 ft* in length overall with 1,82 ha *$4\frac{1}{2}$ acres* of flight deck and have a speed well in excess of 56 km/h *30 knots* from their 4 nuclear-powered 260,000 shp reactors. They have to be refuelled after about 1 450 000 km *900,000 miles* steaming. Their complement is 6300. The total cost of the *Abraham Lincoln*, laid down at Newport News in Dec 1984 will exceed $$3\frac{1}{4}$ billion (*£2.6 billion*), excluding the 90-plus aircraft carried. USS *Enterprise* is, however, 335,8 m *1102 ft* long and thus still the longest warship ever built.

THE SUPER SUB

The world's largest submarines are of the USSR Typhoon class code named Oscar. The launch of the first at the secret covered shipyard at Severodvinsk in the White Sea was announced by NATO on 23 Sept 1980. It is believed to have a dived displacement of 30,000 tonnes, measure *c* 170 m *557.6 ft* overall and is armed with twenty SS NX 20 missiles with a 10 050 km *6250 miles* range, each with 7 warheads. By 1987 two others building in Leningrad will also be operational, each deploying 140 warheads.

RECORD JUNK

The largest junk on record was the sea-going *Cheng Ho*, flagship of Admiral Cheng Ho's 62 treasure ships, of *c* 1420, with a displacement of 3150 tonnes *3100 tons* and a length variously estimated up to 164 m *538 ft* and believed to have had 9 masts.

BIGGEST SAILING SHIP EVER

The largest sailing vessel ever built was the *France II* (5806 gross tons), launched at Bordeaux in 1911. The *France II* was a steel-hulled, five-masted barque (square-rigged on four masts and fore and aft rigged on the aftermost mast). Her hull measured 127,4 m *418 ft* overall. Although principally designed as a sailing vessel with a stump topgallant rig, she was also fitted with two steam engines. She was wrecked off New Caledonia on 13 July 1922.

'The largest tanker ever built – the giant 564,763 ton tanker *Seawise Giant* completed in 1981. She measures more than quarter of a mile in length.'

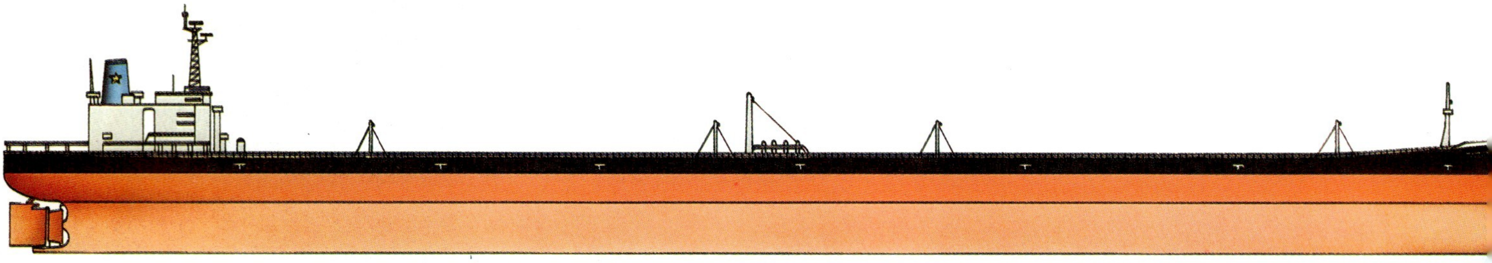

The world's largest ship's propeller is the triple-bladed screw of 11 m *36 ft 1 in* in diameter made by Kawasaki Heavy Industries Ltd on 17 Mar 1982 for the 208,000 ton bulk carrier *Hoei Maru*.

ALL-TIME LARGEST LINER

The RMS *Queen Elizabeth* (finally 82,998 but formerly 83,673 gross tons), of the Cunard fleet, was the largest passenger vessel ever built and had the largest displacement of any liner in the world. She had an overall length of 314 m *1031 ft* and was 36 m *118 ft 7 in* in breadth and was powered by steam turbines which developed 168,000 hp. Her last passenger voyage ended on 15 Nov 1968. In 1970 she was removed to Hong Kong to serve as a floating marine university and renamed *Seawise University*. On 9 Jan 1972 she was fired by 3 simultaneous outbreaks. Most of the gutted hull had been cut up and removed by December 1978. *Seawise* was a pun on the owner's initials – C. Y. Tung (1911–1982).

FASTEST LINER ATLANTIC CROSSING

The fastest Atlantic crossing was made by the *United States* (then 51,988, now 38,216 gross tons), former flagship of the United States Lines. On her maiden voyage between 3 and 7 July 1952 from New York City, to Le Havre, France, and Southampton, England, she averaged 35.59 knots, or 65,95 km/h *40.98 mph* for 3 days 10 hr 40 min (6.36 p.m. GMT, 3 July to 5.16 a.m., 7 July) on a route of 5465 km *2949 nautical miles* from the Ambrose Light Vessel to the Bishop Rock Light, Isles of Scilly, Cornwall. During this run, on 6–7 July 1952, she steamed the greatest distance ever covered by any ship in a day's run (24 hr) – 1609 km *868 nautical miles*, hence averaging 36.17 knots (67,02 km/h *41.65 mph*). The maximum speed attained from her 240,000 shp engines was 38.32 knots (71,01 km/h *44.12 mph*) on trials on 9–10 June 1952.

With 2500 passengers and 600 cars the M/S *Olympia* has in 1986 become the world's largest car ferry.

WORLD'S BIGGEST EVER BATTLESHIP

The Japanese battleship *Yamato* (completed on 16 Dec 1941 and sunk south-west of Kyūshū, Japan, by US planes on 7 Apr 1945) and *Musashi* (sunk in the Philippine Sea by 11 bombs and 16 torpedoes on 24 Oct 1944) were the largest battleships ever commissioned, each with a full load displacement of 73 977 tonnes *72,809 tons*. With an overall length of 263 m *863 ft*, a beam of 38,7 m *127 ft* and a full load draught of 10,8 m *35½ ft* they mounted nine 460 mm *18.1 in* guns in three triple turrets. Each gun weighed 164,6 tonnes *162 tons* and was 22,8 m *75 ft* in length firing a 1451 kg *3200 lb* projectile.

The largest battleship in service in the world is the 270,6 m *887 ft 9 in* long USS *New Jersey* with a full load displacement of 58 000 tonnes *58,000 tons*.

On 16 Dec 1977, 22 miles off South Africa the oil-tanker *Venoil* (330,954 dwt) collided with her sister ship *Venpet* (330,869 dwt) – the world's most heavyweight marine collision.

SPACE FLIGHT RECORDS

Youngest. **Col Gherman S. Titov (25 yrs 329 days) *Vostok 2* 6 Aug 1961.**

Longest on Moon. **Capt Eugene A. Cernan (USN) (b. 14 Mar 1934) (USA), Dr Harrison H. Schmitt (b. 3 July 1935) (USA) 74 hr 59 min *Apollo 17* 7–19 Dec 1972.**

First on Moon. **Neil A. Armstrong (b. 5 Aug 1930) (USA) *Apollo 11* 21 July 1969.**

THE FASTEST ROCKET

The first space vehicle to achieve the Third Cosmic velocity sufficient to break out of the Solar System was *Pioneer 10.* The Atlas SLV-3C launcher with a modified Centaur D second stage and a Thiokol Te-364-4 third stage left the Earth at an unprecedented 51 682 km/h *32,114 mph* on 2 Mar 1972. The highest recorded velocity of any space vehicle has been 240 000 km/h *149,125 mph* in the case of the US-German solar probe *Helios B* launched on 15 Jan 1976.

EARLIEST SUCCESSFUL MANNED SATELLITE

The first successful manned space flight began at 9.07 a.m. (Moscow time), or 6.07 a.m. GMT, on 12 Apr 1961. Cosmonaut Flight Major (later Colonel) Yuriy Alekseyevich Gagarin (b. 9 Mar 1934) completed a single orbit of the Earth in 89.34 min in the 4,72 tonnes *4.65 ton* space vehicle *Vostok* ('East') 1. The take-off was from Tyuratam in Kazakhstan, and the landing was 108 min later near the village of Smelovka, near Engels, in the Saratov region of the USSR. The maximum speed was 28 260 km/h *17,560 mph* and the maximum altitude 327 km *203.2 miles* in a flight of 40 868,6 km *25,394.5 miles.* Major Gagarin, invested a Hero of the Soviet Union and awarded the Order of Lenin and the Gold Star Medal, was killed in a jet plane crash near Moscow on 27 Mar 1968.

FIRST WOMAN IN SPACE

The first woman to orbit the Earth was Junior Lieutenant (now Lt-Col) Valentina Vladimirovna Tereshkova, now Nikolayev, (b. 6 Mar 1937), who was launched in *Vostok 6* from Tyuratam, USSR, at 9.30 a.m. GMT on 16 June 1963, and landed at 8.16 a.m. on 19 June, after a flight of 2 days 22 hr 42 min, during which she completed over 48 orbits (1 971 000 km *1,225,000 miles*) and passed momentarily within 4,8 km *3 miles* of *Vostok 5.* Svetlana Savitskaya (USSR) became the second woman in space on 19 Aug 1982 and Dr Sally K. Ride (US) the third on 18–24 June 1973.

LONGEST MANNED SPACE FLIGHT

The longest time spent in space is 236 days 22 hr 50 min, by Dr Oleg Y. Atkov, 35; Leonid D. Kizim, 43, and Vladimir A. Solovyev on board *Soyuz T-10.* They travelled 158 million km *98.1 million miles* 8 Feb–20 Oct 1984. Valeriy Ryumin holds the aggregate duration record at 362 days in 3 flights.

LARGEST SPACE OBJECT

The heaviest object orbited is the Saturn V third stage with *Apollo 15* (space craft) which, prior to trans-lunar injection in parking orbit weighed 140 512 kg *138.29 tons.* The 200 kg *442 lb* US RAE (radio astronomy explorer) B or *Explorer 49* launched on 10 June 1973 has, however, antennae, 415 m *1500 ft* from tip to tip.

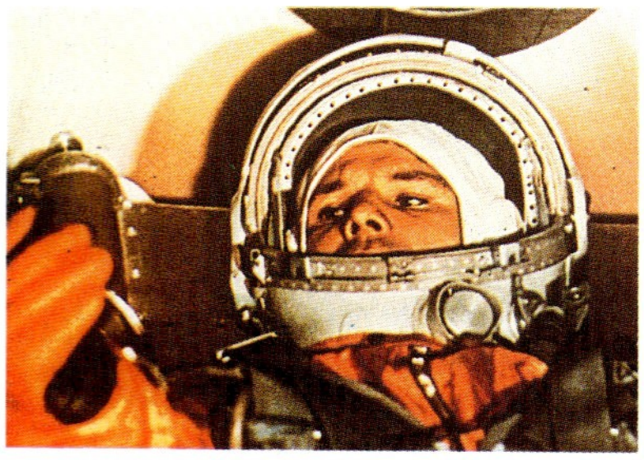

Earliest. **Col Yuriy Gagarin (b. 9 Mar 1934) (USSR) *Vostok 1* 12 Apr 1961.**

First Space Walk. **Lt-Col Aleksey A. Leonov (b. 20 May 1934) (USSR) *Voskhod 2* 18 Mar 1965.**

First Woman. **Lt-Col Valentina Tereshkova-Nikolayev (48 orbits) (b. 6 Mar 1937) (USSR) *Vostok 6* 16 June 1963.**

ASTRONAUTS

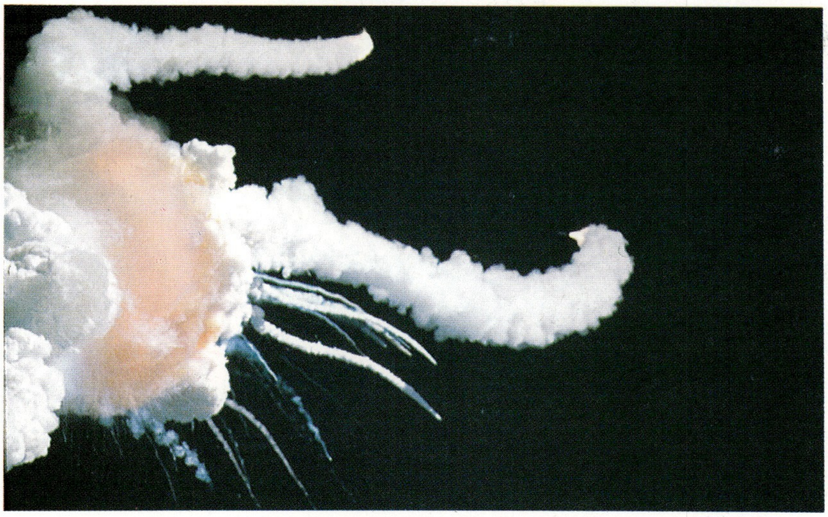

The immediate aftermath of the explosion of *Challenger 51L* that caused the worst human disaster in space flight history. (*SIPA Press*)

First Untethered 'Float' in Space (wearing a Manned Manoeuvring Unit). *Man:* Capt Bruce McCandless (USN) (b. 1938) *Challenger* 7 Feb 1984. *Woman:* Dr Kathryn Sullivan (b. 1952) *Challenger* 11 Oct 1984.

First Undisputed Fatality. Col Vladimir Komarov (b. 16 Mar 1927) (USSR) *Soyuz 1* 23 Apr 1967.

First Feminine Space Walk. Mde Svetlana Savitskaya-Khatkovsky *Salyut 7* 25 July 1984.

Most on One Mission. 5 men and 2 women. 13th Shuttle mission from Cape Canaveral, Florida, USA. *Challenger* 5 Oct 1984. 6 men and 1 woman. 16th Shuttle mission from Cape Canaveral, Florida, USA. *Discovery* 12 Apr 1985. 7 men, 2 monkeys, 24 rats. 17th Shuttle mission from Cape Canaveral, Florida, USA. *Challenger* 24 April 1985.

Oldest. Karl G. Heinz (US), 58 years. *Challenger*. July 1985.

Longest Manned Flight. 236 days 22 hr 50 min Dr Oleg Y. Atkov, 35; Leonid D. Kizim, 43, and Vladimir A. Solovyev. 158 million km *98.1 million miles*. *Soyuz T-10* 8 Feb–20 Oct 1984. Valeriy Ryumin holds the aggregate duration record at 362 days in 3 flights.

SPORTS ENDURANCE RECORDS

Activity	No. in team	Duration	Record holders
BACKGAMMON	Pair	151 hr 11 min	Dick Newcomb and Greg Peterson at Rockford, Illinois, USA 30 June–6 July 1978.
BADMINTON *(singles)*	Pair	78 hr 23 min	Cameron McMullen and Michael Patterson at Blessed Edward Jones HS, Rhyl 1–4 Apr 1986.
(doubles)	4	77 hr 1 min	Paul Farmer, Andrew Hood, Ben Smith and Loraine Storey at Chilwell, Nottingham 29 May–1 June 1984.
BASKETBALL	5	102 hr	Sigma Nu Fraternity at Indiana University, Pennsylvania, USA 13–17 Apr 1983.
BINGO CALLING	2	285 hr 24 min	Phillip Carter and Mark Kiely at the Top Rank Club, Kingston, Surrey 8–20 May 1983.
BOWLING *(Ten Pin)*	1	195 hr 1 min	Jim Webb at Gosford City Bowl, New South Wales, Australia 1984.
BOWLS *(outdoor)*	4	100 hr 2 min	Two teams from Taieri Bowling Club, Mosgiel, New Zealand 27–31 Mar 1986.
(indoor)	4	77 hr	Two teams from Sutton Indoor Bowls Club, Sutton, Surrey 24–27 Apr 1986.
BRIDGE *(Contract)*	4	180 hr	Four students at Edinburgh University 21–28 Apr 1972.
CHESS	Pair	200 hr	Roger Long and Graham Croft at Dingles, Bristol 11–19 May 1984.
CRIBBAGE	4	120 hr	Geoff Lee, Ken Whyatt, Ray Charles and Paul Branson at Mapperley, Nottingham 16–21 Mar 1982.
CRICKET	11	316 hr	Two teams from Belper, Derbyside 14–27 Aug 1983.
CROQUET	4	113 hr 25 min	Hilary Lund-Yates, Hilary Cuthbert, Simon Clay and Roger Swift at Birmingham University 18–23 June 1983.
CURLING	4	67 hr 55 min	Capital Winter Club, Fredericton, New Brunswick, Canada 9–12 Apr 1982.
	Pair	38 hr	Jim Paul and Chris McCrady at the Brockville Country Club, Ontario, Canada 26–28 Mar 1982.
DARTS	Pair	134 hr 54 min	Ray Azzopardi and Alan Alden at Bank of Valletta Sports Club, Marsa, Malta 11–17 Dec 1985.
DOMINOES	Pair	150 hr 5 min	Neil Thomas and Tim Beesley at St. Anselm's College, Wirral, Merseyside 5–11 Aug 1985.
DRAUGHTS	Pair	138 hr 28 min	Greg Davis and Mark Schumacher at Denny's Restaurant, Nunawading, Victoria, Australia 26 Aug–1 Sept 1985.
FOOTBALL *(outdoor)*	11	64 hr 44 min	Two teams from Stewart's, Lake Park, Florida, USA 31 Aug–3 Sept 1984.
(Soccer)	5	74 hr 30 min	Two teams at Liswerry Leisure Centre, Newport, Gwent, Wales 23–26 June 1983.
(indoor)	5	104 hr 10 min	Two teams of students at Summerhill College, Sligo, Ireland 27–31 Mar 1983.
HOCKEY *(outdoor)*	11	35 hr 23 min	Two teams from Hilson Park Hockey Club in Johannesburg, South Africa 25–26 June 1983.
(indoor)	6	44 hr 43 min	Two teams from Nottingham University Men's Hockey Club, 18–20 Mar 1986.
HORSEMANSHIP	1	112 hr 30 min	Ken Northdurft at Kingsthorpe, Australia 31 Aug–4 Sept 1985.
ICE SKATING	1	109 hr 5 min	Austin McKinley at Christchurch, New Zealand 21–25 June 1977.
JUDO	Pair	245 hr 30 min	Five of six people at Smithfield RSL Youth Club, New South Wales, Australia 3–13 Jan 1984.
MONOPOLY *(Parker Bros.)*	4	660 hr	Caara Fritz, Randy Smith, Phil Bennett and Terry Sweatt at Atlanta, Georgia, USA 12 July–Aug 1981.
NETBALL	7	38 hr	The 'Pan-Ems' at the Emerton Youth Centre, Mt. Druitt, NSW, Australia 30 Sept–1 Oct 1984.
POOL	Pair	300 hr 16 min	Barry Wicks and Derek Shaw; also Paul Haslam and Vincent Moore at the New Inn, Galgate, Lancaster 21 May–2 June 1984.
RACQUETBALL	Pair	40 hr 22 min	Daryl Houlden and Eddy Oogjes at Rochester, Victoria, Australia 20–22 July 1984.
ROLLER SKATING	1	344 hr 18 min	Isamu Furugen at Naha Roller Skate Land, Okinawa, Japan 11–27 Dec 1983.
SCRABBLE	Pair	153 hr	Peter Finan and Neil Smith at St. Anselm's College, Wirral, Merseyside 18–25 Aug 1984.
SKIING (Alpine)	1	138 hr	Luc Labrie at Daie Comeau, Quebec, Canada 20–25 Feb 1984.
	Pair	82 hr 9 min	With no waiting for lifts – John Rutter and Andrew Hampel at Silverwood Winter Park, New Brunswick, Canada 25–28 Jan 1984.
	1	83 hr 2 min	Using T-bars only – Pierre Verot, 6–9 Jan 1983.
SKITTLES	6	168 hr	Gloucester & District Irish Society at Gloucester 15–22 Aug 1981.
SNOOKER	Pair	300 hr 30 min	Sam Ellis and Glyn Travis at Bridlington Snooker Centre, Humberside 14–26 May 1985.
SOFTBALL *(fast pitch)*	9	57 hr	Two teams from Austin, Minnesota, USA 24–26 July 1981.
(slow pitch)	10	96 hr 10 min	Two teams from Naval & Marine Corps Reserve Center, Roanoke, Va., USA 22–26 Aug 1985.
SQUASH	2	121 hr 16 min	Paul Holmes and Andy Head at Hove Squash Club, Hove, Sussex 18–23 Apr 1984.
TABLE FOOTBALL	Pair	59 hr 38 min	Nick Huddy and Martin Cordero in the Prince Albert public house, Guildford in Aug 1985.
TABLE TENNIS	Pair	147 hr 47 min	S. Unterslak and J. Boccia at Dewaal Hotel, Cape Town, South Africa 12–18 Nov 1983.
	Doubles	101 hr 1 min	Lance, Phil and Mark Warren and Bill Weir at Sacramento, Cal., USA 9–13 Apr 1979.
TENNIS *(Lawn)*	Pair	117 hr	Mark and Jim Pinchoff at the Fitness Resort, Lafayette, Louisiana, USA 14–19 May 1985.
	Doubles	96 hr 25 min	Ann Wilkinson, Peter Allsopp, John Thorpe and David Dicks at Mansfield Lawn Tennis Club, 17–21 Aug 1983.
TIDDLYWINKS	6	300 hr	Southampton University Tiddlywinks Club 20 Feb–5 Mar 1981.
TRAMPOLINING	1	266 hr 9 min	Jeff Schwartz at Glenview, Illinois, USA 14–25 Aug 1981.
TREADING WATER *(sea)*	1	108 hr 9 min	Albert Rizzo at The Strand, Gzira, Malta 7–12 Sept 1983
(vertical posture in 2,4 m 8 ft square in swimming pool)	1	81 hr 25 min	Thiru Shanmugam at Anna Swimming Pool, Madras, India 26–29 June 1983.
VOLLEYBALL	6	84 hr	Two teams from Beta Theta Pi fraternity, Bethany College, Bethany, West Virginia 27–30 Sept 1984.

CHAPTER 8

SPORTING RECORDS

SPORT AID

'Omar Khalifa, the Sudanese 1500 metres runner and symbol of the world's greatest mass participation sporting event, Sport Aid. Setting out from a relief camp in Khartoum, Khalifa reached the United Nations in New York by air and foot via 12 European cities in eight days. On 25 May 1986, the climax of Sport Aid, a minimum of 15 million runners took part in the 'Race Against Time' in 277 cities in 78 countries. Held simultaneously across the world, runners included lepers in Zimbabwe and early risers in Auckland, New Zealand where the race began at 3 o'clock in the morning.'

ALL-SPORT RECORDS

'Whilst records in mass participation activities continue to fall, the *Round the Bays* race in Auckland, New Zealand still stands out in attracting the most runners.'

FASTEST SPORT
The highest speed reached in a non-mechanical sport is in sky-diving, in which a speed of 298 km/h *185 mph* is attained in a head-down free falling position, even in the lower atmosphere. In delayed drops speeds of 1005 km/h *625 mph* have been recorded at high rarefied altitudes. The highest projectile speed in any moving ball game is *c* 302 km/h *188 mph* in pelota. This compares with 273 km/h *170 mph* (electronically-timed) for a golf ball driven off a tee.

SLOWEST SPORT
In wrestling, before the rules were modified towards 'brighter wrestling', contestants could be locked in holds for so long that a single bout once lasted for 11 hr 40 min. In the extreme case of the 2 hr 41 min pull in the regimental tug o' war in Jubbulpore, India, on 12 Aug 1889, the winning team moved a net distance of 3,6 m *12 ft* at an average speed of 0,00135 km/h *0.00084 mph.*

LONGEST SPORTING EVENT
The most protracted sporting contest was an automobile duration test of 358 273 km *222,621 miles* (equivalent to 8.93 times around the equator) by Appaurchaux and others in a Ford Taunus at Miranas, France. This was contested over 142 days in July–November 1963.

The most protracted non-mechanical sporting event is the *Tour de France* cycling race. In 1926 this was over 5743 km *3569 miles* lasting 29 days but is now reduced to 23 days.

YOUNGEST AND OLDEST RECORD BREAKERS
The youngest at which anybody has broken a non-mechanical world record is 12 yr 298 days for Gertrude Caroline Ederle (USA) (b. 23 Oct 1906) with 13 min 19.0 sec for women's 880 yd freestyle swimming at Indianapolis, USA, on 17 Aug 1919. Gerhard Weidner (W. Germany) (b. 15 Mar 1933) set a 20 mile walk record on 25 May 1974, aged 41 yr 71 days.

YOUNGEST AND OLDEST CHAMPIONS
The youngest successful competitor in a world title event was a French boy, whose name is not recorded, who coxed the Netherlands' Olympic pair at Paris on 26 Aug 1900. He was not more than ten and may have been as young as seven. The youngest individual Olympic winner was Marjorie Gestring (USA) (b. 18 Nov 1922), who took the springboard diving title at the age of 13 yr 268 days at the Olympic Games in Berlin on 12 Aug 1936. Oscar Gomer Swahn (Sweden) (1847–1927) was aged 64 yr 258 days when he won a gold medal in the 1912 Olympic Running Deer team shooting competition.

YOUNGEST AND OLDEST INTERNATIONALS
The youngest age at which any person has won international honours is eight years in the case of Joy Foster, the Jamaican singles and mixed doubles table tennis champion in 1958. The youngest British international has been diver Beverley Williams (b. 5 Jan 1957), who was 10 yr 268 days old when she competed against the USA at Crystal Palace, London, on 30 Sept 1967. It would appear that the greatest age at which anyone has actively competed for his country was 72 yr 280 days in the case of Oscar Swahn (see above) who won a silver medal for shooting in the Olympic Games at Antwerp on 26 July 1920. He qualified for the 1924 Games but was unable to participate due to illness. Britain's oldest international was Hilda Lorna Johnstone (b. 4 Sept 1902) who was 70 yr 5 days when she was placed twelfth in the Dressage competition at the 1972 Games.

ALL-TIME ALL-ROUNDER
Charlotte 'Lottie' Dod (1871–1960) won the Wimbledon Singles tennis title five times between 1887 and 1893, the British Ladies Golf Championship in 1904, an Olympic silver medal for archery in 1908, and represented England at hockey in 1899. She also excelled at skating and tobogganing. Mildred 'Babe' Zaharias (*née* Didrikson) (1914–56) (USA) won two gold medals (80 m hurdles and javelin) and a silver (high jump) at the 1932 Olympic Games. She set world records at those three events in 1930–32. She was an All-American basketball player for three years and set the world record for throwing the baseball 90,22 m *296 ft.* Switching to golf she won the US women's Amateur title in 1946 and the US Women's

Open in 1948, 1950 and 1954. She also excelled at several other sports. Charles Burgess Fry (GB) (1872–1956) was probably the most versatile male sportsman at the highest level. On 4 Mar 1893 he equalled the world long jump record of 7,17 m *23 ft 6½ in.* He represented England *v.* Ireland at soccer (1901) and played first-class rugby for the Barbarians. His greatest achievements were at cricket, where he headed the English batting averages in six seasons and captained England in 1912. He was an excellent angler and tennis player.

CHAMPION RECORD BREAKER

Between 24 Jan 1970 and 1 Nov 1977 Vasili Alexeyev (USSR) (b. 7 Jan 1942) broke 80 official world records in weightlifting.

LONGEST-REIGNING CHAMPION

The longest reign as a world champion is 33 years (1829–62) by Jacques Edmond Barre (France) (1802–73) at real tennis. The longest reign as a British champion is 41 years by the archer Alice Blanche Legh (1855–1948) who first won the Championship in 1881 and for the 23rd and final time in 1922 aged 67.

SHORTEST-REIGNING CHAMPION

Olga Rukavishnikova (USSR) (b. 13 Mar 1955) held the pentathlon world record for 0.4 sec at Moscow on 24 July 1980. That is the difference between her second place time of 2 min 04.8 sec in the final 800 m event of the Olympic five-event competition, and that of third-placed Nadyezhda Tkachenko (USSR), whose overall points were better, 5083 to 4937.

RECORD EARNINGS

The greatest fortune amassed by an individual in sport is an estimated $69 million by the boxer Muhammad Ali (USA) in 1960–81. The highest paid woman athlete in the world is tennis player Martina Navratilova (b. Prague, Czechoslovakia, 18 Oct 1956) whose official career earnings passed $10 million on 8 Mar 1986.

RECORD SPORTS CONTRACT

In March 1982, the National Football League concluded a deal worth $2000 million for five years coverage of American Football by the three major TV networks, ABC, CBS and NBC. This represents $14.2 million for each league team.

LARGEST CROWD

The greatest number of non-TV spectators for any sporting spectacle is the estimated 2,500,000 who annually line the route of the New York Marathon. However, spread over 23 days, it is estimated that more than 10,000,000 see the annual *Tour de France* cycling race along the route.

The total attendance at the 1984 summer Olympic Games was given at 5,797,923 for all sports, including 1,421,627 for soccer and 1,129,465 for track and field athletics.

The largest crowd travelling to any single sporting venue is 'more than 400,000' for the annual *Grand Prix d'Endurance* motor race on the Sarthe circuit near Le Mans, France. The record stadium crowd was one of 199,854 for the Brazil *v.* Uruguay soccer match in the Maracaña Municipal Stadium, Rio de Janeiro, Brazil, on 16 July 1950.

'The largest attendance at a basketball game – 67,596 in the Hoosier Dome, Indianapolis on 9 July 1984. (See p.157).'

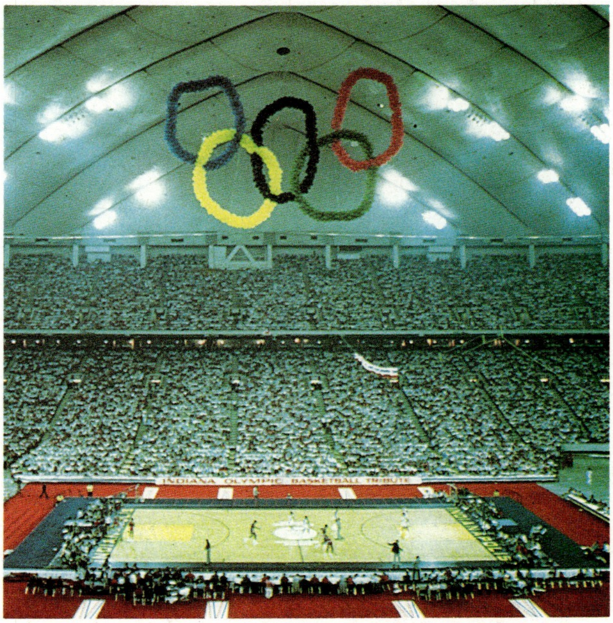

LARGEST TV AUDIENCE

The largest television audience for a single sporting event, excluding Olympic events, was an estimated 1500 million who saw the final of the 1982 soccer World Cup.

MOST PARTICIPANTS

An estimated 90,000 runners contested the 74th annual *Bay to Breakers* 12,2 km *7.6 mile* race in San Francisco in 1985. The 1983 Women's International Bowling Congress Championship tournament attracted 75,480 bowlers for the 83-day event held 7 Apr–1 July at Showboat Lanes, Las Vegas, Nevada, USA.

ALL-TIME HEAVIEST SPORTSMAN

The heaviest sportsman of all-time was the professional wrestler William J. Cobb of Macon, Georgia, USA, who in 1962 was billed as the 802 lb (363 kg *57 st 4 lb*) 'Happy Humphrey'. The heaviest player of a ball-game was the 221 kg *487 lb* Bob Pointer, the US Football tackle formerly on the 1967 Santa Barbara High School Team, California, USA.

SPORTS DISASTERS

The worst sports disaster in recent history was when an estimated 604 were killed after some stands at the Hong Kong Jockey Club racecourse collapsed and caught fire on 26 Feb 1918. During the reign of Antoninus Pius (AD 138–161) the upper wooden tiers in the Circus Maximus, Rome, collapsed during a gladiatorial combat killing some 1112 spectators. Britain's worst sports disaster was when 66 were killed and 145 injured at the Rangers *v.* Celtic football match at Exit 13 of Ibrox Park stadium, Glasgow on 2 Jan 1971.

AEROBATICS

EARLIEST
The first aerobatic 'manoeuvre' is generally considered to be the sustained inverted flight in a Bleriot of Célestin-Adolphe Pégoud (1889–1915), at Buc, France on 21 Sept 1913, but Lieut. Peter Nikolayevich Nesterov (1887–1914), of the Imperial Russian Air Service, performed a loop in a Nieuport Type IV monoplane at Kiev, USSR on 27 Aug 1913.

WORLD CHAMPIONSHIPS
Held biennially since 1960 (excepting 1974), scoring is based on the system devised by Col. José Aresti of Spain. The competition consists of two compulsory and two free programmes. The men's team competition had been won a record five times by the USSR. Igor Egorov (USSR) in 1976 and Petr Jirmus (Czechoslovakia) in 1984 won three out of four programmes. Betty Stewart (USA) won the women's competition in 1980 and 1982. Lidia Leonova (USSR) won a record three medals: first in 1976, second in 1978 and third in 1982. The only medal achieved by Britain has been a bronze in the team event at Kiev, USSR in 1976. The highest individual placing by a Briton is fourth by Neil Williams (1935–77) in 1976.

INVERTED FLIGHT
The duration record for inverted flight is 4 hr 9 min 5 sec by John 'Hal' McClain in a Swick Taylorcraft on 23 Aug 1980 over Houston International Raceways, Texas, USA.

LOOPS
On 21 June 1980, R. Steven Powell performed 2315$\frac{5}{8}$ inside loops in a Bellanca Decathalon over Almont, Michigan, USA. John McClain achieved 180 outside loops in a Bellanca Super Decathalon on 2 Sept 1978 over Houston, Texas, USA.

Ken Ballinger completed 155 consecutive inside loops in a Bellanca Citabria on 6 Aug 1983 over Staverton Airport, Cheltenham, Gloucestershire.

AMERICAN FOOTBALL

SUPER BOWL
First held in 1967 between the winners of the NFL and the AFL. Since 1970 it has been contested by the winners of the National and American Conferences of the NFL. Pittsburgh Steelers have most wins, four, 1975–6 and 1979–80. The highest aggregate score was in 1979 when Pittsburgh beat Dallas Cowboys 35–31. The highest team score and the record victory margin was when the Chicago Bears beat the New England Patriots 46–10 at New Orleans, Louisiana on 26 Jan 1986. The Green Bay Packers won a record 11 NFL titles between 1929 and 1967.

COLLEGE FOOTBALL *HIGHEST TEAM SCORE*
Georgia Tech, Atlanta, Georgia scored 222 points, including a record 32 touchdowns, against Cumberland University, Lebanon, Tennessee (nil) on 7 Oct 1916.

PROFESSIONAL RECORDS – AMERICAN FOOTBALL

Most points	career	2002	George Blanda (Chicago, Baltimore, Houston, Oakland)	1949–75
	season	176	Paul Hornung (Green Bay)	1960
	game	40	Ernie Nevers (Chicago Cardinals)	1929
Most touchdowns	career	126	Jim Brown (Cleveland)	1957–65
	season	24	John Riggins (Washington Redskins)	1983
	game	6	Ernie Nevers (Chicago Cardinals)	1929
		6	William 'Dub' Jones (Cleveland)	1951
		6	Gale Sayers (Chicago)	1965
Most yards gained rushing	career	14,860	Walter Payton (Chicago Bears)	1975–85
	season	2105	Eric Dickerson (Los Angeles Rams)	1985
	game	275	Walter Payton (Chicago Bears)	1977
Most passes completed	career	3686	Fran Tarkenton (Minnesota, NY Giants)	1961–78
	season	362	Dan Marino (Miami Dolphins)	1984
	game	42	Richard Todd (New York Jets)	1980
Most yards gained passing	career	47003	Fran Tarkentin (Minnesota, New York Giants)	1961–78
	season	5084	Dan Marino (Miami Dolphins)	1984
	game	554	Norm Van Brocklin (Los Angeles Rams)	1951
Pass receptions	career	716	Charley Joiner (Houston, Cincinnati, San Diego	1969–85
	season	106	Art Monk (Washington Redskins)	1984
	game	18	Tom Fears (Los Angeles Rams)	1950
Field goals	career	373	Jan Stenerud (Kansas City, Green Bay, Minnesota)	1967–85
	season	35	Ali Haji-Sheikh (New York Giants)	1983
	game	7	Jim Bakken (St Louis Cardinals)	1967

SUPER BOWL INDIVIDUAL GAME RECORDS

Points	18	Roger Craig (San Francisco 49ers)	1985
Touchdowns	2	by many players	
Yards gained rushing	191	Marcus Allen (Los Angeles Raiders)	1984
Yards gained passing	331	Joe Montana (San Francisco 49ers)	1985
Passes completed	29	Dan Marino (Miami Dolphins)	1985
Pass receptions	11	Dan Ross (Cincinnati Bengals)	1982
Field goals	4	Don Chandler (Green Bay Packers)	1968
	4	Ray Wersching (San Francisco 49ers)	1982

The San Francisco 49ers (red shirts) equalled the highest ever score (38) in the XIX Superbowl against the Miami Dolphins.

ANGLING

CATCH *LARGEST SINGLE*

The largest officially ratified fish ever caught on a rod is a man-eating Great white shark (*Carcharodon carcharias*) weighing 1208 kg *2664 lb* and measuring 5,13 m *16 ft 10 in* long, caught on a 58 kg *130 lb* test line by Alf Dean at Denial Bay, near Ceduna, South Australia, on 21 Apr 1959. A Great white shark weighing 1537 kg *3388 lb* was caught by Clive Green off Albany, Western Australia, on 26 Apr 1976 but will remain unratified as whale meat was used as bait. The biggest ever rod-caught fish by a British angler is a 571,5 kg *1260 lb* Black marlin, by Edward A. Crutch off Cairns, Queensland, Australia on 19 Oct 1973.

The largest marine animal ever killed by *hand* harpoon was a Blue whale 29,56 m *97 ft* in length, by Archer Davidson in Twofold Bay, New South Wales, Australia, in 1910. Its tail flukes measured 6,09 m *20 ft* across and its jaw bone 7,11 m *23 ft 4 in*.

The largest officially ratified fish ever caught in a British river was a 176 kg *388 lb* sturgeon (2,79 m *9 ft 2 in* long) landed by Alec Allen (1895–1972), helped by David Price, from the River Towy, between Llandilo and Carmarthen, S. Wales, on 25 July 1933.

SPEAR FISHING

The largest fish ever taken underwater was an 364 kg *804 lb* giant black grouper or jewfish by Don Pinder of the Miami Triton Club, Florida, USA, in 1955. The British spear-fishing record is 40,36 kg *89 lb* for an angler fish by James Brown (Weymouth Association Divers) in 1969.

CHAMPIONSHIP RECORDS *WORLD FRESHWATER*

The *Confédération Internationale de la Pêche Sportive* championships were inaugurated as European championships in 1953. They were recognised as World Championships in 1957. France won twelve times between 1956 and 1981 and Robert Tesse (France) took the individual title uniquely three times, in 1959–60, 1965. The record weight (team) is 34,71 kg *76 lb 8 oz 8 dr* in 3 hr by West Germany on the Neckar at Mannheim, West Germany on 21 Sept 1980. The individual record is 16,99 kg *37 lb 7 oz 3 dr* by Wolf-Rüdiger Kremkus (West Germany) at Mannheim on 20 Sept 1980. The most fish caught is 652 by Jacques Isenbaert (Belgium) at Dunajvaros, Yugoslavia on 27 Aug 1967.

LONGEST FIGHT

The longest recorded individual fight with a fish is 32 hr 5 min by Donal Heatley (b. 1938) (New Zealand) with a black marlin (estimated length 6,09 m *20 ft* and weight 680 kg *1500 lb*) off Mayor Island off Tauranga, North Island on 21–22 Jan 1968. It towed the 12 tonnes/*ton* launch 80 km *50 miles* before breaking the line.

CASTING RECORDS

The longest freshwater cast ratified under ICF (International Casting Federation) rules is 175,01 m *574 ft 2 in* by Walter Kummerow (W. Germany), for the Bait Distance Double-Handed 30 g event held at Lenzerheide, Switzerland in the 1968 Championships. The British National record is 148,78 m *488 ft 1 in* by Andy Dickison on the same occasion. The longest Fly Distance Double-Handed cast is 78,38 m *257 ft 2 in* by Sverne Scheen (Norway), also at Lenzerheide in September 1968. Peter Anderson set a British National professional record of 70,50 m *231 ft 3 in* on water at Scarborough on 11 Sept 1977, and Hugh Newton cast 80,47 m *264 ft* on land at Stockholm, Sweden on 20 Sept 1978. The UK Surfcasting Federation record (150 g *5¼ oz* weight) is 248 m *815 ft* by Neil Mackellow on 4 Sept 1983 at Norwich.

ATHLETICS

EARLIEST LANDMARKS
The first time 10 sec ('even time') was bettered for 100 yd under championship conditions was when John Owen, then aged 30, recorded 9⅘ sec in the AAU Championship at Analostan Island, Washington, DC, USA, on 11 Oct 1890. The first recorded instance of 1,83 m *6 ft* being cleared in the high jump was when Marshall Jones Brooks (1855–1944) jumped 1,832 m *6 ft 0⅛ in* at Marston, near Oxford, on 17 Mar 1876. The breaking of the 'four-minute barrier' in the 1609,34 m *1 mile* was first achieved by Dr (now Sir) Roger Gilbert Bannister, CBE (b. Harrow, London, 23 Mar 1929), when he recorded 3 min 59.4 sec on the Iffley Road track, Oxford, at 6.10 p.m. on 6 May 1954. The first man to pole vault 6.00 m *19 ft 8¼ in* was Sergey Bublca (USSR) in Paris on 13 July 1985.

FASTEST SPEED
The fastest speed recorded in an individual world record is 36,51 km/h *22.69 mph*, but this does not allow for the effects of the delay in reaching peak speed from a standing start. Maximum speeds are likely to exceed 40 km/h *25 mph* for men and 36,5 km/h *22.5 mph* for women. Maximum speeds exceeding 40 km/h *25 mph* for men and 36,5 km/h *22.5 mph* for women have been measured; for instance for Carl Lewis and Evelyn Ashford respectively for their final 100 metres in the 1984 Olympic sprint relays.

HIGHEST HIGH JUMPER ABOVE OWN HEAD
The greatest height cleared above an athlete's own head is 59 cm *23¼ in* by Franklin Jacobs (b. 31 Dec 1957) (USA), who cleared 2,32 m *7 ft 7¼ in* at New York, USA, on 27 Jan 1978. He is only 1,73 m *5 ft 8 in* tall. The greatest height cleared by a woman above her own head is 30,5 cm *12 in* by Cindy John Holmes (b. 29 Aug 1960) (USA), 1,525 m *5 ft* tall, who jumped 1,83 m *6 ft* at Provo, Utah, USA on 1 June 1982.

MOST OLYMPIC TITLES *MEN*
The most Olympic gold medals won is ten (an absolute Olympic record) by Ray C. Ewry (1874–1937) (USA) in the Standing High, Long and Triple Jumps in 1900, 1904, 1906 and 1908.

MOST OLYMPIC TITLES *WOMEN*
The most gold medals won by a woman is four shared by Francina 'Fanny' E. Blankers-Koen (b. 26 Apr 1918) (Netherlands) with 100 m, 200 m, 80 m hurdles and 4×100 m relay, 1948; Betty Cuthbert (b. 20 Apr 1938) (Australia) with 100 m, 200 m, 4×100 m relay, 1956 and 400 m, 1964; and Bärbel Wöckel (*née* Eckert) (b. 21 Mar 1955) (GDR) with 200 m and 4×100 m relay in 1976 and 1980.

MOST WINS AT ONE GAMES
The most gold medals at one celebration is five by Paavo Johannes Nurmi (1897–1973) (Finland) in 1924, and the most individual is four by Alvin C. Kraenzlein (1876–1928) (USA) in 1900, with 60 m, 110 m hurdles, 200 m hurdles and long jump.

WORLD RECORD BREAKERS *OLDEST AND YOUNGEST*
The female record is 35 yr 255 days for Dana Zátopkova, *née* Ingrova (b. 19 Sept 1922) of Czechoslovakia, who broke the women's javelin record with 55,73 m *182 ft 10 in* at Prague, Czechoslovakia, on 1 June 1958. The youngest individual record breaker is Carolina Gisolf (b. 13 July 1913) (Netherlands) who set a women's high jump mark with 1.61 m *5 ft 3⅜ in* at Maastricht, Netherlands on 18 July 1928, aged 15 yr 5 days. The male record is 17 yr 198 days by Thomas Ray (1862–1904) when he pole-vaulted 3.42 m *11 ft 2¾ in* on 19 Sept 1879 (both pre-IAAF records).

Strides ahead . . . Ed Moses has the most successful record in track events, having won 109 consecutive 400 m hurdle races up to 1985. ***(All-Sport)***

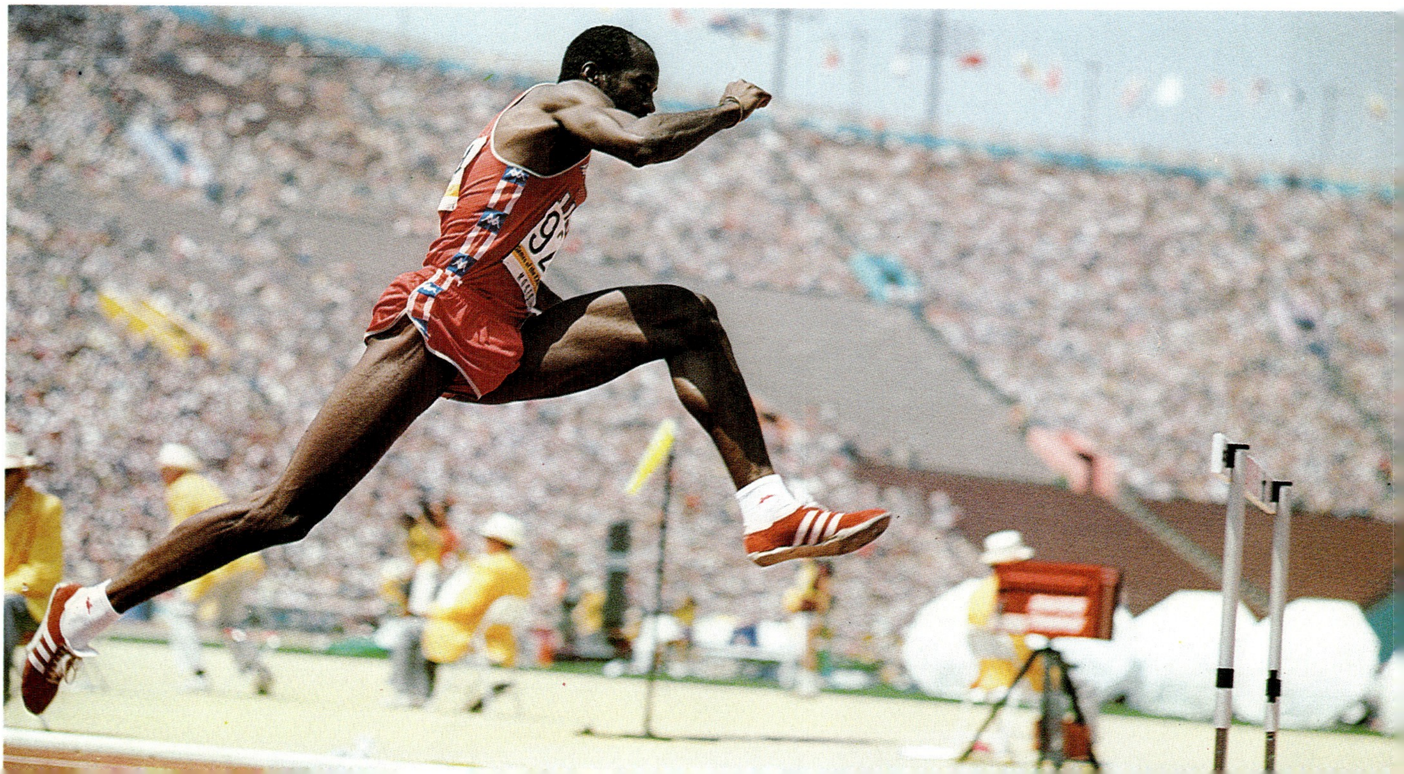

MOST RECORDS IN A DAY
Jesse Owens (1913–80) (USA) set six world records in 45 min at Ann Arbor, Michigan on 25 May 1935 with a 9.4 sec 100 yd at 3.15 p.m., a 8,13 m *26 ft 8¼ in* long jump at 3.25 p.m., a 20.3 sec 220 yd (and 200 m) at 3.45 p.m. and a 22.6 sec 220 yd low hurdles (and 200 m) at 4.00 p.m.

1000 MILES
Siegfried 'Siggy' Bauer (New Zealand) ran 1609 km *1000 miles* in Australia in 12 days 12 hr 36 min 20 sec from Melbourne by road 148 km *92 miles* to Colac and then 2715 laps of a third of a mile track on 15–28 Nov 1983.

LONGEST NON-STOP RUN
The greatest non-stop run recorded is 568 km *352.9 miles* in 121 hr 54 min by Bertil Järlåker (b. 1936) (Sweden) at Norrköping, Sweden, 26–31 May 1980. He was moving for 95.04% of the time.

LONGEST RUNNING RACE
The longest races ever staged were the 1928 (5507 km *3422 miles*) and 1929 (5898 km *3665 miles*) Trans-continental races from New York City, NY, to Los Angeles, California, USA. The Finnish-born Johnny Salo (1893–1931) was the winner in 1929 in 79 days, from 31 Mar to 18 June. His elapsed time of 525 hr 57 min 20 sec (averaging 11,21 km/h *6.97 mph*) left him only 2 min 47 sec ahead of Englishman Pietro 'Peter' Gavuzzi (1905–81).

BACKWARDS RUNNING
Anthony 'Scott' Weiland, 27, ran the Detroit marathon backwards in 4 hr 7 min 54 sec on 3 Oct 1982. Donald Davis (b. 10 Feb 1960) (USA) ran 1 mile backwards in 6 min 7.1 sec at the University of Hawaii on 21 Feb 1983. Ferdie Adoboe (USA) ran 100 yd backwards in 12.8 sec (100 m in 14.0 sec) at Amherst, Mass. on 28 July 1983. Arvind Pandya (India) ran backwards from John O'Groats to Lands End, 1416 km *880 miles* in 29 days, 2–31 Oct 1985.

HIGHEST ONE-LEGGED JUMP
One-legged Arnie Boldt (b. 1958), of Saskatchewan, Canada, cleared 2.04 m *6 ft 8¼ in* in Rome, Italy on 3 Apr 1981.

BADMINTON

MOST WORLD TITLES
The Men's International Championship, the Thomas Cup (inst. 1948) has been won most often by Indonesia, eight times in 1958, 1961, 1964, 1970, 1973, 1976, 1979 and 1984. The Women's Championship, the Uber Cup (inst. 1956) has been won five times by Japan, 1966, 1969, 1972, 1978 and 1981.

MOST INTERNATIONALS
The most capped English internationals are (men) Mike Trodgett with 137, 1970–85 and (women) Gillian Gilks (née Perrin) 108, 1966–85.

SHORTEST GAME
In the 1969 Uber Cup in Tokyo, Japan, Noriko Takagi (Japan) beat Poppy Termengkol (Indonesia) in just nine minutes.

LONGEST HIT
Frank Rugani drove a shuttlecock 24,29 m *79 ft 8½ in* in indoor tests at San José, California, USA on 29 Feb 1964.

'Gillian Gilks, with 108 international appearances for England (1966–85) has also won 11 All-England Championships.'

BASEBALL

EARLIEST GAME
The Rev Thomas Wilson, of Maidstone, Kent, England, wrote disapprovingly, in 1700, of baseball being played on Sundays. The earliest baseball game under the Cartwright (Alexander Joy Cartwright Jr 1820–92) rules was at Hoboken, New Jersey, USA, on 19 June 1846, with the New York Nine beating the Knickerbockers 23–1 in four innings.

HOME RUNS *MOST*
Henry Louis 'Hank' Aaron (Milwaukee and Atlanta Braves) (b. 5 Feb 1934) holds the major league career home run record of 755, from 1954 to 1976. Joshua Gibson (1911–47) of Homestead Grays and Pittsburgh Crawfords, Negro League clubs, achieved a career total of nearly 800 homers including an unofficial total of 75 in 1931. The US major league record for home runs in a season is 61 by Roger Eugene Maris (1934–85) for New York Yankees in 162 games in 1961. George Herman 'Babe' Ruth (1895–1948) hit 60 in 154 games in 1927. The most official home runs in minor leagues is 72 by Joe Bauman of Rosewell, New Mexico in 1954.

BASEBALL

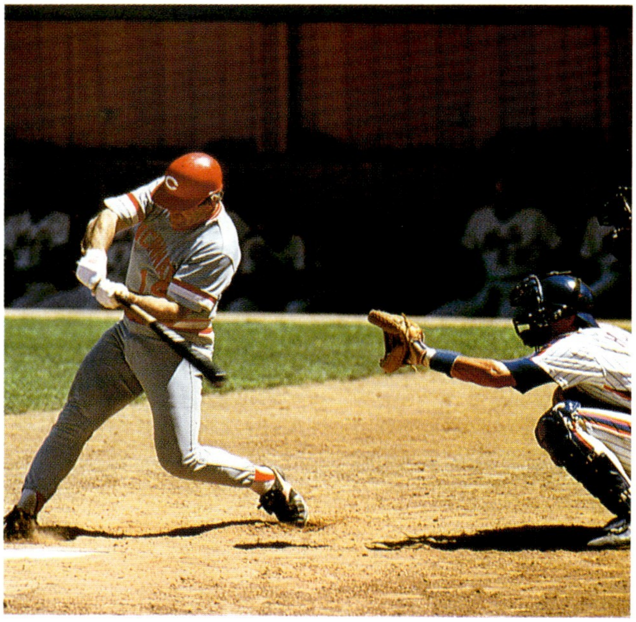

LONGEST HOME RUN
The longest home run ever measured was one of 188,4 m *618 ft* by Roy Edward 'Dizzy' Carlyle (1900–56) in a minor league game at Emeryville Ball Park, California, USA, on 4 July 1929. In 1919 Babe Ruth hit a 178,9 m *587 ft* homer in a Boston Red Sox *v.* New York Giants exhibition match at Tampa, Florida.

LONGEST THROW
The longest throw (ball weighs 141–148 g *5–5¼ oz*) is 135,88 m *445 ft 10 in* by Glen Edward Gorbous (b. Canada 8 July 1930) on 1 Aug 1957. The longest throw by a woman is 90,2 m *296 ft* by Mildred Ella 'Babe' Didrikson (later Mrs Zaharias) (1914–56) (US) at Jersey City, New Jersey, USA on 25 July 1931.

FASTEST BASE RUNNER
The fastest time for circling bases is 13.3 sec by Ernest Evar Swanson (1902–73) at Columbus, Ohio, in 1932, at an average speed of 29,70 km/h *18.45 mph.*

'Pete Rose broke Ty Cobb's record for career base hits in September 1985, 47 years after it had been established.'

BASKETBALL

MOST TITLES *OLYMPIC*
The USA have won nine men's Olympic titles. From the time the sport was introduced to the Games in 1936 until 1972 in Munich they won 63 consecutive matches in the Olympic Games until they lost 50–51 to the USSR in the disputed Final match. They won eighth and ninth titles in 1976 and 1984. The women's title was won by the USSR in 1976 and 1980 and by the USA in 1984.

MOST TITLES *WORLD*
The USSR have won most titles at both the men's World Championships (inst. 1950) with three (1967, 1974 and 1982) and women's (inst. 1953) with six (1959, 1964, 1967, 1971, 1975 and 1983).

MOST TITLES *EUROPEAN*
The most European Champions Cup (inst. 1957) wins is seven by Real Madrid, Spain. The women's title has been won 18 times by Daugawa, Riga, Latvia, USSR. The most wins in the European Nations Championships for men is 13 by the USSR, and in the women's event 17 also by the USSR.

MOST TITLES *AMERICAN PROFESSIONAL*
The most National Basketball Association (NBA) titles (inst. 1947), played for between the leading professional teams in the United States, have been won by the Boston Celtics with 16 victories between 1957 and 1985.

HIGHEST SCORE *INTERNATIONAL*
The highest score recorded in a senior international match is 251 by Iraq against Yemen (33) at New Delhi in November 1982 at the Asian Games. The highest in a British Championship is 125 by England *v.* Wales (54) on 1 Sept 1978. England beat Gibraltar 130–45 on 31 Aug 1978.

HIGHEST SCORE *MATCH*
The highest aggregate score in an NBA match is 370 when the Detroit Pistons (186) beat the Seattle Nuggets

Kareem Abdul-Jabbar has scored more points than anyone else in the history of the NBA. *(All-Sport)*

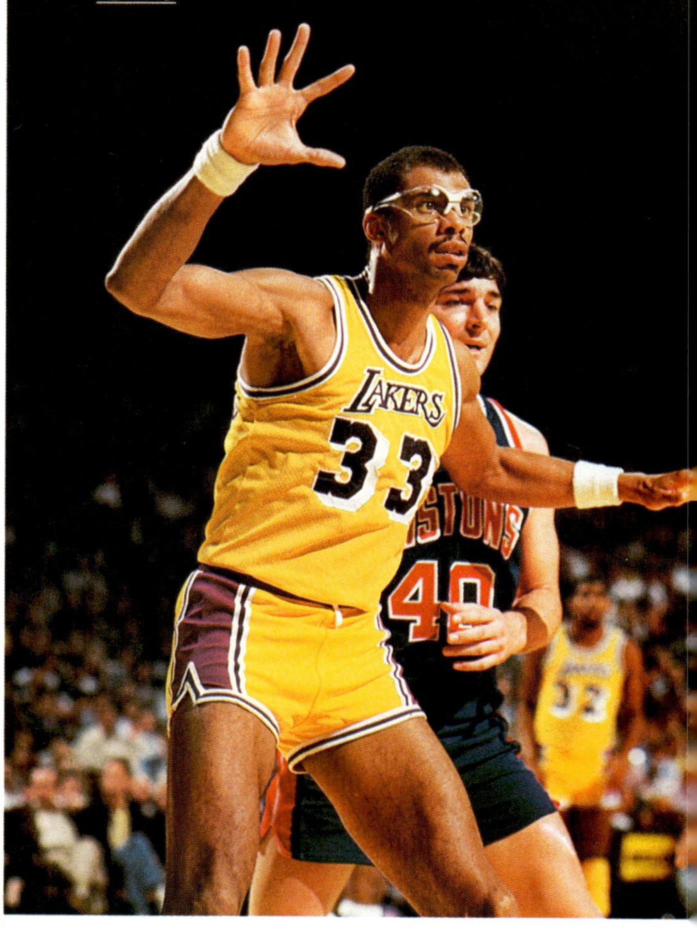

(184) in Denver on 13 Dec 1983. Overtime was played after a 145–145 tie in regulation time.

The highest score in an English National League match was when West Bromwich Kestrels beat Milton Keynes 167 to 69 in February 1983.

HIGHEST SCORE *INDIVIDUAL*
Mats Wermelin, 13, (Sweden) scored all 272 points in a 272-0 win in a regional boys' tournament in Stockholm, Sweden on 5 Feb 1974. The highest single game score in an NBA game is 100 points by Wilton Norman Chamberlain (b. 21 Aug 1936) for Philadelphia *v.* New York on 2 Mar 1962. The most in a college game is 113 points by Clarence 'Bevo' Francis, for Rio Grande College, Ohio *v.* Hillsdale at Jackson, Ohio on 2 Feb 1954. The record score by a woman is 156 points by Marie Boyd (now Eichler) of Central HS, Lonaconing, Maryland, USA in a 163–3 defeat of Ursaline Academy, Cumberland on 25 Feb 1924.

MOST POINTS
Kareem Abdul-Jabbar (formerly Lewis Ferdinand Alcindor) (b. 16 Apr 1947) has scored a career record 35,004 points from 1969 to 31 Mar 1986 for the Milwaukee Bucks and Los Angeles Lakers. The previous record holder, Wilt Chamberlain had a record average of 30.1 points per game for his total of 31,419. He set a season's record 4029 for Philadelphia in 1962. The record for the most points scored in a college career is (women): 4061, Pearl Moore of Francis Marion College, Florence, S. Carolina, 1975–9, (men): 4045 by Travis Grant for Kentucky State in 1969–72. In the English National League, Ian Day (b. 16 May 1953) has scored 3456 points in 203 games, 1973–84.

TALLEST PLAYERS
The tallest player of all time is reputed to be Suleiman Ali Nashnush (b. 1943) who played for the Libyan team in 1962 when measuring 2,45 m *8 ft.* Aleksandr Sizonenko of Kuibyshev Stroitel and USSR is 2,39 m *7 ft 10 in* tall. The tallest woman player was Iuliana Semenova (b. 9 Mar 1952) (USSR) at a reported 2,18 m *7 ft 2 in* and weighing 127,4 kg *281 lb.* The tallest British player has been the 2,29 m *7 ft 6¼ in* tall Christopher Greener of London Latvians whose international debut for England was *v.* France on 17 Dec 1969.

MOST ACCURATE
The greatest goal shooting demonstration has been by Ted St Martin of Jacksonville, Florida, who, on 25 June 1977, scored 2036 consecutive free throws. In a 24-hr period, Jeff Liles (USA) scored 15,138 free throws from a total of 17,862 (84.75% success rate) in Lakeland, Florida, USA, on 11–12 Apr 1986.

LONGEST RECORDED GOAL
The longest recorded field goal in a match is a measured 28,17 m *92 ft 5¼ in* by Bruce Morris for Marshall University *v.* Appalachian State University at Huntington, West Virginia, USA on 8 Feb 1985. A British record of 23,10 m *75 ft 9½ in* is claimed by David Tarbatt (b. 23 Jan 1949) of Altofts Aces *v.* Harrogate Demons at Featherstone, West Yorkshire on 27 Jan 1980.

LARGEST EVER GATE
The Harlem Globetrotters (USA) played an exhibition in front of 75,000 in the Olympic Stadium, West Berlin, Germany, in 1951. The largest indoor basketball attendance was 67,596, including 64,682 tickets sold at the box office, for the Indiana Olympic Basketball Tribute at the Hoosier Dome, Indianapolis, Indiana, USA on 9 July 1984. They saw victories by the US men's and women's Olympic teams over All-Star opposition.

BOARD GAMES

CHESS

HIGHEST RANKED PLAYER
Robert J. 'Bobby' Fischer (USA, b. 9 Mar 1943) has achieved the highest ever rating for any Grand Master on the officially adopted ELO scale with 2785.

MOST OPPONENTS
Erik Knoppert (West Germany) played 500 games of 10-minute chess against opponents averaging 2002 on the ELO scale on 13–16 Sept 1985. He scored 413 points (1 for win, ½ for draw), a success rate of 82.6%.

'Karpov (USSR) concentrates during the world's longest championship match (159 days) against Kasparov (USSR) in 1984/85.'

YOUNGEST AND OLDEST WORLD CHAMPIONS
The youngest men's World Champion is Gary Kasparov (USSR, b. 13 Apr 1963) who defeated Anatoliy Karpov (USSR), winning the title on 9 Nov 1985 aged 22 yr 210 days.

The oldest was Wilhem Steinitz (b. Czechoslovakia, 1836) who was 58 years old when he lost his title to Lasker in 1894.

DRAUGHTS

SHORTEST COMPOSED GAME
The shortest possible game is one of 20 moves composed by Alan Beckerson (GB) in 1977.

SCRABBLE®

HIGHEST SCORES
The highest score achieved in a single turn in competition play is 392 by Dr Saladin Khoshnaw in Manchester in April 1982. He laid down CAZIQUES.

The highest league game score is 849 by Maurice Rocker (GB) at Sheffield on 6 July 1985.

BOXING

LONGEST FIGHTS
The longest recorded fight with gloves was between Andy Bowen of New Orleans (1867–94) and Jack Burke in New Orleans, Louisiana, USA, on 6–7 Apr 1893. The fight lasted 110 rounds and 7 hr 19 min (9.15 p.m.–4.34 a.m.), and was declared no contest (later changed to a draw). Bowen won an 85 round bout on 31 May 1893. The longest bare knuckle fight was 6 hr 15 min between James Kelly and Jack Smith at Fiery Creek, Dalesford, Victoria, Australia on 3 Dec 1855. The longest bare knuckle fight in Britain was 6 hr 3 min (185 rounds) between Bill Hayes and Mike Madden at Edenbridge, Kent, on 17 July 1849. The greatest number of rounds was 276 in 4 hr 30 min when Jack Jones beat Patsy Tunney in Cheshire in 1825.

SHORTEST FIGHTS
There is a distinction between the quickest knock-out and the shortest fight. A knock-out in 10½ sec (including a 10 sec count) occurred on 23 Sept 1946, when Al Couture struck Ralph Walton while the latter was adjusting a gum shield in his corner at Lewiston, Maine, USA. If the time was accurately taken it is clear that Couture must have been more than half-way across the ring from his own corner at the opening bell. The shortest fight on record appears to be one in a Golden Gloves tournament at Minneapolis, Minnesota, USA, on 4 Nov 1947 when Mike Collins floored Pat Brownson with the first punch and the contest was stopped, without a count, 4 sec after the bell.

The fastest officially timed knock-out in British boxing is 11 sec (including a doubtless fast 10 sec count) when Jack Cain beat Harry Deamer, both of Notting Hill, London at the National Sporting Club on 20 Feb 1922. More recently, Hugh Kelly knocked out Steve Cook with the first punch of their contest at the Normandy Hotel, Glasgow on 14 May 1984, again in 11 sec with a 10 sec count.

The shortest world title fight was the James J. Jeffries (1875–1953) – Jack Finnegan heavy-weight bout 6 Apr 1900, won by Jeffries in 55 sec. The shortest ever British title fight was one of 40 sec (including the count), when Dave Charnley knocked out David 'Darkie' Hughes in a lightweight championship defence in Nottingham on 20 Nov 1961.

TALLEST
The tallest boxer to fight professionally was Gogea Mitu (b. 1914) of Romania in 1935. He was 233 cm *7 ft 4 in* and weighed 148 g *327 lb (23 st 5 lb)*. John Rankin, who won a fight in New Orleans, Louisiana, USA, in November 1967, was reputedly also 233 cm *7 ft 4 in*.

LONGEST CAREER
The heavyweight Jem Mace (GB) (1831–1910), known as 'the gypsy', had a career lasting 35 years from 1855 to 1890, but there were several years in which he had only one fight. Bobby Dobbs (USA) (1858–1930) is reported to have had a 39 year career from 1875 to 1914. Walter Edgerton, the 'Kentucky Rosebud', knocked out John Henry Johnson aged 45 in four rounds at the Broadway AC, New York City, USA, on 4 Feb 1916, when aged 63.

MOST FIGHTS
The greatest recorded number of fights in a career is 1024 by Bobby Dobbs (USA) (*see above*). Abraham Hollandersky, *alias* Abe the Newsboy (USA), is reputed to have had up to 1039 fights from 1905 to 1918, but many of them were exhibition bouts.

MOST FIGHTS WITHOUT LOSS
Edward Henry (Harry) Greb (USA) (1894–1926) was unbeaten in 178 bouts, including 117 'No Decision', in 1916–23. Of boxers with complete records Packey McFarland (USA) (1888–1936) had 97 fights (five draws) in 1905–15 without a defeat. Pedro Carrasco (Spain) (b. 7 Nov 1943) won 83 consecutive fights from 22 Apr 1964 to 3 Sept 1970, drew once and had a further nine wins before his loss to Armando Ramos in a WBC lightweight contest on 18 Feb 1972.

MOST KNOCK-OUTS
The greatest number of finishes classed as 'knock-outs' in a career (1936–63) is 145 by Archie Moore (b. Archibald Lee Wright, 13 Dec 1913 or 1916) (USA).

WORLD HEAVYWEIGHT CHAMPIONS

EARLIEST TITLE FIGHT
The first world heavyweight title fight, with gloves and 3 min rounds, was that between John Lawrence Sullivan (1858–1918) and 'Gentleman' James John Corbett (1866–1933) in New Orleans, Louisiana, USA, on 7 Sept 1892. Corbett won in 21 rounds.

LONGEST AND SHORTEST REIGNS
The longest reign of any world heavyweight champion is 11 years 8 months and 7 days by Joe Louis (USA) (b. Joseph Louis Barrow, 1914–81), from 22 June 1937, when he knocked out James Joseph Braddock in the eighth round at Chicago, Illinois, USA, until announcing his retirement on 1 Mar 1949. During his reign Louis made a record 25 defences of his title. The shortest reign was by Leon Spinks (USA) (b. 11 July 1953) for 212 days from 15 Feb to 15 Sept 1978. Ken Norton (USA) (b. 9 Aug 1945) was recognised by the WBC as champion for 83 days from 18 Mar–9 June 1978. The longest lived world heavyweight champion was Jack Dempsey who died on 31 May 1983 aged 87 yr 341 days.

MOST RECAPTURES
Muhammad Ali (b. Cassius Marcellus Clay Jr. 17 Jan 1942) is the only man to regain the heavyweight championship twice. Ali first won the title on 25 Feb 1964 defeating Sonny Liston. He defeated George Foreman on 30 Oct 1974 having been stripped of the title by the world boxing authorities on 28 Apr 1967. He won the WBA title from Leon Spinks on 15 Sept 1978 having previously lost to him on 15 Feb 1978.

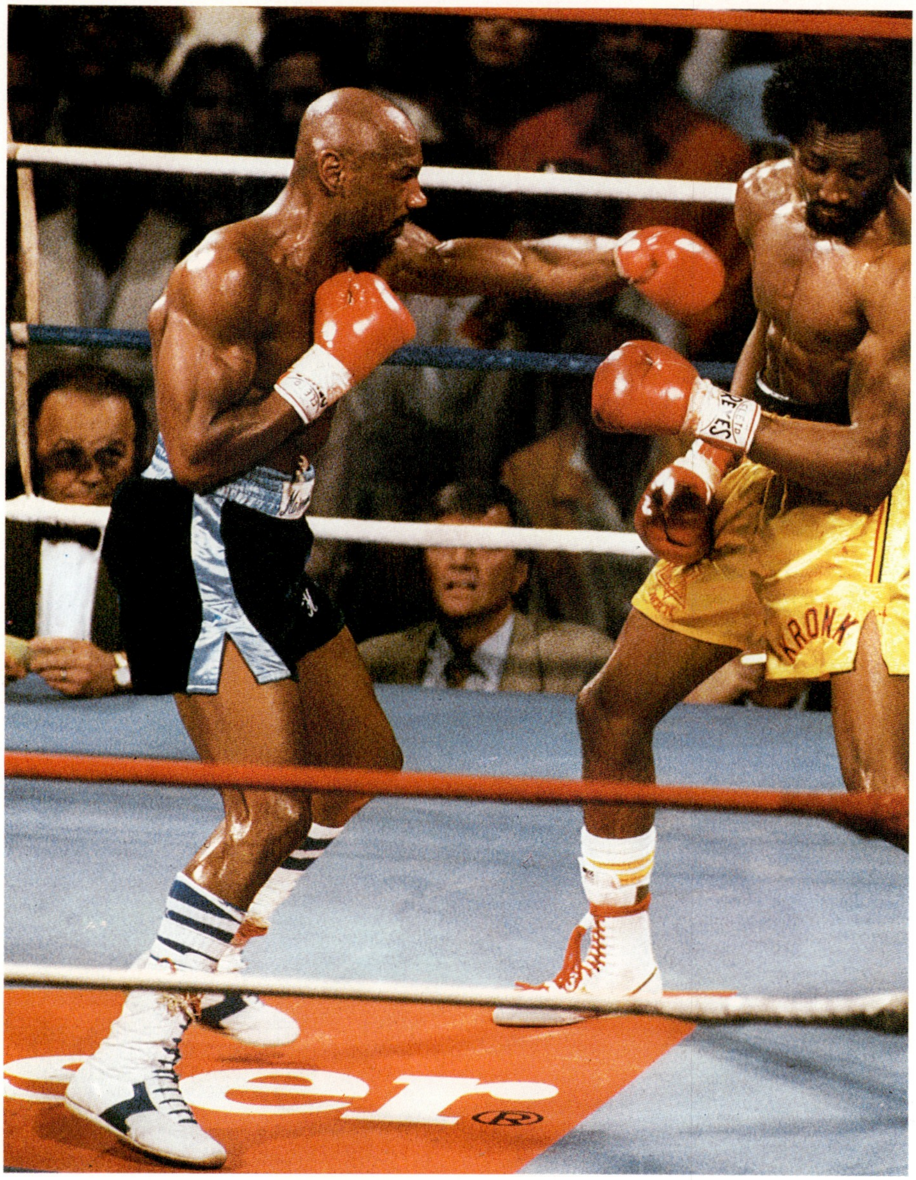

The WBC light middleweight title fight between Marvin Hagler and Thomas Hearns carries the largest ever purse, an estimated $17 million. Hagler won in the third round. *(All-Sport)*

The record for consecutive KO's is 44 by Lamar Clark (b. 1 Dec 1934) (USA) from 1958 to 11 Jan 1960. He knocked out six in one night (five in the first round) at Bingham, Utah, on 1 Dec 1958.

HIGHEST EARNINGS IN CAREER

The largest fortune made in a fighting career is an estimated $69 million (including exhibitions) by Muhammad Ali from October 1960 to December 1981 in 61 fights comprising 549 rounds.

ATTENDANCES *HIGHEST*

The greatest paid attendance at any boxing fight has been 120,757 (with a ringside price of $27.50) for the Tunney *v.* Dempsey world heavyweight title fight at the Sesquicentennial Stadium, Philadelphia, Pennsylvania, USA, on 23 Sept 1926. The indoor record is 63,350 at the Ali *v.* Leon Spinks fight in the Superdrome, New Orleans, Louisiana, on 15 Sept 1978. Record receipts of $7,293,600 were reported for the WBC world heavyweight title fight at Las Vegas on 11 June 1982 when Larry Holmes (USA) (b. 3 Nov 1949) beat Gerry Cooney (USA) (b. 24 Aug 1956). The British attendance record is 82,000 at the Len Harvey *v.* Jock McAvoy fight at White City, London, on 10 July 1939.

The highest non-paying attendance is 135,132 at the Tony Zale *v.* Billy Pryor fight at Juneau Park, Milwaukee, Wisconsin, USA, on 16 Aug 1941.

ATTENDANCES *LOWEST*

The smallest attendance at a world heavyweight title fight was 2434 at the Clay *v.* Liston fight at Lewiston, Maine, USA, on 25 May 1965.

BOXING

WORLD HEAVYWEIGHT CHAMPIONS

UNDEFEATED

Rocky Marciano (b. Rocco Francis Marchegiano) (1923–69) is the only world heavyweight champion to have been undefeated during his entire professional career (1947–56). He won all his 49 fights, 43 by knockouts or stoppages.

Larry Holmes won all 48 of his bouts, including 33 by knockouts and 19 successful heavyweight title defences to May 1985.

OLDEST AND YOUNGEST

The oldest man to win the heavyweight crown was Jersey Joe Walcott (USA) (b. Arnold Raymond Cream, 31 Jan 1914) who knocked out Ezzard Mack Charles (1921–75) on 18 July 1951 in Pittsburgh, Pennsylvania, when aged 37 yr 168 days. Walcott was the oldest holder at 37 yr 236 days, losing his title to Rocky Marciano (1923–69) on 23 Sept 1952. The youngest age at which the world title has been won is 21 yr 331 days by Floyd Patterson (USA) (b. 4 Jan 1935), when he won the vacant title by beating Archie Moore in Chicago, Illinois, USA, on 30 Nov 1956.

HEAVIEST AND LIGHTEST

The heaviest world champion was Primo Carnera (1906–67) (Italy), the 'Ambling Alp', who won the title from Jack Sharkey in six rounds in New York City, NY, USA, on 29 June 1933. He scaled 121 kg *267 lb* for this fight but his peak weight was 122 kg *270 lb*. He had an expanded chest measurement of 134 cm *53 in* and the longest reach at 217 cm *85½ in* (finger tip to finger tip). The lightest champion was Robert James 'Bob' Fitzsimmons (1863–1917), from Helston, Cornwall, who at a weight of 75 kg *167 lb*, won the title by knocking out James Corbett in 14 rounds at Carson City, Nevada, USA, on 17 Mar 1897.

The greatest differential in a world title fight was 39 kg *86 lb* between Carnera (122 kg *270 lb*) and Tommy Loughran (83 kg *184 lb*) of the USA, when the former won on points at Miami, Florida, USA, on 1 Mar 1934.

TALLEST AND SHORTEST

The tallest world champion according to measurements by the Physical Education Director of the Hemingway Gymnasium, Harvard University, was Carnera at 196,6 cm *6 ft 5.4 in* although he was widely reported and believed to be up to 204 cm *6 ft 8½ in*. Jess Willard (1881–1968), who won the title in 1915, often stated to be 199 cm *6 ft 6¼ in* was in fact 196 cm *6 ft 5¼ in*. The shortest was Tommy Burns, world champion from 23 Feb 1906 to 26 Dec 1908, who stood 170 cm *5 ft 7 in* and weighed between 76–81 kg *168–180 lb*.

WORLD CHAMPIONS *ANY WEIGHT*

LONGEST REIGN

Joe Louis's heavyweight duration record of 11 years 252 days stands for all divisions.

YOUNGEST AND OLDEST

The youngest age at which any world championship has been won is 17 yr 176 days by Wilfred Benitez (b. New York, 12 Sept 1958) of Puerto Rico, who won the WBA light welterweight title in San Juan, PR, on 6 Mar 1976. The oldest world champion was Archie Moore who was recognised as a light heavyweight champion up to 10 Feb 1962 when his title was removed. He was then believed to be between 45 and 48. Bob Fitzsimmons had the longest career of any official world titleholder with over 32 years from 1882 to 1914. He won his last world title aged 40 yr 183 days in San Francisco, California on 25 Nov 1903.

LONGEST FIGHT

The longest world title fight (under Queensberry Rules) was that between the lightweights Joe Gans (1874–1910), of the USA, and Oscar Matthew 'Battling' Nelson (1882–1954), the 'Durable Dane', at Goldfield, Nevada, USA, on 3 Sept 1906. It was terminated in the 42nd round when Gans was declared the winner on a foul.

MOST RECAPTURES

The only boxer to win a world title five times at one weight is 'Sugar' Ray Robinson (b. Walker Smith, Jr, 3 May 1921) (USA), who beat Carmen Basilio (USA) in the Chicago Stadium on 25 Mar 1958, to regain the world middleweight title for the fourth time. The record number of title bouts in a career is 33 or 34, at bantam and featherweight, by George Dixon (1870–1909), *alias* 'Little Chocolate', of Canada, between 1890 and 1901.

GREATEST WEIGHT SPAN

The only man to hold world titles at three weights *simultaneously* was Henry 'Homicide Hank' Armstrong (b. 12 Dec 1912), now the Rev Henry Jackson, of the USA, at featherweight, lightweight and welterweight from August to December 1938.

GREATEST 'TONNAGE'

The greatest 'tonnage' recorded in any fight is 317 kg *700 lb* when Claude 'Humphrey' McBride (Oklahoma) 154 kg *340 lb* knocked out Jimmy Black (Houston), who weighed 163 kg *360 lb* in the third round at Oklahoma City on 1 June 1971. The greatest 'tonnage' in a world title fight was 221½ kg *488¾ lb*, when Carnera, then 117½ kg *259¼ lb* fought Paolino Uzcudun, 104 kg *229½ lb* of Spain in Rome on 22 Oct 1933.

MOST KNOCK-DOWNS IN TITLE FIGHTS

Vic Toweel (b. 12 Jan 1929) (South Africa) knocked down Danny O'Sullivan of London 14 times in ten rounds in their world bantamweight fight at Johannesburg on 2 Dec 1950, before the latter retired.

CRICKET

FIRST-CLASS CRICKET (1815 to 1985)

A substantial reduction in the English first-class cricket programme since 1968 has rendered many of the record aggregates for a season unassailable.

BATTING RECORDS – TEAMS

HIGHEST INNINGS
The highest recorded innings by any team was one of 1107 runs in 10 hr 30 min by Victoria against New South Wales in an Australian Sheffield Shield match at Melbourne on 27–28 Dec 1926.

The highest innings in Test cricket and the highest made in England is 903 runs for 7 wickets declared in 15 hr 17 min, by England against Australia at Kennington Oval, London, on 20, 22 and 23 Aug 1938. The highest innings in a County Championship match is 887 in 10 hr 50 min by Yorkshire *v.* Warwickshire at Edgbaston, Birmingham on 7–8 May 1896.

LOWEST INNINGS
The lowest recorded innings is 12 made by Oxford University *v.* the Marylebone Cricket Club (MCC) at Cowley Marsh, Oxford on 24 May 1877, and 12 by Northamptonshire *v.* Gloucestershire at Gloucester on 11 June 1907. On the occasion of the Oxford match, however, the University batted a man short. The lowest in modern times is 14 by Surrey *v.* Essex at Chelmsford on 30 May 1983. The lowest score in a Test innings is 26 by New Zealand *v.* England in the second innings at Auckland on 28 Mar 1955.

The lowest aggregate for two innings is 34 (16 in first and 18 in second) by Border *v.* Natal in the South African Currie Cup at East London on 19 and 21 Dec 1959.

GREATEST VICTORY
The greatest recorded margin of victory is an innings and 851 runs, when Pakistan Railways (910 for 6 wickets declared) beat Dera Ismail Khan (32 and 27) at Lahore on 2–4 Dec 1964. The largest margin in England is an innings and 579 runs by England over Australia at The Oval on 20–24 Aug 1938 when Australia scored 201 and 123 with two men short in both innings. The most one-sided county match was when Surrey (698) defeated Sussex (114 and 99) by an innings and 485 runs at The Oval on 9–11 Aug 1888.

MOST RUNS IN A DAY
The greatest number of runs scored in a day is 721 all out (ten wickets) in 5 hr 48 min by the Australians *v.* Essex at Southchurch Park, Southend-on-Sea on 15 May 1948. The Test record for runs in a day is 588 at Old Trafford, Manchester, on 27 July 1936 when England added 398 and India were 190 for 0 in their second innings by the close.

'The spearhead of the brilliant West Indian pace attack, Malcolm Marshall has achieved the unprecedented feat of taking 20 wickets in seven successive Test series. (All-Sport.)'

CRICKET

(*Left*) Ravi Shastri became only the second man ever to score six sixes off one over, going on in the same innings to the fastest double century. Clive Lloyd (*above*) captained the West Indies in a record 74 Test matches. *(All-Sport)*

BATTING RECORDS – INDIVIDUALS

HIGHEST INNINGS

The highest individual innings recorded is 499 in 10 hr 35 min by Hanif Mohammad (b. 21 Dec 1934) for Karachi *v.* Bahawalpur at Karachi, Pakistan, on 8, 9 and 11 Jan 1959. The highest score in England is 424 in 7 hr 50 m in by Archibald Campbell MacLaren (1871–1944) for Lancashire *v.* Somerset at Taunton on 15–16 July 1895. The record for a Test match is 365 not out in 10 hr 14 min by Sir Garfield St Aubrun Sobers (b. 28 July 1936) playing for West Indies against Pakistan at Sabina Park, Kingston, Jamaica, on 27 Feb–1 Mar 1958. The England Test record is 364 by Sir Leonard Hutton (b. 23 June 1916) *v.* Australia at The Oval on 20, 22 and 23 Aug 1938.

LONGEST INNINGS

The longest innings on record is one of 16 hr 10 min for 337 runs by Hanif Mohammad (Pakistan) *v.* West Indies at Bridgetown, Barbados, on 20–23 Jan 1958. The English record is 13 hr 17 min by Len Hutton in his record Test score of 364.

MOST RUNS *OFF AN OVER*

The first batsman to score 36 runs off a six-ball over was Sir Garfield Sobers (Nottinghamshire) off Malcolm Andrew Nash (b. 9 May 1945) (Glamorgan) at Swansea on 31 Aug 1968. His feat was emulated by Ravishankar Jayadritha Shastri (b. 27 May 1962) for Bombay *v.* Baroda at Bombay, India on 10 Jan 1985 off the bowling of Tilak Raj.

MOST RUNS *OFF A BALL*

The most runs scored off a single hit is ten by Albert Neilson Hornby (1847–1925) off James Street (1839–1906) for Lancashire *v.* Surrey at The Oval on 14 July 1873, and ten by Samuel Hill Wood (later Sir Samuel Hill Hill-Wood) (1872–1949) off Cuthbert James Burnup (1875–1960) in the Derbyshire *v.* MCC match at Lord's, London, on 26 May 1900.

MOST SIXES *IN AN INNINGS*

The highest number of sixes hit in an innings is 15 by John Richard Reid (b. 3 June 1928), in an innings of 296, lasting 3 hr 40 min, for Wellington *v.* Northern Districts in the Plunket Shield Tournament at Wellington, New Zealand, on 14–15 Jan 1963. The Test record is ten by Walter Hammond in an innings of 336 not out for England *v.* New Zealand at Auckland on 31 Mar and 1 Apr 1933.

MOST SIXES *IN A MATCH*

William James Perver Stewart (b. 31 Oct 1934) hit a record 17 sixes (ten in the first innings and seven in the second) for Warwickshire *v.* Lancashire at Blackpool on 29–31 July 1959. His two innings were of 155 and 125.

MOST BOUNDARIES IN AN INNINGS

The highest number of boundaries was 68 (all in fours) by Percival Albert Perrin (1876–1945) in an innings of 343 not out for Essex *v.* Derbyshire at Chesterfield on 18–19 July 1904.

DOUBLE HUNDREDS

The only batsman to score double hundreds in both innings is Arthur Edward Fagg (1915–77), who made 244 and 202 not out for Kent *v.* Essex at Colchester on 13–15 July 1938. Sir Donald Bradman scored a career record 37 double hundreds 1927–49.

'CARRYING BAT'

Cecil John Burditt Wood (1875–1960), of Leicestershire, is the only batsman to carry his bat through both completed innings of a match, and score a hundred in both innings, (107 not out, 117 not out) on 12–14 June 1911 *v.* Yorkshire at Bradford.

FASTEST SCORING

The fastest 50 was completed off 13 balls in 8 min (1.22 to 1.30 p.m.) and in 11 scoring strokes by Clive Clay Inman (b. 29 Jan 1936) in an innings of 57 not out for Leicestershire *v.* Nottinghamshire at Trent Bridge, Nottingham on 20 Aug 1965. Full tosses were bowled to expedite a declaration.

The fastest hundred was completed in 35 min off between 40 and 46 balls by Percy George Herbert Fender (b. 22 Aug 1892), when scoring 113 not out for Surrey *v.* Northamptonshire at Northampton on 26 Aug 1920. Steven Joseph O'Shaughnessy (b. 9 Sept 1961) also scored a hundred in 35 minutes for Lancashire *v.* Leicestershire at Old Trafford, Manchester off 54 balls on 13 Sept 1983. In all he scored 105 and with Graeme Fowler (b. 20 Apr 1957) put on 201 runs for the 1st wicket in 45 mins. The match was 'dead' and irregular bowlers were used.

The hundred in fewest recorded deliveries was by David William Hookes (b. 3 May 1955) in 34 balls, in 43 min, for South Australia *v.* Victoria at Adelaide on 25 Oct 1982. In all he scored 107 from 40 balls in this the second innings, following 137 in the first innings. The most prolific scorer of hundreds in an hour or less was Gilbert Laird Jessop (1874–1955), with 11 between 1897 and 1913. The fastest Test hundred was off 56 balls by Isaac Vivian Alexander Richards (b. 7 Mar 1952) for West Indies *v.* England at Antigua on 15 Apr 1986. He went on to score 110 in 81 minutes. Edwin Boaler Alletson (1884–1963) scored 189 runs in 90 min for Nottinghamshire *v.* Sussex at Hove on 20 May 1911.

A double hundred in 113 min was scored by Ravi Shastri for Bombay *v.* Baroda at Bombay on 10 Jan 1985 (see most runs off an over). He received 123 balls. Clive Hubert Lloyd (b. 31 Aug 1944), for West Indies *v.* Glamorgan at Swansea on 9 Aug 1976, and Gilbert Jessop (286), for Gloucestershire *v.* Sussex at Hove on 1 June 1903, both scored 200 in 120 min. Lloyd received 121 balls but the figure for Jessop is not known.

(*Right*) Viv Richards' 56-ball century against England in Antigua was the fastest in Test cricket.

John Lever of Essex, holder of two career records for one-day cricket. He has taken 100 wickets in a season four times.

CRICKET

CONSECUTIVE DUCKS

A unique distinction of scoring two ducks (known as 'a pair of spectacles') in less than 60 seconds was 'achieved' by Peter Judge (Glamorgan) in the match *v.* India at Cardiff Arms Park, South Wales, 11 June 1946. Glamorgan had reversed their batting order for the second innings and India had agreed to waive the interval between innings.

BOWLING

MOST WICKETS *IN AN INNINGS*

The taking of all ten wickets by a single bowler has been recorded many times but only one bowler has achieved this feat on three occasions – Alfred Freeman of Kent, against Lancashire at Maidstone on 24 July 1929, against Essex at Southend on 13–14 Aug 1930 and against Lancashire at Old Trafford on 27 May 1931. The fewest runs scored off a bowler taking all ten wickets is ten, when Hedley Verity (1905–43) of Yorkshire dismissed (eight caught, one lbw, one stumped) Nottinghamshire at Leeds on 12 July 1932. The only bowler to bowl out all ten was John Wisden (1826–84) of Sussex, playing for North *v.* South at Lord's in 1850.

MOST WICKETS *MATCH*

James Charles Laker (1922–86) of Surrey took 19 wickets for 90 runs (9–37 and 10–53) for England *v.* Australia in the Fourth Test at Old Trafford, on 27–31 July 1956. No other bowler has taken more than 17 wickets in a first-class match.

MOST WICKETS *IN A DAY*

The greatest number of wickets taken in a day's play is 17 (for 48 runs) by Colin Blythe (1879–1917), for Kent *v.* Northamptonshire at Northampton on 1 June 1907; by Hedley Verity for 91 runs, for Yorkshire *v.* Essex at Leyton on 14 July 1933; and by Thomas William John Goddard (1900–66) for 106 runs, for Gloucestershire *v.* Kent at Bristol on 3 July 1939.

MOST CONSECUTIVE WICKETS

No bowler in first-class cricket has yet achieved five wickets with five consecutive balls. The nearest approach was that of Charles Warrington Leonard Parker (1882–1959) (Gloucestershire) in his own benefit match against Yorkshire at Bristol on 10 Aug 1922, when he struck the stumps with five successive balls but the second was called as a no-ball. The only man to have taken four wickets with consecutive balls more than once is Robert James Crisp (b. 28 May 1911) for Western Province *v.* Griqualand West at Johannesburg on 24 Dec 1931 and against Natal at Durban on 3 Mar 1934.

Patrick Ian Pocock (b. 24 Sept 1946) took five wickets in six balls, six in nine balls and seven in eleven balls for Surrey *v.* Sussex at Eastbourne on 15 Aug 1972. In his own benefit match at Lord's on 22 May 1907, Albert Edwin Trott (1873–1914) of Middlesex took four Somerset wickets with four consecutive balls and then later in the same innings achieved a 'hat trick'.

MOST CONSECUTIVE MAIDENS

Hugh Joseph Tayfield (b. 30 Jan 1929) bowled 16 consecutive eight-ball maiden overs (137 balls without conceding a run) for South Africa *v.* England at Durban on 25–26 Jan 1957. The greatest number of consecutive six-ball maiden overs bowled is 21 (131 balls) by Rameshchandra Gangaram 'Bapu' Nadkarni (b. 4 Apr 1932) for India *v.* England at Madras on 12 Jan 1964. The English record is 17 overs (105 balls) by Horace Leslie Hazell (b. 30 Sept 1909) for Somerset *v.* Gloucestershire at Taunton on 4 June 1949. Alfred Shaw (1842–1907) of Nottinghamshire bowled 23 consecutive four-ball maiden overs (92 balls) for North *v.* South at Trent Bridge on 17 July 1876.

MOST BALLS

The most balls bowled in a match is 917 by Cottari Subbanna Nayudu (b. 18 Apr 1914), 6–153 and 5–275, for Holkar *v.* Bombay at Bombay on 4–9 Mar 1945. The most balls bowled in a Test match is 774 by Sonny Ramadhin (b. 1 May 1929) for West Indies *v.* England, 7–49 and 2–179, at Edgbaston on 29 May–4 June 1957. In the second innings he bowled a world record 588 balls (98 overs).

MOST EXPENSIVE BOWLING

The greatest number of runs hit off one bowler in one innings is 362, scored off Arthur Alfred Mailey (1886–1967) in the New South Wales *v.* Victoria match at Melbourne on 24–28 Dec 1926. The greatest number of runs ever conceded by a bowler in one match is 428 by Cottari Subbanna Nayudu in the Holkar *v.* Bombay match above. The most runs conceded in a Test innings is 298 by Leslie O'Brien 'Chuck' Fleetwood-Smith (1910–71) for Australia *v.* England at the Oval on 20–23 Aug 1938.

FASTEST

The highest electronically measured speed for a ball bowled by any bowler is 160,45 km/h *99.7 mph* by Jeffrey Robert Thomson (b. 16 Aug 1950) (Australia) during the Second Test *v.* the West Indies in December 1975. Albert Cotter (1883–1917) of New South Wales, Australia, is reputed to have broken a stump on more than 20 occasions.

FIELDING

MOST CATCHES *INNINGS AND MATCH*

The greatest number of catches in an innings is seven, by Michael James Stewart (b. 16 Sept 1932) for Surrey *v.* Northamptonshire at Northampton on 7 June 1957, and by Anthony Stephen Brown (b. 24 June 1936) for Gloucestershire *v.* Nottinghamshire at Trent Bridge on 26 July 1966.

The most catches in a Test match is seven by Greg Chappell for Australia *v.* England at Perth on 13–17 Dec 1974, and by Yajurvindra Singh (b. 1 Aug 1952) for India *v.* England at Bangalore on 28 Jan–2 Feb 1977.

Walter Hammond held a match record total of ten catches (four in the first innings, six in the second) for Gloucestershire *v.* Surrey at Cheltenham on 16–17 Aug 1928. The record for a wicket-keeper is 11 (see wicket-keeping).

LONGEST THROW

A cricket ball (5½ oz *155 g*) was reputedly thrown 128,6 m *140 yd 2ft* by Robert Percival, a left-hander, on Durham Sands racecourse on Easter Monday, 18 Apr 1881.

CYCLING

HIGHEST SPEED

The highest speed ever achieved on a bicycle is 245,077 km/h *152.284 mph* by John Howard (USA) behind a wind-shield at Bonneville Salt Flats, Utah, USA on 20 July 1985. It should be noted that considerable help is provided by the slipstreaming effect of the lead vehicle. Fred Markham recorded an official unpaced 8.80 sec for 200 m (81,81 km/h *50.84 mph*) on a streamlined bicycle at Ontario, California, USA, on 6 May 1979.

The greatest distance ever covered in one hour is 122,771 km *76 miles 504 yd* by Leon Vanderstuyft (1890–1964) (Belgium) on the Montlhery Motor Circuit, France, on 30 Sept 1928, achieved from a standing start paced by a motorcycle. The 24 hr record behind pace is 1384,367 km *860 miles 367 yd* by Hubert Ferdinand Opperman (later Hon Sir) (b. 29 May 1904) in Melbourne, Australia on 23 May 1932.

MOST TITLES *OLYMPIC*

The most gold medals won is three by Paul Masson (1874–1945) (France) in 1896, Francisco Verri (1885–1945) (Italy) in 1906 and Robert Charpentier (1916–66) (France) in 1936. Daniel Morelon (France) won two in 1968, and a third in 1972. He also won a bronze medal in 1964. In the 'unofficial' 1904 cycling programme, Marcus Hurley (1884–1950) (USA) won four events.

TOUR DE FRANCE

The greatest number of wins in the Tour de France (inaugurated 1903) is five by Jacques Anquetil (b. 8 Jan 1934) (France), 1957, 1961–4, by Eddy Merckx (b. 17 June 1945) (Belgium), 1969–72 and 1974, and by Bernard Hinault (France) (b. 14 Nov 1954), 1978–9, 1981–2 and 1985. The closest race ever was in 1968 when after 4665 km *2898.7 miles* over 25 days (27 June–21 July) Jan Janssen (b. 19 May 1940) (Netherlands) beat Herman van Springel (Belgium) in Paris by 38 sec. The fastest average speed was 37,84 km/h *23.51 mph* by Bernard Hinault in 1981. The longest race was 5745 km *3569 miles* in 1926, and most participants were 170 starters in 1982 and 1984. The longest ever stage was the 486 km from Les Sables d'Olonne to Bayonne in 1919. The longest in 1984 was 338 km *210 miles* from Nantes to Bordeaux.

LONGEST ONE-DAY RACE

The longest single-day 'massed start' road race is the 551–620 km *342–385 miles* Bordeaux–Paris, France, event. Paced over all or part of the route, the highest average speed was in 1981 with 47,186 km/h *29.32 mph* by Herman van Springel (b. 14 Aug 1943) (Belgium) for 584,5 km *363.1 miles* in 13 hr 35 min 18 sec.

CYCLE TOURING

The greatest mileage amassed in a cycle tour was more than 643 700 km *402,000 miles* by the itinerant lecturer Walter Stolle (b. Sudetenland, 1926) from 24 Jan 1959 to 12 Dec 1976. He visited 159 countries starting from Romford, Essex, England. From 1922 to 25 Dec 1973 Tommy Chambers (1903–84) of Glasgow, rode a verified total of 1 286 517 km *799,405 miles*.

Visiting every continent, John W. Hathaway (b. England, 13 Jan 1925) of Vancouver, Canada covered 81 300 km *50,600 miles* from 10 Nov 1974 to 6 Oct 1976. Veronica and Colin Scargill, of Bedford, travelled 29 000 km *18,020 miles* around the world, on a tandem, 25 Feb 1974–27 Aug 1975.

HIGHEST

Nicholas and Richard Crane cycled their mountainbikes to the summit of Mount Kilimanjaro, Tanzania 5894 m *19,340 ft* on 31 Dec 1984.

John Howard holds the world speed cycling record of over 240 kmph *150 mph*. The official land speed record only passed this mark in 1926 and any deviation of the rider behind the car's rear shield would mean certain death.

DARTS

MOST TITLES

Eric Bristow (b. 25 Apr 1957) has most wins in the World Masters Championship (inst. 1974) with five, in 1977, 1979, 1981 and 1983–4, and in the World Professional Championship (inst. 1978) with five, in 1980–1 and 1984–6. Bristow completed a unique treble in 1983 by also winning the World Cup singles. Six men have won the annual *News of the World* individual Championship twice. Most recently Eric Bristow in 1983 and 1984 and Bobby George in 1979 and 1986. John Lowe (b. 21 July 1945) is the only other man to have won each of the four major titles: World Masters, 1976 and 1980; World Professional, 1979; World Cup Singles, 1981; and *News of the World*, 1981

The National Darts Association of Great Britain individual title was won by Tom O'Regan (b. 28 Feb 1939) of the Northern Star, New Southgate, Greater London in 1970–2. Maureen Flowers (b. 6 Dec 1946), in 1979 and 1980, is the only double winner of the NDA women's individual title.

WORLD CUP

The first World Cup was held at the Wembley Conference Centre, London in 1977. Wales were the inaugural champions and England won in 1979, 1981 and 1983.

RECORD PRIZE

John Lowe won £102,000 for achieving the first 501 scored with the minimum nine darts in a major event on 13 Oct 1984 at Slough in the quarter-finals of the World Match-play Championships. His darts were six successive treble 20s, treble 17, treble 18 and double 18.

LONGEST UNBEATEN RUN

Mike Bowell (b. 31 May 1947) of Paulton Darts League, Avon, won 152 consecutive competition games from 9 Feb 1971 to 29 Nov 1974. The White Horse Inn, Ashton-under-Lyne, Manchester, were undefeated in a total of 169 matches from 31 May 1979 to 9 Feb 1981.

FASTEST MATCH

The fastest time taken for a match of three games of 301 is 1 min 47 sec by Keith Deller (GB) on BBC TV's *Record Breakers* in November 1985.

FASTEST 'ROUND THE BOARD'

The record time for going round the board clockwise in 'doubles' at arm's length is 9.2 sec by Dennis Gower at the Millers Arms, Hastings, East Sussex on 12 Oct 1975 and 14.5 sec in numerical order by Jim Pike (1903–60) at the Craven Club, Newmarket in March 1944. The record for this feat at the 2,7 m *9 ft* throwing distance, retrieving own darts, is 2 min 13 sec by Bill Duddy (b. 29 Sept 1932) at The Plough, Haringey, London on 29 Oct 1972.

LEAST DARTS

Scores of 201 in four darts, 301 in six darts, 401 in seven darts and 501 in nine darts, have been achieved on various occasions. The lowest number of darts thrown for a score of 1001 is 19 by Cliff Inglis (b. 27 May 1935) (160, 180, 140, 180, 121, 180, 40) at the Bromfield Men's Club, Devon on 11 Nov 1975. A score of 2001 in 52 darts was achieved by Alan Evans (b. 14 June 1949) at Ferndale, Glamorgan on 3 Sept 1976. 3001 in 75 darts was thrown by Mike Gregory (b. 16 Dec 1956).

TEN HOUR SCORES

The record number of trebles scored in 10 hr is 3056 by Paul Taylor from 7992 darts thrown on 19 Oct 1985 at the Woodhouse Tavern, Leytonstone, London. David Broad scored a record 3085 doubles (out of 9945 darts) in 10 hr at Blantyre on 17 Mar 1984. The greatest score amassed in 10 hr with players retrieving their own darts in 371,428 by Derek Brown and Barry Hajisaava at Morphett Vale, Victoria, Australia on 11 May 1986.

24 HR SCORE

Eight players from Paddock Wood and District Lions Club scored 1,585,445 in 24 hr on one board at the John Brunt VC public house, Paddock Wood, Kent on 16–17 Feb 1985.

MILLION AND ONE UP

Eight players from the Gardeners Arms, Ipswich scored 1,000,001 with 37,809 darts in one session on 28 Feb–2 Mar 1986. Their attempt included 180 180s.

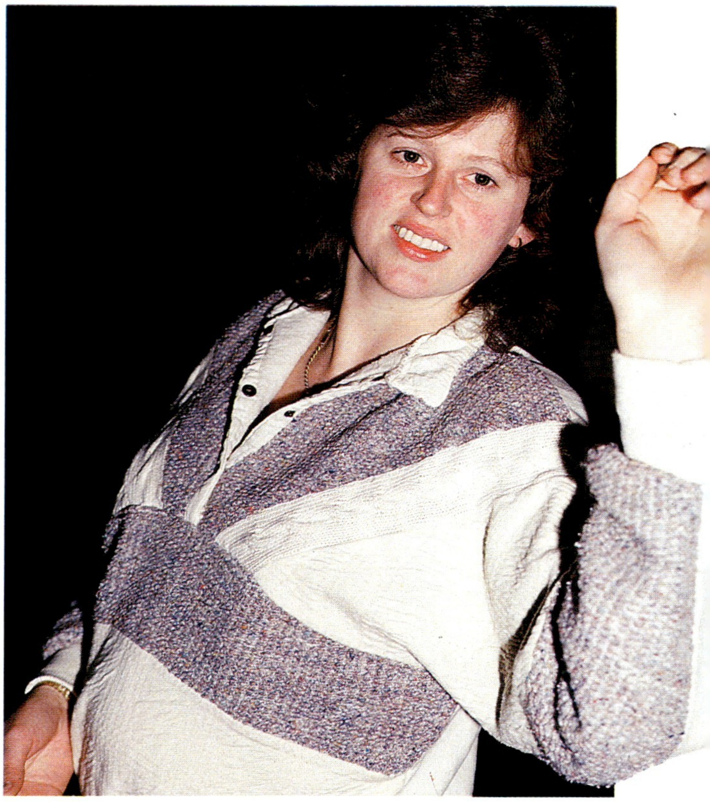

'Linda Batten who finished on a double after 117 darts holds the women's record for 3001.'

EQUESTRIAN SPORTS

Lucinda Green has won the Badminton Three-Day event a record six times, between 1973 and 1984. *(All-Sport)*

MOST OLYMPIC MEDALS

The greatest number of Olympic gold medals is five by Hans-Günter Winkler (b. 24 July 1926) (W. Germany) who won four team gold medals as captain in 1956, 1960, 1964 and 1972 and won the individual Grand Prix in 1956. The most team wins in the Prix des Nations is five by Germany in 1936, 1956, 1960, 1964 and 1972. The lowest score obtained by a winner is no faults by Frantisek Ventura (1895–1969) (Czechoslovakia) on *Eliot*, 1928 and Alwin Schockemöhle (b. 29 May 1937) (W. Germany) on *Warwick Rex*, 1976. Pierre Jonqueres d'Oriola (b. 1 Feb 1920) (France) uniquely won the individual gold medal twice, 1952 and 1964. Richard John Hannay Meade (b. 4 Dec 1938) (Great Britain) is the only British rider to win three gold medals – as an individual in 1972 and team titles in 1968 and 1972, all in the 3-day event.

MOST TITLES *WORLD*

The men's world championships (inst. 1953) have been won twice by Hans-Günter Winkler (W. Germany) (1954–5) and Raimondo d'Inzeo (Italy) (1956 and 1960). The women's title (1965–74) was won twice by Jane 'Janou' Tissot (*née* Lefebvre) (France) (b. Saigon, 14 May 1945) on *Rocket* (1970 and 1974).

KING GEORGE V GOLD CUP AND QUEEN ELIZABETH II CUP

David Broome (b. 1 Mar 1940) has won the King George V Gold Cup (first held 1911) a record five times, 1960 on *Sunsalve*, 1966 on *Mister Softee*, 1972 on *Sportsman*, 1977 on *Philco* and 1981 on *Mr Ross*. The Queen Elizabeth II Cup (first held 1949), for women, has been won four times by Elizabeth Edgar (b. 28 Apr 1943), 1977 on *Everest Wallaby*, 1979 on *Forever*, 1981 and 1982 on *Everest Forever*. The only horse to win both these trophies is *Sunsalve* in 1957 (with Elisabeth Anderson) and 1960.

THE PRINCE PHILIP (WORLD TEAM CHAMPIONSHIP)

Instituted in 1965 as the President's Trophy and renamed in 1985, it has been won a record eleven times by Great Britain, 1965, 1967, 1970, 1972–4, 1977–9, 1983 and 1985.

THREE-DAY EVENT

The Badminton Three-Day Event (inst. 1949) has been won six times by Lucinda Green (*née* Prior-Palmer) (b. 7 Nov 1953) in 1973 (on *Be Fair*), 1976 (*Wide Awake*), 1977 (*George*), 1979 (*Killaire*), 1983 (*Regal Realm*) and 1984 (*Beagle Bay*).

JUMPING RECORDS

The official *Fédération Equestre Internationale* high jump record is 2,47 m *8 ft $1\frac{1}{4}$ in* by *Huasó*, ridden by Capt Alberto Larraguibel Morales (Chile) at Vina del Mar, Santiago, Chile, on 5 Feb 1949, and 8,40 m *27 ft $6\frac{3}{4}$ in* for a long jump over water by *Something*, ridden by André Ferreira (S. Africa) at Johannesburg on 26 Apr 1975.

GOLF

CLUB *OLDEST*
The oldest club of which there is written evidence is the Gentlemen Golfers (now the Honourable Company of Edinburgh Golfers) formed in March 1744 – ten years prior to the institution of the Royal and Ancient Club of St Andrews, Fife. However the Royal Burgess Golfing Society of Edinburgh claim to have been founded in 1735.

COURSE *HIGHEST*
The highest golf course in the world is the Tuctu Golf Club in Morococha, Peru, which is 4369 m *14,335 ft* above sea-level at its lowest point. Golf has, however, been played in Tibet at an altitude of over 4875 m *16,000 ft*.

The highest golf course in Great Britain is one of nine holes at Leadhills, Strathclyde, 457 m *1500 ft* above sea-level.

LONGEST HOLE
The longest hole in the world is the 7th hole (par-7) of the Sano Course, Satsuki GC, Japan, which measures 831 m *909 yd*. In August 1927 the sixth hole at Prescott Country Club in Arkansas, USA, measured 766 m *838 yd*. The longest hole on a championship course in Great Britain is the sixth at Troon, Strathclyde, which stretches 528 m *577 yd*.

LARGEST GREEN
Probably the largest green in the world is that of the par-6 635 m *695 yd* fifth hole at International GC, Bolton, Massachusetts, USA, with an area greater than 2600 m^2 *28,000* ft^2.

BIGGEST BUNKER
The world's biggest bunker (called a trap in the USA) is Hell's Half Acre on the 535 m *585 yd* seventh hole of the Pine Valley course, Clementon, New Jersey, USA, built in 1912 and generally regarded as the world's most trying course.

LONGEST COURSE
The world's longest course is the par-77 7612 m *8325 yd* International GC, (*see also above*), from the 'Tiger' tees, remodelled in 1969 by Robert Trent Jones. Floyd Satterlee Rood used the United States as a course, when he played from the Pacific surf to the Atlantic surf from 14 Sept 1963 to 3 Oct 1964 in 114,737 strokes. He lost 3511 balls on the 5468 km *3397.7 mile* trail.

LONGEST DRIVES
In long-driving contests 300 m *330 yd* is rarely surpassed at sea-level. In officially regulated long driving contests over level ground the greatest distance recorded is 358 m *392 yd* by William Thomas 'Tommie' Campbell (b. 24 July 1927) (Foxrock Golf Club) at Dun Laoghaire, Co. Dublin, in July 1964.

On an airport runway Lian Higgins (Ireland) drove a Spalding Top Flite ball 579,8 m *634.1 yd* at Baldonnel military airport, Dublin, Ireland on 25 Sept 1984. The greatest recorded drive on an ordinary course is one of 471 m *515 yd* by Michael Hoke Austin (b. 17 Feb 1910) of Los Angeles, California, USA, in the US National Seniors Open Championship at Las Vegas, Nevada, on 25 Sept 1974. Austin, 1,88 m *6 ft 2 in* tall and weighing 92 kg *210 lb*, drove the ball to within a yard of the green on the par-4 412 m *450 yd* fifth hole of the Winterwood Course and it rolled 59 m *65 yd* past the flagstick. He was aided by an estimated 56 km/h *35 mph* tailwind.

A drive of 2414 m *2640 yd (1½ miles)* across ice was achieved by an Australian meteorologist named Nils Lied at Mawson Base, Antarctica, in 1962. Arthur Lynskey claimed a drive of 182 m *200 yd* horizontal and 3200 m *2 miles* vertical off Pikes Peak, Colorado (4300 m *14,110 ft*) on 28 June 1968. On the Moon the energy expended on a mundane 274 m *300 yd* drive would achieve, craters permitting, a distance of 1,6 km *1 mile*.

LONGEST PUTT
The longest recorded holed putt in a major tournament was one of 26 m *86 ft* on the vast 13th green at the Augusta National, Georgia by Cary Middlecoff (b. 6 Jan 1921) (USA) in the 1955 Masters' Tournament. Robert Tyre 'Bobby' Jones Jr (1902–71) was reputed to have holed a putt in excess of 30 m *100 ft* at the fifth green in the first round of the 1927 Open at St Andrews.

Bob Cook (USA) sunk a 42.74 m *140 ft 2¾ in* putt on the 18th at St. Andrew's in the International Fourball Pro Am Tournament on 1 Oct 1976.

SCORES

LOWEST 9 HOLES AND 18 HOLES *MEN*
At least four players are recorded to have played a long course (over 5486 m *6000 yd*) in a score of 58, most recently Monte Carlo Money (b. 3 Dec 1954) (USA) the par-72, 6041 m *6607 yd* Las Vegas Municipal GC, Nevada, USA on 11 Mar 1981. The lowest recorded score on a long course in Britain is 58 by Harry Weetman (1920–72) the British Ryder Cup golfer, for the 5642 m *6171 yd* Croham Hurst Course, Croydon, Surrey, on 30 Jan 1956. Alfred Edward Smith (1903–85) the Woolacombe professional, achieved an 18-hole score of 55 (15 under bogey 70) on his home course on 1 Jan 1936. The course measured 3884 m *4248 yd*. The detail was 4, 2, 3, 4, 2, 4, 3, 4, 3=29 out, and 2, 3, 3, 3, 3, 2, 5, 4, 1=26 in.

The United States PGA tournament record for 18 holes is 59 (30+29) by Al Geiberger (b. 1 Sept 1937) in the second round of the Danny Thomas Classic, on the 72-par 6628 m *7249 yd* Colonial GC course, Memphis, Tennessee on 10 June 1977. Three golfers have recorded 59 over 18 holes in non-PGA tournaments; Samuel Jackson Snead (b. 27 May 1912) in the third round of the Sam Snead Festival at White Sulphur Springs, West Virgina, USA on 16 May 1959; Gary Player (b. 1 Nov 1935) (South Africa) in the second round of the Brazilian Open in Rio de Janeiro on 29 Nov 1974, and David Jagger (b. 9 June 1949) (GB) in a Pro-Am tournament prior to the 1973 Nigerian Open at Ikoyi Golf Club, Lagos.

Nine holes in 25 (4, 3, 3, 2, 3, 3, 1, 4, 2) was recorded by A. J. 'Bill' Burke in a round in 57 (32+25) on the 5842 m *6389 yd* par-71 Normandie course St Louis, Missouri, USA on 20 May 1970. The tournament record is 27 by Mike Souchak (b. 10 May 1927) (USA) for the second nine (par-35) first round of the 1955 Texas Open (*see 72 holes*), Andy North (b. 9 Mar 1950) (USA) second nine (par-34), first round, 1975 BC Open at En-Joie GC, Endicott, NY and José Maria Canizares (b. 18 Feb 1947) (Spain), first nine, third round, in the 1978 Swiss Open on the 6228 m *6811 yd* Crans-Sur course.

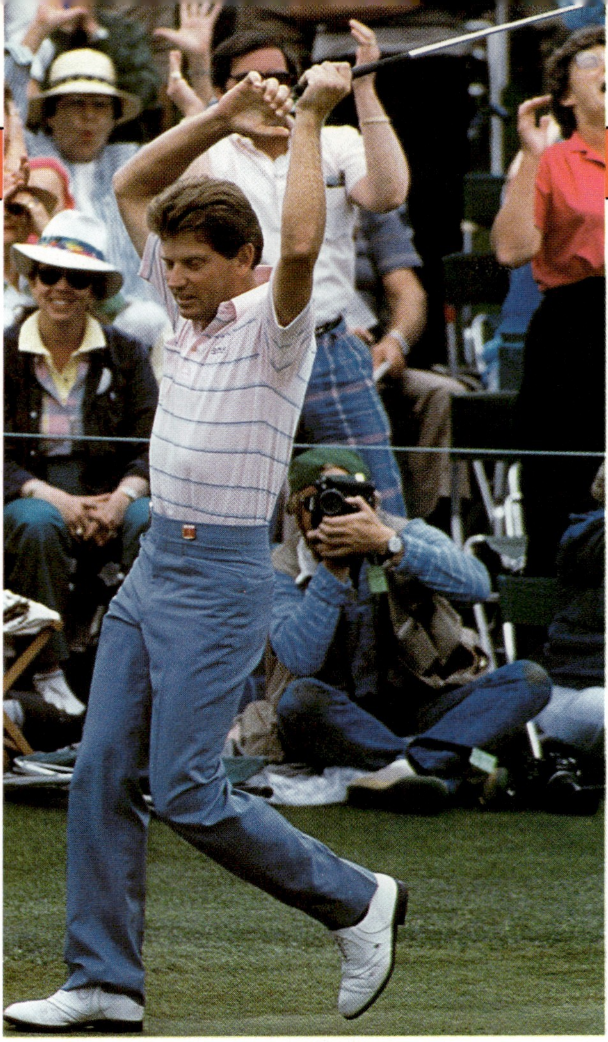

Zimbabwean Nick Price celebrates his record-breaking round of 68 in the 1986 US Masters.

LOWEST 18 HOLES *WOMEN*

The lowest recorded score on an 18-hole course (over 5486 m *6000 yd*) for a woman is 62 (30+32) by Mary 'Mickey' Kathryn Wright (b. 14 Feb 1935) (USA) on the Hogan Park Course (par-71, 5757 m *6286 yd*) at Midland, Texas, USA, in November 1964. Wanda Morgan (b. 22 Mar 1910) recorded a score of 60 (31+29) on the Westgate and Birchington Golf Club course, Kent, over 18 holes (4573 m *5002 yd*) on 11 July 1929.

LOWEST 18 HOLES *GREAT BRITAIN*

The lowest score recorded in a first class professional tournament on a course of more than 5486 m *6000 yd* in Great Britain is 61 (29+32), by Thomas Bruce Haliburton (1915–71) of Wentworth GC in the Spalding Tournament at Worthing, West Sussex, in June 1952, and 61 (32+29) by Peter J. Butler (b. 25 Mar 1932) in the Bowmaker Tournament on the Old Course at Sunningdale, Berkshire, on 4 July 1967.

LOWEST 36 HOLES

The record for 36 holes is 122 (59+63) by Sam Snead in the 1959 Sam Snead Festival on 16–17 May 1959. Horton Smith (1908–63), twice US Master Champion, scored 121 (63+58) on a short course on 21 Dec 1928 (*see 72 holes*). The lowest score by a British golfer has been 124 (61+63) by Alexander Walter Barr 'Sandy' Lyle (b. 9 Feb 1958) in the Nigerian Open at the 5508 m *6024 yd* (par-71) Ikoyi Golf Club, Lagos in 1978.

LOWEST 72 HOLES

The lowest recorded score on a first-class course is 255 (29 under par) by Leonard Peter Tupling (b. 6 Apr 1950) (GB) in the Nigerian Open at Ikoyi Golf Club, Lagon in February 1981, made up of 63, 66, 62 and 64 (average 63.75 per round).

The lowest 72 holes in a US professional event is 257 (60, 68, 64, 65) by Mike Souchak in the 1955 Texas Open at San Antonio.

The lowest 72 holes in an Open championship in Europe is 262 (67, 66, 66, 63) by Percy Alliss (1897–1975) (GB) in the 1932 Italian Open at San Remo, and by Lu Liang Huan (b. 10 Dec 1935) (Taiwan) in the 1971 French Open at Biarritz. Kelvin D. G. Nagle (b. 21 Dec 1920) of Australia shot 261 in the Hong Kong Open in 1961. The lowest for four rounds in a British first class tournament is 262 (66, 63, 66 and 67) by Bernard Hunt in the Piccadilly tournament on the par-68 5655 m *6184 yd* Wentworth East Course, Virginia Water, Surrey on 4–5 Oct 1966. Horton Smith scored 245 (63, 58,61 and 63) for 72 holes on the 4297 m *4700 yd* (par-64) at Catalina Country Club, California, USA, to win the Catalina Open on 21–23 Dec 1928.

HIGHEST SCORE

The highest score for a single hole in the British Open is 21 by a player in the inaugural meeting at Prestwick in 1860. Double figures have been recorded on the card of the winner only once, when Willie Fernie (1851–1924) scored a ten at Musselburgh, Lothian, in 1883. Ray Ainsley of Ojai, California, took 19 strokes for the par-4 16th hole during the second round of the US Open at Cherry Hills Country Club, Denver, Colorado, on 10 June 1938. Most of the strokes were used in trying to extricate the ball from a brook. Hans Merell of Mogadore, Ohio, took 19 strokes on the par-3 16th (203 m *222 yd*) during the third round of the Bing Crosby National Tournament at Cypress Point Club, Del Monte, California, USA, on 17 Jan 1959. It is recorded that Chevalier von Cittern went round 18 holes in 316, averaging 17.55 per hole, at Biarritz, France in 1888. Steven Ward took 222 strokes for the 5680 m *6212 yd* Pecos Course, Reeves County, Texas, USA, on 18 June 1976 – but he was only aged 3 years 286 days.

MOST SHOTS FOR ONE HOLE

A woman player in the qualifying round of the Shawnee Invitational for Ladies at Shawnee-on-Delaware, Pennsylvannia, USA, in *c.* 1912, took 166 strokes for the short 118 m *130 yd* 16th hole. Her tee shot went into the Binniekill River and the ball floated. She put out in a boat with her exemplary but statistically minded husband at the oars. She eventually beached the ball 2,4 km *1½ miles* downstream but was not yet out of the wood. She had to play through one on the home run. In a competition at Peacehaven, Sussex, England in 1890, A. J. Lewis had 156 putts on one green without holing out.

ROUNDS FASTEST *INDIVIDUAL*

With such variations in lengths of courses, speed records, even for rounds under par, are of little comparative value. Rick Baker completed 18 holes (5616 m *6142 yd*) in 25 min 48.47 sec at Surfer's Paradise, Queensland, Australia on 4 Sept 1982, but this test permitted the striking of the ball whilst still moving. The record for a still ball is 28.09 min by Gary Shane Wright (b. 27 Nov 1946) at Tewantin-Noosa Golf Club, Queensland (18 holes, 5522 m *6039 yd*) on 9 Dec 1980.

GOLF

ROUNDS FASTEST *TEAM*
Seventy-seven players completed the 18-hole 5945 m *6502 yd* Kern City course, California, USA in 10 min 30 sec on 24 Aug 1984 using only one ball. They scored 80!

ROUNDS SLOWEST
The slowest stroke play tournament round was one of 6 hr 45 min taken by South Africa in the first round of the 1972 World Cup at the Royal Melbourne GC, Australia. This was a four-ball medal round, everything holed out.

THROWING THE GOLF BALL
The lowest recorded score for throwing a golf ball round 18 holes (over 5500 m *6000 yd*) is 82 by Joe Flynn (USA), 21, at the 5694 m *6228 yd* Port Royal Course, Bermuda, on 27 Mar 1975.

CHAMPIONSHIP RECORDS

THE OPEN
The Open Championship was inaugurated in 1860 at Prestwick, Strathclyde, Scotland. The lowest score for 9 holes is 28 by Denis Durnian (b. 30 June 1950), at Royal Birkdale, Southport, Lancashire in the second round on 15 July 1983.

The all-time professional money winner is Jack Nicklaus with $4,857,494 to 25 May 1986.

The lowest round in The Open is 63 by Mark Hayes (b. 12 July 1949) (USA) at Turnberry, Strathclyde, on 7 July 1977, and Isao Aoki (b. 31 Aug 1942) (Japan) at Muirfield, East Lothian, on 19 July 1980. Thomas Henry Cotton (b. 26 Jan 1907) at Royal St George's, Sandwich, Kent completed the first 36 holes in 132 (67+65) on 27 June 1934. The lowest aggregate is 268 (68, 70, 65, 65) by Tom Watson (b. 4 Sept 1949) (USA) at Turnberry, ending on 9 July 1977.

US OPEN
The United States Open Championship was inaugurated in 1895. The lowest 72-hole aggregate is 272 (63, 71, 70, 68) by Jack Nicklaus (b. 21 Jan 1940) on the Lower Course (6414 m *7015 yd*) at Baltusrol Country Club, Springfield, New Jersey, on 12–15 June 1980. The lowest score for 18 holes is 63 by Johnny Miller (b. 29 Apr 1947) on the 6328 m *6921 yd* par-71 Oakmont Country Club course, Pennsylvania on 17 June 1973, Jack Nicklaus (*see above*) and Tom Weiskopf (b. 9 Nov 1942) (USA), both on 12 June 1980.

US MASTERS'
The lowest score in the US Masters' (instituted on the par-72 6382 m *6980 yd* Augusta National Golf Course, Georgia, in 1934) has been 271 by Jack Nicklaus in 1965 and Raymond Floyd (b. 4 Sept 1942) in 1976. The lowest round was 63 achieved by Nick Price (USA) in 1986.

WORLD CUP (FORMERLY CANADA CUP)
The World Cup (instituted as the Canada Cup in 1953) has been won most often by the USA with 16 victories between 1955 and 1983. The only men to have been on six winning teams have been Arnold Palmer (b. 10 Sept 1929) (1960, 1962–4, 1966–7) and Jack Nicklaus (1963–4, 1966–7, 1971 and 1973). Only Nicklaus has taken the individual title three times (1963–4, 1971). The lowest aggregate score for 144 holes is 544 by Australia, Bruce Devlin (b. 10 Oct 1937) and David Graham (b. 23 May 1946), at San Isidro, Buenos Aires, Argentina on 12–15 Nov 1970. The lowest individual score has been 269 by Roberto de Vicenzo (b. 14 Apr 1923) (Arentina), also in 1970.

RYDER CUP
The biennial Ryder Cup professional match between USA and the British Isles or Great Britain (Europe since 1979) was instituted in 1927. The USA have won 21½ to 3½ to date. William Earl 'Billy' Casper (b. San Diego, California, USA, 24 June 1931) has the record of winning most matches in the Trophy with 20 in 1961–75. Christy O'Connor Sr (b. 21 Dec 1924) (GB) played in ten matches up to 1973.

WALKER CUP
The USA *v.* GB & Ireland series instituted in 1921 (for the Walker Cup since 1922 and now held biennially) has been won by the USA 25½–2½ to date. Joseph Boynton Carr (GB&I) (b. 18 Feb 1922) played in ten contests (1947–67).

CURTIS CUP
The biennial ladies' Curtis Cup match between USA and Great Britain and Ireland was first held in 1932. The USA have won 19, GB&I 2 and two matches have been tied. Mary McKenna (GB&I) (b. 29 Apr 1949) played in a record eighth match in 1984.

RICHEST PRIZES
The greatest first place prize money was $500,000 (total purse $1,100,000) won by Johnny Miller in 1982 and Raymond Floyd in 1983, at Sun City, Bophuthatswana, S. Africa. Both won in play-offs, from Severiano Ballesteros and Craig Stadler respectively.

HIGHEST EARNINGS *EUROPEAN CIRCUIT*
Sandy Lyle won a European record £162,352 in European Order of Merit tournaments (£199,020 in all European events) plus a £25,000 bonus in 1985.

MOST TOURNAMENT WINS
The record for winning tournaments in a single season is 18 (plus one unofficial), including a record 11 consecutively, by John Byron Nelson (b. 4 Feb 1912) (USA), from 8 Mar–4 Aug 1945. Sam Snead won 84 official US PGA Tour events 1936–65, and has been credited with a total 134 tournament victories since 1934. The Ladies PGA record is 85 by Kathy Whitworth (b. 27 Sept 1939) from 1962 to 1984.

BIGGEST WINNING MARGIN
The greatest margin of victory in a major tournament is 21 strokes by Jerry Pate (b. 16 Sept 1953) (USA) in the Colombian Open with 262 on 10–13 Dec 1981.

YOUNGEST AND OLDEST CHAMPIONS
The youngest winner of The Open was Tom Morris, Jr. (1851–75) at Prestwick, Strathclyde in 1868 aged 17 yr 249 days. The youngest winners of The Amateur title were John Charles Beharrell (b. 2 May 1938) at Troon, Strathclyde, on 2 June 1956, and Robert 'Bobby' E. Cole (b. 11 May 1948) (South Africa) at Carnoustie, Tayside, on 11 June 1966, both aged 18 yr 1 month. The oldest Open Champion was 'Old Tom' Morris (1821–1908), aged 46 yr 99 days when he won at Prestwick in 1867. In recent times the 1967 champion, Roberto de Vicenzo was aged 44 yr 93 days. The oldest winner of The Amateur was the Hon Michael Scott (1878–1959) at Hoylake, Merseyside in 1933, when 54 yr 297 days. The oldest United States Amateur Champion was Jack Westland (1904–82) at Seattle, Washington, on 23 Aug 1952, aged 47 yr 253 days.

MOST ROUNDS
The greatest number of rounds played on foot in 24 hr is 22 rounds and five holes (401 holes) by Ian Colston, 35, at Bendigo GC, Victoria (par-73, 5542 m *6061 yd*) on 27–28 Nov 1971. The British record is 360 holes by Antony J. Clark at Childwall GC, Liverpool on 18 July 1983. Gaston Gravelle played 326 holes in 12 hr on the 5940 m *6499 yd* course at Notre-Dame-de-la-Salette, Quebec, Canada, on 2 Sept 1984, being driven between shots in a golf cart. Dr R. C. 'Dick' Hardison, aged 61, played 236 holes under USGA rules in 12 hr at Sea Mountain GC, Punalina, Hawaii on 31 July 1984, maintaining an average score of 76 per round, with an average time per hole of 3.05 min. His best round was a 68, achieved in 49 min 58 sec, including a second nine of 30 in 24 min 28 sec. He used seven fore caddies and 26 electric golf carts, which he drove himself. The most holes played on foot in a week (168 hr) is 1128 by Steve Hylton at the Mason Rudolph Golf Club (5541 m *6060 yd*), Clarkesville, Tennessee, USA, from 25–31 Aug 1980.

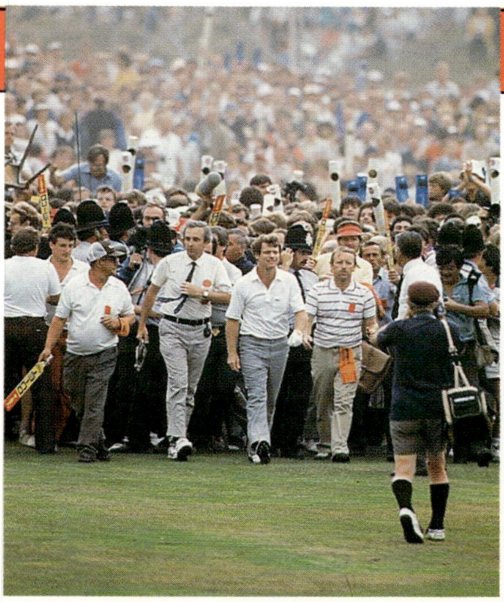

Tom Watson, five times winner of the Open, has the lowest 72-hole aggregate score for the tournament. *(All-Sport)*

HOLES IN ONE

LONGEST
The longest straight hole ever holed in one shot is the tenth (408 m *447 yd*) at Miracle Hills Golf Club, Omaha, Nebraska, USA by Robert Mitera (b. 1944) on 7 Oct 1965. Mitera stood 1,68 m *5 ft 6 in* tall and weighed 75 kg *165 lb (11 st 11 lb)*. He was a two handicap player who normally drove 224 m *245 yd*. A 80 km/h *50 mph* gust carried his shot over a 265 m *290 yd* drop-off. The longest 'dog-leg' hole achieved in one is the 439 m *480 yd* fifth at Hope Country Club, Arkansas by L. Bruce on 15 Nov 1962. The feminine record is 359 m *393 yd* by Marie Robie on the first hole of the Furnace Brook Golf Club, Wollaston, Mass., USA, on 4 Sept 1949. The longest hole in one performed in the British Isles is the seventh (par-4. 359 m *393 yd*) at West Lancashire GC by Peter Richard Parkinson (b. 26 Aug 1947) on 6 June 1972.

MOST
The greatest number of holes-in-one in a career is 66 by Harry Lee Bonner from 1967 to 1983, most at his home 9-hole course of Las Gallinas, San Rafael, California, USA. The British record is 31 by Charles T. Chevalier (1902–73) of Heaton Moor Golf Club, Stockport, Greater Manchester between 20 June 1918 and 1970.

The most holes-in-one in a year is 28 by Scott Palmer from 5 June 1983 to 31 May 1984, all on par-3 or par-4 holes between 119 m *130 yd* and 238 m *260 yd* in length at Ballboa Park, San Diego, California, USA.

CONSECUTIVE
There are at least 16 cases of 'aces' being achieved in two consecutive holes, of which the greatest was Norman L. Manley's unique 'double albatross' on the par-4 301 m *330 yd* seventh and par-4 265 m *290 yd* eighth holes on the Del Valle Country Club Course, Saugus, California, on 2 Sept 1964. The first woman to record consecutive 'aces' was Sue Prell, on the 13th and 14th holes at Chatswood Golf Club, Sydney, Australia on 29 May 1977.

The closest to achieving three consecutive holes in one was the late Dr Joseph Boydstone on the 3rd, 4th and 9th at Bakersfield GC, California, USA, on 10 Oct 1962 and the Rev Harold Snider (b. 4 July 1900) who aced the 8th, 13th and 14th holes of the par-3 Ironwood course, Arizona, USA on 9 June 1976.

GYMNASTICS

EARLIEST REFERENCES

A primitive form of gymnastics was practised in ancient Greece and Rome during the period of the ancient Olympic Games (776 BC to AD 393) but Johann Friedrich Simon was the first teacher of modern gymnastics at Basedow's School, Dessau, Germany in 1776.

MOST TITLES *WORLD*

The greatest number of individual titles won by a man in the World Championships is ten by Boris Shakhlin (b. 27 Jan 1932) (USSR) between 1954 and 1964. He also won three team titles. The female record is ten individual wins and five team titles by Larissa Semyonovna Latynina (b. 27 Dec 1934) of the USSR, between 1956 and 1964. Japan has won the men's team title a record five times (1962, 1966, 1970, 1974, 1978) and the USSR the women's team title on eight occasions (1954, 1958, 1962, 1970, 1974, 1978, 1981 and 1983).

The most overall titles in Modern Rhythmic Gymnastics is three by Maria Gigova (Bulgaria) in 1969, 1971 and 1973 (shared). Galina Shugurova (USSR) (b. 1955) won eight apparatus titles from 1969–77.

MOST TITLES *OLYMPIC*

Japan (1960, 1964, 1968, 1972 and 1976) have won the men's team title most often. The USSR have won the women's title eight times (1952–80). The only men to win six individual gold medals are Boris Shakhlin (USSR), with one in 1956, four (two shared) in 1960 and one in 1964, and Nikolai Andrianov (b. 14 Oct 1952) (USSR), with one in 1972, four in 1976 and one in 1980.

Vera Caslavska-Odlozil (b. 3 May 1942) (Czechoslovakia), has won most individual gold medals with seven, three in 1964 and four (one shared) in 1968. Larissa Latynina won six individual gold medals and was in three winning teams in 1956–64 making nine gold medals. She also won five silver and four bronze making 18 in all – an Olympic record. The most medals for a male gymnast is 15 by Nikolai Andrianov (USSR), 7 gold, 5 silver and 3 bronze in 1972–80. Aleksander Ditiatin (b.7 Aug 1957) (USSR) is the only man to win a medal in all eight categories in the same Games, with 3 gold, 4 silver and 1 bronze at Moscow in 1980.

HIGHEST SCORE *OLYMPICS*

Nadia Comaneci (b. 12 Nov 1961) (Romania) was the first to achieve a perfect score, with seven of 10.00 at the Montreal Olympics in July 1976.

YOUNGEST INTERNATIONAL AND WORLD CHAMPION

Pasakevi 'Voula' Kouna (b. 6 Dec 1971) was aged 9 yr 299 days at the start of the Balkan Games at Serres, Greece on 1–4 Oct 1981, when she represented Greece. Olga Bicherova (b. 26 Oct 1966) (USSR) won the women's world title at 15 yr 33 days on 28 Nov 1981. The youngest male world champion was Dmitri Belozerchev (b. 17 Dec 1966) (USSR) at 16 years 315 days at Budapest, Hungary on 28 Oct 1983.

GYMNASTICS FEATS

24 Hr Press-Ups – 25,573 by Paul Lynch at the Hippodrome Club, London on 17–18 July 1985.
24 Hr Sit-Ups – 43,418 by Lou Scripa (USA) at Jack La Lanne's Health Club, Sacramento, California, USA on 6–7 Oct 1984.
5 Hr One Arm Push-Ups – 3856 by Colin Hewick (GB) at Bodyworld Health Club, Hull, Humberside, 13 June 1986.

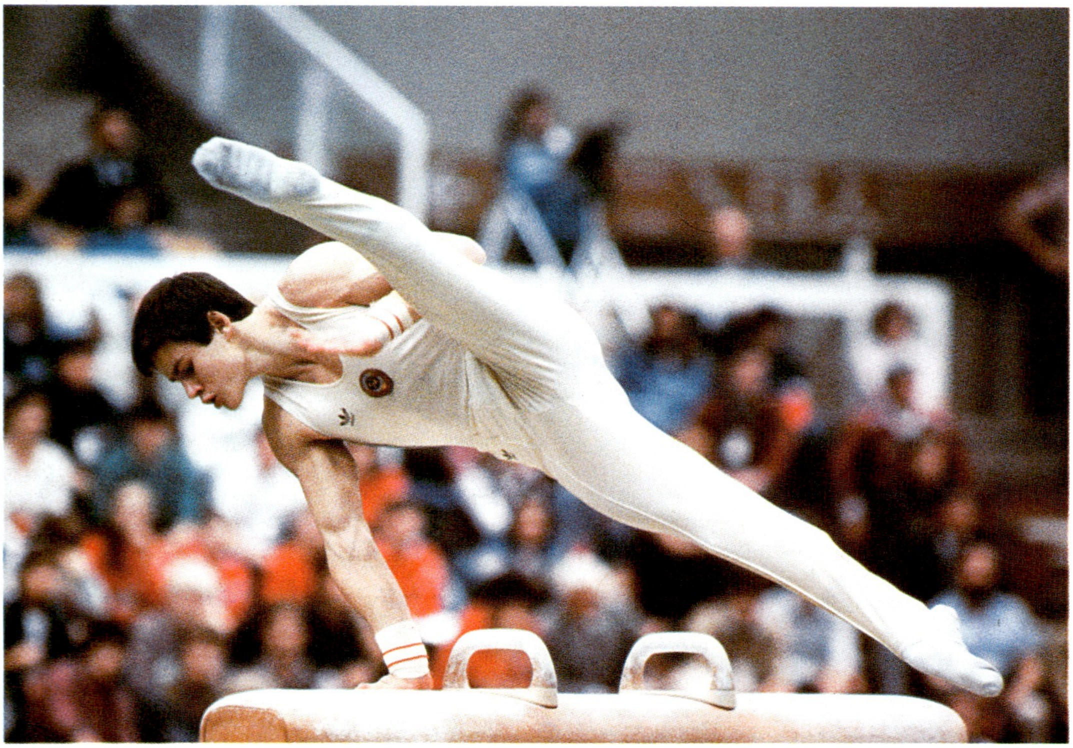

Dimitri Belozerchev of Russia became the youngest ever Men's World Gymnastics Champion at the age of 16. *(All-Sport)*

HORSE RACING

ORIGINS
Horsemanship was an important part of the Hittite culture of Anatolia, Turkey dating from 1400 BC. The 33rd ancient Olympic Games of 648 BC in Greece featured horse racing. The earliest races recorded in England were those held in about AD 200 at Netherby, Cumbria, between Arab horses imported by the Romans.

RACECOURSE *LARGEST*
The world's largest racecourse is at Newmarket. It now comprises the Rowley Mile Course and the July Course, whose grandstands are about a mile apart, although a portion of the course is common to both. The Beacon Course of 6,80 km *4 miles 397 yd*, is no longer in use. The course is situated in the middle of Newmarket Heath, *c.* 2500 acres, the largest training area in the world.

LARGEST PRIZES
The richest day's racing ever was staged at Hollywood Park, Los Angeles, USA on 10 Nov 1984, when the prize money totalled $10 million for the seven races. Included was a record $3 million for the Breeders' Cup Classic. A record $2.6 million was received by *Spend A Buck*, $600,000 for winning the Jersey Derby, Garden Hote Park, NJ, USA on 27 May 1985, together with a $2 million bonus for also winning the Kentucky Derby and two preparatory races at Garden State Park.

MOST RUNNERS
The most horses in a race was 66 in the Grand National on 22 Mar 1929. The record for the Flat is 58 in the Lincolnshire Handicap at Lincoln on 13 Mar 1948. The most runners at a meeting were 214 (Flat) in seven races at Newmarket on 15 June 1915 and 229 (National Hunt) in eight races at Worcester on 13 Jan 1965.

DEAD-HEATS
There is no recorded case in Turf history of a quintuple dead-heat. The nearest approach was in the Astley Stakes, at Lewes, Sussex, on 6 Aug 1880 when *Mazurka*, *Wandering Nun* and *Scobell* triple dead-heated for first place a head in front of *Cumberland* and *Thora*, who dead-heated for fourth place. Each of the five jockeys thought he had won. The only three known examples of a quadruple dead-heat were between *Honest Harry*, *Miss Decoy*, *Young Daffodil* and *Peteria* at Bogside, on 7 June 1808, between *Defaulter*, *The Squire of Malton*, *Reindeer* and *Pulcherrima* in the Omnibus Stakes at The Hoo, Hertfordshire, on 26 Apr 1851, and between *Overreach*, *Lady Golightly*, *Gamester* and *The Unexpected* at Newmarket on 22 Oct 1855. Since the introduction of the photo-finish, the highest number of horses dead-heating has been three, on several occasions.

HORSES *MOST SUCCESSFUL*
The horse with the best win-loss record was *Kincsem*, a Hungarian mare foaled in 1874, who was unbeaten in 54 races (1876–9) throughout Europe, including the Goodwood Cup of 1878. *Camerero*, foaled in 1951, won his first 56 races in Puerto Rico from 19 Apr 1953 to 17 Aug 1955. (In his career to 1956 he won 73 of 77 races.) The most wins in a career is 137 from 159 starts by *Galgo Jr* (foaled 1928) in Puerto Rico between 1930 and 1936; in 1931 he won a record 30 races in one year.

'Steve Cauthen (in red) and Oh So Sharp hold the time record for the 1000 Guineas at 1 min 36.8 sec.'

HORSE *HIGHEST PRICE*
The most expensive horse ever is *Shareef Dancer* syndicated for $40 million in August 1983 by his owner Sheikh Maktoum al Maktoumi, 40 shares were issued at $1 million each. The most paid for a yearling is $10.2 m for *Snaafi Dancer* on 20 July 1983 at Keeneland, Kentucky, by Sheikh Mohammed al Maktoum.

HORSES *GREATEST WINNINGS*
The career earnings record is $6,597,947 by the gelding *John Henry* (foaled 1975) with 39 wins from 83 races, from 1977 to 1984. The leading money-winning mare is *All Along* (foaled 1979) with $3,018,420 in France and the USA, 1981–4.

HORSES *BIGGEST WEIGHT*
The biggest weight ever carried is 190 kg *30 stone* by both Mr Maynard's mare and Mr Baker's horse in a match won by the former over a mile at York on 21 May 1788.

JOCKEYS *MOST SUCCESSFUL*
The most successful jockey of all time has been William Lee 'Bill' Shoemaker (USA) (b. weighing 1,1 kg *2½ lb*, 19 Aug 1931) now weighing 43 kg *94 lb* and standing 1,50 m *4 ft 11 in*. He rode 8514 winners from 38,201 mounts, earning $103,848,268 from his first ride on 19 Mar 1949 and first winner on 20 Apr 1949 to 29 Jan 1986. Lanffitt Pincay Jr. (B. 29 Dec 1946, Panama City) has earned a record $106,595,202 from over 6000 winners, 1966–86.

JOCKEYS *YOUNGEST AND OLDEST*
The youngest jockey was Australian-born Frank Wootton (1893–1940) (English champion jockey 1909–12), who rode his first winner in South Africa aged 9 years 10 months. The oldest jockey was Harry Beasley, who rode his last race at Baldoyle, Co. Dublin, Ireland on 10 June 1935 aged 83.

ICE HOCKEY

WORLD CHAMPIONSHIPS AND OLYMPIC GAMES
World Championships were first held for amateurs in 1920 in conjunction with the Olympic Games, which were also considered as World Championships up to 1968. From 1977 World Championships have been open to professionals. The USSR have won 19 world titles between 1954 and 1983, including the Olympic titles of 1956, 1964 and 1968. They have won three further Olympic titles in 1972, 1976 and 1984. Canada have also won 19 titles, between 1920 and 1961, including 6 Olympic titles (1920, 1924, 1928, 1932, 1948 and 1952). The longest Olympic career is that of Richard Torriani (b. 1 Oct 1911) (Switzerland) from 1928 to 1948. The most gold medals won by any player is three achieved by USSR players Vitaliy Davidov, Anatoliy Firssov, Viktor Kuzkin and Aleksandr Ragulin in 1964, 1968 and 1972, and by Vladislav Tretyak in 1972, 1976 and 1984.

STANLEY CUP
The Stanley Cup, presented by the Governor-General, Lord Stanley (original cost $48.67), became emblematic of National Hockey League supremacy 33 years after the first contest at Montreal in 1893. It has been won most often by the Montreal Canadiens with 22 wins in 1916, 1924, 1930–1, 1944, 1946, 1953, 1956–60, 1965–6, 1968–9, 1971, 1973, 1976–9.

MOST GOALS *TEAM*
The greatest number of goals recorded in a world championship match was when Canada beat Denmark 47–0 in Stockholm, Sweden on 12 Feb 1949. The NHL record is 21 goals when Montreal Canadiens beat Toronto St Patrick's, at Montreal, 14–7 on 10 Jan 1920.

LONGEST MATCH
The longest match was 2 hr 56 min 30 sec (playing time) when Detroit Red Wings beat Montreal Maroons 1–0 in the sixth period of overtime at the Forum, Montreal, at 2.25 a.m. on 25 Mar 1936. Norm Smith, the Red Wings goaltender, turned aside 92 shots for the NHL's longest single shutout.

MOST GOALS AND POINTS *INDIVIDUAL*
The most goals scored in a season in the NHL is 92 in the 1981–2 season by Wayne Gretzky (b. 26 Jan 1961) (Edmonton Oilers). He also scored a record 212 points (including 120 assists). He scored an additional 12 points (5 goals, 7 assists) in the Stanley Cup playoffs and 14 points (6 goals, 8 assists) for Canada in the World Championships in April 1982. He scored a record 125 assists the following season, 1982–83. Gretzky scored his 400th NHL goal on 13 Jan 1985 for an average .915 goals per game. The North American career record for goals is 1071 (801 in the NHL) by Gordie Howe (b. 31 Mar 1928) (Detroit Red Wings, Houston Aeros, New England Whalers and Hartford Whalers) from 16 Oct 1946 in 32 seasons ending in 1979–80. He took 2204 games to achieve the 1000th goal, but Robert Marvin 'Bobby' Hull (b. 3 Jan 1939) (Chicago Black Hawks and Winnipeg Jets) scored his 1000th in 1600 games on 12 Mar 1978.

MOST POINTS ONE GAME
The North American major league record for most points scored in one game is ten (3 goals, 7 assists) by Jim Harrison (b. 9 July 1947) (for Alberta, later Edmonton Oilers) in a World Hockey Association match at Edmonton on 30 Jan 1973, and by Darryl Sittler (b. 18 Sept 1950) (6 goals, 4 assists) for Toronto Maple Leafs in a NHL match at Toronto on 7 Feb 1976.

FASTEST SCORING *WORLD*
In the NHL the fastest goal was after 4 sec in the second period by Joseph Antoine Claude Provost (b. 17 Sept 1933) (Montreal Canadiens) *v* Boston Bruins at Montreal on 9 Nov 1957. Doug Smail of the Winnipeg Jets scored 5 sec from the opening whistle against St Louis on 20 Dec 1981. Canadian Bill Mosienko (b. 2 Nov 1921) (Chicago Black Hawks) scored three goals in 21 sec *v* New York Rangers on 23 Mar 1952. Toronto scored eight goals in 4 min 52 sec *v* New York Americans on 19 Mar 1938.

Vladeslav Tretyak (*left*) has won three gold medals for Russia preventing goals, whilst Wayne Gretzky (*below*) has rewritten the American League record books scoring them. *(All-Sport)*

ICE SKATING

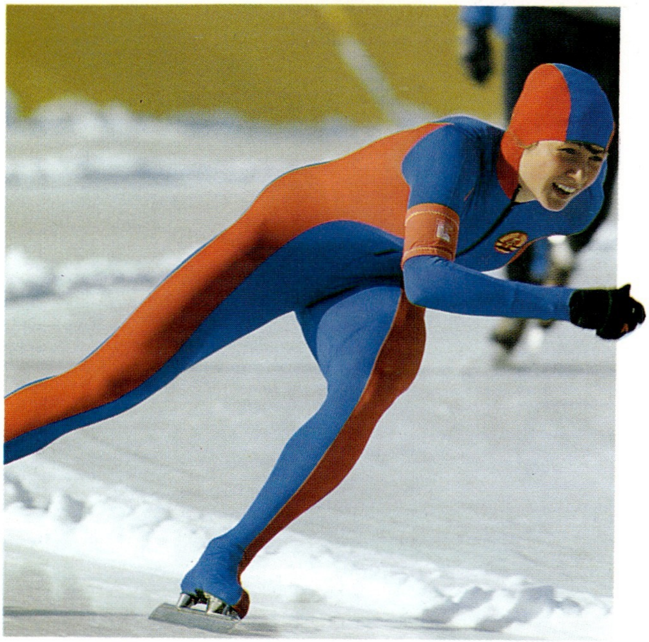

Karin Kania of East Germany regained four of her world speed records in 1986.

FIGURE SKATING

MOST TITLES *OLYMPIC*
The most Olympic gold medals won by a figure skater is three by Gillis Grafström (1893–1938) of Sweden in 1920, 1924 and 1928 (also silver medal in 1932); by Sonja Henie (1912–69) of Norway in 1928, 1932 and 1936; and by Irina Rodnina (b. 12 Sept 1949) (USSR) with two different partners in the Pairs event in 1972, 1976 and 1980.

MOST TITLES *WORLD*
The greatest number of individual world figure skating titles (inst. 1896) is ten by Ulrich Salchow (1877–1949) of Sweden, in 1901–5 and 1907–11. The women's record (inst. 1906) is also ten individual titles by Sonja Henie between 1927 and 1936. Irina Rodnina has won ten pairs titles (inst. 1908), four with Aleksey Ulanov (b. 4 Nov 1947) 1969–72, and six with her husband Aleksandr Zaitsev (b. 16 June 1952) 1973–8. The most ice dance titles (inst. 1952) won is six by Ludmila Pakhomova (1946–86) and Aleksandr Gorshkov (b. 8 Oct 1946) (USSR) 1970–4 and 1976.

TRIPLE CROWN
The only British skaters to win the 'Grand Slam' of World, Olympic and European titles in the same year are John Anthony Curry (b. 9 Sept 1949) in 1976 and the ice dancers Jayne Torvill and Christopher Dean in 1984. Karl Schäfer (Austria) (1909–76) and Sonja Henie achieved double 'Grand Slams', both in the years 1932 and 1936.

HIGHEST MARKS
The highest tally of maximum six marks awarded in an international championship was 29 to Jayne Torvill and Christopher Dean (GB) in the World ice dance championships at Ottawa, Canada on 22–24 Mar 1984. This comprised seven in the compulsory dances, a perfect set of nine for presentation in the set pattern dance and 13 in the free dance including another perfect set from all nine judges for artistic presentation. They previously gained a perfect set of nine sixes for artistic presentation in the free dance at the 1983 World Championships in Helsinki, Finland and at the 1984 Olympic Games in Sarajevo, Yugoslavia. In their career Torvill and Dean received a record total of 136 sixes.
The most by a soloist was seven to Donald Jackson (b. 2 Apr 1940) (Canada) in the world men's championship at Prague, Czechoslovakia, in 1962.

DISTANCE
Robin Cousins (b. 17 Mar 1957) (GB) achieved 5,81 m *19 ft 1 in* in an Axel jump and 5,48 m *18 ft* with a back flip at Richmond Ice Rink, Surrey on 16 Nov 1983.

LARGEST RINK
The world's largest indoor ice rink is in the Moscow Olympic arena which has an ice area of 8064 m² *86,800 ft²*. The five rinks at Fujikyu Highland Skating Centre, Japan total 25 500 m² *285,243 ft²*.

SPEED SKATING

MOST TITLES *OLYMPIC*
The most Olympic gold medals won in speed skating is six by Lidia Skoblikova (b. 8 Mar 1939) of Chelyabinsk, USSR, in 1960 (two) and 1964 (four). The male record is by Clas Thunberg (1893–1973) (Finland) with five gold (including one tied), and also one silver and one tied bronze in 1924 and 1928. Eric Heiden (b. 14 June 1958) (USA) also won five gold medals, all at Lake Placid, NY, USA, in 1980.

MOST TITLES *WORLD*
The greatest number of world overall titles (inst. 1893) won by any skater is five by Oscar Mathisen (1888–1954) (Norway) in 1908–9 and 1912–14, and Clas Thunberg in 1923, 1925, 1928–9 and 1931. The most titles won in the women's events (inst. 1936) is four by Inga Voronina (*née* Artomonova) (1936–66) (USSR) in 1957, 1958, 1962 and 1964 and Atje Keulen-Deelstra (b. 31 Dec 1939) (Netherlands) 1970, 1972–4.

The record score achieved in the world overall title is 160.807 points by Viktor Shasherin (b. 23 July 1962) (USSR) at Medeo, USSR, 23–24 Mar 1984. The record women's score is 171.760 points by Andrea Schöne (b. 1 Dec 1960) (GDR) at Medeo, 23–24 Mar 1984.

LONGEST RACE
The 'Elfstedentocht' ('Tour of the Eleven Towns') was held in the Netherlands from the 1800s to 1963, covering 200 km *124 miles 483 yd*. It was transferred first to Lake Vesijärvi, near Lahti, Finland and in 1984 to Canada as the International Race of 11 Cities on the Ottawa River. The record time for 200 km is 6 hr 5 min 12 sec by Jan-Roelof Kruithof (Netherlands) on 25 Feb 1979 at Oulu, Finland

24 HOURS
Ton Smits (Netherlands) skated 506,375 km *314.65 miles* in 24 hr in Eindhoven, Netherlands on 15–16 Dec 1984.

MOTORCYCLE RACING

FASTEST CIRCUITS *WORLD*
The highest average lap speed attained on any closed circuit is 257,958 km/h *160.288 mph* by Yvon du Hamel (b. 1941) (Canada) on a modified 903 cc four-cylinder Kawasaki Z1 at the 31 degree banked 4,02 km *2.5 mile* Daytona International Speedway, Florida, USA, in March 1973. His lap time was 56.149 sec.

The fastest road circuit is the Francorchamps circuit near Spa, Belgium. It is 14,12 km *8.74 miles* in length and was lapped in 3 min 50.3 sec (average speed 220,721 km/h *137.150 mph*) by Barry Stephen Frank Sheene (b. 11 Sept 1950) (GB) on a 495 cc four-cylinder Suzuki during the Belgian Grand Prix on 3 July 1977.

FASTEST RACE *WORLD*
The fastest road race is the 500 cc Belgian Grand Prix held on the Francorchamps circuit. The record time for this ten lap (141,20 km *87.74 mile*) race is 38 min 58.5 sec (average speed 217,370 km/h *135.068 mph*) by Barry Sheene, on a 495 cc four-cylinder Suzuki, on 3 July 1977.

FASTEST RACE *UNITED KINGDOM*
The fastest race in the United Kingdom is the 750 cc event of the North-West 200 held on the Londonderry circuit. The record lap speed is 205,395 km/h *127.63 mph* by Tom Herron (1949–79) on a 747 cc Yamaha in 1978.

LONGEST RACE
The longest race is the Liège 24 hr. The greatest distance ever covered is 4444,8 km *2761.9 miles* (average speed 185,20 km/h *115.08 mph*) by Jean-Claude Chemarin and Christian Leon, both of France, on a 941 cc four-cylinder Honda on the Francorchamps circuit on 14–15 Aug 1976.

Mike Hailwood has won the Isle of Mann TT races a record 14 times in an 18 year career. *(All-Sport)*

LONGEST CIRCUIT
The 60,72 km *37.73 mile* 'Mountain' circuit, over which the principal TT races have been run since 1911 (with minor amendments in 1920), has 264 curves and corners and is the longest used for any motorcycle race.

MOST SUCCESSFUL RIDERS *TOURIST TROPHY*
The record number of victories in the Isle of Man TT races is 14 by Stanley Michael Bailey Hailwood (1940–81) between 1961 and 1979. The first man to win three consecutive TT titles in two events was James A. Redman (b. 8 Nov 1931) (Rhodesia). He won the 250 cc and 350 cc events in 1963–5. Mike Hailwood won three events in one year, in 1961 and 1967. This feat was emulated by Joey Dunlop in 1985.

The TT circuit speed record is 190,66 km/h *118.47 mph* by Joey Dunlop on a Honda on 4 June 1984.

MOST SUCCESSFUL RIDERS *WORLD CHAMPIONSHIPS*
The most world championship titles (instituted by the *Fédération Internationale Motocycliste* in 1949) won are 15 by Giacomo Agostini (b. 16 June 1942) (Italy), the 350 cc in 1968–74, and 500 cc in 1966–72, 1975. He is the only man to win two world championships in five consecutive years (350 and 500 cc titles 1968–72).

Agostini won 122 races in the world championship series between 24 Apr 1965 and 29 Aug 1976, including a record 19 in 1970, also achieved by Mike Hailwood in 1966. Klaus Enders (b. 1937) (W. Germany) won six world side-car titles, 1967, 1969–70, 1972–4.

MOST SUCCESSFUL RIDERS *TRIALS*
Yrjo Vesterinen (Finland) won a record three World trials championships, 1976–8. Samuel Hamilton Miller (b. 11 Nov 1935) won eleven A-CU Solo Trials Drivers' Stars in 1959–69.

MOST SUCCESSFUL RIDERS *MOTO-CROSS*
Joël Robert (b. 11 Nov 1943) (Belgium) won six 250 cc moto-cross world championships (1964, 1968–72). Between 25 Apr 1964 and 18 June 1972 he won a record fifty 250 cc Grands Prix. He became the youngest moto-cross world champion on 12 July 1964 when he won the 250 cc title aged 20 yr 244 days.

MOST SUCCESSFUL MACHINES
Italian MV-Agusta machines won 37 world championships between 1952 and 1973, and 276 world championship races between 1952 and 1976. Japanese Honda machines won 29 world championship races and five world championships in 1966. In the seven years they contested the championship (1961–7) their annual average was 20 race wins.

YOUNGEST AND OLDEST WORLD CHAMPIONS
Alberto 'Johnny' Cecotto (b. 25 Jan 1956) (Venezuela) is the youngest to win a world championship. He was 19 yr 211 days when he won the 350 cc title on 24 Aug 1975. The oldest was Hermann-Peter Müller (1909–76) of W. Germany, who won the 250 cc title in 1955 aged 46.

HIGHEST SPEEDS
Official world speed records must be set with two runs over a measured distance made in opposite directions within a time limit – 1 hr for FIM records and 2 hr for AMA records.

Donald A. Vesco (b. 8 Apr 1939) (USA) riding his 6,4 m *21 ft* long *Lightning Bolt* streamliner, powered by two 1016 cc Kawasaki engines on Bonneville Salt Flats, Utah, USA on 28 Aug 1978 set AMA and FIM absolute records with an overall average of 512,733 km/h *318.598 mph* and had a fastest run at an average of 513,165 km/h *318.66 mph*.

The highest speed achieved over two runs in the UK is 308,82 km/h *191.897 mph* by Roy Francis Daniel (b. 7 Dec 1938) on his 998 cc supercharged twin-engined RDS Triumph at Elvington, N Yorks on 29 July 1978. His average time for the flying 402 m *440 yd* was 4.69 sec.

The world record for 1 km *1093.6 yd* from a standing start is 16.68 sec by Henk Vink (b. 24 July 1939) (Netherlands) on his supercharged 984 cc four-cylinder Kawasaki, at Elvington Airfield, North Yorkshire on 24 July 1977. The faster run was made in 16.09 sec.

The world record for 402 m *440 yd* from a standing start is 8.805 sec by Henk Vink on his supercharged 1132 cc four-cylinder Kawasaki at Elvington Airfield, North Yorkshire on 23 July 1977. The faster run was made in 8.55 sec.

The fastest time for a single run over 402 m *440 yd* from a standing start is 7.08 sec by Bo O'Brechta (USA) riding a supercharged 1200 cc Kawasaki-based machine at Ontario, California, in 1980. The highest terminal velocity recorded at the end of a 402 m *440 yd* run from a standing start is 321,14 km/h *199.55 mph* by Russ Collins (USA) at Ontario on 7 Oct 1978.

Barry Sheene won the Belgian Grand Prix, the fastest race in the world, in the fastest ever time.

MOTOR RACING

FASTEST CIRCUITS

The highest average lap speed attained on any closed circuit is 403,878 km/h *250.958 mph* in a trial by Dr Hans Liebold (b. 12 Oct 1926) (Germany) who lapped the 12,64 km *7.85 mile* high-speed track at Nardo, Italy in 1 min 52.67 sec in a Mercedes-Benz C111-IV experimental coupé on 5 May 1979. It was powered by a V8 engine with two KKK turbochargers with an output of 500 hp at 6200 rpm.

The highest average race lap speed for a closed circuit is 344,654 km/h *214.158 mph* by Mario Gabriele Andretti (b. Trieste, Italy, 28 Feb 1940) (USA) driving a 2.6 litre turbocharged Viceroy Parnelli-Offenhauser on the 3,2 km *2 mile*, 22 degree banked oval at Texas World Speedway, College Station, Texas, USA on 6 Oct 1973.

The fastest road circuit was the Francorchamps circuit near Spa, Belgium, then 14,10 km *8.761 miles* in length which was lapped in 3 min 13.4 sec (average speed 262,461 km/h *163.086 mph*) on 6 May 1973, by Henri Pescarolo (b. 25 Sept 1942) (France) driving a 2993 cc V12 Matra-Simca MS670 Group 5 sports car. The race lap average speed record at Berlin's AVUS track was 276,38 km/h *171.75 mph* by Bernd Rosemeyer (1909–38) (Germany) in a 6-litre V16 Auto Union in 1937.

FASTEST RACE

The fastest race is the Busch Clash at Daytona, Florida over 201 km *125 miles* on a $2\frac{1}{2}$ miles 31 degree banked track. In 1979 Elzie Wylie 'Buddy' Baker (b. 25 Jan 1941) averaged 312,831 km/h *194.384 mph* in an Oldsmobile.

MOST RACE WINS BY DRIVER

Richard Lee Petty (b. 2 July 1937) (USA) won 200 NASCAR Grand National races in 947 starts, 1958–84. His best season was 1967 with 27 wins. His total earnings reached a record $5,504,877 on 29 July 1984. Geoff Bodine (b. 18 Apr 1949) won 55 races in 1978.

WORLD CHAMPIONSHIP GRAND PRIX MOTOR RACING

The World Drivers' Championship, inaugurated in 1950, has been won a record five times by Juan-Manuel Fangio (Argentina) (b. 24 June 1911) in 1951, 1954–7. He retired in 1958, after having won 24 Grand Prix races (two shared).

The most Grand Prix victories is 27 by John Young 'Jackie' Stewart (b. 11 June 1939) (GB) between 12 Sept 1965 and 5 Aug 1973. The most Grand Prix points is $418\frac{1}{2}$ by Niki Lauda (b. 22 Feb 1949) (Austria) in 171 Grands Prix, with 25 wins from 1971 to 1985. The most Grand Prix victories in a year is seven by James 'Jim' Clark (1936–68) (GB) in 1963 and by Alain Prost (b. 24 Feb 1955) (France) in 1984. The most Grand Prix starts is 176 (out of a possible 184) between 18 May 1958 and 26 Jan 1975 by Norman Graham Hill (1929–75) (GB). Between 20 Nov 1960 and 5 Oct 1969 he took part in 90 consecutive Grands Prix.

'Big Daddy' Don Garlits set a terminal velocity record of over 431 kmph *268 mph.*

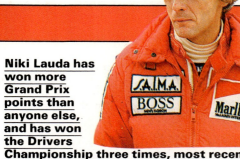

Niki Lauda has won more Grand Prix points than anyone else, and has won the Drivers Championship three times, most recently in his McClaren (pictured left) in 1984. *(All-Sport)*

OLDEST AND YOUNGEST

The youngest world champion was Emerson Fittipaldi (b. 12 Dec 1946) (Brazil) who won his first world championship on 10 Sept 1972 aged 25 yr 273 days. The oldest world champion was Juan-Manuel Fangio who won his last world championship on 18 Aug 1957 aged 46 yr 55 days.

The youngest Grand Prix winner was Bruce Leslie McLaren (1937–70) of New Zealand, who won the United States Grand Prix at Sebring, Florida, on 12 Dec 1959 aged 22 yr 104 days. The oldest Grand Prix winner (in pre-World Championship days) was Tazio Giorgio Nuvolari (1892–1953) (Italy), who won the Albi Grand Prix at Albi, France on 14 July 1946 aged 53 yr 240 days. The oldest Grand Prix driver was Louis Alexandre Chiron (1899–1979) (Monaco), who finished 6th in the Monaco Grand Prix on 22 May 1955 aged 55 yr 292 days. The youngest Grand Prix driver was Michael Christopher Thackwell (b. 30 Mar 1961) (New Zealand) who took part in the Canadian GP on 28 Sept 1980, aged 19 yr 182 days.

MANUFACTURERS

Ferrari have won a record eight manufacturers' world championships, 1961, 1964, 1975–7, 1979, 1982–3. Ferrari have 91 race wins in 390 Grands Prix, 1950–85.

FASTEST RACE

The fastest overall average speed for a Grand Prix race on a circuit in current use is 224,050 km/h *139.218 mph* in the 1983 British Grand Prix (see below). The fastest qualifying speed was set in the Austrian Grand Prix at Zeltweg on 18 Aug 1984 at 248,235 km/h *154.250 mph* by Nelson Piquet in a Brabham BMW. The race itself, on 19 Aug 1984, was won by Niki Lauda in a McLaren TAG at an average 223,883 km/h, including a race lap record of 230,305 km/h *143.109 mph.*

TOUGHEST CIRCUIT

The most gruelling and slowest Grand Prix circuit is that for the Monaco Grand Prix (first run on 14 Apr 1929), round the streets and the harbour of Monte Carlo. It is 3,312 km *2.058 miles* in length and has eleven pronounced corners and several sharp changes of gradient. The race is run over 76 laps (251,7 km *156.4 miles*) and involves on average about 1600 gear changes. The record time for the race is 1 hr 54 min 11.259 sec (average speed 132,30 km/h *82.21 mph* by Riccardo Patrese (b. 17 Apr 1954) (Italy) in a Brabham-Ford on 23 May 1982. The race lap record is 1 min 26.35 sec (average speed 138,073 km/h *85.79 mph*) by Patrese in 1982. The practice lap record is 1 min 22.66 sec (average speed 144,242 km/h *89.63 mph*) by Alain Prost (b. 24 Feb 1955) (France) in a McLaren TAG Porsche on 2 June 1984.

CLOSEST FINISH

The closest finish to a World Championship race was in the Italian Grand Prix at Monza on 5 Sept 1971. Just 0.61 sec separated winner Peter Gethin (GB) from the fifth placer.

LE MANS

The greatest distance ever covered in the 24 hour *Grand Prix d'Endurance* (first held on 26–27 May 1923) on the old Sarthe circuit at Le Mans, France is 5333,724 km *3314.222 miles* by Dr Helmut Marko (b. 27 Apr 1943) (Austria) and Jonkheer Gijs van Lennep (b. 16 Mar 1942) (Netherlands) in a 4907 cc flat-12 Porsche 917K Group 5 sports car, on 12–13 June 1971. The record for the current circuit is 5088,507 km *3161.938 miles* (average speed 212,021 km/h *131.747 mph*) by Klaus Ludwig (W. Germany), Paolo Barilla (Italy), and John Winter (W. Germany) in a Porsche 956 on 15–16 June 1985. The race lap record (13,64 km *8.475 mile* lap) is 3 min 28.1 sec (average speed 239,16 km/h *148.61 mph*) by Jacky Ickx (Belgium) in a Porsche 962C in 1985.

MOST WINS

The race has been won by Porsche cars 11 times, in 1970–1, 1976–7, 1979, 1981–6. The most wins by one man is six by Jacky Ickx, 1969, 1975–7 and 1981–2.

The race has been won 13 times by British cars: Bentley in 1924 and 1927–30, Lagonda in 1935, Jaguar in 1951, 1953 and 1955–7, Aston Martin in 1959 and a Gulf-Ford in 1975.

RALLIES

EARLIEST

The earliest long rally was promoted by the Parisian daily *Le Matin* in 1907 from Peking, China to Paris over about 12 000 km *7500 miles* on 10 June. The winner, Prince Scipione Borghese (1872–1927) of Italy, arrived in Paris on 10 Aug 1907 in his 40 hp Itala accompanied by his chauffeur, Ettore, and Luigi Barzini.

LONGEST

The longest ever rally was the *Singapore Airlines* London–Sydney Rally over 31 107 km *19,329 miles* from Covent Garden, London on 14 Aug 1977 to Sydney Opera House, won on 28 Sept 1977 by Andrew Cowan, Colin Malkin and Michael Broad in a Mercedes 280E. The longest held annually is the Safari Rally (first run 1953 through Kenya, Tanzania and Uganda) which is up to 6234 km *3874 miles* long, as in the 17th Safari held between 8 and 12 Apr 1971. It has been won a record five times by Shekhar Mehta (b. Uganda 1945) in 1973, 1979–82.

MONTE CARLO

The Monte Carlo Rally (first run 1911) has been won a record four times by Sandro Munari (b. 1940) (Italy) in 1972, 1975, 1976 and 1977 and by Walter Röhrl (b. 7 Mar 1947) (with co-driver Christian Geistdorfer) in 1980, 1982–84, each time in a different car. The smallest car to win was an 851 cc Saab driven by Erik Carlsson (b. 5 Mar 1929) (Sweden) and Gunnar Häggbom (Sweden) on 25 Jan 1962, and by Carlsson and Gunnar Palm on 24 Jan 1963.

RUGBY LEAGUE FOOTBALL

MOST TITLES

There have been seven World Cup Competitions. Australia have most wins, with four, 1957, 1968, 1970 and 1977 as well as a win in the International Championship of 1975.

The Northern Rugby League was formed in 1901. The word Northern was dropped in 1980. Wigan have won the League Championship a record nine times (1909, 1922, 1926, 1934, 1946, 1947, 1950, 1952 and 1960).

In the Rugby League Challenge Cup (inaugurated 1896–7 season) Leeds have most wins with ten, 1910, 1923, 1932, 1936, 1941–2 (wartime), 1957, 1968, 1977–8. Oldham is the only club to appear in four consecutive Cup Finals (1924–7).

Since 1974 there have been five major competitions for RL clubs: Challenge Cup, League Championship, Premiership, John Player Trophy and County Cup. Over this period only Widnes have won three in one season (Challenge Cup, John Player Trophy and Lancashire Cup) in 1978–79. Wigan has a record 34 wins in these five competitions.

Three clubs have won all possible major Rugby League trophies in one season: Hunslet, 1907–8 season, Huddersfield, 1914–15 and Swinton, 1927–8, all won the Challenge Cup, League Championship, County Cup and County League (now defunct).

HIGHEST SCORES

SENIOR MATCH

The highest aggregate score in a game where a senior club has been concerned was 121 points, when Huddersfield beat Swinton Park Rangers by 119 (19 goals, 27 tries) to 2 (one goal) in the first round of the Northern Union Cup on 28 Feb 1914. The highest score in League football is 112 points by Leeds *v.* Coventry (nil) on 12 Apr 1913.

CHALLENGE CUP FINAL

The highest score in a Challenge Cup Final is 38 points (8 tries, 7 goals) by Wakefield Trinity *v.* Hull (5) at Wembley on 14 May 1960. The record aggregate is 52 points when Wigan beat Hull 28–24 at Wembley on 4 May 1985. The greatest winning margin was 34 points when Huddersfield beat St Helens 37–3 at Oldham on 1 May 1915.

INTERNATIONAL MATCH

The highest score in an international match is Australia's 63–13 defeat of England at Paris, France on 31 Dec 1933. The highest score in a World Cup match is the 53–19 win by Great Britain over New Zealand at Hameau, Paris on 4 Nov 1972.

TOURING TEAMS

The record score for a British team touring Australasia is 101 points by England *v.* South Australia (nil) at Adelaide in May 1914. The record for a touring team in Britain is 92 (10 goals, 24 tries) by Australia against Bramley's 7 (2 goals, 1 try) at the Barley Mow Ground, Bramley, near Leeds, on 9 Nov 1921.

Wigan (*in red*) and Hull were involved in the highest scoring rugby league cup final in 1985. Wigan won 28–24 for their eighth success. *(All-Sport)*

MOST POINTS *SEASON*

Leigh scored a record 1436 points (258 tries, 199 goals, 6 drop goals) in the 1985–6 season.

INDIVIDUAL INTERNATIONAL RECORDS

Jim Sullivan (Wigan) played in most internationals (60 for Wales and Great Britain) kicked most goals (160) and scored most points (329).

Mick Sullivan (no kin) (b. 12 Jan 1934) of Huddersfield, Wigan, St Helens and York played in 51 international games for England and Great Britain and scored a record 45 tries.

MOST AND LEAST SUCCESSFUL TEAMS

Wigan won 31 consecutive league games from February 1970 to February 1971. Hull won all 26 League Division II matches in the 1978–9 season. Doncaster hold the record of losing 40 consecutive League games from 16 Nov 1975 to 21 Apr 1977.

RECORD TRANSFER FEES

The highest RL transfer fee is £100,000 paid to Widnes for Joe Lydon (b. 26 Nov 1963) by Wigan on 20 Jan 1986.

GREATEST CROWDS

The greatest attendance at any Rugby League match is 102,569 for the Warrington *v.* Halifax Challenge Cup Final replay at Odsal Stadium, Bradford, on 5 May 1954.

The record attendance for any international match is 70,204 for the Test between Australia and England on the Sydney Cricket Ground on 6 June 1932. The highest international attendance in Britain is 43,500 for the Test between Great Britain and Australia at Odsal Stadium, Bradford on 29 Jan 1949.

RUGBY UNION FOOTBALL

HIGHEST INDIVIDUAL SCORES

INTERNATIONALS
Colin Mair scored 30 points (9 conversions, 4 penalty goals) for Scotland *v.* Japan at Tokyo on 18 Sept 1977. The highest individual points score in any match between members of the International Board is 26 by Alan Hewson (b. 1953) (1 try, 2 conversions, 5 penalty goals and a drop goal) for New Zealand against Australia at Auckland on 11 Sept 1982.

Ian Scott Smith (1903–72) (Scotland) scored a record six consecutive international tries in 1925; comprised of the last three *v.* France and two weeks later, the first three *v.* Wales. His 24 tries, 1924–33, is the record for an international career.

The most points scored in an international career is 301 by Andrew Robertson Irvine (Heriots) (b. 16 Sept 1951), 273 for Scotland (including 12 *v.* Romania) and 28 for the British Lions from 1973 to 1982.

SEASON
The first-class rugby scoring record for a season is 581 points by Samuel Arthur Doble (1944–77) of Moseley, in 52 matches in 1971–2. He also scored 47 points for England in South Africa out of season.

CAREER
William Henry 'Dusty' Hare (b. 29 Nov 1952) of Leicester, scored 5926 points in first-class games from 1971–86, comprising 1800 for Nottingham, 3202 for Leicester, 240 for England, 88 for the British Lions and 596 in other representative matches.

MATCH
Jannie van der Westhuizen scored 80 points (14 tries, 9 conversions, 1 dropped goal, 1 penalty goal) for Carnarvon (88) *v.* Williston (12) at North West Cape, S. Africa on 11 March 1972.

In a junior house match in February 1967 at William Ellis School, Edgware, Greater London, between Cumberland and Nunn, Thanos Morphitis, 12, contributed 90 points (13 tries and 19 conversions) (77) to Cumberland's winning score.

ALL-ROUNDER
Canadian international, Barrie Burnham, scored all possible ways – try, conversion, penalty goal, drop goal, goal from mark – for Meralomas *v.* Georgians (20–11) at Vancouver, BC, on 26 Feb 1966.

LONGEST KICKS
The longest recorded successful drop-goal is 82 m *90 yd* by Gerald Hamilton 'Gerry' Brand (b. 8 Oct 1906) for South Africa *v.* England at Twickenham, Greater London, on 2 Jan 1932. This was taken 6 m *7 yd* inside the England 'half ' 50 m *55 yd* from the posts and dropped over the dead ball line.

The place kick record is reputed to be 91 m *100 yd* at Richmond Athletic Ground, Greater London, by Douglas Francis Theodore Morkel (b. 1886) in an unsuccessful penalty for South Africa *v.* Surrey on 19 Dec 1906. This was not measured until 1932. In the match Bridlington School 1st XV *v.* an Army XV at Bridlington, Humberside on 29 Jan 1944, Ernie Cooper (b. 21 May 1926), captaining the school, landed a penalty from a measured 74 m *81 yd* from the post with a kick which carried over the dead ball line.

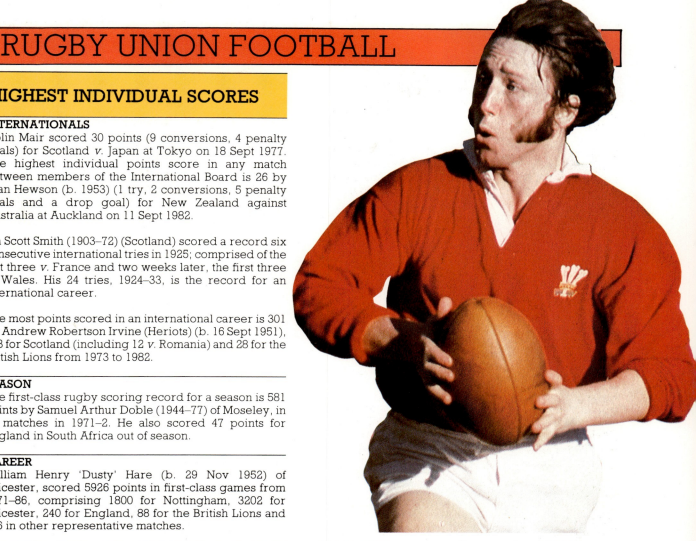

J. P. R. Williams was capped a record 55 times by Wales in a twelve year career from 1969 to 1981. *(All-Sport)*

FASTEST TRY
The fastest try in an international game was when H. L. 'Bart' Price scored for England *v.* Wales at Twickenham on 20 Jan 1923 less than 10 sec after kick off.

MOST TRIES
Alan Morley (b. 25 June 1950) has scored 447 tries in senior rugby in 1968–85 including 355 for Bristol, a record for one club. John Huins scored 85 tries in 1953–4, 73 for St Luke's College, Exeter and 12 more for Neath and in trial games.

LONGEST TRY
The longest 'try' ever executed is by a team of 15, from Power-House RUFC, Victoria, Australia, who ran a try of 2366,7 km *1470.6 miles* on 4–13 Mar 1983 around Albert Park Lake, Victoria. There were no forward passes or knock-ons, and the ball was touched down between the posts in the prescribed manner (Law 12).

SKIING

Franz Weber holds the world's downhill speed record at 208,936 km/h *129.827 mph*.

SKI-JUMPING

The longest ski-jump ever recorded is 191 m *626 ft 7 in* by Matti Nykaenen (Finland) at Planica, Yugoslavia on 15 Mar 1985 and equalled by Andreas Felder (Austria) at Bas Mittendorf, Austria on 9 Mar 1986. The female record is 110 m *361 ft* by Tiina Lehtola (b. 3 Aug 1962) (Finland) at Ruka, Finland on 29 Mar 1981. The longest dry ski-jump is 92 m *302 ft* by Hubert Schwarz (W. Germany) at Berchtesgarten, W. Germany on 30 June 1981.

HIGHEST SPEED – DOWNHILL

The highest speed claimed for a skier is 208,936 km/h *129.827 mph* by Franz Weber (Austria) and the fastest by a woman is 200,780 km/h *124.759 mph* by Melissa Dimino (USA) both at Les Arcs, France on 19 Apr 1984. The highest average speed in the Olympic downhill race was 104,53 km/h *64.95 mph* by William D. Johnson (b. 30 Mar 1960) (USA) at Sarajevo, Yugoslavia on 16 Feb 1984. The fastest in a World Cup downhill is 107,82 km/h *67.00 mph* by Harti Weirather (b. 25 Jan 1958) (Austria) at Kitzbühl, Austria on 15 Jan 1982.

HIGHEST SPEED – CROSS COUNTRY

Bill Koch (b. 13 Apr 1943) (USA) on 26 Mar 1981 skied ten times round a 5 km *3.11 mile* loop on Marlborough Pond, near Putney, Vermont, USA. He completed the 50 km in 1 hr 59 min 47 sec, an average speed of 25,045 km/h *15.57 mph*. A race includes uphill and downhill sections; the record time for a 50 km race is 2 hr 10 min 49.9 sec by Gunde Svan (b. 12 Jan 1962) (Sweden) in the 1985 World Championships, an average speed of 22,93 km/h *14.25 mph*. The record for a 15 km Olympic or World Championship race is 38 min 52.5 sec by Oddvar Braa (b. 16 Mar 1951) (Norway) at the 1982 World Championships, an average speed of 23,15 km/h *14.38 mph*.

LONGEST RACES

The world's longest ski races are the Grenader, run just north of Oslo, Norway and the Konig Ludwig Lauf in Oberammergau, W. Germany. Both are of 90 km *55.9 miles*. The Canadian Ski Marathon at 160 km *99 miles* from Lachute, Quebec to Ottawa, Ontario is longer, but is run in two parts on consecutive days.

The world's greatest Nordic ski race is the Vasaloppet, which commemorates an event of 1521 when Gustav Vasa (1496–1560), later King Gustavus Eriksson, fled 85,8 km *53.3 miles* from Mora to Sälen, Sweden. He was overtaken by loyal, speedy scouts on skis, who persuaded him to return eastwards to Mora to lead a rebellion and become the king of Sweden. The re-enactment of this return journey is now an annual event at 89 km *55.3 miles*, contested by about 12,000 skiers. The fastest time is 3 hr 58 min 8 sec by Konrad Hallenbarter (Switzerland) on 6 Mar 1983. The Vasaloppet is now the longest of ten long distance races in ten countries constituting the World loppet.

The longest downhill race is the *Inferno* in Switzerland, 14 km *8.7 miles* from the top of the Schilthorn to Lauterbrunnen. In 1981 there was a record entry of 1401, with Heinz Fringer (Switzerland) winning in a record 15 min 44.57 sec.

HIGHEST ALTITUDE

Jean Atanassilf and Nicolas Jaeger skied from 8200 m *26,900 ft* to 6200 m *20,340 ft* on the 1978 French Expedition on Mt Everest.

LONGEST RUN

The longest all-downhill ski run in the world is the Weissfluhjoch–Küblis Parsenn course, near Davos, Switzerland, which measures 12,23 km *7.6 miles*. The run from the Aiguille du Midi top of the Chamonix lift (vertical lift 2759 m *9052 ft*) across the Vallée Blanche is 20,9 km *13 miles*.

Michela Figini, the youngest ever Olympic skiing champion. She won the downhill in 1984 aged 17 years 315 days. *(All-Sport)*

SNOOKER

ORIGINS
Research shows that snooker was originated by Colonel Sir Neville Francis Fitzgerald Chamberlain (1856–1944) as a hybrid of 'black pool', 'pyramids' and billiards, in Jubbulpore, India in 1875. It did not reach England until 1885, where the modern scoring system was adopted in 1891. Championships were not instituted until 1916. The World Professional Championship was instituted in 1927.

MOST TITLES *WORLD*
The world professional title (instituted 1927) was won a record 15 times by Joe Davis, 1927–40 and 1946. The most wins in the amateur championships (instituted 1963) have been two by Gary Owen (England) in 1963 and 1966, and Ray Edmonds (England) 1972 and 1974.

MOST TITLES *WOMEN*
Maureen Baynton (*née* Barrett) won a record eight women's amateur championships between 1954 and 1968, as well as seven at billiards.

WORLD CHAMPIONSHIPS *YOUNGEST*
The youngest player to win a world title is Jimmy White (GB) (b. 2 May 1962) who was 18 yr 191 days when he won the World Amateur Snooker championship in Launceston, Tasmania, Australia on 9 Nov 1980. The youngest to win the professional world title was Alex 'Hurricane' Higgins of Northern Ireland who was 22 yr 345 days old when he won the 1972 title at Birmingham.

HIGHEST BREAKS
Over 100 players have achieved the 'maximum' break of 147. The first to do so was E. J. 'Murt' O'Donoghue (b. New Zealand 1901) at Griffiths, NSW, Australia on 26 Sept 1934. The first officially ratified 147 was by Joe Davis against Willie Smith at Leicester Square Hall, London on 22 Jan 1955. The first maximum achieved in a major tournament was by John Spencer (b. 18 Sept 1935) at Slough, Berkshire on 13 Jan 1979, but the table had oversized pockets. Steve Davis (b. 22 Aug 1957) had a ratified break of 147 against John Spencer in the Lada Classic at Oldham on 11 Jan 1982. The first 147 scored in the World Championships was by Cliff Thorburn (Canada) (b. 16 Jan 1948) against Terry Griffiths at the Crucible Theatre, Sheffield on 23 Apr 1983, thereby winning a £10,000 jackpot prize.
The official world amateur record break is 140 set by Joe Johnson (England) (b. 29 July 1952) in the TUC Club, Middlesbrough, Cleveland in 1978. David Taylor (b. 29 July 1943) made three consecutive frame clearances of 130, 140 and 139 (total 409) at Minehead, Somerset, on 1 June 1978. Jim Meadowcroft (b. 15 Dec 1946) made four consecutive frame clearances of 105, 115, 117 and 125 at Connaught Leisure Centre, Worthing on 27 Jan 1982.

Cliff Thorburn seen celebrating after becoming the first man to score a maximum 147 break in snooker's world championships. *(All-Sport)*

'In 1978 Joe Johnson set the world amateur break record at 140. In 1986 he became World Champion.'

BAR BILLIARDS

HIGHEST SCORING RATE
The record scoring rate in a league game has been 28,530 in 19 min 5 sec by Keith Sheard at the Crown and Thistle, Headington, Oxford on 9 July 1984.

24 HOURS
The highest bar billiards score in 24 hr by a team of five is 1,506,570 by John Burrows, Kent Murray, Ray Hussey, Roy Buckle and Brian Ray of 'The Hour Glass', Sands, High Wycombe, Buckinghamshire on 26–27 Nov 1983.

POOL

Pool or championship pocket billiards with numbered balls began to become standardized *c.* 1890. The greatest exponents were Ralph Greenleaf (USA) (1899–1950) who won the 'world' professional title 19 times (1919–37) and William Mosconi (USA) (b. 27 June 1913) who dominated the game from 1941 to 1957.
The greatest number of balls pocketed in 24 hr is 15,780 by Vic Elliott at the Royal George, Lincoln on 2–3 Apr 1985.
The record time for potting all 15 balls in a speed competition is 40.06 sec by Ross McInnes (b. 19 Jan 1955) at Clacton, Essex on 11 Sept 1983.

SOCCER

PROFESSIONAL

LONGEST MATCH

The duration record for first-class fixtures was set in the Copa Libertadores in Santos, Brazil, on 2–3 Aug 1962, when Santos drew 3–3 with Penarol FC of Montevideo, Uruguay. The game lasted 3 hr 30 min (with interruptions), from 9.30 pm to 1 am.

The longest British match on record was one of 3 hr 23 min between Stockport County and Doncaster Rovers in the second leg of the Third Division (North) Cup at Edgeley Park, Stockport, Greater Manchester on 30 Mar 1946.

LONGEST UNBEATEN STREAK

Nottingham Forest were undefeated in 42 consecutive Division I matches from 20 Nov 1977 to 9 Dec 1978. In Scottish football Glasgow Celtic were undefeated in 62 matches (49 won, 13 drawn), 13 Nov 1915–21 Apr 1917.

MOST POSTPONEMENTS

The Scottish Cup tie between Inverness Thistle and Falkirk during the winter of 1978–9 was postponed a record 29 times due to weather conditions. Finally Falkirk won the game 4–0.

GOAL SCORING

TEAMS

The highest score recorded in a British first-class match is 36. This occurred in the Scottish Cup match between Arbroath and Bon Accord on 12 Sept 1885, when Arbroath won 36–0 on their home ground. But for the lack of nets and the consequent waste of retrieval time the score must have been even higher. Seven further goals were disallowed for offside.

The highest margin recorded in an international match is 17, when England beat Australia 17–0 at Sydney on 30 June 1951. This match is not listed by England as a *full* international. The highest in the British Isles was when England beat Ireland 13–0 at Belfast on 18 Feb 1882.

The highest score between English clubs in any major competition is 26, when Preston North End beat Hyde 26–0 in an FA Cup tie at Deepdale, Lancashire on 15 Oct 1887. The biggest victory in an FA Cup Final is six when Bury beat Derby County 6–0 at Crystal Palace on 18 Apr 1903, in which year Bury did not concede a single goal in the five Cup matches.

The highest score by one side in an English Football League (Division I) match is 12 goals when West Bromwich Albion beat Darwen 12–0 at West Bromwich, West Midlands on 4 Apr 1892; when Nottingham Forest beat Leicester Fosse by the same score at Nottingham on 21 Apr 1909; and when Aston Villa beat Accrington 12–2 at Perry Barr, W. Midlands on 12 Mar 1892.

SEASON

The most goals in a League season is 60 in 39 games by William Ralph 'Dixie' Dean (1907–80) for Everton (Division I) in 1927–8 and 66 in 38 games by James Smith (1902–76) for Ayr United (Scottish Division II) in the same season. With three more in Cup ties and 19 in representative matches Dean's total was 82.

CAREER

Artur Friedenreich (1892–1969) (Brazil) scored an undocumented 1329 goals in a 43 year first-class football career. The most goals scored in a specified period is 1216 by Edson Arantes do Nascimento (b. 23 Oct 1940) (Brazil), known as Pelé, from 7 Sept 1956 to 2 Oct 1974 in 1254 games. His best year was 1959 with 126 and the *milesimo* (1000th) came in a penalty for his club Santos in the Maracaña Stadium, Rio de Janeiro on 19 Nov 1969 when playing his 909th first-class match. He later played for New York Cosmos and on his retirement on 1 Oct 1977 his total had reached 1281, in 1363 games. He added two more goals later in special appearances. Franz 'Bimbo' Binder (b. 1 Dec 1911) scored 1006 goals in 756 games in Austria and Germany between 1930 and 1950.

The international career record for England is 49 goals by Robert 'Bobby' Charlton (b. 11 Oct 1937). His first was *v.* Scotland on 19 Apr 1958 and his last on 20 May 1970 *v.* Colombia.

The greatest number of goals scored in British first-class football is 550 (410 in Scottish League matches) by James McGrory of Glasgow Celtic (1922–38). The most scored

'The faces of Everton's unique double in the 1984/85 season. Above, they hold aloft the League Championship and, below, the Cup Winner's Cup.'

in League matches is 434, for West Bromwich Albion, Fulham, Leicester City and Shrewsbury Town, by George Arthur Rowley (b. 21 Apr 1926) between 1946 and April 1965. Rowley also scored 32 goals in the FA Cup and one for England 'B'.

INDIVIDUAL

The most scored by one player in a first-class match is 16 by Stephan Stanis (*né* Stanikowski, b. Poland, 15 July 1913) for Racing Club de Lens *v.* Aubry-Asturies, in Lens, France, in a wartime French Cup game on 13 Dec 1942.

The record number of goals scored by one player in an international match is ten by Sofus Nielson (1888–1963) for Denmark *v.* France (17–1) in the 1908 Olympics and by Gottfried Fuchs (1889–1972) for Germany who beat Russia 16–0 in the 1912 Olympic tournament (consolation event) in Sweden.

FASTEST GOALS

The fastest Football League goals on record were scored in 6 sec by Albert E. Mundy (b. 12 May 1926) (Aldershot) in a Division IV match *v.* Hartlepool United at Victoria Ground, Hartlepool, Cleveland on 25 Oct 1958, by Barrie Jones (b. 31 Oct 1938) (Notts Co) in a Division III match *v.* Torquay United on 31 Mar 1962, by Keith Smith (b. 15 Sept 1940) (Crystal Palace) in a Division II match *v.* Derby County at the Baseball Ground, Derby on 12 Dec 1964 and by Tommy W. Langley (b. 8 Feb 1958) (Queen's Park Rangers) in a Division II match *v.* Bolton Wanderers on 11 Oct 1980.

The fastest confirmed hat-trick is in 2½ minutes by Ephraim 'Jock' Dobbs (b. 7 Sept 1915) for Blackpool *v.* Tranmere Rovers on 28 Feb 1943, and by Jimmy Scarth (b. 26 Aug 1920) for Gillingham *v.* Leyton Orient in Division III (Southern) on 1 Nov 1952. A hat-trick in 1 min 50 sec is claimed for Maglioni of Independiente *v.* Gimnasia y Escrima de la Plata in Argentina on 18 Mar 1973. John McIntyre (Blackburn Rovers) scored four goals in 5 min *v.* Everton at Ewood Park, Blackburn, Lancashire on 16 Sept 1922. William 'Ginger' Richardson (West Bromwich Albion) scored four goals in 5 min from the kick-off against West Ham United at Upton Park on 7 Nov 1931. Frank Keetley scored six goals in 21 min in the 2nd half of the Lincoln City *v.* Halifax Town league match on 16 Jan 1932. The international record is three goals in 3½ min by Willie Hall (Tottenham Hotspur) for England against Ireland on 16 Nov 1938 at Old Trafford, Greater Manchester.

FASTEST OWN GOAL

Torquay United's Pat Kruse (b. 30 Nov 1953) equalled the fastest goal on Football League record when he headed the ball into his own net only 6 sec after kick-off *v.* Cambridge United on 3 Jan 1977.

THE WORLD CUP

The Fédération Internationale de Football Association (FIFA), which was founded on 21 May 1904, instituted the first World Cup on 13 July 1930, in Montevideo, Uruguay.

GOAL SCORING AND APPEARANCES

Antonio Carbayal (b. 1923) (Mexico) is the only player to have appeared in five World Cup final tournaments, keeping goal for Mexico in 1950, 1954, 1958, 1962 and 1966, playing 11 games in all. Uwe Seeler (b. 5 Nov 1936) (West Germany) holds the record for the most appearances in final tournaments, playing as a centre forward in 21 games in the 1958–1970 events, whilst Pelé is the only player to have been with three World Cup winning teams, in 1958, 1962 and 1970. The youngest ever to play in the World Cup is Norman Whiteside who played for Northern Ireland *v.* Yugoslavia aged 17 yr 42 days on 17 June 1982. The record goal scorer is Just Fontaine (b. Marrakesh, Morocco, 18 Aug 1933) of France who scored 13 goals in six matches in the final stages of the 1958 competition in Sweden.

Fontaine and Jairzinho (Brazil) are the only two players to have scored in every match in a final series, as Jairzinho scored seven in six games in 1970.

The most goals scored in a final is three by Geoff Hurst (b. 8 Dec 1941) for England *v.* West Germany on 30 July 1966. Three players have scored in two finals, Vava (real name Edwaldo Izito Neto) (Brazil) in 1958 and 1962, Pelé (Brazil) in 1958 and 1970 and Paul Breitner (West Germany) in 1974 and 1982. The fastest goal in World Cup competition was one in 27 sec by Bryan Robson (b. 11 Jan 1957) for England *v.* France in Bilbao on 16 June 1982.

MEXICO 1986

The 13th World Cup Final was won by Argentina at the Azteca Stadium, Mexico City, Mexico on 29 June 1986, when they beat West Germany 3–2.

Only six nations have won the World Cup. Argentina became the third to have won it twice, along with Uruguay (1930 and 1950) and West Germany (1954 and 1974), who were making a record fifth appearance in the final.

The attendance in the Azteca, 114,590, was the second highest ever for a final. Gary Lineker (England) (b. 30 Nov 1960) was the tournament's highest scorer with six, whilst the goals-per-game average was 2.54 (excluding penalty shoot outs), the lowest in the history of the tournament.

'Diego Maradona, captain of the victorious Argentinian side, illuminated the tournament with his sparkling individual skills. He is widely regarded as the world's greatest footballer' (All Sport).

SOCCER

Norman Whiteside, the youngest player to appear in the World Cup, is also the youngest to have scored in an FA Cup final. ***(All-Sport)***

The highest score in a World Cup match occurred in a qualifying match in Auckland on 15 Aug 1981 when New Zealand beat Fiji 13–0. The highest score during the final stages is 10, scored by Hungary in a 10–1 win over El Salvador at Elche, Spain on 15 June 1982. The highest match aggregate during the finals is 12 when Austria beat Switzerland 7–5 in 1954.

The highest scoring team in a final tournament has been West Germany who scored 25 in six matches in 1954, for the highest average of 4.17 goals per game.

The best defensive record belongs to England, who in six matches in 1966 conceded only three goals. Curiously, no team has ever failed to score in a World Cup Final.

GREATEST CROWDS

The greatest recorded crowd at any football match was 205,000 (199,859 paid) for the Brazil *v.* Uruguay World Cup match in the Maracaña Municipal Stadium, Rio de Janeiro, Brazil on 16 July 1950. The record attendance for a European Cup match is 136,505 at the semi-final between Glasgow Celtic and Leeds United at Hampden Park, Glasgow on 15 Apr 1970.

The British record paid attendance is 149,547 at the Scotland *v.* England international at Hampden Park,

‘Zararov scores one of Dynamo Kiev's goals in their 3–0 win over Atletico Madrid in the 1986 Cup Winner's Cup Final. They became only the fourth club to win it twice.’

Glasgow, on 17 Apr 1937. It is, however, probable that this total was exceeded (estimated 160,000) at the FA Cup Final between Bolton Wanderers and West Ham United at Wembley Stadium on 28 Apr 1923, when the crowd broke in on the pitch and the start was delayed 40 min until the pitch was cleared. The counted admissions were 126,047.

The Scottish Cup record attendance is 146,433 when Celtic played Aberdeen at Hampden Park on 24 Apr 1937. The record attendance for a League match in Britain is 118,567 for Rangers *v.* Celtic at Ibrox Park, Glasgow on 2 Jan 1939.

The highest attendance at an amateur match has been 120,000 in Senayan Stadium, Jakarta, Indonesia, on 26 Feb 1976 for the Pre-Olympic Group II final, North Korea *v.* Indonesia.

OLDEST AND YOUNGEST INTERNATIONAL CAPS

The oldest cap has been William Henry 'Billy' Meredith (1874–1958) (Manchester City and United) who played outside right for Wales *v.* England at Highbury, London, on 15 Mar 1920 when aged 45 yr 229 days. He played internationally for a record span of 26 years (1895–1920).

The youngest British international was Norman Whiteside, who played for Northern Ireland *v.* Yugoslavia, at 17 yr 42 days on 17 June 1982.

England's youngest international was Duncan Edwards (1936–58) of Manchester United *v.* Scotland at Wembley on 2 Apr 1955, at 18 yr 183 days. The youngest Welsh cap was John Charles (b. 27 Dec 1931), of Leeds United *v.* Ireland at Wrexham on 8 Mar 1950, aged 18 yr 71 days. Scotland's youngest international has been Johnny Lambie of Queen's Park, at 17 yr 92 days *v.* Ireland on 20 Mar 1886. The youngest for the Republic of Ireland was James Holmes (b. 11 Nov 1953) of Coventry City, at 17 yr 200 days *v.* Austria in Dublin on 30 May 1971.

MOST INTERNATIONAL APPEARANCES

The greatest number of appearances for a national team is 150 by Hector Chumpitaz (b. 12 Apr 1943) (Peru) from 1963 to 1982. This includes all matches played by the national team. The record for full internationals against other national teams is 119 by Pat Jennings (b. 12 June 1945) (Northern Ireland) from 1964–86.

The most women's internationals is 56 (49 as captain) by Carol Thomas (b. 5 June 1955) for England, 1974–86.

BALL CONTROL

Mikael Palmquist (Sweden) juggled a regulation soccer-ball for 14 hr 14 min non-stop with feet, legs and head without the ball ever touching the ground at Göteborg, Sweden on 6 Apr 1986. Palmquist also headed a regulation football non-stop for 4½ hr at Göteborg, Sweden in 1984. Uno Lindström of Boden, Sweden kept a football up while he travelled a distance of 21,097 km *13.11 miles* in 2 hr 55 min 49 sec on 10 Aug 1985.

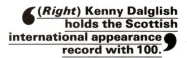

(*Left*) Joey Jones shares the Welsh international cap record of 68 with Ivor Allchurch.

(*Right*) Kenny Dalglish holds the Scottish international appearance record with 100.

BRITISH RECORD HOLDERS

ENGLAND	108 appearances	Robert Frederick 'Bobby' Moore (b. 12 Apr 1941)	West Ham U/Fulham	1962–73
NORTHERN IRELAND	119 appearances	Patrick A. Jennings (b. 12 June 1945)	Watford/Tottenham H/Arsenal	1964–86
SCOTLAND	100 appearances	Kenneth M. Dalglish (b. 4 Mar 1951)	Celtic/Liverpool	1971–86
WALES	68 appearances	Ivor Allchurch (b. 29 Dec 1929)	Swansea C/Newcastle/Cardiff C/Worcester C	1950–68
		Joseph P. 'Joey' Jones (b. 4 Mar 1955)	Wrexham/Liverpool/Chelsea/Huddersfield T	1972–86
REPUBLIC OF IRELAND	60 appearances	Michael J. 'Johnny' Giles (b. 6 Jan 1940)	Manchester U/Leeds U/West Bromwich A	1960–79

SOCCER

'In the local Cup match between Tongham Youth Club, Surrey and Hawley, Hampshire, on 3 Nov 1969 the referee booked all 22 players including one who went to hospital, and one of the linesmen. The match, won by Tongham 2–0, was described by a player as 'A good, hard game'.
In a Gancia Cup match at Waltham Abbey, Essex on 23 Dec 1973, the referee, Michael J Woodhams, sent off the entire Juventus-Cross team and some club officials. Glencraig United, Faifley, near Clydebank, had all 11 team members and two substitutes for their match against Goldenhill Boys' Club on 2 Feb 1975 booked in the dressing room before a ball was kicked. The referee, Mr Tarbet of Bearsden, took exception to the chant which greeted his arrival. It was not his first meeting with Glencraig. The teams drew 2–2.'

WORLD CLUB CHAMPIONSHIP
This club tournament was started in 1960 between the winners of the European Cup and the Copa Libertadores, the South American equivalent. The most wins is three by Penarol, Uruguay in 1961, 1966 and 1982. Independiente, Argentina won in 1973 and 1984, and in 1975 reached the final but couldn't agree dates for the matches with Bayern Munich.

EUROPEAN CHAMPIONSHIP (*FORMERLY NATIONS CUP*)
The European equivalent of the World Cup started in 1958 and is staged every four years. West Germany are the only country to have won twice, in 1972 and 1980.

EUROPEAN CHAMPION CLUBS CUP
The European Cup for the League champions of the respective nations was approved by FIFA on 8 May 1955 and was run by the European governing body UEFA (Union of European Football Associations) which came into being in the previous year. Real Madrid won the first final, and have won a record six times including five times consecutively 1956–60, 1966. The highest score in a final was Real Madrid's 7–3 win over Eintracht Frankfurt at Hampden Park, Glasgow on 18 May 1960.

Glasgow Celtic became the first British club to win the Cup beating Inter-Milan 2–1 in Lisbon, Portugal, on 25 May 1967. They also became the first British club to win the European Cup and the two senior domestic tournaments (League and Cup) in the same season. Liverpool, winners in 1977, 1978, 1981 and 1984, have been the most successful British club and in the 1983–4 season emulated Celtic by also winning two domestic competitions – League Championship and Milk Cup.

EUROPEAN CUP WINNERS CUP
A tournament for the national Cup winners started in 1960–1. Clubs to win twice have been AC Milan 1968 and 1973, Anderlecht 1976 and 1978, Barcelona 1979 and 1982 and Dynamo Kiev in 1975 and 1986. Tottenham Hotspur were the first British club to win the trophy, beating Atletico Madrid 5–1 in Rotterdam in 1963.

UEFA CUP
Originally known as the International Inter-City Industrial Fairs Cup, this club tournament began in 1955. The first competition lasted three years, the second two years. In 1960–1 it became an annual tournament and since 1971–2 has been replaced by the UEFA Cup. The first British club to win the trophy was Leeds United in 1968. The most wins is three by Barcelona in 1958, 1960 and 1966.

PLAYERS

MOST DURABLE PLAYER
The most durable player in League history has been Terence Lionel Paine (b. 23 Mar 1939) who made 824 league appearances from 1957 to 1977 playing for Southampton and Hereford Utd. Norman John Trollope (b. 14 June 1943) made 770 League appearances for one club, Swindon Town, between 1960 and 1980.

TRANSFER FEES
The greatest transfer fee quoted for a player is 15,895 million lire (£6.9 million) by Napoli in 1984 for Diego Maradona (b. 30 Oct 1960) (Argentina) from Barcelona. This exceeded the *c* £5 million that Barcelona paid for Maradona in 1982.

The record fee between British clubs was £1,500,000 (incl. VAT and other levies) paid by Manchester United to West Bromwich Albion for Bryan Robson on 3 Oct 1981.

HEAVIEST GOALKEEPER
The biggest goalkeeper in representative football was the England international Willie. J. 'Fatty' Foulke (1874–1916), who stood 1,90 m *6 ft 3 in* and weighed 141 kg *22 st 3 lb*. His last games were for Bradford City, by which time he was 165 kg *26 st*. He once stopped a game by snapping the cross bar.

GOALKEEPING *INDIVIDUAL RECORD*
The longest that any goalkeeper has succeeded in preventing any goals being scored past him in international matches is 1142 min for Dino Zoff (Italy), from September 1972 to June 1974. The Football League record is 1103 min by Steve Death (b. 19 Sept 1949) for Reading in Division IV from 24 March to 18 Aug 1979.

SWIMMING

FASTEST SWIMMER
The fastest 50 m in a 50 m pool is *men:* Matt Blondi (USA) 8,06 km/h *5.01 mph*; *women:* Tamara Costache (Romania) 7,10 km/h *4.41 mph*.

MOST WORLD RECORDS
Men: 32, Arne Borg (b. 18 Aug 1901) (Sweden), 1921–9. *Women:* 42, Ragnhild Hveger (b. 10 Dec 1920) (Denmark), 1936–42. Under modern conditions (only metric distances in 50 m pools) the most is 26 by Mark Andrew Spitz (b. 10 Feb 1950) (USA), 1967–72, and 23 by Kornelia Ender (b. 25 Oct 1958) (GDR), 1973–6.

MOST WORLD TITLES
In the world championships (inst. 1973) the most medals won is ten by Kornelia Ender with eight gold and two silver in 1973 and 1975. The most by a man is eight by Ambrose 'Rowdy' Gaines (b. 17 Feb 1959) (USA), five gold and three silver, in 1978 and 1982. The most gold medals is six by James Montgomery (b. 24 Jan 1955) (USA) in 1973 and 1975. The most medals in a single championship is six by Tracy Caulkins (b. 11 Jan 1963) (USA) in 1978 with five golds and a silver.

OLYMPIC RECORDS

MOST GOLD MEDALS *MEN*
The greatest number of Olympic gold medals won is nine by Mark Spitz (USA): 100 m and 200 m freestyle 1972; 100 m and 200 m butterfly 1972; 4×100 m freestyle 1968 and 1972; 4×200 m freestyle 1968 and 1972; 4×100 m medley 1972. *All but one of these performances (the 4×200 m freestyle of 1968) were also new world records.*

Matt Blondi (USA) the world's fastest man over 50 m.

MOST GOLD MEDALS *WOMEN*
The record number of gold medals won by a woman is four shared by Patricia McCormick (*née* Keller) (b. 12 May 1930) (USA), the high and springboard diving double in 1952 and 1956 (also the female record for individual golds), Dawn Fraser (b. 4 Sept 1937) (Australia), the 100 m freestyle (1956, 1960 and 1964) and the 4×100 m freestyle (1956) and Kornelia Ender (GDR) the 100 and 200 m freestyle, 100 m butterfly and 4×100 m medley in 1976. Dawn Fraser is the only swimmer to win the same event on three successive occasions.

CLOSEST VERDICT
The closest recorded win in the Olympic Games was in the Munich 400 m individual medley final of 30 Aug 1972 when Gunnar Larsson (b. 12 May 1951) (Sweden) got the verdict over Tim McKee (b. 14 Mar 1953) (USA) by 21000th of a second in 4 min 31.981 sec to 4 min 31.983 sec – a margin of 3 mm or the length grown by a finger nail in three weeks. This led to a change in international rules with timings and places decided only to hundredths.

SQUASH

WORLD CHAMPIONSHIPS
Geoffrey B. Hunt (b. 11 Mar 1947) (Australia) won a record four World Open (inst. 1976) titles, 1976–7 and 1979–80, and three World Amateur (inst. 1967) titles. Australia have won a record four amateur team titles, 1967, 1969, 1971 and 1973.

MOST TITLES *OPEN CHAMPIONSHIP*
The most wins in the Open Championship (amateurs or professionals), held annually in Britain, is eight by Geoffrey Hunt in 1969, 1974, 1976–81. Hashim Khan (b. 1915) (Pakistan) won seven times, 1950–5 and 1957, and has also won the Vintage title six times in 1978–83.

The most wins in the Women's Squash Rackets Championship is 16 by Heather Pamela McKay (*née* Blundell) (b. 31 July 1941) (Australia) from 1961 to 1977. She also won the World Open title in 1976 and 1979. In her career from 1959 to 1980 she only lost two games (one in 1960, one in 1962).

MOST TITLES *AMATEUR CHAMPIONSHIP*
The most wins in the Amateur Championship is six by Abdel Fattah Amr Bey (b. 14 Feb 1910) (Egypt) later appointed Ambassador in London, who won in 1931–3 and 1935–7. Norman Francis Borrett (b. 1 Oct 1917) of England won in 1946–50.

LONGEST AND SHORTEST CHAMPIONSHIP MATCHES
The longest recorded competitive match was one of 2 hr 45 min when Jahangir Khan (b. 10 Dec 1963) (Pakistan) beat Gamal Awad (b. 8 Sept 1955) (Egypt) 9–10, 9–5, 9–7, 9–2, the first game lasting a record 1 hr 11 min, in the final of the Patrick International Festival at Chichester, West Sussex, England on 30 Mar 1983. Deanna Murray beat Christine Rees in only 9½ min in a Ladies Welsh title match at Rhos-on-Sea, Clwyd, on 21 Oct 1979.

TENNIS

FASTEST SERVICE
The fastest service timed with modern equipment is 222 km/h *138 mph* by Steve Denton (USA) at Beaver Creek, Colorado, USA, on 29 July 1984. The fastest *ever* measured was one of 263 km/h *163.6 mph* by William Tatem Tilden (1893–1953) (USA) in 1931.

LONGEST GAME
The longest known singles game was one of 37 deuces (80 points) between Anthony Fawcett (Rhodesia) and Keith Glass (GB) in the first round of the Surrey championships at Surbiton, Surrey, on 26 May 1975. It lasted 31 min.

The longest tiebreaker was 26–24 for the fourth and decisive set of a first round men's doubles at the Wimbledon Championships on 1 July 1985. Jan Gunnarsson (Sweden) and Michael Mortensen (Denmark) defeated John Frawley (Australia) and Victor Pecci (Paraguay) 6–3, 4–6, 3–6, 7–6.

MOST WIMBLEDON WINS (*WOMEN*)
Six times singles champion Billie-Jean King has won ten women's doubles and four mixed doubles during the period 1961 to 1979, to total a record 20 titles. Elizabeth Montague Ryan (1892–1979) (USA) won a record 19 doubles (12 women's, 7 mixed) titles from 1914 to 1934.

MOST WIMBLEDON WINS (*MEN*)
The greatest number of wins by a man has been 13 by Hugh Laurence Doherty (1875–1919) (GB) with five singles titles (1902–6) and a record eight men's doubles (1897–1901, 1903–5) partnered by his brother Reginald Frank (1872–1910).

YOUNGEST WIMBLEDON CHAMPIONS
The youngest champion was Charlotte 'Lottie' Dod (1871–1906), who was 15 yr 285 days when she won in 1887. The youngest men's champion was Boris Becker (b. 22 Nov 1967) (W. Germany) who won the men's title in 1985 at 17 yr 227 days. The youngest ever player at Wimbledon is reputedly Mita Klima (Austria) who was 13 yr in the 1907 singles competition. The youngest player to win a match at Wimbledon is Kathy Rinaldi (b. 24 Mar 1967) (USA), at 14 yr 91 days on 23 June 1981.

OLDEST WIMBLEDON CHAMPIONS
The oldest champion was Margaret Evelyn du Pont (*née* Osborne) (b. Mar 1918) (USA) at 44 yr 125 days when she won the mixed doubles in 1962 with Neale Fraser (Aus). The oldest singles champion was Arthur Gore (GB) in 1909 at 41 yr 182 days.

Boris Becker, the youngest ever Wimbledon men's champion in 1985, retained it in 1986.

ATHLETICS WORLD RECORDS MEN

World records for the men's events scheduled by the International Amateur Athletic Federation. Fully automatic electric timing is mandatory for events up to 400 metres.

RUNNING	**Record**	**Name and Country**	**Place**	**Date**
100 metres	9.93 sec	Calvin Smith (USA) (b. 8 Jan 1961)	Colorado Springs, Colorado, USA	3 July 1983
200 metres	19.72 sec	Pietro Mennea (Italy) (b. 28 June 1952)	Mexico City, Mexico	12 Sept 1979
400 metres	43.86 sec	Lee Edward Evans (USA) (b. 25 Feb 1947)	Mexico City, Mexico	18 Oct 1968
800 metres	1 min 41.73 sec	Sebastian Newbold Coe (GB) (b. 29 Sept 1956)	Florence, Italy	10 June 1981
1000 metres	2 min 12.18 sec	Sebastian Newbold Coe (GB)	Oslo, Norway	11 July 1981
1500 metres	3 min 29.45 sec	Said Aouita (Morocco) (b. 2 Nov 1960)	Berlin, West Germany	23 Aug 1985
1 mile	3 min 46.32 sec	Steven Cram (GB)	Oslo, Norway	27 July 1985
2000 metres	4 min 51.39 sec	Steven Cram (GB)	Budapest, Hungary	4 Aug 1985
3000 metres	7 min 32.1 sec	Henry Rono (Kenya) (b. 12 Feb 1952)	Oslo, Norway	27 June 1978
5000 metres	13 min 0.40 sec	Said Aouita (Morocco)	Oslo, Norway	27 July 1985
10 000 metres	27 min 13.81 sec	Fernando Mameda (Portugal) (b. 1 Nov 1951)	Stockholm, Sweden	2 July 1984
20 000 metres	57 min 24.2 sec	Josephus Hermens (Netherlands) (b. Jan 1950)	Papendal, Netherlands	1 May 1976
25 000 metres	1 hr 13 min 55.8 sec	Toshihiko Seko (Japan) (b. 15 July 1956)	Christchurch, New Zealand	22 Mar 1981
30 000 metres	1 hr 29 min 18.8 sec	Toshihiko Seko (Japan)	Christchurch, New Zealand	22 Mar 1981
1 hour	20,944 m *13 miles 24 yd 2 ft*	Josephus Hermens (Netherlands)	Papendal, Netherlands	1 May 1976

HURDLING				
110 metres (106 cm *3 ft 6 in*)	12.93 sec	Renaldo Nehemiah (USA) (b. 24 Mar 1959)	Zürich, Switzerland	19 Aug 1981
400 metres (91,4 cm *3 ft 0 in*)	47.02 sec	Edwin Corley Moses (USA) (b. 31 Aug 1955)	Koblenz, W. Germany	31 Aug 1983
3000 metres steeplechase	8 min 5.4 sec	Henry Rono (Kenya)	Seattle, Washington, USA	13 May 1978

RELAYS				
4×100 metres	37.83 sec	United States National Team: Sam Graddy, Ronald James Brown, Calvin Smith, Frederick Carlton Lewis	Los Angeles, USA	11 Aug 1984
4×200 metres	1 min 20.26 sec	University of Southern California, USA: Joel Andres, James Sanford, William Mullins, Clancy Edwards	Tempe, Arizona, USA	27 May 1978
4×400 metres	2 min 56.16 sec	United States National Team: Vincent Edward Matthews, Ronald J. Freeman, George Lawrence James, Lee Edward Evans	Mexico City, Mexico	20 Oct 1968
4×800 metres	7 min 3.89 sec	Great Britain: Peter Elliot, Gary Peter Cook, Steven Cram, Sebastian Newbold Coe	Crystal Palace, London	30 Aug 1982
4×1500 metres	14 min 38.8 sec	West Germany: Thomas Wessinghage, Harald Hudak, Michael Lederer, Karl Fleschen	Cologne, W. Germany	17 Aug 1977

† *The time of 1 min 20.23 sec achieved by the Tobias Striders (Guy Abrahams, Mike Simmons, Donald O'Riley Quarrie, James Gilkes) at Tempe, Ariz., USA on 27 May 1978 was not ratified as the team was composed of varied nationalities.*

FIELD EVENTS				
High Jump	2,41 m *7 ft 10¾ in*	Igor Paklin (USSR)	Kobe, Japan	4 Sept 1985
Pole Vault	6,01 m *19 ft 8¾ in*	Sergey Bubka (USSR) (b. 4 Dec 1963)	Moscow, USSR	8 July 1986
Long Jump	8,90 m *29 ft 2 in*	Robert Beamon (USA) (b. 29 Aug 1946)	Mexico City, Mexico	18 Oct 1968
Triple Jump	17,97 m *58 ft 11 in*	William Augustus 'Willie' Banks (b. 11 Mar 1956)	Indianapolis, USA	16 June 1985
Shot 7,26 kg *16 lb*	22,62 m *74 ft 2½ in*‡	Olf Timmerman (GDR)	Berlin, East Germany	22 Sept 1985
Discus 2 kg *4 lb 6.55 oz*	74,08 m *243 ft 0 in*	Jürgen Schult (GDR) (b. 11 May 1960	Neubrandenburg, GDR	6 June 1986
Hammer 7,26 kg *16 lb*	86,34 m *283 ft 3 in*	Yuri Georgiyevich Sedykh (USSR) (b. 11 Jun 1955)	Cork, Ireland	3 July 1984
Javelin 800 g *28.22 oz*	104,80 m *343 ft 10 in*	Uwe Hohn (GDR) (b. 16 July 1962)	East Berlin, GDR	20 July 1984

DECATHLON (1984 Scoring Table)				
	8847 points	Francis Morgan 'Daley' Thompson (GB) (b. 30 July 1958)	Los Angeles, USA	8–9 Aug 1984

(1st day: 100 m 10.44 sec. Long Jump 8,01 m *26 ft 3½ in*, Shot Put 15,72 m *51 ft 7 in*, High Jump 2,03 m *6 ft 8 in*, 400 m 46.97 sec) (2nd day: 110 m Hurdles 14.33 sec, Discus 48,56 m *152 ft 9 in*, Pole Vault 5,00 m *16 ft 4¾ in*, Javelin 65,24 m *214 ft 0 in*, 1500 m 4 min 35.00 sec)

ATHLETICS WORLD RECORDS WOMEN

World records for the women's events scheduled by the International Amateur Athletic Federation. The same stipulation about automatically timed events applies in the six events up to 400 metres as in the men's list.

RUNNING	Record	Name and Country	Place	Date
100 metres	10.76 sec	Evelyn Ashford (USA) (b. 15 Apr 1957)	Zürich, Switzerland	22 Aug 1984
200 metres	21.71 sec	Marita Koch (GDR) (b. 18 Feb 1957)	Karl Marx Stadt, GDR	10 June 1979
		Marita Koch	Potsdam, GDR	21 July 1984
400 metres	47.60 sec	Marita Koch (GDR)	Canberra, Australia	6 Oct 1985
800 metres	1 min 53.28 sec	Jarmila Kratochvilova (Czechoslovakia)	Munich, W. Germany	26 July 1983
1000 metres	2 min 30.6 sec	Tatyana Providokhina (USSR) (b. 26 Mar 1953)	Podolsk, USSR	20 Aug 1978
1500 metres	3 min 52.47 sec	Tatyana Kazankina (USSR) (b. 17 Dec 1951)	Zürich, Switzerland	13 Aug 1980
1 mile	4 min 16.71 sec	Mary Slaney (née Decker) (USA) (b. 4 Aug 1958)	Zürich, Switzerland	21 Aug 1985
2000 metres	5 min 28.69 sec	Maricica Puica (Rom)	London	1st July 1986
3000 metres	8 min 22.62 sec	Tatyana Kazankina (USSR)	Leningrad, USSR	26 Aug 1984
5000 metres	14 min 48.07 sec	Zola Budd (GB)	London, GB	26 Aug 1985
10 000 metres	30 min 13.74 sec	Ingrid Kristiansen (Norway)	Oslo, Norway	5 July 1986
HURDLING				
100 metres (84 cm *2 ft 9 in*)	12.36 sec	Grazyna Rabsztyn (Poland) (b. 20 Sept 1952)	Warsaw, Poland	13 June 1980
400 metres (76 cm *2 ft6 in*)	53.55 sec	Sabine Busch (GDR)	Berlin, East Germany	22 Sept 1985
RELAYS				
4×100 metres	41.37 sec	GDR: Silke Gladisch, Sabine Reiger, Ingrid Auerswald, Marlies Göhr [*née* Oelsner]	Canberra, Australia	6 Oct 1985
4×200 metres	1 min 28.15 sec	GDR: Marlies Göhr [*née* Oelsner], Romy Müller [*née* Schneider], Bärbel Wöckel [*née* Eckert], Marita Koch	Jena, GDR	9 Aug 1980
4×400 metres	3 min 15.92 sec	GDR: Gesine Walther, Sabine Busch, Dagmar Rübsam, Marita Koch	Erfurt, GDR	3 June 1984
4×800 metres	7 min 50.17 sec	USSR: Nadezha Olizarenko, Lyubov Gurina, Lyudmila Borisova, Irina Podyalovskaya	Moscow, USSR	4 Aug 1984
FIELD EVENTS				
High Jump	2,07 m *6 ft 9 in*	Lyudmila Andonova (Bulgaria) (b. 12 May 1960)	East Berlin, GDR	20 July 1984
Long Jump	7,44 m *24 ft 5 in*	Heike Drechsler [*née* Daute] (GDR)	Berlin, East Germany	22 Sept 1985
Shot 4 kg *8 lb 13 oz*	22,53 m *73 ft 11 in*	Natalya Lisovskaya (USSR) (b. 16 July 1962)	Sochi, USSR	27 May 1984
Discus 1 kg *2 lb 3.27 oz*	74,56 m *244 ft 7 in*	Zdenka Silhava (Czechoslovakia) (b. 15 June 1954)	Nitra, Czechoslovakia	26 Aug 1984
Javelin 600g *24.74 oz*	75,40 m *247 ft 4 in*	Petra Felke (GDR) (b. 30 July 1959)	Schwerin, GDR	4 June 1985
HEPTATHLON				
	7148 points	Jacqueline Joyner (USA) (b. 3 Mar 1962)	Moscow, USSR	6–7 July 1986

(100 m hurdles 12.85 sec; High Jump 1,88 m *6 ft 2 in*; Shot 14,76 m *48 ft 5¼ in*; 200 m 23.00 sec; Long Jump 7,01 m *23 ft*; Javelin 49,86 m *163 ft 7 in*; 800 m 2 min 10.02 sec

Steve Cram who altered this record book several times in 1985